The Utopia Reader

The
Utopia Reader

EDITED BY

Gregory Claeys and Lyman Tower Sargent

New York University Press

New York and London

NEW YORK UNIVERSITY PRESS
New York and London

Acknowledgment is made to the following for permission to quote from copyrighted material: Reprinted by permission of the publishers and the Loeb Classical Library from *Plutarch: the Parallel Lives,* Volume I, edited by B. Perrin (Cambridge, Mass.: Harvard University Press, 1914). Reprinted by permission of the publishers and the Loeb Classical Library from Iambulus, *Diodorus Siculus,* Volume I and Volume 3, translated by C. H. Oldfather (Cambridge, Mass.: Harvard University Press, 1939). Reprinted by permission of the publishers and the Loeb Classical Library from Lucian, *Lucian,* Volume 6, translated by K. Kilburn (Cambridge, Mass.: Harvard University Press, 1959). From *The Land of Cokaygyne* in *The English Utopia,* by A. L. Morton, reprinted by permission of Lawrence and Wishart. From *L'Andrographe,* by Nicolas-Edme Restif de la Bretonne, reprinted with the permission of The Free Press, a Division of Simon & Schuster. From *French Utopias: An Anthology of Ideal Societies,* edited and translated by Frank E. and Fritzie P. Manuel. Copyright © 1966 by The Free Press. From *Amana That Was and Amana That Is,* by Bertha M. H. Shambaugh, reprinted by permission of the State Historical Society of Iowa. From *Journey through Utopia,* by Marie Louis Berneri, reprinted by permission of Routledge. From *A Modern Utopia,* by H. G. Wells, reprinted by permission of A. P. Watt, Ltd., on behalf of The Literary Executors of the Estate of H. G. Wells. From *Darkness and the Light,* by Olaf Stapledon, reprinted by permission of the Estate of Olaf Stapledon. From *We,* by Yevgeni Zamiatin, translated by Gregory Zilboorg, translation copyright © 1924 by E. P. Dutton & Co., Inc. Renewed copyright © 1952 by Gregory Zilboorg. Used by permission of Dutton, a division of Penguin Putnam, Inc. From *Galaxy,* by Ursula K. Le Guin. Copyright © 1974 by Ursula K. Le Guin; first appeared in *Galaxy,* reprinted by permission of the author and the author's agent, Virginia Kidd. From *Walden Two,* reprinted by permission of the B. F. Skinner Foundation. Chapters One and Two from *Brave New World,* by Aldous Huxley. Copyright © 1932, 1960 by Aldous Huxley. Reprinted by permission of HarperCollins Publishers, Inc. "The Principles of Newspeak" from *Nineteen Eighty-Four,* by George Orwell. Copyright © 1949 by Harcourt Brace & Company, renewed 1977 by Sonia Orwell, reprinted by permission of the publisher and Mark Hamilton as the Literary Executor of the Estate of the Late Sonia Brownell Orwell and Martin Secker & Warburg.

Library of Congress Cataloging-in-Publication Data
The utopia reader / edited by Gregory Claeys and Lyman Tower Sargent.
p. cm.
Includes bibliographical references and index.
ISBN 0-8147-1571-0 (pbk.)
ISBN 0-8147-1570-2 (cloth)
I. Utopias. I. Claeys, Gregory. II. Sargent, Lyman Tower, 1940–
PN6071.U85 U88 1999
809'.93372—dc21   99-6660
CIP

10 9 8 7 6 5 4 3 2

To Evan, Jennifer, Ian, and Kieran Sargent and
Christine Lattek and Anna, Christopher, and Daniel Claeys

Contents

6. The Nineteenth Century

Preface

This collection is designed to provide an overview of the history of utopianism through selections from well-known as well as more obscure authors and texts. Any anthology represents a series of compromises, and ours is no exception. We could easily have created a volume four times this size; in fact, our first selection of texts did just that. But the realities of acceptable length, untranslated texts, and permission fees force editors to make choices. We have chosen to include more excerpts than complete works to better represent the range of materials available and have included the most important sections of each work while trying to give the flavor of the work.

Most selections in this book come from the Anglo-American utopian tradition with a few from France and Germany, as well as some that represent the origins of utopianism before the invention of the literary genre in 1516. Although most utopias are portrayed in fictional form, we have also included some nonfiction to represent both major influences on the development of utopian thought or to include some expressions of utopia that were originally presented as non-fiction. In a few cases we deliberately chose a relatively unknown but important text that is not generally available over a well-known text by the same author that is easily obtainable.

Acknowledgments

The editors wish to thank Deborah Altus, Carol Farley Kessler, and Kenneth M. Roemer for their assistance in suggesting specific texts. We also wish to thank Nicole Pohl for providing us with her transcription of "The Inventory of Judgments Commonwealth." Michelle Pandolfo transcribed a number of texts in the early stages of compiling this anthology. A few years ago, one of the editors participated in a panel discussion at the annual meeting of the Society for Utopian Studies on the issue of whether there is or should be a "canon" of utopian texts (the general answers were "no" and "no") and raised the possibility of this anthology as part of the discussion. He wishes to thank the members of the audience for many suggestions.

ONE

Introduction

❧

Utopianism generally is the imaginative projection, positive or negative, of a society that is substantially different from the one in which the author lives. The word *utopia* or *outopia* was derived from Greek and means "no (or not) place" (*u* or *ou,* no, not; *topos,* place). Thomas More (1478–1535), inventor of the word, punned on *eutopia,* or good place, and we have since added *dystopia,* or bad place. Thus, the primary characteristic of the utopia is its nonexistence combined with a *topos*—a location in time and space—to give verisimilitude. In addition, the place must be recognizably good or bad to the intended reader. All fiction describes a no-place; utopian fiction generally describes good or bad no-places. Fashions change in utopias; most sixteenth-century eutopias horrify today's reader even though the authors' intentions are clear. On the other hand, a sixteenth-century reader would consider most twentieth-century eutopias as dys-topias worthy of being burnt as works of the devil.

As a literary genre, utopia refers to works that describe an imaginary society in some detail. Utopian thought construed more widely, however, is not restricted to fiction and includes visionary, millenarian, and apocalyptic as well as constitutional writings united by their willingness to envision a dramatically different form of society as either a social ideal-type or its negative inversion. Not all forms of imaginative literature and social and political thought, however, should be called utopian. The following categories may prove helpful:

Utopianism—social dreaming
Utopia—a nonexistent society described in detail and normally located in time and space
Eutopia or *positive utopia*—a utopia that the author intended a contemporaneous reader to view as considerably better than the society in which the reader lived

I

Dystopia or *negative utopia*—a utopia that the author intended a contemporaneous reader to view as considerably worse than the society in which the reader lived

Utopian satire—a utopia that the author intended a contemporaneous reader to view as a criticism of the existing society

Anti-utopia—a utopia that the author intended a contemporaneous reader to view as a criticism of utopianism or of some particular eutopia

Critical utopia—a utopia that the author intended a contemporaneous reader to view as better than contemporary society but with difficult problems that the described society may or may not be able to solve, and which takes a critical view of the utopian genre

Bearing these categories in mind, we may distinguish between two fundamental utopian traditions: utopias of sensual gratification and utopias of human contrivance. These traditions represent alternate ways of expressing the utopian impulse—that need to dream of a better life, even when we are reasonably content.

The first eutopias we know of are myths that look to the past of the human race or beyond death for a time when human life was or will be easier and more gratifying. They have various labels—golden ages, Arcadias, earthly paradises, fortunate isles, isles of the blest. They are peopled with our earliest ancestors; heroes and, very rarely, heroines; the virtuous dead; or, in some cases, contemporaneous but little-known noble savages. These eutopias have certain features in common—simplicity, security, immortality or an easy death, unity among the people; unity between the people and God or the gods, abundance without labor, and no enmity between human beings and the other animals. If women are included (they often are not), they give birth without pain. These eutopias are achieved without human effort and are seen as a gift of nature or the gods. Well-known examples are Hesiod's golden age, Eden, some versions of the millennium, and various Greek and Roman myths. These utopias of sensual gratification are social dreaming at its simplest. Every culture has some such stories.

But human beings do not like depending on the whims of nature or gods. As a first step toward taking control of our dreams, and when it becomes intellectually possible, identical imagery is projected into future life on earth, rather than after death. Vergil's fourth Eclogue is an example of this. Although such changes are still not under human control, there is at least the suggestion that human beings can control their destiny. A second step can be seen in the existence of festivals such as Saturnalia, the Feast of Fools, and Carnival, where the world is turned upside down for a few days and at least temporarily the poor possess plenty and experience reverie. A third step is found in Cockaigne and its variants, in which permanent utopia of sensual gratification is described and, in most versions, presented as possible for some people after going through an almost incredible rite of passage.

The fourth and most important step is to imagine that every aspect of social order can be susceptible to human control, thus creating an entirely new tradition—utopias of human contrivance, often cast in the form of the imaginary city. Plato's Republic is the most cited early Western example.

In 1516 Thomas More invented the genre to which these works are precursors. Though the propensity to social dreaming existed well before there was any utopian genre, from that point on utopian literature began to have the formal characteristics specified in the definitions above.

Utopias and the changes they undergo both help bring about and are reflections of paradigm shifts in the way a culture views itself. Sometimes it is possible to identify fairly precisely the role of a utopia or a group of utopias in this process, but all such shifts take place unevenly, and, therefore, different utopias in any time and place may reflect different stages in the paradigm shift, including reactions against it.

Following More, we may enumerate four main historical stages in the evolution of the utopian tradition. First, religious radicalism in the sixteenth and seventeenth centuries spawned a variety of egalitarian schemes in which communal property-holding, linked to Spartan ideals as well as Christian monasticism, was given a high priority. These strands of thought would eventually give rise to socialism in the nineteenth century.

Second, voyages of discovery from the sixteenth century on encouraged a heated debate over the virtues and vices of primitive peoples, their relation to pagan and Christian traditions of an original age of innocence, and the moral any such discussion held out for societies concerned that their increasing wealth threatened moral degeneration.

Third, scientific discovery and technological innovation from the seventeenth century on began to hold out the promise of an indefinite progress of the human species toward better health, a longer life, and the domination of nature in the interests of humankind. Twentieth-century science fiction emerges as the characteristic genre expressing both the hopes and fears of our own era. The modern dystopia crystallizes the anxieties that increasingly accompanied the onward march of progress.

Finally, aspirations for much greater social equality emerged in the revolutionary movements of late eighteenth-century North America and France, in which the utopian promise of a society of greater virtue, equality, and social justice was now projected onto a national scale. This was matched by the transformation of socialism after 1848, in which the ethos of small-scale communitarianism was replaced by the ideal of centralized state socialism. Small-scale communitarianism was refiected in the establishment of many communes or intentional communities, groups of five or more adults and their children, if any, who come from more than one nuclear family and who have chosen to live together to enhance their shared values or for some other mutually agreed-upon purpose. Many such communities have been founded, sometimes linked to the formation of states (American frontier communities, the Kibbutzim in Israel) and at other times to movements for social reform (the Hippie communes of the 1960s), and many continue to exist. In such communities, and in a continued outpouring of utopian literature, the imaginative aspiration for social and human improvement continues to provide models for forward movement, as well as dangers to be avoided.

FURTHER READING

Bibliography

Sargent, Lyman Tower. *British and American Utopian Literature, 1516–1985: An Annotated, Chronological Bibliography.* New York: Garland, 1988.

Definition

Sargent, Lyman Tower. "The Three Faces of Utopianism Revisited." *Utopian Studies* 5, no. 1 (1994): 1–37.

Collections

Claeys, Gregory, ed. *Modern British Utopias 1700–1850.* 8 volumes. London: Pickering & Chatto, 1997.
———. *Utopias of the British Enlightenment.* Cambridge: Cambridge University Press, 1994.
Manuel, Frank E., and Fritzie P. Manuel, eds. and trans. *French Utopias.* New York: Free Press, 1966.

Studies

Davis, J. C. *Utopia and the Ideal Society: A Study of English Utopian Writing 1516–1700.* Cambridge: Cambridge University Press, 1981.
Eliav-Feldon, Miriam. *Realistic Utopias: The Ideal Imaginary Societies of the Renaissance, 1516–1630.* Oxford: Clarendon Press, 1982.
Ferguson, John. *Utopias of the Classical World.* London: Thames and Hudson, 1975.
Goodwin, Barbara, and Keith Taylor. *The Politics of Utopia: A Study in Theory and Practice.* London: Hutchinson, 1982.
Kumar, Krishan. *Utopia and Anti-Utopia in Modern Times.* Oxford: Basil Blackwell, 1987.

————. *Utopianism*. Milton Keynes, England: Open University Press; Minneapolis: University of Minnesota Press, 1991.

Levitas, Ruth. *The Concept of Utopia*. Hemel Hempstead, England: Philip Allan; Syracuse, N.Y.: Syracuse University Press, 1990.

Manuel, Frank E., and Fritzie P. Manuel. *Utopian Thought in the Western World*. Cambridge: Belknap Press of Harvard University Press, 1979.

Moylan, Tom. *Demand the Impossible: Science Fiction and the Utopian Imagination*. London: Methuen, 1986.

Roemer, Kenneth M. *The Obsolete Necessity: America in Utopian Writings, 1888–1900*. Kent, Ohio: Kent State University Press, 1976.

————, ed. *America as Utopia*. New York: Burt Franklin, 1981.

TWO

Utopianism before Thomas More

⟡

Although Thomas More created the form of the modern utopia, he was not the first to write a utopia. Indeed, better places have been described at least since the earliest forms of writing, and many such descriptions are clearly the result of earlier oral traditions. The earliest utopian works are myths of a golden age or race in the past and earthly paradises like Eden.

Christianity is one of the dominating influences in the development of utopianism. It contains strong utopian currents that flow like a torrent into secular utopianism. The originality and importance of Christianity in the utopian tradition is twofold—first, for the way it put the elements of utopia together into a more or less coherent pattern; and second, for the way it stressed utopian aspects in its eschatology. The utopian elements of Christian belief are Eden, the earthly paradise (Eden to be rediscovered), the apocalypse and millennium, and heaven.

Much of the imagery of medieval Christian utopianism derives from the early images of a golden age or earthly paradise. These earlier descriptions are often changed only by throwing in a few references to God or Christ. At the same time, the forms in which the early images of utopia were expressed proliferated. Scholars looking back on the Middle Ages have identified a growing number of utopian forms that would not have been apparent as such at the time.

The growth in the ways in which utopianism was expressed seems to reflect a more complex awareness of both place and time. Christianity provided a more complex understanding of time in relationship to utopia. There is utopia past or Eden; utopia future, or the millennium; and utopia outside of time, or heaven. The growth of geographical knowledge also provided places to put utopias, and travelers both real and imaginary provided a rationale for putting the utopias in these new or imagined places.

The result was various tales of Eden rediscovered and the story of the king-dom of Prester John. In addition, there were other loosely contemporaneous forms of utopianism, such as the myth of Cockaigne. This period also saw the development of the first monastic orders, whose rules were designed to create an ideal commonwealth.

The Golden Age

The most famous depiction of a golden age in the past is that of Hesiod, who invented the image as a contrast to the horrors of his own time.

Hesiod
Works and Days

> The gods who own Olympus as dwelling-place
> deathless, made first of mortals a Golden Race,
> (this was the time when Kronos in heaven dwelt)
> and they lived like gods and no sorrow of heart they felt.
> Nothing for toil or pitiful age they cared,
> but in strength of hand and foot still unimpaired
> they feasted gaily, undarkened by sufferings.
> They died as if falling asleep; and all good things
> were theirs, for the fruitful earth unstintingly bore
> unforced her plenty, and they, amid their store
> enjoyed their landed ease which nothing stirred
> loved by the gods and rich in many of herd.

Hesiod had little positive to say of his own time:

> Fifth is the race that I call my own and abhor.
> O to die, or be later born, or born before!
> This is the Race of Iron. Dark is their plight.
> Toil and sorrow is theirs, and by night
> The anguish of death and the gods afflict them and kill,
> Though there's yet a trifle of good amid manifold ill.

Hesiod (eighth century B.C.) is generally considered the father of Greek didactic poetry.

Source: Hesiod, "Works and Days," trans. Jack Lindsay in THE OXFORD BOOK OF GREEK VERSE IN TRANSLATION, ed. T. F. Higham and C. M. Bowra (Oxford: Clarendon Press, 1938), 133, 135.

Ovid

Metamorphosis

In the beginning was the Golden Age, when men of their own accord, without threat of punishment, without laws, maintained good faith and did what was right. There were no penalties to be afraid of, no bronze tablets were erected, carrying threats of legal action, no crowd of wrong-doers, anxious for mercy, trembled before the face of their judge: indeed, there were no judges, men lived securely without them. Never yet had any pine tree, cut down from its home on the mountains been launched on ocean's waves, to visit foreign lands: men knew only their own shores. Their cities were not yet surrounded by sheer moats; they had no straight brass trumpets, no coiling brass helmets and no swords. The peoples of the world, untroubled by any fears, enjoyed a leisurely and peaceful existence, and had no use for soldiers. The earth itself, without compulsion, untouched by the hoe, unfurrowed by any share, produced things spontaneously, and men were content with foods that grew without cultivation. They gathered arbute berries and mountain strawberries, wild cherries and blackberries that cling to thorny bramble bushes: or acorns, fallen from Jupiter's spreading oak. It was a season of everlasting spring, when peaceful zephyrs, with their warm breath, caressed the flowers that sprang up without having been planted. In time the earth, though untilled, produced corn too, and fields that never lay fallow whitened with heavy ears of grain. Then there flowed rivers of milk and rivers of nectar, and golden honey dripped from the green holmoak.

Ovid 43 B.C.–A.D. 17?) was a Roman poet.

Source: Ovid, METAMORPHOSES, I: 89–112, trans. Mary M. Innes (Harmondsworth, Eng.: Penguin, 1955), 33–34.

Vergil

Fourth Eclogue

Vergil presented a more complex picture and changed his images of the golden age from work to work. His famous fourth Eclogue, known as the messianic Eclogue, is the clearest example of the shift to the future.

Next, when now the strength of years has made thee man, even the trader shall quit the sea, nor shall the ship of pine exchange wares; every land shall bear all fruits. The earth shall not feel the harrow, nor the vine the pruning-hook; the sturdy ploughman, too, shall now loose his oxen from the yoke. Wool shall no more learn to counterfeit varied hues, but of himself the ram in the meadows shall change his fleece, now to sweetly blushing purple, now to saffron yellow; of its own will shall scarlet clothe the grazing lamb.

Vergil (70–19 B.C.) was a Roman poet.

Source: Vergil, ECLOGUES, IV: 37–45, in VERGIL, 2 vols., trans. H. Rushton Fairclough (London: William Heinemann, 1906), 31, 33.

Earthly Paradises

Earthly paradises are myths of origin that help explain the current human condition. In the Judeo-Christian earthly paradise, Eden, God provides everything necessary for human life. Sin leads to expulsion from Eden.

THE GARDEN OF EDEN

Genesis

2:8 And the LORD God planted a garden eastward in Eden; and there he put the man whom he had formed.

9 And out of the ground made the LORD God to grow every tree that is pleasant to the sight, and good for food; the tree of life also in the midst of the garden, and the tree of knowledge of good and evil.

10 And a river went out of Eden to water the garden; and from thence it was parted, and became into four heads.

11 The name of the first is Pison: that is it which compasseth the whole land of Havilah, where there is gold;

12 And the gold of that land is good: there is bdellium and the onyx stone.

13 And the name of the second river is Gihon: the same is it that compasseth the whole land of Ethiopia.

14 And the name of the third river is Hiddekel: that is it which goeth toward the east of Assyria. And the fourth river is Euphrates.

15 And the LORD God took the man, and put him into the garden of Eden to dress it and to keep it.

16 And the LORD God commanded the man, saying, Of every tree of the garden thou mayest freely eat:

17 But of the tree of the knowledge of good and evil, thou shalt not eat of it: for in the day that thou eatest thereof thou shalt surely die.

18 And the LORD God said, It is not good that the man should be alone; I will make him an help meet for him.

19 And out of the ground the LORD God formed every beast of the field, and every fowl of the air; and brought them unto Adam to see what he would call them: and whatsoever Adam called every living creature, that was the name thereof.

20 And Adam gave names to all cattle, and to the fowl of the air, and to every beast of the field; but for Adam there was not found an help meet for him.

21 And the LORD God caused a deep sleep to fall upon Adam, and he slept: and he took one of his ribs, and closed up the flesh instead thereof;

22 And the rib, which the LORD God had taken from man, made he a woman, and brought her unto the man.

23 And Adam said, This is now bone of my bones, and flesh of my flesh: she shall be called Woman, because she was taken out of Man.

24 Therefore shall a man leave his father and his mother, and shall cleave unto his wife: and they shall be one flesh.

25 And they were both naked, the man and his wife, and were not ashamed.
3:1 Now the serpent was more subtil than any beast of the field which the LORD God had made. And he said unto the woman, Yea, hath God said, Ye shall not eat of every tree of the garden?

2 And the woman said unto the serpent, We may eat of the fruit of the trees of the garden:

3 But of the fruit of the tree which is in the midst of the garden, God hath said, Ye shall not eat of it, neither shall ye touch it, lest ye die.

4 And the serpent said unto the woman, Ye shall not surely die:

5 For God doth know that in the day ye eat thereof, then your eyes shall be opened, and ye shall be as gods, knowing good and evil.

6 And when the woman saw that the tree was good for food, and that it was pleasant to the eyes, and a tree to be desired to make one wise, she took of the fruit thereof, and did eat, and gave also unto her husband with her; and he did eat.

7 And the eyes of them both were opened, and they knew that they were naked; and they sewed fig leaves together, and made themselves aprons.

8 And they heard the voice of the LORD God walking in the garden in the cool of the day: and Adam and his wife hid themselves from the presence of the LORD God amongst the trees of the garden.

9 And the LORD God called unto Adam, and said unto him, Where art thou?

10 And he said, I heard thy voice in the garden, and I was afraid, because I was naked; and I hid myself.

11 And he said, Who told thee that thou wast naked? Hast thou eaten of the tree, whereof I commanded thee that thou shouldest not eat?

12 And the man said, The woman whom thou gavest to be with me, she gave me of the tree, and I did eat.

13 And the LORD God said unto the woman, What is this that thou hast done? And the woman said, The serpent beguiled me, and I did eat.

14 And the LORD God said unto the serpent, Because thou hast done this, thou art cursed above all cattle, and above every beast of the field; upon thy belly shalt thou go, and dust shalt thou eat all the days of thy life:

15 And I will put enmity between thee and the woman, and between thy seed and her seed; it shall bruise thy head, and thou shalt bruise his heel.

16 Unto the woman he said, I will greatly multiply thy sorrow and thy conception; in sorrow thou shalt bring forth children; and thy desire shall be to thy husband, and he shall rule over thee.

17 And unto Adam he said, Because thou hast hearkened unto the voice of thy wife, and hast eaten of the tree, of which I commanded thee, saying, Thou shalt not eat of it: cursed is the ground for thy sake; in sorrow shalt thou eat of it all the days of thy life;

18 Thorns also and thistles shall it bring forth to thee; and thou shalt eat the herb of the field;

19 In the sweat of thy face shalt thou eat bread, till thou return unto the ground; for out of it wast thou taken: for dust thou art, and unto dust shalt thou return.

20 And Adam called his wife's name Eve; because she was the mother of all living.

21 Unto Adam also and to his wife did the LORD God make coats of skins, and clothed them.

22 And the LORD God said, Behold, the man is become as one of us, to know good and evil: and now, lest he put forth his hand, and take also of the tree of life, and eat, and live for ever:

23 Therefore the LORD God sent him forth from the garden of Eden, to till the ground from whence he was taken.

24 So he drove out the man; and he placed at the east of the garden of Eden Cherubims, and a flaming sword which turned every way, to keep the way of the tree of life.

Compare Genesis 2:21–22 with 1:26–27, which reads:

1:26 And God said, Let us make man in our image, after our likeness: and let them have dominion over the fish of the sea, and over the fowl of the air, and over the cattle, and over all the earth, and over every creeping thing that creepeth upon the earth.

27 So God created man in his own image, in the image of God created he him; male and female created he them.

Source: Genesis 1:26–27, 2:8–3:24, King James Version

Pindar

Fragments

But in sunshine ever fair
    Abide the Good, and all their nights and days
    An equal splendour wear.
And never as of old with thankless toil
For their poor empty needs they vex the soil,
    And plough the watery seas,
But dwelling with the glorious gods in ease
    A tearless life they pass
    Whose joy on earth it was
To keep their plighted word; but far from these
Torments the rest sustain too dark for human gaze.

Some of them delight themselves with horses and with
wrestling; others with draughts; and with lyres; while
beside them bloometh the fair flower of perfect bliss.
And o'er that lovely land fragrance is ever shed,
while they mingle all manner of incense with the far-
shining fire on the altars of the gods.

Pindar (522?–443 B.C.) was a lyric poet.

Source: Pindar, Fragments 129 and 130 (95), in THE ODES OF PINDAR INCLUDING THE PRIN-
CIPAL FRAGMENTS, trans. Sir John Sandys (Cambridge: Harvard University Press, 1937), 591.

ISLANDS OF THE BLEST

Horace

Epode 16

let us seek the fields,
    the happy fields and the islands of the blest,
where the earth is not plowed, but yearly it yields the grain,
    and the vine is not trimmed, but forever flourishes,
and the branch of the olive never fails to blossom,
    and the black fig, ungrafted, adorns its own tree,
honey drips from the hollow oak, from the lofty hills

the light-stepping spring comes splashing down.
There the goats need no orders to come to the milking pails,
    and the flock returns gladly with swelling udders,
and the bear does not growl as he circles the sheepfold at evening,
    and the earth does not swell up with vipers.
And we shall wonder at greater blessings: the rainy Eastwind
    does not wash away crops with a flood of showers,
and the fertile seeds are not scorched in the dried-up clods,
    for the heat and cold are controlled by the king of the gods.
No diseases infect the flock, no raging heat
    from a star can dry up the herd with drought.
Never did a ship manned by Argive rowers reach here,
    nor a shameless Cochian set foot on this soil,
no Phoenician sailors swing their yardarms this way,
    nor did the long-suffering crew of Ulysses.

Horace (65–8 B.C.) was a Roman lyric poet and satirist.

Source: Horace, Epode 16, in THE ODES AND EPODES OF HORACE, trans. Joseph P. Clancy (Chicago: University of Chicago Press, 1960), 224–225.

The Middle Ages

EDEN

Dracontius

This description of the Garden of Eden by Dracontius includes all the elements of the standard description.

> A place there is diffusing rivers four,
> With flowers ambrosial decked; where jewelled turf,
> Where fragrant herbs abound that never fade,
> The fairest garden in this world of God.
> There fruit knows naught of season, but the year,
> There ever blossoms earth's eternal spring.
> Fair vesture clothes the trees, a goodly band;
> With leaves and sturdy branches well entwined
> A dense-grown wall arises; from each tree
> Depends its store, or lies in meadows strewn.
> In sun's hot rays it burneth not, by blasts

Is never shaken, or doth whirlwind rage
With fierce-conspiring gales; no ice can quell,
No hailstorm strike, nor under hoary frost
Grow white the fields. But there are breezes calm,
Rising from softer gust by gleaming springs.
Each tree is lightly stirred; by this mild breath
From moving leaves the tranquil show strays.

Dracontius was a Christian poet of the late fifth century.

Source: Eleanor S. Duckett, LATIN WRITERS OF THE FIFTH CENTURY (New York: Henry Holt, 1930), 85.

THE LAND OF PRESTER JOHN

The land of Prester John became one of the great myths of the late middle ages. Many explorers set out to find it; many reported back that they had. Found or not, the basic characteristics of Prester John's land remained roughly the same. Prester John was the essence of the holy, Christian ruler, and the land he ruled was one where a true Christian could lead a fully Christian life, something not possible elsewhere.

21. Our land flows with honey and abounds with milk. In some parts of our land, no poisons harm nor garrulous frogs croak, no scorpion is there nor serpent winding through the grass. Poisonous beasts cannot live in that place nor harm anyone.

22. In the country through one of our provinces flows a river called Ydonus. This river, flowing out of Paradise, winds through the whole province at various speeds and there are found in it natural jewels, emeralds, sapphires, carbuncles, topazes, onyx, beryls, amethysts, carnelians, and several other precious stones.

23. In the same place grows a plant which is called *assidios,* the root of which, when carried, puts to flight unclean spirits and forces one to say who he may be and whence and what his name is. Wherefore unclean spirits never dare to enter anyone in that country.

24. In another province of ours whole pepper grows and is gathered; it is exchanged for wheat and corn and hides and cloth. . . .

27. This grove is situated near the foot of Mount Olympus, whence a transparent spring arises, possessing every kind of taste. The flavor varies, however, each hour of the day and night, and lasts a three days journey, not far from Paradise from which Adam was expelled.

28. If anyone, even if he has fasted for three days, tastes of that spring, he will suffer no weakness from that day on, and will always be as a man thirty two years old, however long he may live.

29. There are stones there which are called *midriosi,* which eagles often are accustomed to carry off to our land, by which they rejuvenate and restore their sight.

30. If anyone should wear one on his finger, his sight would not fail, and, if diminished, it is restored, and the more he uses his eyes, the sharper his vision becomes. Blessed by the right charm, it makes a man invisible, banishes hatred, prepares the way for peace, routs envy. . . .

42. In certain other provinces near the torrid zone are reptiles which in our tongue are called salamanders. These reptiles live only in fire, and they produce a sort of membrane about them as other worms do, which make silk.

43. These membranes are carefully worked by the ladies of our palace, and from them we have garments and cloths for every service of our excellency. These cloths are washed only in a strong fire.

Source: "The Letter of Prester John," quoted in George Boas, PRIMITIVISM AND RE-LATED IDEAS IN THE MIDDLE AGES (Baltimore: Johns Hopkins University Press, 1948), 162.

The Lawgivers

Among the founts of early utopianism were the activities of two Greek law-givers or constitution makers: Solon, the lawgiver of Athens; and the probably fictional Lycurgus, the lawgiver of Sparta. Appropriately, Lycurgus has been the most influential on the utopian tradition.

SOLON

Of Solon, Aristotle wrote:

The following seem to be the three most popular features of Solon's constitution: first and most important, that nobody might borrow money on the security of anyone's freedom; secondly, that anyone might seek redress on behalf of those who were wronged; thirdly, the feature which is said to have contributed most to the strength of the democracy, the right to appeal to the *dikasterion* [popular courts], for when the people have the right to vote in the courts they control the constitution.

Source: Aristotle, "Constitution of Athens," in J. M. Moore, ARISTOTLE AND XENOPHON ON DEMOCRACY AND OLIGARCHY (Berkeley: University of California Press, 1975). Quoted in Stephen Everson, ed., THE POLITICS AND CONSTITUTION OF ATHENS (Cambridge: Cambridge University Press, 1996), 216.

Solon himself wrote:

For I gave the common folk such privilege as is sufficient for them, neither adding nor taking away; and such as had power and were admired for their riches, I provided that they too should not suffer undue wrong. Nay, I stood with a strong shield thrown before the both sorts, and would have neither to prevail unrighteously over the other.

Solon (638?–559? B.C.) was the lawgiver of Athens.

Source: SOLON, ELEGY AND IAMBUS, trans. J. M. Edmonds (London: William Heinemann, 1931), 121.

LYCURGUS

Up to the present day, classical Sparta was renowned for both its extreme militarism and its highly collectivist system of social organization, best known through the description of the Greek historian Plutarch (A.D. 46?–120?).

He distributed the rest of the Laconian land among the "perioeci," or free provincials, in thirty thousand lots, and that which belonged to the city of Sparta, in nine thousand lots, to as many genuine Spartans. . . . The lot of each was large enough to produce annually seventy bushels of barley for a man and twelve for his wife, with a proportionate amount of wine and oil. Lycurgus thought that a lot of this size would be sufficient for them, since they needed sustenance enough to promote vigour and health of body, and nothing else. And it is said that on returning from a journey some time afterwards, as he traversed the land just after the harvest, and saw the heaps of grain standing parallel and equal to one another, he smiled, and said to them that were by: "All Laconia looks like a family estate newly divided among many brothers."

IX. Next, he undertook to divide up their movable property also, in order that every vestige of unevenness and inequality might be removed; and when he saw that they could not bear to have it taken from them directly, he took another course, and overcame their avarice by political devices. In the first place, he withdrew all gold and silver money from currency, and ordained the use of iron money only. Then to a great weight and mass of this he gave a trifling value, so that ten minas' worth [a very small amount] required a large storeroom in the house, and a yoke of cattle to transport it. When this money obtained currency, many sorts of iniquity went into exile from Lacedaemon. For who would steal, or receive as a bribe, or rob, or plunder that which could neither be concealed, nor possessed with satisfaction, nay, nor even cut to pieces with any profit? For vinegar was used, as we are told, to quench the red-hot iron, robbing it of its temper and making it worthless for any other purpose, when once it had become brittle and hard to work.

In the next place, he banished the unnecessary and superfluous arts. And even without such banishment most of them would have departed with the old coinage, since there was no sale for their products. For the iron money could not be carried into the rest of Greece, nor had it any value there, but was rather held in ridicule. It was not possible, therefore, to buy any foreign wares or bric-a-brac; no merchant-seamen brought freight into their harbours; no rhetoric teacher set foot on Laconian soil, no vagabond soothsayer, no keeper of harlots, no gold- or silver-smith, since there was no money there. But luxury, thus gradually deprived of that which stimulated and supported it, died away of itself, and men of large possessions had no advantage over the poor, because their wealth found no public outlet, but had to be stored up at home in idleness. In this way it came about that such common and necessary utensils as bedsteads, chairs, and tables were most excellently made among them, and the Laconian "kothon," or drinking-cup, was in very high repute for usefulness among soldiers in active service, as Critias tells us. For its colour concealed the disagreeable appearance of the water which they were often compelled to drink, and its curving lips caught the muddy sediment and held it inside, so that only the purer part reached the mouth of the drinker. For all this they had to thank their lawgiver; since their artisans were now freed from useless tasks, and displayed the beauty of their workmanship in objects of constant and necessary use.

X. With a view to attack luxury still more and remove the thirst for wealth, he introduced his third and most exquisite political device, namely, the institution of common messes, so that they might eat with one another in companies, of common and specified foods, and not take their meals at home, reclining on costly couches at costly tables, delivering themselves into the hands of servants and cooks to be fattened in the dark, like voracious animals, and ruining not only their characters but also their bodies, by surrendering them to every desire and all sorts of surfeit, which call for long sleeps, hot baths, abundant rest, and, as it were, daily nursing and tending. This was surely a great achievement, but it was a still greater one to make wealth "an object of no desire," as Theophrastus says, and even "unwealth," by this community of meals and simplicity of diet. For the rich man could neither use nor enjoy nor even see or display his abundant means, when he went to the same meal as the poor man; so that it was in Sparta alone, of all the cities under the sun, that men could have that far-famed sight, a Plutus [God of Wealth] blind, and lying as lifeless and motionless as a picture. For the rich could not even dine beforehand at home and then go to the common mess with full stomachs, but the rest kept careful watch of him who did not eat and drink with them, and reviled him as a weakling, and one too effeminate for the common diet. . . .

XII. They met in companies of fifteen, a few more or less, and each one of the mess-mates contributed monthly a bushel of barley-meal, eight gallons of wine, five pounds of cheese, two and a half pounds of figs, and in addition to this, a very small sum of money for such relishes as flesh and fish. Besides this, whenever any one made a sacrifice of first fruits, or brought home game from the hunt, he sent a portion to his mess. For whenever any one was belated by a sacrifice or the chase, he was allowed to sup at home, but the rest had to be at the mess. For a long time this custom of eating at common mess-tables was rigidly observed. . . .

Boys also used to come to these public messes, as if they were attending schools of sobriety; there they would listen to political discussions and see instructive models of liberal breeding. There they themselves also became accustomed to sport and jest without scurrility, and to endure jesting without displeasure. Indeed, it seems to have been especially characteristic of a Spartan to endure jesting; but if any one could not bear up under it, he had only to ask it, and the jester ceased. As each one came in, the eldest of the company pointed to the door and said to him: "Through that door no word goes forth outside." And they say that a candidate for membership in one of these messes underwent the following ordeal. Each of the mess-mates took in his hand a bit of soft bread, and when a servant came along with a bowl upon his head, then they cast it into this without a word, like a ballot, leaving it just as it was if he approved of the candidate, but if he disapproved, squeezing it tight in his hand first. For the flattened piece of bread had the force of a perforated, or negative, ballot. And if one such is found in the bowl, the candidate is not admitted to the mess, because they wish all its members to be congenial. The candidate thus rejected is said to have been "caddished," for "caddichus" is the name of the bowl into which they cast the pieces of bread. Of their dishes, the black broth is held in the highest esteem, so that the elderly men do not even ask for a bit of meat, but leave it for the young men, while they themselves have the broth poured out for their meals. . . . After drinking moderately, they go off home without a torch; for they are not allowed to walk with a light, either on this or any other occasion, that they may accustom themselves to marching boldly and without fear in the darkness of night. Such, then, is the fashion of their common messes.

XIII. None of his laws were put into writing by Lycurgus, indeed, one of the so-called "rhetras" [decrees] forbids it. For he thought that if the most important and binding principles which conduce to the prosperity and virtue of a city were implanted in the habits and training of its citizens, they would remain unchanged and secure, having a stronger bond than compulsion in the fixed purposes imparted to the young by education, which performs the office of a law-giver for every one of them. And as for minor matters, such as business contracts, and cases where the needs vary from time to time, it was better, as he thought, not to hamper them by written constraints or fixed usages, but to suffer them, as occasion demanded, to receive such modifications as educated men should determine. Indeed, he assigned the function of law-making wholly and entirely to education.

One of his rhetras accordingly, as I have said, prohibited the use of written laws. Another was directed against extravagance, ordaining that every house should have its roof fashioned by the axe, and its doors by the saw only, and by no other tool. For, as in later times Epaminondas is reported to have said at his own table, that such a meal did not comport with treachery, so Lycurgus was the first to see clearly that such a house does not comport with luxury and extravagance. Nor is any man so vulgar and senseless as to introduce into a simple and common house silver-footed couches, purple coverlets, gold drinking-cups, and all the extravagance which goes along with these, but one must of necessity adapt and proportion his couch to his house, his coverlets to his couch, and to this the rest of his supplies and equipment. It was because he was used to this simplicity that Leotychides the Elder, as we are told, when he was dining in Corinth, and saw the roof of the house adorned with costly panellings, asked his host if trees grew square in that country. . . .

XIV. In the matter of education, which he regarded as the greatest and noblest task of the law-giver, he began at the very source, by carefully regulating marriages and births. For it is not true that, as Aristotle says, he tried to bring the women under proper restraint, but desisted, because he could not overcome the great licence and power which the women enjoyed on account of the many expeditions in which their husbands were engaged. During these the men were indeed obliged to leave their wives in sole control at home, and for this reason paid them greater deference than was their due, and gave them the title of Mistress. But even to the women Lycurgus paid all possible attention. He made the maidens exercise their bodies in running, wrestling, casting the discus, and hurling the javelin, in order that the fruit of their wombs might have vigorous root in vigorous bodies and come to better maturity, and that they themselves might come with vigour to the fulness of their times, and struggle successfully and easily with the pangs of child-birth. He freed them from softness and delicacy and all effeminacy by accustoming the maidens no less than the youths to wear tunics only in processions, and at certain festivals to dance and sing when the young men were present as spectators. There they sometimes even mocked and railed good-naturedly at any youth who had misbehaved himself; and again they would sing the praises of those who had shown themselves worthy, and so inspire the young men with great ambition and ardour. For he who was thus extolled for his valour and held in honour among the maidens, went away exalted by their praises; while the sting of their playful raillery was no less sharp than that of serious admonitions, especially as the kings and senators, together with the rest of the citizens, were all present at the spectacle.

Nor was there anything disgraceful in this scant clothing of the maidens, for modesty attended them, and wantonness was banished; nay, rather, it produced in them habits of simplicity and an ardent desire for health and beauty of body. It gave also to woman-kind a taste of lofty sentiment, for they felt that they too had a place in the arena of bravery and ambition. Wherefore they were led to think and speak as Gorgo, the wife of Leonidas, is said to have done. When some foreign woman, as it would seem, said to her: "You Spartan women are the only ones who rule their men," she answered: "Yes, we are the only ones that give birth to men."

XV. Moreover, there were incentives to marriage in these things,—I mean such things as the appearance of the maidens without much clothing in processions and athletic contests where young men were looking on, for these were drawn on by necessity, "not geometrical, but the sort of necessity which lovers know," as Plato says. Nor was this all; Lycurgus also put a kind of public stigma upon confirmed bachelors. They were excluded from the sight of the young men and maidens at their exercises, and in winter the magistrates ordered them to march round the market-place in their tunics only, and as they marched, they sang a certain song about themselves, and its burden was that they were justly punished for disobeying the laws. Besides this, they were deprived of the honour and gracious attentions which the young men habitually paid to their elders. Therefore there was no one to find fault with what was said to Dercyllidas, reputable general though he was. As he entered a company, namely, one of the younger men would not offer him his seat, but said: "Indeed, thou has begotten no son who will one day give his seat to me."

For their marriages the women were carried off by force, not when they were small and unfit for wedlock, but when they were in full bloom and wholly ripe. After the woman was thus carried off, the bride's-maid, so called, took her in charge, cut her hair off close to the head, put a man's cloak and sandals on her, and laid her down on a pallet, on the floor, alone, in the dark. The bride-groom, not flown with wine nor enfeeble by excesses, but composed and sober, after supping at his public mess-table as usual, slipped stealthily into the room where the bride lay, loosed her virgin's zone, and bore her in his arms to the marriage-bed. Then, after spending a short time with his bride, he went away composedly to his usual quarters, there to sleep with the other young men. And so he continued to do from that time on, spending his days with his comrades, and sleeping with them at night, but visiting his bride by stealth and with every precaution, full of dread and fear lest any of her household should be aware of his visits, his bride also contriving and conspiring with him that they might have stolen interviews as occasion offered. And this they did not for a short time only, but long enough for some of them to become fathers before they had looked upon their own wives by daylight. Such interviews not only brought into exercise self-restraint and moderation, but united husbands and wives when their bodies were full of creative energy and their affections new and fresh, not when they were sated and dulled by unrestricted intercourse; and there was always left behind in their hearts some residual spark of mutual longing and delight.

After giving marriage such traits of reserve and decorum, he none the less freed men from the empty and womanish passion of jealous possession, by making it honourable for them, while keeping the marriage relation free from all wanton irregularities, to share with other worthy men in the begetting of children, laughing to scorn those who regard such common privileges as intolerable, and resort to murder and war rather than grant them. For example, an elderly man with a young wife, if he looked with favour and esteem on some fair and noble young man, might introduce him to her, and adopt her offspring by such a noble father as his own. And again, a worthy man who admired some woman for the fine children that she bore her husband and the modesty of her behaviour as a wife, might enjoy her favours, if her husband would consent, thus planting, as it were, in a soil of beautiful fruitage, and begetting for himself noble sons, who would have the blood of noble men in their veins. For in the first place, Lycurgus did not regard sons as the peculiar property of their fathers, but rather as the common property of the state, and therefore would not have his citizens spring from random parentage, but from the best there was. In the second place, he saw much folly and vanity in what other peoples enacted for the regulation of these matters; in the breeding of dogs and horses they insist on having the best sires which money or favour can secure, but they keep their wives under lock and key, demanding that they have children by none but themselves, even though they be foolish, or infirm, or diseased; as though children of bad stock did not show their badness to those first who possessed and reared them, and children of good stock, contrariwise, their goodness. The freedom which thus prevailed at that time in marriage relations was aimed at physical and political well-being, and was far removed from the licentiousness which was afterwards attributed to their women, so much so that adultery was wholly unknown among them. And a saying is reported of one Geradas, a Spartan of very ancient type, who, on being asked by a stranger what the punishment for adulterers was among them, answered: "Stranger, there is no adulterer among us." "Suppose, then," replied the stranger, "there should be one." "A bull," said Geradas, "would be his forfeit, a bull so large that it could stretch over Mount Taygetus and drink from the river Eurotas." Then the stranger was astonished and said: "But how could there be a bull so large?" To which Geradas replied, with a smile: "But how could there be an adulterer in Sparta?" Such, then, are the accounts we find of their marriages.

XVI. Offspring was not reared at the will of the father, but was taken and carried by him to a place called Lesche, where the elders of the tribes officially examined the infant, and if it was well-built and sturdy, they ordered the father to rear it, and assigned it one of the nine thousand lots of land; but if it was ill-born and deformed, they sent it to the so-called Apothetae, a chasm-like place at the foot of Mount Taygetus, in the conviction that the life of that which nature had not well equipped at the very beginning for health and strength, was of no advantage either to itself or the state. On the same principle, the women used to bathe their new-born babes not with water, but with wine, thus making a sort of test of their constitutions. For it is said that epileptic and sickly infants are thrown into convulsions by the strong wine and loose their senses, while the healthy ones are rather tempered by it, like steel, and given a firm habit of body. Their nurses, too, exercised great care and skill; they reared infants without swaddling-bands, and thus left their limbs and figures free to develop; besides, they taught them to be contented and happy, not dainty about their food, nor fearful of the dark, nor afraid to be left alone, nor given to contemptible peevishness and whimpering. . . .

Of reading and writing, they learned only enough to serve their turn; all the rest of their training was calculated to make them obey commands well, endure hardships, and conquer in battle. Therefore, as they grew in age, their bodily exercise was increased; their heads were close-clipped, and they were accustomed to going bare-foot, and to playing for the most part without clothes. When they were twelve years old, they no longer had tunics to wear, received one cloak a year, had hard, dry flesh, and knew little of baths and ointments; only on certain days of the year, and few at that, did they indulge in such amenities. They slept together, in troops and companies, on pallet-beds which they collected for themselves, breaking off with their hands—no knives allowed—the tops of the rushes which grew along the river Eurotas. In the winter-time, they added to the stuff of these pallets the so-called "lycophon," or *thistle-down,* which was thought to have warmth in it.

XVII. When the boys reached this age, they were favoured with the society of lovers from among the reputable young men. The elderly men also kept close watch of them, coming more frequently to their places of exercise, and observing their contests of strength and wit, not cursorily, but with the idea that they were all in a sense the fathers and tutors and governors of all the boys. In this way, at every fitting time and in every place, the boy who went wrong had someone to admonish and chastise him. Nor was this all; one of the noblest and best men of the city was appointed paedonome, or inspector of the boys, and under his directions the boys, in their several companies, put themselves under the command of the most prudent and warlike of the so-called Eirens. This was the name given to those who had been for two years out of the class of boys, and Melleirens, or *Would-be Eirens,* was the name for the oldest of the boys. This eiren, then, a youth of twenty years, commands his subordinates in their mimic battles, and in doors makes them serve him at his meals. He commissions the larger ones to fetch wood, and the smaller one potherbs. And they steal what they fetch, some of them entering the gardens, and others creeping right slyly and cautiously into the public messes of the men; but if a boy is caught stealing, he is soundly flogged, as a careless and unskillful thief. They steal, too, whatever food they can, and learn to be adept in setting upon people when asleep or off their guard. But the boy who is caught gets a flogging and must go hungry. For the meals allowed them are scanty, in order that they may take into their own hands the fight against hunger, and so be forced into boldness and cunning. . . .

XVIII. The boys make such a serious matter of their stealing, that one of them, as the story goes, who was carrying concealed under his cloak a young fox which he had stolen, suffered the animal to tear out his bowels with its teeth and claws, and died rather than have his theft detected. And even this story gains credence from what their youths now endure, many of whom I have seen expiring under the lash at the altar of Artemis Orthia [a Spartan cult].

The eiren, as he reclined after supper, would order one of the boys to sing a song, and to another would put a question requiring a careful and deliberate answer, as, for instance, "Who is the best man in the city?" or, "What thinkest thou of this man's conduct?" In this way the boys were accustomed to pass right judgements and interest themselves at the very outset in the conduct of the citizens. For if one of them was asked who was a good citizen, or who an infamous one, and had no answer to make, he was judged to have a torpid spirit, and one that would not aspire to excellence. And the answer must not only have reasons and proof given for it, but also be couched in very brief and concise language, and the one who gave a faulty answer was punished with a bite in the thumb from the eiren. Often-times, too, the eiren punished the boys in the presence of the elders and magistrates, thus showing whether his punishments were reasonable and proper or not. While he was punishing them, he suffered no restraint, but after the boys were gone, he was brought to an account if his punishments were harsher than was necessary, or, on the other hand, too mild and gentle.

The boys' lovers also shared with them in their honour or disgrace; and it is said that one of them was once fined by the magistrates because his favourite boy had let an ungenerous cry escape him while he was fighting. Moreover, though this sort of love was so approved among them that even the maidens found lovers in good and noble women, still, there was no jealous rivalry in it, but those who fixed their affections on the same boys made this rather a foundation for friendship with one another, and persevered in common efforts to make their loved one as noble as possible.

XIX. The boys were also taught to use a discourse which combined pungency with grace, and condensed much observation into a few words. His iron money, indeed, Lycurgus made of large weight and small value, as I have observed, but the current coin of discourse he adapted to the expression of deep and abundant meaning with simple and brief diction, by contriving that the general habit of silence should make the boys sententious and correct in their answers. For as sexual incontinence generally produces unfruitfulness and sterility, so intemperance in talking makes discourse empty and vapid. King Agis, accordingly, when a certain Athenian decried the Spartan swords for being so short, and said that jugglers on the stage easily swallowed them, replied: "And yet we certainly reach our enemies with these daggers." And I observe that although the speech also of the Spartans seems short, yet it certainly reaches the point, and arrests the thought of the listener. . . .

XXI. Nor was their training in music and poetry any less serious a concern than the emulous purity of their speech, nay, their very songs had a stimulus that roused the spirit and awoke enthusiastic and effectual effort; the style of them was simple and unaffected, and their themes were serious and edifying. They were for the most part praises of men who had died for Sparta, calling them blessed and happy; censure of men who had played the coward, picturing their grievous and ill-starred life; and such promises and boasts of valour as befitted the different ages. . . .

XXIV. The training of the Spartans lasted into the years of full maturity. No man was allowed to live as he pleased, but in their city, as in a military encampment, they always had a prescribed regimen and employment in public service, considering that they belonged entirely to their country and not to themselves, watching over the boys, if no other duty was laid upon them, and either teaching them some useful thing, or learning it themselves from their elders. For one of the noble and blessed privileges which Lycurgus provided for his fellow-citizens, was abundance of leisure, since he forbade their engaging in any mechanical art whatsoever, and as for money-making, with its laborious efforts to amass wealth, there was no need of it all, since wealth awakened no envy and brought no honour. Besides, the Helots [slaves] tilled their ground for them, and paid them the produce. . . . Therefore it was that one of them who was sojourning at Athens when the courts were in session, and learned that a certain Athenian had been fined for idleness and was going home in great distress of mind and attended on his way by sympathetic and sorrowing friends, begged the bystanders to show him the man who had been fined for living like a freeman. So servile a thing did they regard the devotion to the mechanical arts and to money-making. And law-suits, of course, vanished from among them with their gold and silver coinage, for they knew neither greed nor want, but equality in well-being was established there, and easy living based on simple wants. Choral dances and feasts and festivals and hunting and bodily exercise and social converse occupied their whole time, when they were not on a military expedition.

XXV. Those who were under thirty years of age did not go into the market-place at all, but had their household wants supplied at the hands of their kins-folk and lovers. And it was disreputable for the elderly men to be continually seen loitering there, instead of spending the greater part of the day in the places of exercise that are called "leschai." For if they gathered in these, they spent their time suitably with one another, making no allusions to the problems of money-making or of exchange, nay, they were chiefly occupied there in prais-ing some noble action or censuring some base one, with jesting and laughter which made the path to instruction and correction easy and natural. For not even Lycurgus himself was immoderately severe; indeed, Sosibius tells us that he actually dedicated a little statue of Laughter, and introduced seasonable jest-ing into their drinking parties and like diversions, to sweeten, as it were, their hardships and meagre fare.

In a word, he trained his fellow-citizens to have neither the wish nor the abil-ity to live for themselves; but like bees they were to make themselves always in-tegral parts of the whole community, clustering together about their leader, al-most beside themselves with enthusiasm and noble ambition, and to belong wholly to their country. This idea can be traced also in some of their utterances. For instance, Paedaretus, when he failed to be chosen among the three hundred best men, went away with a very glad countenance, as if rejoicing that the city had three hundred better men than himself. And again, Polycratida, one of an embassy to the generals of the Persian king, on being asked by them whether the embassy was there in a private or a public capacity, replied: "If we succeed, in a public capacity; if we fail, in a private." Again, Argileonis, the mother of Brasidas, when some Amphipolitans who had come to Sparta paid her a visit, asked them if Brasidas had died nobly and in a manner worthy of Sparta. Then they greatly extolled the man and said that Sparta had not such another, to which she answered: "Say not so, Strangers; Brasidas was noble and brave, but Sparta has many better men than he."

XXVI. The senators were at first appointed by Lycurgus himself . . . from those who shared his counsels; but afterwards he arranged that any vacancy caused by death should be filled by the man elected as most deserving out of those above sixty years of age. And of all the contests in the world this would seem to have been the greatest and the most hotly disputed. For it was not the swiftest of the swift, nor the strongest of the strong, but the best and wisest of the good and wise who was to be elected, and have for the rest of his life, as a victor's prize for excellence, what I may call the supreme power in the state, lord as he was of life and death, honour and dishonour, and all the greatest issues of life. The election was made in the following manner. An assembly of the people having been convened, chosen men were shut up in a room near by so that they could neither see nor be seen, but only hear the shouts of the assembly. For as in other matters, so here, the cries of the assembly decided between the competitors. These did not appear in a body, but each one was introduced separately, as the lot fell, and passed silently through the assembly. Then the secluded judges, who had writing-tablets with them, recorded in each case the loudness of the shouting, not knowing for whom it was given, but only that he was introduced first, second, or third, and so on. Whoever was greeted with the most and loudest shouting, him they declared elected. The victor then set a wreath upon his head and visited in order the temples of the gods. He was followed by great numbers of young men, who praised and extolled him, as well as by many women, who celebrated his excellence in songs, and dwelt on the happiness of his life. Each of his relations and friends set a repast before him, saying: "the city honours thee with this table." When he had finished his circuit, he went off to his mess-table. Here he fared in other ways as usual, but a second portion of food was set before him, which he took and put by. After the supper was over, the women who were related to him being now assembled at the door of the mess-hall, he called to him the one whom he most esteemed and gave her the portion he had saved, saying that he had received it as a meed of excellence, and as such gave it to her. Upon this, she too was lauded by the rest of the women and escorted by them to her home.

XXVII. Furthermore, Lycurgus made most excellent regulations in the matter of their burials. To begin with, he did away with all superstitious terror by allowing them to bury their dead within the city, and to have memorials of them near the sacred places, thus making the youth familiar with such sights and accustomed to them, so that they were not confounded by them, and had no horror of death as polluting those who touched a corpse or walked among graves. In the second place, he permitted nothing to be buried with the dead; they simply covered the body with a scarlet robe and olive leaves when they laid it away. To inscribe the name of the dead upon the tomb was not allowed, unless it were that of a man who had fallen in war, or that of a woman who had died in sacred office. He set apart only a short time for mourning, eleven days; on the twelfth, they were to sacrifice to Demeter [the Goddess of Corn] and cease their sorrowing. Indeed, nothing was left untouched and neglected, but with all the necessary details of life he blended some commendation of virtue or rebuke of vice; and he filled the city full of good examples, whose continual presence and society must of necessity exercise a controlling and moulding influence upon those who were walking the path of honour.

Lycurgus is described as the lawgiver of Sparta. He is now generally thought to have been mythical.

Source: Plutarch, PLUTARCH'S LIVES, trans. Bernadotte Perrin. 11 vols. (Cambridge: Harvard University Press, 1914), 1: 229–35, 237–43, 245–65, 271, 279–87.

Utopias and Utopian Satires

Classical Greece provides both the earliest works we now call utopias, descriptions of much better societies, and satires on those societies. In the dialogue that follows Socrates is the main speaker with Glaucon primarily acting as a respondent.

Plato
Republic

For men born and educated like our citizens, the only way, in my opinion, of arriving at a right conclusion about the possession and use of women and children is to follow the path on which we originally started, when we said that the men were to be the guardians and watchdogs of the herd.

True.

Let us further suppose the birth and education of our women to be subject to similar or nearly similar regulations; then we shall see whether the result accords with our design.

What do you mean?

What I mean may be put into the form of a question, I said: Are dogs divided into hes and shes, or do they both share equally in hunting and in keeping watch and in the other duties of dogs? or do we entrust to the males the entire and exclusive care of the flocks, while we leave the females at home, under the idea that the bearing and suckling their puppies is labour enough for them?

No, he said, they share alike; the only difference between them is that the males are stronger and the females weaker.

But can you use different animals for the same purpose, unless they are bred and fed in the same way?

You cannot.

Then, if women are to have the same duties as men, they must have the same nurture and education?

Yes.

The education which was assigned to the men was music and gymnastic.

Yes.

Then women must be taught music and gymnastic and also the art of war, which they must practise like the men? . . .

First, then, whether the question is to be put in jest or in earnest, let us come to an understanding about the nature of woman: Is she capable of sharing either wholly or partially in the actions of men, or not at all? And is the art of war one of those arts in which she can or can not share? That will be the best way of commencing the enquiry, and will probably lead to the fairest conclusion.

That will be much the best way.

Shall we take the other side first and begin by arguing against ourselves; in this manner the adversary's position will not be undefended.

Why not? he said.

Then let us put a speech into the mouths of our opponents. They will say: 'Socrates and Glaucon, no adversary need convict you, for you yourselves, at the first foundation of the State, admitted the principle that everybody was to do the one work suited to his own nature.' And certainly, if I am not mistaken, such an admission was made by us. 'And do not the natures of men and women differ very much indeed?' And we shall reply: Of course they do. Then we shall be asked, 'Whether the tasks assigned to men and to women should not be different, and such as are agreeable to their different natures?'

Certainly they should. 'But if so, have you not fallen into a serious inconsistency in saying that men and women, whose natures are so entirely different, ought to perform the same actions?'

What defence will you make for us, my good Sir, against any one who offers these objections?

That is not an easy question to answer when asked suddenly; and I shall and I do beg of you to draw out the case on our side.

These are the objections, Glaucon, and there are many others of a like kind, which I foresaw long ago; they made me afraid and reluctant to take in hand any law about the possession and nurture of women and children.

By Zeus, he said, the problem to be solved is anything but easy.

Why yes, I said, but the fact is that when a man is out of his depth, whether he has fallen into a little swimming bath or into mid-ocean, he has to swim all the same.

Very true.

And must not we swim and try to reach the shore: we will hope that Arion's dolphin or some other miraculous help may save us?

I suppose so, he said.

Well then, let us see if any way of escape can be found. We acknowledged—did we not? that different natures ought to have different pursuits, and that men's and women's natures are different. And now what are we saying?—that different natures ought to have the same pursuits,—this is the inconsistency which is charged upon us.

Precisely.

Verily, Glaucon, I said, glorious is the power of the art of contradiction!

Why do you say so?

Because I think that many a man falls into the practice against his will. When he thinks that he is reasoning he is really disputing, just because he cannot define and divide, and so know that of which he is speaking; and he will pursue a merely verbal opposition in the spirit of contention and not of fair discussion.

Yes, he replied, such is very often the case; but what has that to do with us and our argument?

A great deal; for there is certainly a danger of our getting unintentionally into a verbal opposition.

In what way?

Why, we valiantly and pugnaciously insist upon the verbal truth, that different natures ought to have different pursuits, but we never considered at all what was the meaning of sameness or difference of nature, or why we distinguished them when we assigned different pursuits to different natures and the same to the same natures.

Why, no, he said, that was never considered by us.

I said: Suppose that by way of illustration we were to ask the question whether there is not an opposition in nature between bald men and hairy men; and if this is admitted by us, then, if bald men are cobblers, we should forbid the hairy men to be cobblers, and conversely?

That would be a jest, he said.

Yes, I said, a jest; and why? because we never meant when we constructed the State, that the opposition of natures should extend to every difference, but only to those differences which affected the pursuit in which the individual is engaged; we should have argued, for example, that a physician and one who is in mind a physician may be said to have the same nature.

True.

Whereas the physician and the carpenter have different natures?

Certainly.

And if, I said, the male and female sex appear to differ in their fitness for any art or pursuit, we should say that such pursuit or art ought to be assigned to one or the other of them; but if the difference consists only in women bearing and men begetting children, this does not amount to a proof that a woman differs from a man in respect of the sort of education she should receive; and we shall therefore continue to maintain that our guardians and their wives ought to have the same pursuits.

Very true, he said.

Next, we shall ask our opponent how, in reference to any of the pursuits or arts of civic life, the nature of a woman differs from that of a man?

That will be quite fair.

And perhaps he, like yourself, will reply that to give a sufficient answer on the instant is not easy; but after a little reflection there is no difficulty.

Yes, perhaps.

Suppose then that we invite him to accompany us in the argument, and then we may hope to show him that there is nothing peculiar in the constitution of women which would affect them in the administration of the State.

By all means.

Let us say to him: Come now, and we will ask you a question:—when you spoke of a nature gifted or not gifted in any respect, did you mean to say that one man will acquire a thing easily, another with difficulty; a little learning will lead the one to discover a great deal; whereas the other, after much study and application, no sooner learns than he forgets; or again, did you mean, that the one has a body which is a good servant to his mind, while the body of the other is a hindrance to him?—would not these be the sort of differences which distinguish the man gifted by nature from the one who is ungifted?

No one will deny that.

And can you mention any pursuit of mankind in which the male sex has not all these gifts and qualities in a higher degree than the female? Need I waste time in speaking of the art of weaving, and the management of pancakes and preserves, in which womankind does really appear to be great, and in which for her to be beaten by a man is of all things the most absurd?

You are quite right, he replied, in maintaining the general inferiority of the female sex: although many women are in many things superior to many men, yet on the whole what you say is true.

And if so, my friend, I said, there is no special faculty of administration in a state which a woman has because she is a woman, or which a man has by virtue of his sex, but the gifts of nature are alike diffused in both; all the pursuits of men are the pursuits of women also, but in all of them a woman is inferior to a man.

Very true.

Then are we to impose all our enactments on men and none of them on women?

That will never do.

One woman has a gift of healing, another not; one is a musician, and another has no music in her nature?

Very true.

And one woman has a turn for gymnastic and military exercises, and another is unwarlike and hates gymnastics?

Certainly.

And one woman is a philosopher, and another is an enemy of philosophy; one has spirit, and another is without spirit?

That is also true.

Then one woman will have the temper of a guardian, and another not. Was not the selection of the male guardians determined by differences of this sort?

Yes.

Men and women alike possess the qualities which make a guardian; they differ only in their comparative strength or weakness.

Obviously.

And those women who have such qualities are to be selected as the companions and colleagues of men who have similar qualities and whom they resemble in capacity and in character?

Very true.

And ought not the same natures to have the same pursuits?

They ought.

Then, as we were saying before, there is nothing unnatural in assigning music and gymnastic to the wives of the guardians—to that point we come round again.

Certainly not.

The law which we then enacted was agreeable to nature, and therefore not an impossibility or mere aspiration; and the contrary practice, which prevails at present, is in reality a violation of nature.

That appears to be true.

We had to consider, first, whether our proposals were possible, and secondly whether they were the most beneficial?

Yes.

And the possibility has been acknowledged?

Yes.

The very great benefit has next to be established?

Quite so.

You will admit that the same education which makes a man a good guardian will make a woman a good guardian; for their original nature is the same?

Yes.

I should like to ask you a question.

What is it?

Would you say that all men are equal in excellence, or is one man better than another?

The latter.

And in the commonwealth which we were founding do you conceive the guardians who have been brought up on our model system to be more perfect men, or the cobblers whose education has been cobbling?

What a ridiculous question!

You have answered me, I replied: Well, and may we not further say that our guardians are the best of our citizens?

By far the best.

And will not their wives be the best women?

Yes, by far the best.

And can there be anything better for the interests of the State than that the men and women of a State should be as good as possible?

There can be nothing better.

And this is what the arts of music and gymnastic, when present in such manner as we have described, will accomplish?

Certainly.

Then we have made an enactment not only possible but in the highest degree beneficial to the State?

True.

Then let the wives of our guardians strip, for their virtue will be their robe, and let them share in the toils of war and the defence of their country; only in the distribution of labours the lighter are to be assigned to the women, who are the weaker natures, but in other respects their duties are to be the same. And as for the man who laughs at naked women exercising their bodies from the best of motives, in his laughter he is plucking 'A fruit of unripe wisdom,' and he himself is ignorant of what he is laughing at, or what he is about;—for that is, and ever will be, the best of sayings, That the useful is the noble and the hurtful is the base.

Very true.

Here, then, is one difficulty in our law about women, which we may say that we have now escaped; the wave has not swallowed us up alive for enacting that the guardians of either sex should have all their pursuits in common; to the utility and also to the possibility of this arrangement the consistency of the argument with itself bears witness.

Yes, that was a mighty wave which you have escaped.

Yes, I said, but a greater is coming; you will of this when you see the next.

Go on; let me see.

The law, I said, which is the sequel of this and of all that has preceded, is to the following effect,—'that the wives of our guardians are to be common, and their children are to be common, and no parent is to know his own child, nor any child his parent.'

Yes, he said, that is a much greater wave than the other; and the possibility as well as the utility of such a law are far more questionable.

I do not think, I said, that there can be any dispute about the very great utility of having wives and children in common; the possibility is quite another matter, and will be very much disputed.

I think that a good many doubts may be raised about both.

You imply that the two questions must be combined, I replied. Now I meant that you should admit the utility; and in this way, as I thought; I should escape from one of them, and then there would remain only the possibility.

But that little attempt is detected, and therefore you will please to give a defence of both.

Well, I said, I submit to my fate. Yet grant me a little favour: let me feast my mind with the dream as day dreamers are in the habit of feasting themselves when they are walking alone; for before they have discovered any means of effecting their wishes—that is a matter which never troubles them—they would rather not tire themselves by thinking about possibilities; but assuming that what they desire is already granted to them, they proceed with their plan, and delight in detailing what they mean to do when their wish has come true—that is a way which they have of not doing much good to a capacity which was never good for much. Now I myself am beginning to lose heart, and I should like, with your permission, to pass over the question of possibility at present. Assuming therefore the possibility of the proposal, I shall now proceed to enquire how the rulers will carry out these arrangements, and I shall demonstrate that our plan, if executed, will be of the greatest benefit to the State and to the guardians. First of all, then, if you have no objection, I will endeavour with your help to consider the advantages of the measure; and hereafter the question of possibility.

I have no objection; proceed.

First, I think that if our rulers and their auxiliaries are to be worthy of the name which they bear, there must be willingness to obey in the one and the power of command in the other; the guardians must themselves obey the laws, and they must also imitate the spirit of them in any details which are entrusted to their care.

That is right, he said.

You, I said, who are their legislator, having selected the men, will now select the women and give them to them;—they must be as far as possible of like natures with them; and they must live in common houses and meet at common meals. None of them will have anything specially his or her own; they will be together, and will be brought up together, and will associate at gymnastic exercises. And so they will be drawn by a necessity of their natures to have intercourse with each other—necessity is not too strong a word, I think?

Yes, he said;—necessity, not geometrical, but another sort of necessity which lovers know, and which is far more convincing and constraining to the mass of mankind.

True, I said; and this, Glaucon, like all the rest, must proceed after an orderly fashion; in a city of the blessed, licentiousness is an unholy thing which the rulers will forbid.

Yes, he said, and it ought not to be permitted.

Then clearly the next thing will be to make matrimony sacred in the highest degree, and what is most beneficial will be deemed sacred?

Exactly.

And how can marriages be made most beneficial?—that is a question which I put to you, because I see in your house dogs for hunting, and of the nobler sort of birds not a few. Now, I beseech you, do tell me, have you ever attended to their pairing and breeding?

In what particulars?

Why, in the first place, although they are all of a good sort, are not some better than others?

True.

And do you breed from them all indifferently, or do you take care to breed from the best only?

From the best.

And do you take the oldest or the youngest, or only those of ripe age?

I choose only those of ripe age.

And if care was not taken in the breeding, your dogs and birds would greatly deteriorate?

Certainly.

And the same of horses and animals in general?

Undoubtedly.

Good heavens! my dear friend, I said, what consummate skill will our rulers need if the same principle holds of the human species!

Certainly, the same principle holds; but why does this involve any particular skill?

Because, I said, our rulers will often have to practise upon the body corporate with medicines. Now you know that when patients do not require medicines, but have only to be put under a regimen, the inferior sort of practitioner is deemed to be good enough; but when medicine has to be given, then the doctor should be more of a man.

That is quite true, he said; but to what are you alluding?

I mean, I replied, that our rulers will find a considerable dose of falsehood and deceit necessary for the good of their subjects: we were saying that the use of all these things regarded as medicines might be of advantage.

And we were very right.

And this lawful use of them seems likely to be often needed in the regulations of marriages and births.

How so?

Why, I said, the principle has been already laid down that the best of either sex should be united with the best as often, and the inferior with the inferior, as seldom as possible; and that they should rear the offspring of the one sort of union, but not of the other, if the flock is to be maintained in first-rate condition. Now these goings on must be a secret which the rulers only know, or there will be a further danger of our herd, as the guardians may be termed, breaking out into rebellion.

Very true.

Had we not better appoint certain festivals at which we will bring together the brides and bridegrooms, and sacrifices will be offered and suitable hymeneal songs composed by our poets: the number of weddings is a matter which must be left to the discretion of the rulers, whose aim will be to preserve the average of population? There are many other things which they will have to consider, such as the effects of wars and diseases and any similar agencies, in order as far as this is possible to prevent the State from becoming either too large or too small.

Certainly, he replied.

We shall have to invent some ingenious kind of lots which the less worthy may draw on each occasion of our bringing them together, and then they will accuse their own ill-luck and not the rulers.

To be sure, he said.

And I think that our braver and better youth, besides their other honours and rewards, might have greater facilities of intercourse with women given them; their bravery will be a reason, and such fathers ought to have as many sons as possible.

True.

And the proper officers, whether male or female or both, for offices are to be held by women as well as by men—

Yes—The proper officers will take the offspring of the good parents to the pen or fold, and there they will deposit them with certain nurses who dwell in a separate quarter; but the offspring of the inferior, or of the better when they chance to be deformed, will be put away in some mysterious, unknown place, as they should be.

Yes, he said, that must be done if the breed of the guardians is to be kept pure.

They will provide for their nurture, and will bring the mothers to the fold when they are full of milk, taking the greatest possible care that no mother recognizes her own child; and other wet-nurses may be engaged if more are required. Care will also be taken that the process of suckling shall not be protracted too long; and the mothers will have no getting up at night or other trouble, but will hand over all this sort of thing to the nurses and attendants.

You suppose the wives of our guardians to have a fine easy time of it when they are having children.

Why, said I, and so they ought. Let us, however, proceed with our scheme. We were saying that the parents should be in the prime of life?

Very true.

And what is the prime of life? May it not be defined as a period of about twenty years in a woman's life, and thirty in a man's?

Which years do you mean to include?

A woman, I said, at twenty years of age may begin to bear children to the State, and continue to bear them until forty; a man may begin at five-and-twenty, when he has passed the point at which the pulse of life beats quickest, and continue to beget children until he be fifty-five.

Certainly, he said, both in men and women those years are the prime of physical as well as of intellectual vigour.

Any one above or below the prescribed ages who takes part in the public hymeneals shall be said to have done an unholy and unrighteous thing; the child of which he is the father, if it steals into life, will have been conceived under auspices very unlike the sacrifices and prayers, which at each hymeneal priestesses and priest and the whole city will offer, that the new generation may be better and more useful than their good and useful parents, whereas his child will be the offspring of darkness and strange lust.

Very true, he replied.

And the same law will apply to any one of those within the prescribed age who forms a connection with any woman in the prime of life without the sanction of the rulers; for we shall say that he is raising up a bastard to the State, uncertified and unconsecrated.

Very true, he replied.

This applies, however, only to those who are within the specified age: after that we allow them to range at will, except that a man may not marry his daughter or his daughter's daughter, or his mother or his mother's mother; and women, on the other hand, are prohibited from marrying their sons or fathers, or son's son or father's father, and so on in either direction. And we grant all this, accompanying the permission with strict orders to prevent any embryo which may come into being from seeing the light; and if any force a way to the birth, the parents must understand that the offspring of such an union cannot be maintained, and arrange accordingly.

That also, he said, is a reasonable proposition. But how will they know who are fathers and daughters, and so on?

They will never know. The way will be this:—dating from the day of the hymeneal, the bridegroom who was then married will call all the male children who are born in the seventh and tenth month afterwards his sons, and the female children his daughters, and they will call him father, and he will call their children his grandchildren, and they will call the elder generation grandfathers and grandmothers. All who were begotten at the time when their fathers and mothers came together will be called their brothers and sisters, and these, as I was saying, will be forbidden to inter-marry. This, however, is not to be understood as an absolute prohibition of the marriage of brothers and sisters; if the lot favours them, and they receive the sanction of the Pythian oracle [a variant of the Delphic oracle who was consulted on a wide variety of questions], the law will allow them.

Quite right, he replied.

Such is the scheme, Glaucon, according to which the guardians of our State are to have their wives and families in common. And now you would have the argument show that this community is consistent with the rest of our polity, and also that nothing can be better—would you not?

Yes, certainly.

Shall we try to find a common basis by asking of ourselves what ought to be the chief aim of the legislator in making laws and in the organization of a State,—what is the greatest good, and what is the greatest evil, and then consider whether our previous description has the stamp of the good or of the evil?

By all means.

Can there be any greater evil than discord and distraction and plurality where unity ought to reign? or any greater good than the bond of unity?

There cannot.

And there is unity where there is community of pleasures and pains—where all the citizens are glad or grieved on the same occasions of joy and sorrow?

No doubt.

Yes; and where there is no common but only private feeling a State is disorganized—when you have one half of the world triumphing and the other plunged in grief at the same events happening to the city or the citizens?

Certainly.

Such differences commonly originate in a disagreement about the use of the terms 'mine' and 'not mine,' 'his' and 'not his.'

Exactly so.

And is not that the best-ordered State in which the greatest number of persons apply the terms 'mine' and 'not mine' in the same way to the same thing?

Quite true.

Or that again which most nearly approaches to the condition of the individual—as in the body, when but a finger of one of us is hurt, the whole frame, drawn towards the soul as a center and forming one kingdom under the ruling power therein, feels the hurt and sympathizes all together with the part affected, and we say that the man has a pain in his finger; and the same expression is used about any other part of the body, which has a sensation of pain at suffering or of pleasure at the alleviation of suffering.

Very true, he replied; and I agree with you that in the best-ordered State there is the nearest approach to this common feeling which you describe.

Then when any one of the citizens experiences any good or evil, the whole State will make his case their own, and will either rejoice or sorrow with him?

Yes, he said, that is what will happen in a well-ordered State.

It will now be time, I said, for us to return to our State and see whether this or some other form is most in accordance with these fundamental principles.

Very good.

Our State like every other has rulers and subjects?

True.

All of whom will call one another citizens?

Of course.

But is there not another name which people give to their rulers in other States?

Generally they call them masters, but in democratic States they simply call them rulers.

And in our State what other name besides that of citizens do the people give the rulers?

They are called saviours and helpers, he replied.

And what do the rulers call the people?

Their maintainers and foster-fathers.

And what do they call them in other States?

Slaves.

And what do the rulers call one another in other States?

Fellow-rulers.

And what in ours?

Fellow-guardians.

Did you ever know an example in any other State of a ruler who would speak of one of his colleagues as his friend and of another as not being his friend?

Yes, very often.

And the friend he regards and describes as one in whom he has an interest, and the other as a stranger in whom he has no interest?

Exactly.

But would any of your guardians think or speak of any other guardian as a stranger?

Certainly he would not; for every one whom they meet will be regarded by them either as a brother or sister, or father or mother, or son or daughter, or as the child or parent of those who are thus connected with him.

Capital, I said; but let me ask you once more: Shall they be a family in name only; or shall they in all their actions be true to the name? For example, in the use of the word 'father,' would the care of a father be implied and the filial reverence and duty and obedience to him which the law commands; and is the violator of these duties to be regarded as an impious and unrighteous person who is not likely to receive much good either at the hands of God or of man?

Are these to be or not to be the strains which the children will hear repeated in their ears by all the citizens about those who are intimated to them to be their parents and the rest of their kinsfolk?

These, he said, and none other; for what can be more ridiculous than for them to utter the names of family ties with the lips only and not to act in the spirit of them?

Then in our city the language of harmony and concord will be more often beard than in any other. As I was describing before, when any one is well or ill, the universal word will be with me 'it is well' or 'it is ill.'

Most true.

And agreeably to this mode of thinking and speaking, were we not saying that they will have their pleasures and pains in common?

Yes, and so they will.

And they will have a common interest in the same thing which they will alike call 'my own,' and having this common interest they will have a common feeling of pleasure and pain?

Yes, far more so than in other States.

And the reason of this, over and above the general constitution of the State, will be that the guardians will have a community of women and children?

That will be the chief reason.

And this unity of feeling we admitted to be the greatest good, as was implied in our own comparison of a well-ordered State to the relation of the body and the members, when affected by pleasure or pain?

That we acknowledged, and very rightly.

Then the community of wives and children among our citizens is clearly the source of the greatest good to the State?

Certainly.

And this agrees with the other principle which we were affirming,—that the guardians were not to have houses or lands or any other property; their pay was to be their food, which they were to receive from the other citizens, and they were to have no private expenses; for we intended them to preserve their true character of guardians.

Right, he replied.

Both the community of property and the community of families, as I am saying, tend to make them more truly guardians; they will not tear the city in pieces by differing about 'mine' and 'not mine;' each man dragging any acquisition which he has made into a separate house of his own, where he has a separate wife and children and private pleasures and pains; but all will be affected as far as may be by the same pleasures and pains because they are all of one opinion about what is near and dear to them, and therefore they all tend towards a common end.

Certainly, he replied.

And as they have nothing but their persons which they can call their own, suits and complaints will have no existence among them; they will be delivered from all those quarrels of which money or children or relations are the occasion.

Of course they will.

Neither will trials for assault or insult ever be likely to occur among them. For that equals should defend themselves against equals we shall maintain to be honourable and right; we shall make the protection of the person a matter of necessity.

That is good, he said.

Yes; and there is a further good in the law; viz. that if a man has a quarrel with another he will satisfy his resentment then and there, and not proceed to more dangerous lengths.

Certainly.

To the elder shall be assigned the duty of ruling and chastising the younger.

Clearly.

Nor can there be a doubt that the younger will not strike or do any other violence to an elder, unless the magistrates command him; nor will he slight him in any way. For there are two guardians, shame and fear, mighty to prevent him: shame, which makes men refrain from laying hands on those who are to them in the relation of parents; fear, that the injured one will be succoured by the others who are his brothers, sons, fathers.

That is true, he replied.

Then in every way the laws will help the citizens to keep the peace with one another?

Yes, there will be no want of peace.

And as the guardians will never quarrel among themselves there will be no danger of the rest of the city being divided either against them or against one another.

None whatever.

I hardly like even to mention the little meannesses of which they will be rid, for they are beneath notice: such, for example, as the flattery of the rich by the poor, and all the pains and pangs which men experience in bringing up a family, and in finding money to buy necessaries for their household, borrowing and then repudiating, getting how they can, and giving the money into the hands of women and slaves to keep—the many evils of so many kinds which people suffer in this way are mean enough and obvious enough, and not worth speaking of.

Yes, he said, a man has no need of eyes in order to perceive that.

And from all these evils they will be delivered, and their life will be blessed as the life of Olympic victors and yet more blessed.

How so?

The Olympic victor, I said, is deemed happy in receiving a part only of the blessedness which is secured to our citizens, who have won a more glorious victory and have a more complete maintenance at the public cost. For the victory which they have won is the salvation of the whole State; and the crown with which they and their children are crowned is the fulness of all that life needs; they receive rewards from the hands of their country while living, and after death have an honourable burial.

Yes, he said, and glorious rewards they are.

Do you remember, I said, how in the course of the previous discussion some one who shall be nameless accused us of making our guardians unhappy—they had nothing and might have possessed all things—to whom we replied that, if an occasion offered, we might perhaps hereafter consider this question, but that, as at present advised, we would make our guardians truly guardians, and that we were fashioning the State with a view to the greatest happiness, not of any particular class, but of the whole?

Yes, I remember.

And what do you say, now that the life of our protectors is made out to be far better and nobler than that of Olympic victors—is the life of shoemakers, or any other artisans, or of husbandmen, to be compared with it?

Certainly not.

At the same time I ought here to repeat what I have said elsewhere, that if any of our guardians shall try to be happy in such a manner that he will cease to be a guardian, and is not content with this safe and harmonious life, which, in our judgment, is of all lives the best, but infatuated by some youthful conceit of happiness which gets up into his head shall seek to appropriate the whole State to himself, then he will have to learn how wisely Hesiod spoke, when he said, 'half is more than the whole.'

If he were to consult me, I should say to him: Stay where you are, when you have the offer of such a life. You agree then, I said, that men and women are to have a common way of life such as we have described—common education, common children; and they are to watch over the citizens in common whether abiding in the city or going out to war; they are to keep watch together, and to hunt together like dogs; and always and in all things, as far as they are able, women are to share with the men?

And in so doing they will do what is best, and will not violate, but preserve the natural relation of the sexes.

I agree with you, he replied. . . .

I said: *Until philosophers are kings, or the kings and princes of this world have the spirit and power of philosophy, and political greatness and wisdom meet in one, and those commoner natures who pursue either to the exclusion of the other are compelled to stand aside, cities will never have rest from their evils,—nor the human race, as I believe,—and then only will this our State have a possibility of life and behold the light of day.* Such was the thought, my dear Glaucon, which I would fain have uttered if it had not seemed too extravagant; for to be convinced that in no other State can there be happiness private or public is indeed a hard thing.

Socrates, what do you mean? I would have you consider that the word which you have uttered is one at which numerous persons, and very respectable persons too, in a figure pulling off their coats all in a moment, and seizing any weapon that comes to hand, will run at you might and main, before you know where you are, intending to do heaven knows what; and if you don't prepare an answer, and put yourself in motion, you will be 'prepared by their fine wits,' and no mistake.

You got me into the scrape, I said.

And I was quite right; however, I will do all I can to get you out of it; but I can only give you good-will and good advice, and, perhaps, I may be able to fit answers to your questions better than another—that is all. And now, having such an auxiliary, you must do your best to show the unbelievers that you are right.

I ought to try, I said, since you offer me such invaluable assistance. And I think that, if there is to be a chance of our escaping, we must explain to them whom we mean when we say that philosophers are to rule in the State; then we shall be able to defend ourselves: There will be discovered to be some natures who ought to study philosophy and to be leaders in the State; and others who are not born to be philosophers, and are meant to be followers rather than leaders.

Then now for a definition, he said.

Follow me, I said, and I hope that I may in some way or other be able to give you a satisfactory explanation.

Proceed.

I dare say that you remember, and therefore I need not remind you, that a lover, if he is worthy of the name, ought to show his love, not to some one part of that which he loves, but to the whole.

I really do not understand, and therefore beg of you to assist my memory.

Another person, I said, might fairly reply as you do; but a man of pleasure like yourself ought to know that all who are in the flower of youth do somehow or other raise a pang or emotion in a lover's breast, and are thought by him to be worthy of his affectionate regards. Is not this a way which you have with the fair: one has a snub nose, and you praise his charming face; the hook-nose of another has, you say, a royal look; while he who is neither snub nor hooked has the grace of regularity: the dark visage is manly, the fair are children of the gods; and as to the sweet 'honey pale,' as they are called, what is the very name but the invention of a lover who talks in diminutives, and is not adverse to paleness if appearing on the cheek of youth? In a word, there is no excuse which you will not make, and nothing which you will not say, in order not to lose a single flower that blooms in the spring-time of youth.

If you make me an authority in matters of love, for the sake of the argument, I assent.

And what do you say of lovers of wine? Do you not see them doing the same? They are glad of any pretext of drinking any wine.

Very good.

And the same is true of ambitious men; if they cannot command an army, they are willing to command a file; and if they cannot be honoured by really great and important persons, they are glad to be honoured by lesser and meaner people, but honour of some kind they must have.

Exactly.

Once more let me ask: Does he who desires any class of goods, desire the whole class or a part only?

The whole.

And may we not say of the philosopher that he is a lover, not of a part of wisdom only, but of the whole?

Yes, of the whole.

And he who dislikes learnings, especially in youth, when he has no power of judging what is good and what is not, such an one we maintain not to be a philosopher or a lover of knowledge, just as he who refuses his food is not hungry, and may be said to have a bad appetite and not a good one?

Very true, he said.

Whereas he who has a taste for every sort of knowledge and who is curious to learn and is never satisfied, may be justly termed a philosopher? Am I not right?

Glaucon said: If curiosity makes a philosopher, you will find many a strange being will have a title to the name. All the lovers of sights have a delight in learning, and must therefore be included.

Musical amateurs, too, are a folk strangely out of place among philosophers, for they are the last persons in the world who would come to anything like a philosophical discussion, if they could help, while they run about at the Dionysiac[1] festivals as if they had let out their ears to hear every chorus; whether the performance is in town or country—that makes no difference—they are there. Now are we to maintain that all these and any who have similar tastes, as well as the professors of quite minor arts, are philosophers?

Certainly not, I replied; they are only an imitation.

He said: Who then are the true philosophers?

Those, I said, who are lovers of the vision of truth.

That is also good, he said; but I should like to know what you mean?

To another, I replied, I might have a difficulty in explaining; but I am sure that you will admit a proposition which I am about to make.

What is the proposition?

That since beauty is the opposite of ugliness, they are two?

Certainly.

And inasmuch as they are two, each of them is one?

True again.

And of just and unjust, good and evil, and of every other class, the same remark holds: taken singly, each of them one; but from the various combinations of them with actions and things and with one another, they are seen in all sorts of lights and appear many?

Very true.

And this is the distinction which I draw between the sight-loving, art-loving, practical class and those of whom I am speaking, and who are alone worthy of the name of philosophers.

How do you distinguish them? he said.

The lovers of sounds and sights, I replied, are, as I conceive, fond of fine tones and colours and forms and all the artificial products that are made out of them, but their mind is incapable of seeing or loving absolute beauty.

True, he replied.

Few are they who are able to attain to the sight of this.

Very true.

---

1. Dionysis was the God of wine and intoxication, and his festivals were a release from reason. *Ed.*

And he who, having a sense of beautiful things has no sense of absolute beauty, or who, if another lead him to a knowledge of that beauty is unable to follow—of such an one I ask, Is he awake or in a dream only? Reflect: is not the dreamer, sleeping or waking, one who likens dissimilar things, who puts the copy in the place of the real object?

I should certainly say that such an one was dreaming.

But take the case of the other, who recognises the existence of absolute beauty and is able to distinguish the idea from the objects which participate in the idea, neither putting the objects in the place of the idea nor the idea in the place of the objects—is he a dreamer, or is he awake?

He is wide awake.

And may we not say that the mind of the one who knows has knowledge, and that the mind of the other, who opines only, has opinion.

Certainly.

But suppose that the latter should quarrel with us and dispute our statement, can we administer any soothing cordial or advice to him, without revealing to him that there is sad disorder in his wits?

We must certainly offer him some good advice, he replied.

Come, then, and let us think of something to say to him. Shall we begin by assuring him that he is welcome to any knowledge which he may have, and that we are rejoiced at his having it? But we should like to ask him a question: Does he who has knowledge know something or nothing? (You must answer for him.)

I answer that he knows something.

Something that is or is not?

Something that is; for how can that which is not ever be known?

And are we assured, after looking at the matter from many points of view, that absolute being is or may be absolutely known, but that the utterly non-existent is utterly unknown?

Nothing can be more certain.

Good. But if there be anything which is of such a nature as to be and not to be, that will have a place intermediate between pure being and the absolute negation of being?

Yes, between them.

And, as knowledge corresponded to being and ignorance of necessity to not-being, for that intermediate between being and not-being there has to be discovered a corresponding intermediate between ignorance and knowledge, if there be such?

Certainly.

Do we admit the existence of opinion?

Undoubtedly.

As being the same with knowledge, or another faculty?

Another faculty.

Then opinion and knowledge have to do with different kinds of matter corresponding to this difference of faculties?

Yes.

And knowledge is relative to being and knows being. But before I proceed further I will make a division.

What division?

I will begin by placing faculties in a class by themselves: they are powers in us, and in all other things, by which we do as we do.

Sight and hearing, for example, I should call faculties. Have I clearly explained the class which I mean?

Yes, I quite understand.

Then let me tell you my view about them. I do not see them, and therefore the distinctions of fire, colour, and the like, which enable me to discern the differences of some things, do not apply to them. In speaking of a faculty I think only of its sphere and its result; and that which has the same sphere and the same result I call the same faculty, but that which has another sphere and another result I call different. Would that be your way of speaking?

Yes.

And will you be so very good as to answer one more question? Would you say that knowledge is a faculty, or in what class would you place it?

Certainly knowledge is a faculty, and the mightiest of all faculties.

And is opinion also a faculty?

Certainly, he said; for opinion is that with which we are able to form an opinion.

And yet you were acknowledging a little while ago that knowledge is not the same as opinion?

Why, yes, he said: how can any reasonable being ever identify that which is infallible with that which errs?

An excellent answer, proving, I said, that we are quite conscious of a distinction between them.

Yes.

Then knowledge and opinion having distinct powers have also distinct spheres or subject-matters?

That is certain.

Being is the sphere or subject-matter of knowledge, and knowledge is to know the nature of being?

Yes.

And opinion is to have an opinion?

Yes.

And do we know what we opine? or is the subject-matter of opinion the same as the subject-matter of knowledge?

Nay, he replied, that has been already disproven; if difference in faculty implies difference in the sphere or subject matter, and if, as we were saying, opinion and knowledge are distinct faculties, then the sphere of knowledge and of opinion cannot be the same.

Then if being is the subject-matter of knowledge, something else must be the subject-matter of opinion?

Yes, something else.

Well then, is not-being the subject-matter of opinion? or, rather, how can there be an opinion at all about not-being? Reflect: when a man has an opinion, has he not an opinion about something? Can he have an opinion which is an opinion about nothing?

Impossible.

He who has an opinion has an opinion about some one thing?

Yes.

And not-being is not one thing but, properly speaking, nothing?

True.

Of not-being, ignorance was assumed to be the necessary correlative; of being, knowledge?

True, he said.

Then opinion is not concerned either with being or with not-being?

Not with either.

And can therefore neither be ignorance nor knowledge?

That seems to be true.

But is opinion to be sought without and beyond either of them, in a greater clearness than knowledge, or in a greater darkness than ignorance?

In neither.

Then I suppose that opinion appears to you to be darker than knowledge, but lighter than ignorance?

Both; and in no small degree.

And also to be within and between them?

Yes.

Then you would infer that opinion is intermediate?

No question.

But were we not saying before, that if anything appeared to be of a sort which is and is not at the same time, that sort of thing would appear also to lie in the interval between pure being and absolute not-being; and that the corresponding faculty is neither knowledge nor ignorance, but will be found in the interval between them?

True.

And in that interval there has now been discovered something which we call opinion?

There has.

Then what remains to be discovered is the object which partakes equally of the nature of being and not-being, and cannot rightly be termed either, pure and simple; this unknown term, when discovered, we may truly call the subject of opinion, and assign each to its proper faculty,—the extremes to the faculties of the extremes and the mean to the faculty of the mean.

True.

This being premised, I would ask the gentleman who is of opinion that there is no absolute or unchangeable idea of beauty—in whose opinion the beautiful is the manifold—he, I say, your lover of beautiful sights, who cannot bear to be told that the beautiful is one, and the just is one, or that anything is one—to him I would appeal, saying, Will you be so very kind, sir, as to tell us whether, of all these beautiful things, there is one which will not be found ugly; or of the just, which will not be found unjust; or of the holy, which will not also be unholy?

No, he replied; the beautiful will in some point of view be found ugly; and the same is true of the rest.

And may not the many which are doubles be also halves?—doubles, that is, of one thing, and halves of another?

Quite true.

And things great and small, heavy and light, as they are termed, will not be denoted by these any more than by the opposite names?

True; both these and the opposite names will always attach to all of them.

And can any one of those many things which are called by particular names be said to be this rather than not to be this?

He replied: They are like the punning riddles which are asked at feasts or the children's puzzle about the eunuch aiming at the bat, with what he hit him, as they say in the puzzle, and upon what the bat was sitting. The individual objects of which I am speaking are also a riddle, and have a double sense: nor can you fix them in your mind, either as being or not-being, or both, or neither.

Then what will you do with them? I said. Can they have a better place than between being and not-being? For they are clearly not in greater darkness or negation than not-being, or more full of light and existence than being.

That is quite true, he said.

Thus then we seem to have discovered that the many ideas which the multitude entertain about the beautiful and about all other things are tossing about in some region which is halfway between pure being and pure not-being?

We have.

Yes; and we had before agreed that anything of this kind which we might find was to be described as matter of opinion, and not as matter of knowledge; being the intermediate flux which is caught and detained by the intermediate faculty.

Quite true.

Then those who see the many beautiful, and who yet neither see absolute beauty, nor can follow any guide who points the way thither; who see the many just, and not absolute justice, and the like,—such persons may be said to have opinion but not knowledge?

That is certain.

But those who see the absolute and eternal and immutable may be said to know, and not to have opinion only?

Neither can that be denied.

The one loves and embraces the subjects of knowledge, the other those of opinion? The latter are the same, as I dare say will remember, who listened to sweet sounds and gazed upon fair colours, but would not tolerate the existence of absolute beauty.

Yes, I remember.

Shall we then be guilty of any impropriety in calling them lovers of opinion rather than lovers of wisdom, and will they be very angry with us for thus describing them?

I shall tell them not to be angry; no man should be angry at what is true.

But those who love the truth in each thing are to be called lovers of wisdom and not lovers of opinion.

Assuredly.

And thus, Glaucon, after the argument has gone a weary way, the true and the false philosophers have at length appeared in view.

I do not think, he said, that the way could have been shortened.

I suppose not, I said; and yet I believe that we might have had a better view of both of them if the discussion could have been confined to this one subject and if there were not many other questions awaiting us, which he who desires to see in what respect the life of the just differs from that of the unjust must consider.

And what is the next question? he asked.

Surely, I said, the one which follows next in order. Inasmuch as philosophers only are able to grasp the eternal and unchangeable, and those who wander in the region of the many and variable are not philosophers, I must ask you which of the two classes should be the rulers of our State?

And how can we rightly answer that question?

Whichever of the two are best able to guard the laws and institutions of our State—let them be our guardians.

Very good.

Neither, I said, can there be any question that the guardian who is to keep anything should have eyes rather than no eyes?

There can be no question of that.

And are not those who are verily and indeed wanting in the knowledge of the true being of each thing, and who have in their souls no clear pattern, and are unable as with a painter's eye to look at the absolute truth and to that original to repair, and having perfect vision of the other world to order the laws about beauty, goodness, justice in this, if not already ordered, and to guard and preserve the order of them—are not such persons, I ask, simply blind?

Truly, he replied, they are much in that condition.

And shall they be our guardians when there are others who, besides being their equals in experience and falling short of them in no particular of virtue, also know the very truth of each thing?

There can be no reason, he said, for rejecting those who have this greatest of all great qualities; they must always have the first place unless they fail in some other respect.

Suppose then, I said, that we determine how far they can unite this and the other excellences.

By all means.

In the first place, as we began by observing, the nature of the philosopher has to be ascertained. We must come to an understanding about him, and, when we have done so, then, if I am not mistaken, we shall also acknowledge that such an union of qualities is possible, and that those in whom they are united, and those only, should be rulers in the State.

What do you mean?

Let us suppose that philosophical minds always love knowledge of a sort which shows them the eternal nature not varying from generation and corruption.

Agreed.

And further, I said, let us agree that they are lovers of all true being; there is no part whether greater or less, or more or less honourable, which they are willing to renounce; as we said before of the lover and the man of ambition.

True.

And if they are to be what we were describing, is there not another quality which they should also possess?

What quality?

Truthfulness: they will never intentionally receive into their mind falsehood, which is their detestation, and they will love the truth.

Yes, that may be safely affirmed of them.

'May be,' my friend, I replied, is not the word; say rather 'must be affirmed:' for he whose nature is amorous of anything cannot help loving all that belongs or is akin to the object of his affections.

Right, he said.

And is there anything more akin to wisdom than truth?

How can there be?

Can the same nature be a lover of wisdom and a lover of falsehood?

Never.

The true lover of learning then must from his earliest youth, as far as in him lies, desire all truth?

Assuredly.

But then again, as we know by experience, he whose desires are strong in one direction will have them weaker in others; they will be like a stream which has been drawn off into another channel.

True.

He whose desires are drawn towards knowledge in every form will be absorbed in the pleasures of the soul, and will hardly feel bodily pleasure—I mean, if he be a true philosopher and not a sham one.

That is most certain.

Such an one is sure to be temperate and the reverse of covetous; for the motives which make another man desirous of having and spending, have no place in his character.

Very true.

Another criterion of the philosophical nature has also to be considered.

What is that?

There should be no secret corner of illiberality; nothing can be more antagonistic than meanness to a soul which is ever longing after the whole of things both divine and human.

Most true, he replied.

Then how can he who has magnificence of mind and is the spectator of all time and all existence, think much of human life?

He cannot.

Or can such an one account death fearful?

No indeed.

Then the cowardly and mean nature has no part in true philosophy?

Certainly not.

Or again: can he who is harmoniously constituted, who is not covetous or mean, or a boaster, or a coward—can he, I say, ever be unjust or hard in his dealings?

Impossible.

Then you will soon observe whether a man is just and gentle, or rude and unsociable; these are the signs which distinguish even in youth the philosophical nature from the unphilosophical.

True.

There is another point which should be remarked.

What point?

Whether he has or has not a pleasure in learning; for no one will love that which gives him pain, and in which after much toil he makes little progress.

Certainly not.

And again, if he is forgetful and retains nothing of what he learns, will he not be an empty vessel?

That is certain.

Labouring in vain, he must end in hating himself and his fruitless occupation?

Yes.

Then a soul which forgets cannot be ranked among genuine philosophic natures; we must insist that the philosopher should have a good memory?

Certainly.

And once more, the inharmonious and unseemly nature can only tend to disproportion?

Undoubtedly.

And do you consider truth to be akin to proportion or to disproportion?

To proportion.

Then, besides other qualities, we must try to find a naturally well-proportioned and gracious mind, which will move spontaneously towards the true being of everything.

Certainly.

Well, and do not all these qualities, which we have been enumerating, go together, and are they not, in a manner, necessary to a soul, which is to have a full and perfect participation of being?

They are absolutely necessary, he replied.

And must not that be a blameless study which he only can pursue who has the gift of a good memory, and is quick to learn,—noble, gracious, the friend of truth, justice, courage, temperance, who are his kindred?

The god of jealousy himself, he said, could find no fault with such a study.

And to men like him, I said, when perfected by years and education, and to these only you will entrust the State. . . .

And now, I said, let me show in a figure how far our nature is enlightened or unenlightened:—Behold! human beings living in an underground den, which has a mouth open towards the light and reaching all along the den; here they have been from their childhood, and have their legs and necks chained so that they cannot move, and can only see before them, being prevented by the chains from turning round their heads. Above and behind them a fire is blazing at a distance, and between the fire and the prisoners there is a raised way; and you will see, if you look, a low wall built along the way, like the screen which marionette players have in front of them, over which they show the puppets.

I see.

And do you see, I said, men passing along the wall carrying all sorts of vessels, and statues and figures of animals made of wood and stone and various materials, which appear over the wall? Some of them are talking, others silent.

You have shown me a strange image, and they are strange prisoners.

Like ourselves, I replied; and they see only their own shadows, or the shadows of one another, which the fire throws on the opposite wall of the cave?

True, he said; how could they see anything but the shadows if they were never allowed to move their heads?

And of the objects which are being carried in like manner they would only see the shadows?

Yes, he said.

And if they were able to converse with one another, would they not suppose that they were naming what was actually before them?

Very true.

And suppose further that the prison had an echo which came from the other side, would they not be sure to fancy when one of the passers-by spoke that the voice which they heard came from the passing shadow?

No question, he replied.

To them, I said, the truth would be literally nothing but the shadows of the images.

That is certain.

And now look again, and see what will naturally follow if the prisoners are released and disabused of their error. At first, when any of them is liberated and compelled suddenly to stand up and turn his neck round and walk and look towards the light, he will suffer sharp pains; the glare will distress him, and he will be unable to see the realities of which in his former state he had seen the shadows; and then conceive some one saying to him, that what he saw before was an illusion, but that now, when he is approaching nearer to being and his eye is turned towards more real existence, he has a clearer vision,—what will be his reply? And you may further imagine that his instructor is pointing to the objects as they pass and requiring him to name them,—will he not be perplexed? Will he not fancy that the shadows which he formerly saw are truer than the objects which are now shown to him?

Far truer.

And if he is compelled to look straight at the light, will he not have a pain in his eyes which will make him turn away to take refuge in the objects of vision which he can see, and which he will conceive to be in reality clearer than the things which are now being shown to him?

True, he said.

And suppose once more, that he is reluctantly dragged up a steep and rugged ascent, and held fast until he's forced into the presence of the sun himself, is he not likely to be pained and irritated? When he approaches the light his eyes will be dazzled, and he will not be able to see anything at all of what are now called realities.

Not all in a moment, he said.

He will require to grow accustomed to the sight of the upper world. And first he will see the shadows best, next the reflections of men and other objects in the water, and then the objects themselves; then he will gaze upon the light of the moon and the stars and the spangled heaven; and he will see the sky and the stars by night better than the sun or the light of the sun by day?

Certainly.

Last of all he will be able to see the sun, and not mere reflections of him in the water, but he will see him in his own proper place, and not in another; and he will contemplate him as he is.

Certainly.

He will then proceed to argue that this is he who gives the season and the years, and is the guardian of all that is in the visible world, and in a certain way the cause of all things which he and his fellows have been accustomed to behold?

Clearly, he said, he would first see the sun and then reason about him.

And when he remembered his old habitation, and the wisdom of the den and his fellow-prisoners, do you not suppose that he would felicitate himself on the change, and pity them?

Certainly, he would.

And if they were in the habit of conferring honours among themselves on those who were quickest to observe the passing shadows and to remark which of them went before, and which followed after, and which were together; and who were therefore best able to draw conclusions as to the future, do you think that he would care for such honours and glories, or envy the possessors of them? Would he not say with Homer, 'Better to be the poor servant of a poor master,' and to endure anything, rather than think as they do and live after their manner?

Yes, he said, I think that he would rather suffer anything than entertain these false notions and live in this miserable manner.

Imagine once more, I said, such an one coming suddenly out of the sun to be replaced in his old situation; would he not be certain to have his eyes full of darkness?

To be sure, he said.

And if there were a contest, and he had to compete in measuring the shadows with the prisoners who had never moved out of the den, while his sight was still weak, and before his eyes had become steady (and the time which would be needed to acquire this new habit of sight might be very considerable) would he not be ridiculous? Men would say of him that up he went and down he came without his eyes; and that it was better not even to think of ascending; and if any one tried to loose another and lead him up to the light, let them only catch the offender, and they would put him to death.

No question, he said.

This entire allegory, I said, you may now append, dear Glaucon, to the previous argument; the prison-house is the world of sight, the light of the fire is the sun, and you will not misapprehend me if you interpret the journey upwards to be the ascent of the soul into the intellectual world according to my poor belief, which, at your desire, I have expressed whether rightly or wrongly God knows. But, whether true or false, my opinion is that in the world of knowledge the idea of good appears last of all, and is seen only with an effort; and, when seen, is also inferred to be the universal author of all things beautiful and right, parent of light and of the lord of light in this visible world, and the immediate source of reason and truth in the intellectual; and that this is the power upon which he who would act rationally, either in public or private life must have his eye fixed.

I agree, he said, as far as I am able to understand you.

Moreover, I said, you must not wonder that those who attain to this beatific vision are unwilling to descend to human affairs; for their souls are ever hastening into the upper world where they desire to dwell; which desire of theirs is very natural, if our allegory may be trusted.

Yes, very natural.

And is there anything surprising in one who passes from divine contemplations to the evil state of man, misbehaving himself in a ridiculous manner; if, while his eyes are blinking and before he has become accustomed to the surrounding darkness, he is compelled to fight in courts of law, or in other places, about the images or the shadows of images of justice, and is endeavouring to meet the conceptions of those who have never yet seen absolute justice?

Anything but surprising, he replied.

Any one who has common sense will remember that the bewilderments of the eyes are of two kinds, and arise from two causes, either from coming out of the light or from going into the light, which is true of the mind's eye, quite as much as of the bodily eye; and he who remembers this when he sees any one whose vision is perplexed and weak, will not be too ready to laugh; he will first ask whether that soul of man has come out of the brighter light, and is unable to see because unaccustomed to the dark, or having turned from darkness to the day is dazzled by excess of light. And he will count the one happy in his condition and state of being, and he will pity the other; or, if he have a mind to laugh at the soul which comes from below into the light, there will be more reason in this than in the laugh which greets him who returns from above out of the light into the den.

That, he said, is a very just distinction.

Plato (427?–347 B.C.) was a famous Greek philosopher. He was a disciple of Socrates and teacher of Aristotle. He can be thought of as the founder of Western social philosophy.

Source: Plato, REPUBLIC, trans. B[enjamin] Jowett, 3d ed. (Oxford: Clarendon Press, 1888), 143, 144–62, 170–84, 214–18.

Aristophanes

Ecclesiazusae

Aristophanes wrote the earliest utopian satires. In addition to *Ecclesiazusae*, excerpted here, his utopian works include *Lysistrata* and *Thesmophoriazusae*, satires on the role of women in society, and *Birds*, which presents a simple utopia of pleasure.

Praxagora. The rule which I dare to enact and declare, is that all shall be equal, and equally share all wealth and enjoyments, nor longer endure that one should be rich, and another be poor, that one should have acres, far-stretching and wide, and another not even enough to provide himself with a grave: that this at his call should have hundreds of servants, and that none at all. All this I intend to correct and amend: now all of all blessings shall freely partake, one life and one system for all men I make.

Blepyrus. And how will you manage it?

PR. First, I'll provide that the silver, and land, and whatever beside each man shall possess, shall be common and free, one fund for the public; then out of it we will feed and maintain you, like housekeepers true, dispensing, and sparing, and caring for you.

BL. With regard to the land, I can quite understand, but how, if a man have his money in hand, not farms, which you see, and he cannot withhold, but talents of silver and Darics of gold?

PR. All this to the stores he must bring.

BL. But suppose he choose to retain it, and nobody knows; rank perjury doubtless; but what if it be? 'Twas by that he acquired it at first.

PR. I agree. But now 'twill be useless; he'll need it no more.

BL. How mean you?

PR. All pressure from want will be o'er. Now each will have all that a man can desire, cakes, barley-loaves, chestnuts, abundant attire, wine, garlands and fish: then why should he wish the wealth he has gotten by fraud to retain? If you know any reason, I hope you'll explain.

BL. 'Tis those that have most of these goods, I believe, that are always the worst and the keenest to thieve.

PR. I grant you, my friend, in the days that are past, in your old-fashioned system, abolished at last; but what he's to gain, though his wealth he retain, when all things are common, I'd have you explain.

BL. If a youth to a girl his devotion would show, he surely must woo her with presents.

PR. O no. All women and men will be common and free, no marriage or other restraint there will be.

BL. But if all should aspire to the favours of one, to the girl that is fairest, what then will be done?

PR. By the side of the beauty so stately and grand, the dwarf, the deformed, and the ugly will stand; and before you're entitled the beauty to woo, your court you must pay to the hag and the shrew.

BL. For the ladies you've nicely provided no doubt; no woman will now be a lover without. But what of the men? For the girls, I suspect, the handsome will choose, and the ugly reject.

PR. No girl will of course be permitted to mate except in accord with the rules of the State. By the side of her lover, so handsome and tall, will be stationed the squat, the ungainly and small. And before she's entitled the beau to obtain, her love she must grant to the awkward and plain.

BL. O then such a nose as Lysicrates shows will vie with the fairest and best, I suppose.

PR. O yes, 'tis a nice democratic device, a popular system as ever was tried, a jape on the swells with their rings and their pride. *Now, fopling, away,* Gaffer Hobnail will say, *stand aside: it is I have precedence to-day.*

BL. But how, may I ask, will the children be known? And how can a father distinguish his own?

PR. They will never be known: it can never be told; all youths will in common be sons of the old.

BL. If in vain to distinguish our children we seek, pray what will become of the agèd and weak? At present I own, though a father be known, sons throttle and choke him with hearty goodwill; but will they not do it more cheerily still, when the sonship is doubtful?

PR. No, certainly not. For now if a boy should a parent annoy, the lads who are near will of course interfere; for they may themselves be his children, I wot. . . .

BL. But who will attend to the work of the farm?

PR. All labour and toil to your slaves you will leave; *your* business 'twill be, when the shadows of eve ten feet on the face of the dial are cast [just before sunset], to scurry away to your evening repast.

BL. Our clothes, what of them?

PR. You have plenty in store, when these are worn out, we will weave you some more.

BL. Just one other thing. If an action they bring, what funds will be mine for discharging the fine? You won't pay it out of the stores, I opine.

PR. A fine to be paid when an action they bring! Why bless you, our people won't know such a thing as an action.

BL. No actions! I feel a misgiving. Pray what are "our people" to do for a living?

Chremes. You are right: there are many will rue it.

PR. No doubt. But what can one then bring an action about?

BL. There are reasons in plenty; I'll just mention one. If a debtor won't pay you, pray what's to be done?

PR. If a debtor won't pay! Nay, but tell me, my friend, how the creditor came by the money to lend? All money, I thought, to the stores had been brought. I've got a suspicion, I say it with grief, your creditor's surely a bit of a thief.

CHR. Now that is an answer acute and befitting.

BL. But what if a man should be fined for committing some common assault, when elated with wine; pray what are his means for discharging that fine? I have posed you, I think.

PR. Why, his victuals and drink will be stopped by command for awhile; and I guess that he will not again in a hurry transgress, When he pays with his stomach.

BL. Will thieves be unknown?

PR. Why, how should they steal what is partly their own?

BL. No chance then to meet at night in the street some highwayman coming our cloaks to abstract?

PR. No, not if you're sleeping at home; nor, in fact, though you choose to go out. That trade, why pursue it? There's plenty for all: but suppose him to do it, Don't fight and resist him; what need of a pother? You can go to the stores, and they'll give you another.

BL. Shall we gambling forsake?

PR. Why, what could you stake?

BL. But what is the style of our living to be?

PR. One common to all, independent and free, all bars and partitions for ever undone, all private establishments fused into one.

BL. Then where, may I ask, will our dinners be laid?

PR. Each court and arcade of the law shall be made a banqueting-hall for the citizens.

BL. Right. But what will you do with the desk for the speakers?

PR. I'll make it a stand for the cups and the beakers; and there shall the striplings be ranged to recite the deeds of the brave, and the joys of the fight, and the cowards' disgrace; till out of the place each coward shall slink with a very red face, Not stopping to dine. . . .

PR. There'll be plenty for all, and to spare. No stint and no grudging our system will know, but each will away from the revelry go, elated and grand, with a torch in his hand and a garland of flowers in his hair. And then through the streets as they wander, a lot of women will round them be creeping, "O come to my lodging," says one, "I have got such a beautiful girl in my keeping." "But here is the sweetest and fairest, my boy," from a window another will say, "but ere you're entitled her love to enjoy your toll to myself you must pay." Then a sorry companion, flat-visaged and old, will shout to the youngster "Avast! And where are *you* going, so gallant and bold, and where are *you* hieing so fast? 'tis in vain; you must yield to the laws of the State, and I shall be courting the fair, whilst you must without in the vestibule wait, and strive to amuse yourself there, dear boy. . . ." There now, what think ye of my scheme?

Aristophanes (448?–380 B.C.) was the most important Greek comedic playwright.

Source: Aristophanes, ECCLESIAZUSAE, 580–709, trans. Benjamin Bickley Rogers (London: William Heinemann; Cambridge: Harvard University Press, 1924), 299–307, 309–15.

THE PROPHETS

The Hebrew prophets regularly both warned that unless Israel reformed it would be punished and held out the hope that reform would be rewarded by a better life.

Isaiah

11:1 And there shall come forth a rod out of the stem of Jesse, and a Branch shall grow out of his roots:

2 And the spirit of the LORD shall rest upon him, the spirit of wisdom and understanding, the spirit of counsel and might, the spirit of knowledge and of the fear of the LORD;

3 And shall make him of quick understanding in the fear of the LORD: and he shall not judge after the sight of his eyes, neither reprove after the hearing of his ears:

4 But with righteousness shall he judge the poor, and reprove with equity for the meek of the earth: and he shall smite the earth: with the rod of his mouth, and with the breath of his lips shall he slay the wicked.

5 And righteousness shall be the girdle of his loins, and faithfulness the girdle of his reins.

6 The wolf also shall dwell with the lamb, and the leopard shall lie down with the kid; and the calf and the young lion and the fatling together; and a little child shall lead them.

7 And the cow and the bear shall feed; their young ones shall lie down together: and the lion shall eat straw like the ox.

8 And the sucking child shall play on the hole of the asp, and the weaned child shall put his hand on the cockatrice' den.

9 They shall not hurt nor destroy in all my holy mountain: for the earth shall be full of the knowledge of the LORD, as the waters cover the sea.

Source: Isaiah 11:6–8, King James Version.

HELLENISTIC UTOPIAS

In the period between the height of Greek civilization and the growth of Roman civilization, many late Greek or early Roman writers produced utopias of which we now have only fragments.

Iambulus
Heliopolis

The dwellers upon this island differ greatly both in the characteristics of their bodies and in their manners from the men in our part of the inhabited world; for they are all nearly alike in the shape of their bodies and are over four cubits[1] in height, but the bones of the body have the ability to bend to a certain extent

---

1. A cubit was an ancient unit of linear measure, originally equal to the length of the forearm from the elbow to the tip of the middle finger, approximately 17 to 22 inches. *Ed.*

and then straighten out again, like the sinewy parts. They are also exceedingly tender in respect to their bodies and yet more vigorous than is the case among us; for when they have seized any object in their hands no man can extract it from the grasp of their fingers. There is absolutely no hair on any part of their bodies except on the head, eyebrows and eyelids, and on the chin, but the other parts of the body are so smooth that not even the least down can be seen on them. They are also remarkably beautiful and well-proportioned in the outline of the body. The openings of their ears are much more spacious than ours and growths have developed that serve as valves, so to speak, to close them. And they have a peculiarity in regard to the tongue, partly the work of nature and congenital with them and partly intentionally brought about by artifice; among them, namely, the tongue is double for a certain distance, but they divide the inner portions still further, with the result that it becomes a double tongue as far as its base. Consequently they are very versatile as to the sounds they can utter, since they imitate not only every articulate language used by man but also the varied chatterings of the birds, and, in general, they can reproduce any peculiarity of sound. And the most remarkable thing of all is that at one and the same time they can converse perfectly with two persons discoursing pertinently on the circumstances of the moment; for with one division of the tongue they can converse with the one person, and likewise with the other talk with the second.

Their climate is most temperate, we are told, considering that they live at the equator, and they suffer neither from heat not from cold. Moreover, the fruits in their island ripen throughout the entire year, even as the poet writes (*Odyssey,* 7. 120–121),

> Here pear on pear grows old, and apple close
> On apple, yea, and clustered grapes on grapes,
> And fig on fig.

And with them the day is always the same length as the night, and at midday no shadow is cast of any object because the sun is in the zenith.

57. These islanders, they go on to say, live in groups which are based on kinship and on political organizations, no more than four hundred kinsmen being gathered together in this way; and the members spend their time in the meadows, the land supplying them with many things for sustenance; for by reason of the fertility of the island and the mildness of the climate, food-stuffs are produced of themselves in greater quantity than is sufficient for their needs. For instance, a reed grows there in abundance, and bears a fruit in great plenty that is very similar to the white vetch. Now when they have gathered this they steep it in warm water until it has become about the size of a pigeon's egg; then after they have crushed it and rubbed it skillfully with their hands, they mould it

into loaves, which are baked and eaten, and they are of surprising sweetness. There are also in the island, they say, abundant springs of water, the warm springs serving well for bathing and the relief of fatigue, the cold excelling in sweetness and possessing the power to contribute to good health. Moreover, the inhabitants give attention to every branch of learning and especially to astrology; and they use letters which, according to the value of the sounds they represent, are twenty-eight in number, but the characters are only seven, each one of which can be formed in four different ways. Nor do they write their lines horizontally, as we do, but from the top to the bottom perpendicularly. And the inhabitants, they tell us, are extremely long-lived, living even to the age of one hundred and fifty years, and experiencing for the most part no illness. Anyone also among them who has become crippled or suffers, in general, from any physical infirmity is forced by them, in accordance with an inexorable law, to remove himself from life. And there is also a law among them that they should live only for a stipulated number of years, and that at the completion of this period they should make away with themselves of their own accord, by a strange manner of death; for there grows among them a plant of a peculiar nature, and whenever a man lies down upon it, imperceptibly and gently he falls asleep and dies.

58. They do not marry, we are told, but possess their children in common, and maintaining the children who are born as if they belonged to all, they love them equally; and while the children are infants those who suckle the babes often change them around in order that not even the mothers may know their own offspring. Consequently, since there is no rivalry among them, they never experience civil disorders and they never cease placing the highest value upon internal harmony.

There are also animals among them, we are told, which are small in size but the object of wonder by reason of the nature of their bodies and the potency of their blood; for they are round in form and very similar to tortoises, but they are marked on the surface by two diagonal yellow stripes, at each end of which they have an eye and a mouth; consequently, though seeing with four eyes and using as many mouths, yet it gathers its food into one gullet, and down this its nourishment is swallowed and all flows together into one stomach; and in like manner its other organs and all its inner parts are single. It also has beneath it all around its body many feet, by means of which it can move in whatever direction it pleases. And the blood of this animal, they say, has a marvellous potency; for it immediately glues on to its place any living member that has been severed; even if a hand or the like should happen to have been cut off, by the use of this blood it is glued on again, provided that the cut is fresh, and the same thing is true of such other parts of the body as are not connected with the regions which are vital and sustain the person's life. Each group of the inhabitants also keeps a bird of great size and of a nature peculiar to itself, by means of which a test is made of the infant children to learn what their spiritual disposition is; for they place them upon the birds, and such of them as are able to endure the flight through the air as the birds take wing they rear, but such as become nauseated and filled with consternation they cast out, as not likely either to live many years and being, besides, of no account because of their dispositions.

In each group the oldest man regularly exercises the leadership, just as if he were a kind of king, and is obeyed by all the members; and when the first such ruler makes an end of his life in accordance with the law upon the completion of his one hundred and fiftieth year, the next oldest succeeds to the leadership. The sea about the island has strong currents and is subject to great flooding and ebbing of the tides and is sweet in taste. And as for the stars of our heavens, the Bears and many more, we are informed, are not visible at all. The number of these islands was seven, and they are very much the same in size and at about equal distances from one another, and all follow the same customs and laws.

59. Although all the inhabitants enjoy an abundant provision of everything from what grows of itself in these islands, yet they do not indulge in the enjoyment of this abundance without restraint, but they practise simplicity and take for their food only what suffices for their needs. Meat and whatever else is roasted or boiled in water are prepared by them, but of all the other dishes ingeniously concocted by professional cooks, such as sauces and the various kinds of seasonings, they have no notion whatsoever. And they worship as gods that which encompasses all things and the sun, and, in general, all the heavenly bodies. Fishes of every kind in great numbers are caught by them by sundry devices and not a few birds. There is also found among them an abundance of fruit trees growing wild, and olive trees and vines grow there, from which they make both olive oil and wine in abundance. Snakes also, we are told, which are of immense size and yet do no harm to the inhabitants, have a meat which is edible and exceedingly sweet. And their clothing they make themselves from a certain reed which contains in the centre a downy substance that is bright to the eye and soft, which they gather and mingle with crushed sea-shells and thus make remarkable garments of a purple hue. As for the animals of the islands, their natures are peculiar and so amazing as to defy credence.

All the details of their diet, we are told, follow a prescribed arrangement, since they do not all take their food at the same time nor is it always the same; but it has been ordained that on certain fixed days they shall eat at one time fish, at another time fowl, sometimes the flesh of land animals, and sometimes olives and the most simple side-dishes. They also take turns in ministering to the needs of one another, some of them fishing, others working at the crafts, others occupying themselves in other useful tasks, and still others, with the exception of those who have come to old age, performing the services of the group in a definite cycle. And at the festivals and feasts which are held among them, there are both pronounced and sung in honour of the gods hymns and spoken laudations, and especially in honour of the sun, after whom they name both the islands and themselves.

They inter their dead at the time when the tide is at the ebb, burying them in the sand along the beach, the result being that at flood-tide the place has fresh sand heaped upon it. The reeds, they say, from which the fruit for their nourishment is derived, being sweet and health-giving, maintains its heat and never becomes cold, save when it is mixed with cold water or wine.

Iambulus (third century B.C.?) is known only for this work.

Source: DIODORUS SICULUS (DIODORUS OF SICILY), trans. C. H. Oldfather, 12 vols. (Cambridge: Harvard University Press, 1939), 256.2–59.9.

SATURNALIA

The Saturnalia was a Roman festival honoring the god Saturn or Cronus. During the festival, all were equal and there was much feasting and celebration.

Lucian
Saturnalia

1. First Laws

No one is to do any business, public or private, during the festival, except what pertains to sport, luxurious living and entertainment: cooks and confectioners alone shall work.

Let every man be treated equal, slave and freeman poor and rich.

No one may be ill-tempered or cross or threaten anybody.

No one may audit accounts during the festival of Cronus.

No one may inspect or list his silver or clothing during the festival, nor take part in athletics, nor practise public-speaking, nor deliver lectures, except wits and jolly fellows purveying jokes and entertainment.

2. Second Laws

Long before the festival the rich shall write on a tablet the name of each of their friends, and shall hold in readiness the cash value of a tenth of their yearly income, any surplus clothing they possess, furniture too crude for them, and a good proportion of their silver. They shall keep this ready at hand.

On the day before the festival a purificatory sacrifice shall be carried round, and they shall purge their houses of meanness, avarice, greed, and all such vices that dwell with most of them.

When they have purified the house, they shall sacrifice to Zeus the Giver of Wealth, Hermes the Bestower, and Apollo of the Great Gifts.

Then in the late afternoon, that list of friends shall be read to them. They shall divide the gifts according to each man's worth, and before sunset send them to their friends. The bearers shall not exceed three or four, the most trustworthy of their servants, well advanced in years. The nature and quantity of what is sent shall be written on a slip, that neither party may suspect the bearers. Each servant shall drink one cup and then run off and make no more demands. To men of letters double quantities shall be sent; they deserve a double share. The messages with the gifts shall be as modest and brief as possible. No one shall send an odious message with them, or cry up what is sent.

Rich man shall not send to rich man or at Cronus's festival entertain anyone of equal standing. He shall keep nothing of what is already prepared for sending, nor change his mind about a gift.

Anyone who the year before missed his share through absence shall be given it now as an extra gift.

The rich shall pay debts for their impecunious friends (including their rent if they owe this too and cannot pay). In general they shall make it their business to know long beforehand what is their greatest need.

Those who receive shall not complain, but think the gift, whatever it is, generous. A jar of wine, a hare, or a plump bird shall not be reckoned a gift for Cronus's festival, nor shall Cronian gifts be laughed at.

In return the poor scholar shall send the rich man any pleasant, convivial, old book he may have, or a work of his own, the best he can. The rich man shall receive this gift with a glad countenance and then read it at once. If he rejects it or throws it away, he shall know that he is liable to what the sickle threatens, even if what he sends is adequate. The other poor recipients shall send garlands of flowers or grains of frankincense.

If a poor man sends clothing or silver or gold beyond his means to a rich man, his gift shall be declared public property and sold, the money going into the treasury of Cronus; and the poor man on the next day shall receive from the rich man strokes on his hands with a cane to the number of not less than two hundred and fifty.

3. Laws for Banquets

The time for bathing shall be when the shadow of the sundial is six feet long; before the bath there shall be nuts and gaming.

Each man shall take the couch where he happens to be. Rank, family, or wealth shall have little influence on privilege.

All shall drink the same wine, and neither stomach trouble nor headache shall give the rich man an excuse for being the only one to drink the better quality.

All shall have their meat on equal terms. The waiters shall not show favour to anyone, but shall neither be too slow nor be dismissed until the guests choose what they are to take home. Neither are large portions to be placed before one and tiny ones before another, nor a ham for one and a pig's jaw for another— all must be treated equally.

The man who pours the wine shall keep a sharp eye on each guest from a vantage-point; he shall pay less attention to his master, and his ears shall be sharper than usual. The cups shall be of all kinds. It shall be permissible to pass a loving-cup, if desired. Everyone shall drink to everyone else, if desired, when the rich man has set the example. No one shall be made to drink if he cannot.

It shall not be permissible for anyone who wishes it to introduce into the banquet a dancer or lyre-player who is still learning.

Jesting shall be limited in all cases to what is inoffensive.

All gambling shall be for nuts. If anyone gambles for money he shall go without food for the next day.

Each guest shall stay and go as he likes.

When a rich man gives a banquet to his servants, his friends shall aid him in waiting on them.

Every rich man shall inscribe these laws on a slab of bronze and keep it in the centre of his hall, and read them. And it must be realised that as long as this slab shall last neither famine nor plague nor fire nor any other harm shall come to their house.—May it never be taken down! For if it is, Heaven avert what is in store for them!

Lucian (born c. A.D. 120) was a comic writer.

Source: Lucian, "Saturnalia," in LUCIAN, trans. K. Kilburn, 8 vols. (Cambridge: Harvard University Press; London: William Heinemann, 1959), 6:107, 109, 111, 113, 115.

The Millennium

The millennium is one of the rewards of the faithful but it is clear, as with all Christian utopias, that it is not accessible to the human race without the in-

tervention of God. **Even the righteous do not simply choose themselves but are chosen by God.**

The Revelation of St. John

21:1 And I saw a new heaven and a new earth: for the first heaven and the first earth were passed away; and there was no more sea.

2 And I John saw the holy city, new Jerusalem, coming down from God out of heaven, prepared as a bride adorned for her husband.

3 And I heard a great voice out of heaven saying, Behold, the tabernacle of God is with men, and he will dwell with them, and they shall be his people, and God himself shall be with them, and be their God.

4 And God shall wipe away all tears from their eyes; and there shall be no more death, neither sorrow, nor crying, neither shall there be any more pain: for the former things are passed away.

Source: Revelation (Apocalypse) 21:1–4 King James Version.

II Baruch

And it shall come to pass, when He has brought low everything that is in the
    world,
And has sat down in peace for the age on the throne of His kingdom,
That joy shall be revealed,
And rest shall appear.
And then healing shall descend in dew,
And disease shall withdraw,
And anxiety and anguish and lamentation pass from amongst men,
And gladness proceed through the whole earth.
And no one shall again die untimely,
Nor shall any adversity suddenly befall.
And judgements, and revilings, and contentions, and revenges,
And blood, and passions, and envy, and hatred,
And whatsoever things are like these shall go into condemnation when they are
    removed.
For it is these very things which have filled the world with evils,
And on account of these the life of man has been greatly troubled.
And wild beasts shall come from the forest and minister unto men,

And asps and dragons shall come forth from their holes to submit themselves
   to a little child.
And women shall no longer then have pain when they bear,
Nor shall they suffer torment when they yield the fruit of the womb.
And it shall come to pass in those days that the reapers shall not grow weary,
Nor those that build be toilworn;
For the works shall of themselves speedily advance
Together with those who do them in much tranquility.
For that time is the consummation of that which is corruptible,
And the beginning of that which is not corruptible.

Source: Apocalypse of Baruch (II Baruch) 73:1–74:2, R. H. Charles, ed., THE APOCRYPHA
AND PSEUDEPIGRAPHA OF THE OLD TESTAMENT IN ENGLISH, 2 vols. (Oxford: Clarendon
Press, 1913).

Monasticism

**The medieval monastery was both a rejection of the Eastern tradition of
eremetical isolation and an affirmation of community. The first major step toward this model was the Rule of St. Benedict (probably completed 530–540).
Benedict founded an order designed to provide an organized alternative to
both the solitary life of the hermit and the poverty-stricken, godless life of the
layman. Benedict's order was hierarchical and communal. St. Francis also
stressed the need for reform and proposed a wandering order of friars who
were to practise poverty. Francis's approach was subverted by conservatives
within the church, and a more traditional Franciscan order was ultimately
founded. The rule excerpted here is from 1223.**

The Rule of St. Benedict

22 HOW THE MONKS ARE TO SLEEP. Let them Sleep each one in a separate bed.
Let their beds be assigned them in accordance with the date of their conversion,
subject to the abbot's dispositions. If it be possible, let them all sleep in one
place; but if their numbers do not allow of this, let them sleep by tens or twen-
ties, with seniors to supervise them. There shall be a light burning in the dormitory throughout the night. Let them sleep clothed and girt with girdles or
cords, *but not with their belts,* so that they may not have their knives at their
sides while they are sleeping, and be cut by them in their sleep. Being clothed
they will thus be always ready, and rising at the signal without any delay may
hasten to forestall one another to the Work of God; yet this with all gravity and

self-restraint. The younger brethren shall not have their beds by themselves, but shall be mixed with the seniors. When they rise for the Work of God, let them gently encourage one another, on account of the excuses to which the sleepy are addicted. . . .

33 WHETHER MONKS SHOULD HAVE ANYTHING OF THEIR OWN. This vice especially ought to be utterly rooted out of the monastery. Let no one presume to give or receive anything without the abbot's leave, or to have anything as his own, anything whatever, whether book or tablets or pen or whatever it may be; for monks should not have even their bodies and wills at their own disposal. But let them look to the father of the monastery for all that they require, and let it be unlawful to have anything which the abbot has not given or allowed. And, as the Scripture saith, *let all things be common to all, nor let anyone say that anything is his own* [Acts iv. 32] or claim it for himself. But if anyone shall be found to indulge in this most wicked vice, let him be admonished once and a second time; if he do not amend, let him undergo punishment. . . .

39 THE MEASURE OF FOOD. We believe it to be sufficient for the daily meal, whether that be at the sixth or the ninth hour, that every table should have two cooked dishes, on account of individual infirmities, so that he who perchance cannot eat of the one, may make his meal of the other. Therefore, let two cooked dishes suffice for all the brethren; and if any fruit or young vegetables are available, let a third be added. Let a good pound of bread suffice for the day, whether there be one meal only, or both dinner and supper. . . . .

40 OF THE MEASURE OF DRINK. *Every man hath his proper gift from God, one after this manner, and another after that* [I Cor. vii. 7]. It is therefore with some misgiving that we determine how much others should eat or drink. Nevertheless, keeping in view the needs of weaker brethren, we believe that a hemina [about a pint] of wine a day is sufficient for each. But those upon whom God bestows the gift of abstinence, should know that they shall have a special reward.

But if the circumstances of the place, or their work, or the heat of summer require more, let the superior be free to grant it. Yet let him always take care that neither surfeit nor drunkenness supervene. We do, indeed, read that wine is no drink for monks; but since nowadays, monks cannot be persuaded of this, let us agree upon this, to drink temperately and not to satiety: for *wine maketh even the wise to fall away* [Ecclus. xix. 2]. . . .

48 OF THE DAILY MANUAL LABOUR. Idleness is the enemy of the soul. The brethren, therefore, must be occupied at stated hours in manual labour, and again at other hours in sacred reading.

Benedict of Nursia (480?–?543) was the founder of monasticism in Western Europe.

Source: THE RULE OF SAINT BENEDICT, ed. and trans. Abbot Justin McCann (London: Burns Oates, 1952), 85, 95–96, 97.

The Rule of St. Francis

1. This is the Rule and way of life of the brothers minor; to observe the holy Gospel of our Lord Jesus Christ, living in obedience, without personal possessions, and in chastity. Brother Francis promises obedience and reverence to our Lord Pope Honorius, and to his canonical successors, and to the Roman Church. And the other brothers shall be bound to obey brother Francis and his successors. . . .

4. I strictly command all the brothers never to receive coin or money either directly or through an intermediary. The ministers and guardians alone shall make provision, through spiritual friends, for the needs of the infirm and for other brothers who need clothing, according to the locality, season or cold climate, at their discretion. . . .

5. Those brothers, to whom God has given the ability to work, shall work faithfully and devotedly and in such a way that, avoiding idleness, the enemy of the soul, they do not quench the spirit of holy prayer and devotion, to which other and temporal activities should be subordinate. As the wages of their labour they may receive corporal necessities for themselves and their brothers but not coin nor money, and this with humility as is fitting for servants of God, and followers of holy poverty.

6. The brothers shall possess nothing, neither a house, nor a place, nor anything. But, as pilgrims and strangers in this world, serving God in poverty and humility, they shall confidently seek alms, and not be ashamed, for the Lord made Himself poor in this world for us. This is the highest degree of that sublime poverty, which has made you, my dearly beloved brethren, heirs and kings of the Kingdom of Heaven; which has made you poor in goods but exalted in virtues. Let this be 'your portion,' which leads you to 'the land of the living' [Ps. cxlii. 5]. . . .

11. I strictly charge all the brethren not to hold conversation with women so as to arouse suspicion, nor to take counsel with them. And, with the exception of those to whom special permission has been given by the Apostolic Chair, let them not enter nunneries. Neither may they become fellow god-parents with men or women, lest from this cause a scandal may arise among the brethren or concerning brethren.

Francis of Assisi (1182–1226) was the founder of the Franciscan order.

Source: "The Rule of Saint Francis," in Documents of the Christian Church, ed. Henry Bettenson. 2d ed. (London: Oxford University Press, 1963), 179–84.

The Cockaigne

The Cockaigne, or Cokaygne, is a form of utopia springing, as Robert Elliott suggests, from the golden age.[1] The derivation of the word is obscure, but it emphasizes the immediate gratification of physical needs, and the most frequent images are of food. The most famous Cockaignes are from the Middle Ages (the English version is reprinted below), but there are many earlier examples such as this one from Telecleides. Telecleides shows the link to the golden age, but one very different from those we have seen thus far.

Telecleides

I will, then, tell of the life of old which I provided for mortals. First, there was peace over all, like water over hands. The earth produced no terror and no disease; on the other hand, things needful came of their own accord. Every torrent flowed with wine, barley-cakes strove with wheat-loaves for men's lips, beseeching that they be swallowed if men loved the whitest. Fishes would come to the house and bake themselves, then serve themselves on the tables. A river of broth, whirling hot slices of meat, would flow by the couches; conduits full of piquant sauces for the meat were close at hand for the asking, so that there was plenty for moistening a mouthful and swallowing tender. On dishes there would be honey-cakes all sprinkled with spices, and roast thrushes served up with milk-cakes were flying into the gullet. The flat-cakes jostled each other at the jaws and set up a racket, the slaves would shoot dice with slices of paunch and tid-bits. Men were fat in those days and every bit mighty giants.

Telecleides (fifth century B.C.) was a comic poet.

Source: Quoted in Athenaeus, THE DEIPONOSOPHISTS, VI:268, trans. Charles Burton Gulick, 7 vols. (Cambridge: Harvard University Press, 1929), 3:205–6.

Cockaigne

Out to sea, far west of Spain,
Lies the land men call Cokaygne.
No land that under heaven is,

---

1. Robert C. Elliott, *The Shape of Utopia: Studies in a Literary Genre* (Chicago: University of Chicago Press, 1970), 15.

For wealth and goodness comes near this;
Though Paradise is merry and bright
Cokaygne is a fairer sight.
For what is there in Paradise
But grass and flowers and greeneries?
Though there is joy and great delight,
There's nothing good but fruit to bite,
And only water thirst to quench.
And of men there are but two,
Elijah and Enoch also;
Sadly thither would I come
Where but two men have their home.

    In Cokaygne we drink and eat
Freely without care and sweat,
The food is choice and clear the wine,
At fourses and at supper time,
I say again, and I dare swear,
No land is like it anywhere,
Under heaven no land like this
Of such joy and endless bliss.

    There is many a sweet sight,
All is day, there is no night,
There no quarreling nor strife,
There no death, but endless life;
There no lack of food or cloth,
There no man or woman wroth.
There no serpent, wolf or fox,
Horse or nag or cow or ox,
Neither sheep nor swine nor goat,
Nor creeping groom, I'd have you note,
Neither stallion there nor stud.
Other things you'll find are good.
In bed or garment or in house,
There's neither flea nor fly nor louse.
Neither thunder, sleet nor hail,
No vile worm nor any snail,
Never a storm, nor rain nor wind,
There's no man or woman blind.
All is sporting, joy and glee,
Lucky the man that there may be.

There are rivers broad and fine
Of oil, milk, honey and of wine;
Water serveth there no thing
But for sight and for washing.
Many fruits grow in that place
For all delight and sweet solace.

There is a mighty fine Abbey,
Thronged with monks both white and grey,
Ah, those chambers and those halls!
All of pasties stand the walls,
of fish and flesh and all rich meat,
The tastiest that men can eat.
Wheaten cakes the shingles all,
Of church, of cloister, bower and hall.
The pinnacles are fat puddings,
Good food for princes or for kings.
Every man takes what he will,
As of right, to eat his fill.
All is common to young and old,
To stout and strong, to meek and bold.

There is a cloister, fair and light,
Broad and long, a goodly sight.
The pillars of that place are all
Fashioned out of clear crystal,
And every base and capital
Of jasper green and red coral.
In the garth there stands a tree
Pleasant truly for to see.
Ginger and cyperus the roots,
And valerian all the shoots,
Choicest nutmegs flower thereon,
The bark it is of cinnamon.
The fruit is scented gillyflower,
Of every spice is ample store.
There the roses, red of hue,
And the lovely lily, too,
Never fade through day and night,
But endure to please men's sight.
In that Abbey are four springs,
Healing and health their water brings,

Balm they are, and wine indeed,
Running freely for men's need,
And the bank about those streams
With gold and with rich jewels gleams.
There is sapphire and uniune,
Garnet red and astiune,
Emerald, ligure and prassiune,
Beryl, onyx, topasiune,
Amethyst and chrystolite,
Chalcedony and epetite.

There are birds in every bush,
Throstle, nightingale and thrush,
Woodpecker and the soaring lark,
More there are than man may mark,
Singing with all their merry might,
Never ceasing day or night,
Yet this wonder add to it—
That geese fly roasted on the spit,
As God's my witness, to that spot,
Crying out, 'Geese, all hot, all hot!'
Every goose in garlic crest,
Of all food the seemliest.
And the larks that are so couth
Fly right down into man's mouth,
Smothered in stew, and thereupon
Piles of powdered cinnamon.
Every man may drink his fill
And needn't sweat to pay the bill.

When the monks go in to mass,
All the windows that were glass,
Turn them into crystal bright
To give the monks a clearer light;
And when the mass has all been said,
And the mass-books up are laid,
The crystal pane turns back to glass,
The very way it always was.

Now the young monks every day
After dinner go to play,
No hawk nor any bird can fly

Half so fast across the sky
As the monk in joyous mood
In his wide sleeves and his hood.
The Abbot counts it goodly sport
To see his monks in haste depart,
But presently he comes along
To summon them to evensong.
The monks refrain not from their play,
But fast and far they flee away,
And when the Abbot plain can see
How all his monks inconstant flee,
A wench upon the road he'll find,
And turning up her white behind,
He beats upon it as a drum
To call his monks to vespers home.
When the monks behold that sport
Unto the maiden all resort,
And going all the wench about,
Every one stroketh her white toute.
So they end their busy day
With drinking half the night away,
And so to the long tables spread
In sumptuous procession tread.

Another Abbey is near by,
In sooth, a splendid nunnery,
Upon a river of sweet milk,
Where is plenteous store of silk.
When the summer day is hot
The younger nuns take out a boat,
And forth upon the river clear,
Some do row and some do steer.
When they are far from their Abbey,
They strip them naked for their play,
And, plunging in the river's brim,
Slyly address themselves to swim.
When the young monks see that sport,
Straightway thither they resort,
And coming to the nuns anon,
Each monk taketh to him one,
And, swiftly bearing forth his prey,

Carries her to the Abbey gray,
And teaches her an orison,
Jigging up and jigging down.
The monk that is a stallion good,
And can manage well his hood,
He shall have, without a doubt,
Twelve wives before the year is out,
All of right and nought through grace,
So he may himself solace.
And the monk that sleepeth best,
And gives his body ample rest,
He, God knows, may presently
Hope an Abbot for to be.

Whoso will come that land unto
Full great penance he must do,
He must wade for seven years
In the dirt a swine-pen bears,
Seven years right to the chin,
Ere he may hope that land to win.
Listen Lords, both good and kind,
Never will you that country find
Till through the ordeal you've gone
And that penance has been done.
So you may that land attain
And never more return again,
Pray to God that so it be,
Amen, by holy charity.

Source: "The Land of Cokaygne," in A. L. Morton, THE ENGLISH UTOPIA (London: Lawrence & Wishart, 1952), 217–22.

THREE

The Sixteenth Century

✌

The sixteenth century saw the creation of the utopian genre of literature and the redevelopment of the noble savage as an important theme. The most important book in this new genre was, of course, Thomas More's *Utopia* (1516).

Thomas More
Utopia

The pivotal point in the creation of British utopianism and the beginning of the formal genre of utopian literature was the 1516 publication in Latin in Louvain of Thomas More's *Libellus vere aureus nec minus salutaris quam festivius de optimo reip[ublicae] statu, deq[ue] nova Insula Vtopia*. The *Utopia*, as it fortunately has become known, produced imitators almost immediately. The words utopia and utopian passed into the language remarkably soon—often with negative connotations. *Utopia* struck a chord that had not been sounded recently, and it became the fount for the outpouring of what we now call utopias. *Utopia* and More have been many things to many people. As a result, many layers of commentary overwhelm the little book, which is almost lost under the essays and books (many longer than the original) written about it.

Of Their Trades, and Manner of Life

AGRICULTURE is that which is so universally understood among them, that no person, either man or woman, is ignorant of it; they are instructed in it from their childhood, partly by what they learn at school, and partly by practice; they being led out often into the fields, about the town, where they not only see others at work, but are likewise exercised in it themselves. Besides agriculture, which is so common to them all, every man has some peculiar trade to which he applies himself, such as the manufacture of wool, or flax, masonry, smith's work, or carpenter's work; for there is no sort of trade that is in great esteem among them. Throughout the island they wear the same sort of clothes without any other distinction, except what is necessary to distinguish the two sexes, and the married and unmarried. The fashion never alters; and as it is neither disagreeable nor uneasy, so it is suited to the climate, and calculated both for their summers and winters. Every family makes their own clothes; but all among them, women as well as men, learn one or other of the trades formerly mentioned. Women, for the most part, deal in wool and flax, which suit best with their weakness, leaving the ruder trades to the men. The same trade generally passes down from father to son, inclinations often following descent; but if any man's genius lies another way, he is by adoption translated into a family that deals in the trade to which he is inclined: and when that is to be done, care is taken not only by his father, but by the magistrate, that he may be put to a discreet and good man. And if after a person has learned one trade, he desires to acquire another, that is also allowed, and is managed in the same manner as the former. When he has learned both, he follows that which he likes best, unless the public has more occasion for the other.

The chief, and almost the only business of the Syphogrants [lower officials] is to take care that no man may live idle, but that every one may follow his trade diligently: yet they do not wear themselves out with perpetual toil, from morning to night, as if they were beasts of burden, which as it is indeed a heavy slavery, so it is everywhere the common course of life amongst all mechanics except the Utopians; but they dividing the day and night into twenty-four hours, appoint six of these for work; three of which are before dinner; and three after. They then sup, and at eight o'clock, counting from noon, go to bed and sleep eight hours. The rest of their time besides that taken up in work, eating and sleeping, is left to every man's discretion; yet they are not to abuse that interval to luxury and idleness, but must employ it in some proper exercise according to their various inclinations, which is for the most part reading. It is ordinary to have public lectures every morning before daybreak; at which none are obliged to appear but those who are marked out for literature; yet a great many, both men and women of all ranks, go to hear lectures of one sort or other, according to their inclinations. But if others, that are not made for contemplation, choose rather to employ themselves at that time in their trades, as many of them do, they are not hindered, but are rather commended, as men that take care to serve their country. After supper, they spend an hour in some diversion, in summer in their gardens, and in winter in the halls where they eat; where they entertain each other, either with music or discourse. They do not so much as know dice, or any such foolish and mischievous games: they have, however, two sorts of games not unlike our chess; the one is between several numbers, in which one number, as it were, consumes another: the other resembles a battle between the virtues and the vices, in which the enmity in the vices among themselves, and their agreement against virtue is not unpleasantly represented; together with the special oppositions between the particular virtues and vices; as also the methods by which vice either openly assaults or secretly undermines virtue; and virtue on the other hand resists it. But the time appointed for labour is to be narrowly examined, otherwise you may imagine, that since there are only six hours appointed for work, they may fall under a scarcity of necessary provisions. But it is so far from being true, that this time is not sufficient for supplying them with plenty of all things, either necessary or convenient; that it is rather too much; and this you will easily apprehend, if you consider how great a part of all other nations is quite idle. First, women generally do little, who are the half of mankind; and if some few women are diligent, their husbands are idle: then consider the great company of idle priests, and of those that are called religious men; add to these all rich men, chiefly those that have estates in land, who are called noblemen and gentlemen, together with their families, made up of idle persons, that are kept more for show than use; add to these, all those strong and lusty beggars, that go about pretending some disease, in excuse for their begging; and upon the whole account you will find that the number of those by whose labours mankind is supplied, is much less than you perhaps imagined. Then consider how few of those that work are employed in labours that are of real service; for we who measure all things by money, give rise to many trades that are both vain and superfluous, and serve only to support riot and luxury. For if those who work were employed only in such things as the conveniences of life require, there would be such an abundance of them, that the prices of them would so sink, that tradesmen could not be maintained by their gains; if all those who labour about useless things, were set to more profitable employments, and if all they that languish out their lives in sloth and idleness, every one of whom consumes as much as any two of the men that are at work, were forced to labour, you may easily imagine that a small proportion of time would serve for doing all that is either necessary, profitable, or pleasant to mankind, especially while pleasure is kept within its due bounds. This appears very plainly in Utopia, for there, in a great city, and in all the territory that lies round it, you can scarce find five hundred, either men or women, by their age and strength, are capable of labour, that are not engaged in it; even the Syphogrants, though excused by the law, yet do not excuse themselves, but work, that by their examples they may excite the industry of the rest of the people. The like exemption is allowed to those, who being recommended to the people by the priests, are by the secret suffrages of the Syphogrants privileged from labour, that they may apply themselves wholly to study; and if any of these fall short of those hopes that they seemed at first to give, they are obliged to return to work. And sometimes a mechanic, that so employs his leisure hours, as to make a considerable advancement in learning, is eased from being a tradesman, and ranked among their learned men. Out of these they choose their ambassadors, their priests, their Tranibors [higher officials], and the Prince himself; anciently called their Barzenes, but is called of late their Ademus.

And thus from the great numbers among them that are neither suffered to be idle, nor to be employed in any fruitless labour, you may easily make the estimate how much may be done in those few hours in which they are obliged to labour. But besides all that has been already said, it is to be considered that the needful arts among them are managed with less labour than anywhere else. The building or the repairing of houses among us employ many hands, because often a thriftless heir suffers a house that his father built to fall into decay, so that his successor must, at a great cost, repair that which he might have kept up with a small charge: it frequently happens, that the same house which one person built at a vast expense, is neglected by another, who thinks he has a more delicate sense of the beauties of architecture; and he suffering it to fall to ruin, builds another at no less charge. But among the Utopians, all things are so regulated that men very seldom build upon a new piece of ground; and are not only very quick in repairing their houses, but show their foresight in preventing their decay: so that their buildings are preserved very long, with but little labour; and thus the builders to whom that care belongs are often without employment, except the hewing of timber, and the squaring of stones, that the materials may be in readiness for raising a building very suddenly, when there is any occasion for it. As to their clothes, observe how; little work is spent in them: while they are at labour, they are clothed with leather and skins, cast carelessly about them, which will last seven years; and when they appear in public they put on an upper garment, which hides the other; and these are all of one colour, and that is the natural colour of the wool. As they need less woollen cloth than is used anywhere else, so that which they make use of is much less costly. They use linen cloth more; but that is prepared with less labour, and they value cloth only by the whiteness of the linen, or the cleanness of the wool, without much regard to the fineness of the thread: while in other places, four or five upper garments of woollen cloth, of different colours, and as many vests of silk, will scarce serve one man; and while those that are nicer think ten too few, every man there is content with one, which very often serves him two years. Nor is there anything that can tempt a man to desire more; for if he had them, he would neither be the warmer, nor would he make one jot the better appearance for it. And thus, since they are all employed in some useful labour, and since they content themselves with fewer things, it falls out that there is a great abundance of all things among them: so that it frequently happens, that for want of other work, vast numbers are sent out to mend the highways. But when no public undertaking is to be performed, the hours of working are lessened. The magistrates never engage the people in unnecessary labour, since the chief end of the constitution is to regulate labour by the necessities of the public, and to allow all the people as much time as is necessary for the improvement of their minds, in which they think the happiness of life consists.

Of Their Traffic

BUT it is now time to explain to you the mutual intercourse of this people, their commerce, and the rules by which all things are distributed among them.

As their cities are composed of families, so their families are made up of those that are nearly related to one another. Their women, when they grow up, are married out; but all the males, both children and grandchildren, live still in the same house, in great obedience to their common parent, unless age has weakened his understanding; and in that case, he that is next to him in age comes in his room. But lest any city should become either too great, or by any accident be dispeopled, provision is made that none of their cities may contain above six thousand families, besides those of the country round it. No family may have less than ten, and more than sixteen persons in it; but there can be no determined number for the children under age. This rule is easily observed, by removing some of the children of a more fruitful couple to any other family that does not abound so much in them. By the same rule, they supply cities that do not increase so fast, from others that breed faster; and if there is any increase over the whole island, then they draw out a number of their citizens out of the several towns, and send them over to the neighbouring continent; where, if they find that the inhabitants have more soil than they can well cultivate, they fix a colony, taking the inhabitants into their society, if they are willing to live with them; and where they do that of their own accord, they quickly enter into their method of life, and conform to their rules, and this proves a happiness to both nations for according to their constitution, such care is taken of the soil, that it becomes fruitful enough for both, though it might be otherwise too narrow and barren for any one of them. But if the natives refuse to conform themselves to their laws, they drive them out of those bounds which they mark out for themselves, and use force if they resist. For they account it a very just cause of war, for a nation to hinder others from possessing a part of that soil, of which they make no use, but which is suffered to lie idle and uncultivated; since every man has by the law of Nature a right to such a waste portion of the earth as is necessary for his subsistence. If an accident has so lessened the number of the inhabitants of any of their towns, that it cannot be made up from the other towns of the island, without diminishing them too much, which is said to have fallen out but twice since they were first a people, when great numbers were carried off by the plague; the loss is then supplied by recalling as many as are wanted from their colonies; for they will abandon these, rather than suffer the towns in the island to sink too low.

But to return to their manner of living in society, the oldest man of every family, as has been already said, is its governor. Wives serve their husbands, and children their parents, and always the younger serves the elder. Every city is divided into four equal parts, and in the middle of each there is a market-place: what is brought thither, and manufactured by the several families, is carried from thence to houses appointed for that purpose, in which all things of a sort are laid by themselves; and thither every father goes and takes whatsoever he or his family stand in need of, without either paying for it, or leaving anything in exchange. There is no reason for giving a denial to any person, since there is such plenty of everything among them; and there is no danger of a man's asking for more than he needs; they have no inducements to do this, since they are sure that they shall always be supplied. It is the fear of want that makes any of the whole race of animals either greedy or ravenous; but besides fear, there is in man a pride that makes him fancy it a particular glory to excel others in pomp and excess. But by the laws of the Utopians, there is no room for this. Near these markets there are others for all sorts of provisions, where there are not only herbs, fruits, and bread, but also fish, fowl, and cattle. There are also, without their towns, places appointed near some running water, for killing their beasts, and for washing away their filth; which is done by their slaves: for they suffer none of their citizens to kill their cattle, because they think that pity and good-nature, which are among the best of those affections that are born with us, are much impaired by the butchering of animals: nor do they suffer anything that is foul or unclean to be brought within their towns, lest the air should be infected by ill smells which might prejudice their health. In every street there are great halls that lie at an equal distance from each other, distinguished by particular names. The Syphogrants dwell in those that are set over thirty families, fifteen lying on one side of it, and as many on the other. In these halls they all meet and have their repasts. The stewards of every one of them come to the market-place at an appointed hour; and according to the number of those that belong to the hall, they carry home provisions. But they take more care of their sick than of any others: these are lodged and provided for in public hospitals: they have belonging to every town four hospitals, that are built without their walls, and are so large that they may pass for little towns: by this means, if they had ever such a number of sick persons, they could lodge them conveniently, and at such a distance, that such of them as are sick of infectious diseases may be kept so far from the rest that there can be no danger of contagion. The hospitals are furnished and stored with all things that are convenient for the ease and recovery of the sick; and those that are put in them are looked after with such tender and watchful care, and are so constantly attended by their skilful physicians, that as none is sent to them against their will, so there is scarce one in a whole town that, if he should fall ill, would not choose rather to go thither than lie sick at home.

After the steward of the hospitals has taken for the sick whatsoever the physician prescribes, then the best things that are left in the market are distributed equally among the halls, in proportion to their numbers, only, in the first place, they serve the Prince, the chief priest, the Tranibors, the ambassadors, and strangers, if there are any, which indeed falls out but seldom, and for whom there are houses well furnished, particularly appointed for their reception when they come among them. At the hours of dinner and supper, the whole Syphogranty being called together by sound of trumpet, they meet and eat together, except only such as are in the hospitals, or lie sick at home. Yet after the halls are served, no man is hindered to carry provisions home from the market-place; for they know that none does that but for some good reason; for though any that will may eat at home, yet none does it willingly, since it is both ridiculous and foolish for any to give themselves the trouble to make ready an ill dinner at home, when there is a much more plentiful one made ready for him so near at hand. All the uneasy and sordid services about these halls are performed by their slaves; but the dressing and cooking their meat, and the ordering their tables, belong only to the women, all those of every family taking it by turns. They sit at three or more tables, according to their number; the men sit towards the wall, and the women sit on the other side, that if any of them should be taken suddenly ill, which is no uncommon case amongst women with child, she may, without disturbing the rest, rise and go to the nurse's room, who are there with the sucking children; where there is always clean water at hand, and cradles in which they may lay the young children, if there is occasion for it, and a fire that they may shift and dress them before it. Every child is nursed by its own mother, if death or sickness does not intervene; and in that case the Syphogrants' wives find out a nurse quickly, which is no hard matter; for any one that can do it, offers herself cheerfully; for as they are much inclined to that piece of mercy, so the child whom they nurse considers the nurse as its mother. All the children under five years old sit among the nurses, the rest of the younger sort of both sexes, till they are fit for marriage, either serve those that sit at table; or if they are not strong enough for that, stand by them in great silence, and eat what is given them; nor have they any other formality of dining. In the middle of the first table, which stands across the upper end of the hall, sit the Syphogrant and his wife; for that is the chief and most conspicuous place; next to him sit two of the most ancient, for there go always four to a mess. If there is a temple within that Syphogranty, the priest and his wife sit with the Syphogrant above all the rest: next them there is a mixture of old and young, who are so placed, that as the young are set near others, so they are mixed with the more ancient; which they say was appointed on this account, that the gravity of the old people, and the reverence that is due to them, might restrain the younger from all indecent words and gestures. Dishes are not served up to the whole table at first, but the best are first set before the old, whose seats are distinguished from the young, and after them all the rest are served alike. The old men distribute to the younger any curious meats that happen to be set before them, if there is not such an abundance of them that the whole company may be served alike.

Thus old men are honoured with a particular respect; yet all the rest fare as well as they. Both dinner and supper are begun with some lecture of morality that is read to them; but it is so short, that it is not tedious nor uneasy to them to hear it: from hence the old men take occasion to entertain those about them, with some useful and pleasant enlargements; but they do not engross the whole discourse so to themselves, during their meals, that the younger may not put in for a share: on the contrary, they engage them to talk, that so they may in that free way of conversation find out the force of every one's spirit, and observe his temper. They despatch their dinners quickly, but sit long at supper; because they go to work after the one, and are to sleep after the other, during which they think the stomach carries on the concoction more vigorously. They never sup without music; and there is always fruit served up after meat; while they are at table, some burn perfumes, and sprinkle about fragrant ointments and sweet waters: in short, they want nothing that may cheer up their spirits: they give themselves a large allowance that way, and indulge themselves in all such pleasures as are attended with no inconvenience. Thus do those that are in the towns live together; but in the country, where they live at great distance, every one eats at home, and no family wants any necessary sort of provision, for it is from them that provisions are sent unto those that live in the towns.

Of the Travelling of the Utopians

If any man has a mind to visit his friends that live in some other town, or desires to travel and see the rest of the country, he obtains leave very easily from the Syphogrant and Tranibors, when there is no particular occasion for him at home: such as travel, carry with them a passport from the Prince, which both certifies the license that is granted for travelling, and limits the time of their return. They are furnished with a waggon and a slave, who drives the oxen, and looks after them: but unless there are women in the company, the waggon is sent back at the end of the journey as a needless encumbrance: while they are on the road, they carry no provisions with them; yet they want nothing, but are everywhere treated as if they were at home. If they stay in any place longer than a night, every one follows his proper occupation, and is very well used by those of his own trade: but if any man goes out of the city to which he belongs, without leave, and is found rambling without a passport, he is severely treated, he is punished as a fugitive, and sent home disgracefully; and if he falls again into the like fault, is condemned to slavery. If any man has a mind to travel only over the precinct of his own city, he may freely do it, with his father's permission and his wife's consent; but when he comes into any of the country houses, if he expects to be entertained by them, he must labour with them and conform to their rules: and if he does this, he may freely go over the whole precinct; being thus as useful to the city to which he belongs, as if he were still within it. Thus you see that there are no idle persons among them, nor pretences of excusing any from labour. There are no taverns, no alehouses nor stews among them; nor any other occasions of corrupting each other, of getting into corners, or forming themselves into parties: all men live in full view, so that all are obliged, both to perform their ordinary task, and to employ themselves well in their spare hours. And it is certain that a people thus ordered must live in great abundance of all things; and these being equally distributed among them, no man can want, or be obliged to beg.

In their great council at Amaurot, to which there are three sent from every town once a year, they examine what towns abound in provisions, and what are under any scarcity, that so the one may be furnished from the other; and this is done freely, without any sort of exchange; for according to their plenty or scarcity, they supply, or are supplied from one another; so that indeed the whole island is, as it were, one family. When they have thus taken care of their whole country, and laid up stores for two years, which they do to prevent the ill consequences of an unfavourable season, they order an exportation of the overplus, both of corn, honey, wool, flax, wood, wax, tallow, leather, and cattle; which they send out commonly in great quantities to other nations. They order a seventh part of all these goods to be freely given to the poor of the countries to which they send them, and sell the rest at moderate rates. And by this exchange, they not only bring back those few things that they need at home (for indeed they scarce need anything but iron), but likewise a great deal of gold and silver; and by their driving this trade so long, it is not to be imagined how vast a treasure they have got among them: so that now they do not much care whether they sell off their merchandise for money in hand, or upon trust. A great part of their treasure is now in bonds; but in all their contracts no private man stands bound, but the writing runs in the name of the town; and the towns that owe them money, raise it from those private hands that owe it to them, lay it up in their public chamber, or enjoy the profit of it till the Utopians call for it;

and they choose rather to let the greatest part of it lie in their hands who make advantage by it, than to call for it themselves: but if they see that any of their other neighbours stand more in need of it, then they call it in and lend it to them: whenever they are engaged in war, which is the only occasion in which their treasure can be usefully employed, they make use of it themselves. In great extremities or sudden accidents they employ it in hiring foreign troops, whom they more willingly expose to danger than their own people: they give them great pay, knowing well that this will work even on their enemies, that it will engage them either to betray their own side, or at least to desert it, and that it is the best means of raising mutual jealousies among them: for this end they have an incredible treasure; but they do not keep it as a treasure, but in such a manner as I am almost afraid to tell, lest you think it so extravagant, as to be hardly credible. This I have the more reason to apprehend, because if I had not seen it myself, I could not have been easily persuaded to have believed it upon any man's report.

It is certain that all things appear incredible to us, in proportion as they differ from own customs. But one who can judge aright, will not wonder to find, that since their constitution differs so much from ours, their value of gold and silver should be measured by a very different standard; for since they have no use for money among themselves, but keep it as a provision against events which seldom happen, and between which there are generally long intervening intervals; they value it no farther than it deserves, that is, in proportion to its use. So that it is plain, they must prefer iron either to gold or silver: for men can no more live without iron, than without fire or water; but Nature has marked out no use for the other metals, so essential as not easily to be dispensed with. The folly of men has enhanced the value of gold and silver, because of their scarcity. Whereas, on the contrary, it is their opinion that Nature, as an indulgent parent, has freely given us all the best things in great abundance, such as water and earth, but has laid up and hid from us the things that are vain and useless.

If these metals were laid up in any tower in the kingdom, it would raise a jealousy of the Prince and Senate, and give birth to that foolish mistrust into which the people are apt to fall, a jealousy of their intending to sacrifice the interest of the public to their own private advantage. If they should work it into vessels, or any sort of plate, they fear that the people might grow too fond of it, and so be unwilling to let the plate be run down, if a war made it necessary to employ it in paying their soldiers. To prevent all these inconveniences, they have fallen upon an expedient, which as it agrees with their other policy, so is it very different from ours, and will scarce gain belief among us, who value gold so much, and lay it up so carefully. They eat and drink out of vessels of earth, or glass, which make an agreeable appearance though formed of brittle materials: while they make their chamber-pots and close-stools of gold and silver; and that not only in their public halls, but in their private houses: of the same metals they likewise make chains and fetters for their slaves; to some of which, as a badge of infamy, they hang an ear-ring of gold, and make others wear a chain or a coronet of the same metal; and thus they take care, by all possible means, to render gold and silver of no esteem. And from hence it is, that while other nations part with their gold and silver, as unwillingly as if one tore out their bowels, those of Utopia would look on their giving in all they possess of those (metals, when there were any use for them) but as the parting with a trifle, or as we would esteem the loss of a penny. They find pearls on their coast; and diamonds and carbuncles on their rocks; they do not look after them, but if they find them by chance, they polish them, and with them they adorn their children, who are delighted with them, and glory in them during their childhood; but when they grow to years, and see that none but children use such baubles, they of their own accord, without being bid by their parents, lay them aside; and would be as much ashamed to use them afterwards, as children among us, when they come to years, are of their puppets and other toys. . . .

They reckon up several sorts of pleasures, which they call true ones: some belong to the body and others to the mind. The pleasures of the mind lie in knowledge, and in that delight which the contemplation of truth carries with it; to which they add the joyful reflections on a well-spent life, and the assured hopes of a future happiness. They divide the pleasures of the body into two sorts; the one is that which gives our senses some real delight, and is performed, either by recruiting nature, and supplying those parts which feed the internal heat of life by eating and drinking; or when nature is eased of any surcharge that oppresses it; when we are relieved from sudden pain, or that which arises from satisfying the appetite which Nature has wisely given to lead us to the propagation of the species. There is another kind of pleasure that arises neither from our receiving what the body requires, nor its being relieved when overcharged, and yet by a secret, unseen virtue affects the senses, raises the passions, and strikes the mind with generous impressions; this is the pleasure that arises from music. Another kind of bodily pleasure is that which results from an undisturbed and vigorous constitution of body, when life and active spirits seem to actuate every part. This lively health, when entirely free from all mixture of pain, of itself gives an inward pleasure, independent of all external objects of delight; and though this pleasure does not so powerfully affect us, nor act so strongly on the senses as some of the others, yet it may be esteemed as the greatest of all pleasures, and almost all the Utopians reckon it the foundation and basis of all the other joys of life; since this alone makes the state of life easy and desirable; and when this is wanting, a man is really capable of no other pleasure. . . . If it is said that health cannot be felt, they absolutely deny it; for what man is in health that does not perceive it when he is awake? Is there any man that is so dull and stupid as not to acknowledge that he feels a delight in health? And what is delight but another name for pleasure?

But of all pleasures, they esteem those to be most value able that lie in the mind; the chief of which arises out of true virtue, and the witness of a good conscience. They account health the chief pleasure that belongs to the body; for they think that the pleasure of eating and drinking, and all the other delights of sense, are only so far desirable as they give or maintain health. But they are not pleasant in themselves, otherwise than as they resist those impressions that our natural infirmities are still making upon us: for as a wise man desires rather to avoid diseases than to take physic; and to be freed from pain, rather than to find ease by remedies; so it is more desirable not to need this sort of pleasure, than to be obliged to indulge it. If any man imagines that there is a real happiness in these enjoyments, he must then confess that he would be the happiest of all men if he were to lead his life in perpetual hunger, thirst, and itching, and by consequence in perpetual eating, drinking, and scratching himself; which any one may easily see would be not only a base, but a miserable state of a life. These are indeed the lowest of pleasures, and the least pure; for we can never relish them, but when they are mixed with the contrary pains. The pain of hunger must give us the pleasure of eating; and here the pain outbalances the pleasure; and as the pain is more vehement, so it lasts much longer; for as it begins before the pleasure, so it does not cease but with the pleasure that extinguishes it, and both expire together. They think, therefore, none of those pleasures are to be valued any further than as they are necessary; yet they rejoice in them, and with due gratitude acknowledge the tenderness of the great Author of Nature, who has planted in us appetites, by which those things that are necessary for our preservation are likewise made pleasant to us. For how miserable a thing would life be, if those daily diseases of hunger and thirst were to be carried off by such bitter drugs as we must use for those diseases that return seldomer upon us? And thus these pleasant as well as proper gifts of Nature maintain the strength and the sprightliness of our bodies.

They also entertain themselves with the other delights let in at their eyes, their ears, and their nostrils, as the pleasant relishes and seasonings of life, which Nature seems to have marked out peculiarly for man; since no other sort of animals contemplates the figure and beauty of the universe; nor is delighted with smells, any farther than as they distinguish meats by them; nor do they apprehend the concords or discords of sound; yet in all pleasures whatsoever they take care that a lesser joy does not hinder a greater, and that pleasure may never breed pain, which they think always follows dishonest pleasures. But they think it madness for a man to wear out the beauty of his face, or the force of his natural strength; to corrupt the sprightliness of his body by sloth and laziness, or to waste it by fasting; that it is madness to weaken the strength of his constitution, and reject the other delights of life; unless by renouncing his own satisfaction, he can either serve the public or promote the happiness of others, for which he expects a greater recompense from God. So that they look on such a course of life as the mark of a mind that is both cruel to itself, and ungrateful to the Author of Nature, as if we would not be beholden to Him for His favours, and therefore rejects all His blessings; as one who should afflict himself for the empty shadow of virtue; or for no better end than to render himself capable of bearing those misfortunes which possibly will never happen.

This is their notion of virtue and of pleasure; they think that no man's reason can carry him to a truer idea of them, unless some discovery from Heaven should inspire him with sublimer notions. I have not now the leisure to examine whether they think right or wrong in this matter: nor do I judge it necessary, for I have only undertaken to give you an account of their constitution, but not to defend all their principles. I am sure, that whatsoever may be said of their notions, there is not in the whole world either a better people or a happier government: their bodies are vigorous and lively; and though they are but of a middle stature, and have neither the fruitfullest soil nor the purest air in the world, yet they fortify themselves so well by their temperate course of life, against the unhealthiness of their air, and by their industry they so cultivate their soil, that there is nowhere to be seen a greater increase both of corn and cattle nor are there anywhere healthier men, and freer from diseases: for one may there see reduced to practice, not only all the art that the husbandman employs in manuring and improving an ill soil, but whole woods plucked up by the roots, and in other places new ones planted, where there were none before. Their principal motive for this is the convenience of carriage, that their timber may be either near their towns, or growing on the banks of the sea, or of some rivers, so as to be floated to them; for it is a harder work to carry wood at any distance over land, than corn. The people are industrious, apt to learn, as well as cheerful and pleasant; and none can endure more labour, when it is necessary; but except in that case they love their ease. They are unwearied pursuers of knowledge; for when we had given them some hints of the learning and discipline of the Greeks, concerning whom we only instructed them (for we know that there was nothing among the Romans, except their historians and their poets, that they would value much), it was strange to see how eagerly they were set on learning that language. We began to read a little of it to them rather in compliance with their importunity, than out of any hopes of their reaping from it any great advantage. But after a very short trial we found they made such progress that we saw our labour was like to be more successful than we could have expected. They learned to write their characters, and to pronounce their language so exactly, had so quick an apprehension, they remembered it so faithfully, and became so ready and correct in the use of it, that it would have looked like a miracle if the greater part of those whom we taught had not been men both of extraordinary capacity and of a fit age for instruction. They were for the greatest part chosen from among their learned men, by their chief council, though some studied it of their own accord. In three years' time they became masters of the whole language, so that they read the best of the Greek authors very exactly. I am indeed apt to think that they learned that language the more easily, from its having some relation to their own. I believe that they were a colony of the Greeks; for though the language comes nearer the Persian, yet they retain many names, both for their towns and magistrates, that are of Greek derivation. I happened to carry a great many books with me, instead of merchandise, when I sailed my fourth voyage; for I was so far from thinking of soon coming back, that I rather thought never to have returned at all, and I gave them all my books, among which were many of Plato's and some of Aristotle's works. . . . One of my companions, Thricius Apinatus, happened to carry with him some of Hippocrates's works, and Galen's Microtechne, which they hold in great estimation; for though there is no nation in the world that needs physic so little as they do, yet there is not any that honours it so much: they reckon the knowledge of it one of the pleasantest and most profitable parts of philosophy, by which, as they search into the secrets of Nature, so they not only find this study highly agreeable, but think that such inquiries are very acceptable to the Author of Nature; and imagine that as He, like the inventors of curious engines amongst mankind, has exposed this great machine of the universe to the view of the only creatures capable of contemplating it, so an exact and curious observer, who admires His workmanship, is much more acceptable to Him than one of the herd, who like a beast incapable of reason, looks on this glorious scene with the eyes of a dull and unconcerned spectator. . . .

Of Their Slaves, and of Their Marriages

THEY do not make slaves of prisoners of war, except those that are taken in battle; nor of the sons of their slaves, nor of those of other nations: the slaves among them are only such as are condemned to that state of life for the commission of some crime, or, which is more common, such as their merchants find condemned to die in those parts to which they trade, whom they sometimes redeem at low rates; and in other places have them for nothing. They are kept at perpetual labour, and are always chained, but with this difference, that their own natives are treated much worse than others; they are considered as more profligate than the rest, and since they could not be restrained by the advantages of so excellent an education, are judged worthy of harder usage. Another sort of slaves are the poor of the neighbouring countries, who offer of their own accord to come and serve them; they treat these better, and use them in all other respects as well as their own countrymen, except their imposing more labour upon them, which is no hard task to those that have been accustomed to it; and if any of these have a mind to go back to their own country, which indeed falls out but seldom, as they do not force them to stay, so they do not send them away empty-handed.

I have already told you with what care they look after their sick, so that nothing is left undone that can contribute either to their ease or health: and for those who are taken with fixed and incurable diseases, they use all possible ways to cherish them, and to make their lives as comfortable as possible. They visit them often, and take great pains to make their time pass off easily: but when any is taken with a torturing and lingering pain, so that there is no hope, either of recovery or ease, the priests and magistrates come and exhort them, that since they are now unable to go on with the business of life, are become a burden to themselves and to all about them, and they have really outlived themselves, they should no longer nourish such a rooted distemper, but choose rather to die, since they cannot live but in much misery: being assured, that if they thus deliver themselves from torture, or are willing that others should do it, they shall be happy after death. Since by their acting thus, they lose none of the pleasures, but only the troubles of life; they think they behave not only reasonably, but in a manner consistent with religion and piety; because they follow the advice given them by their priests, who are the expounders of the will of God. Such as are wrought on by these persuasions, either starve themselves of their own accord, or take opium, and by that means die without pain. But no man is forced on this way of ending his life; and if they cannot be persuaded to it, this does not induce them to fail in their attendance and care of them; but as they believe that a voluntary death, when it is chosen upon such an authority, is very honourable, so if any man takes away his own life, without the approbation of the priests and the Senate, they give him none of the honours of a decent funeral, but throw his body into a ditch.

Their women are not married before eighteen, nor their men before two-and-twenty, and if any of them run into forbidden embraces before marriage they are severely punished, and the privilege of marriage is denied them, unless they can obtain a special warrant from the Prince. Such disorders cast a great reproach upon the master and mistress of the family in which they happen, for it is supposed that they have failed in their duty. The reason of punishing this so severely is, because they think that if they were not strictly restrained from all vagrant appetites, very few would engage in a state in which they venture the quiet of their whole lives, by being confined to one person, and are obliged to endure all the inconveniences with which it is accompanied. In choosing their wives they use a method that would appear to us very absurd and ridiculous, but it is constantly observed among them, and is accounted perfectly consistent with wisdom. Before marriage some grave matron presents the bride naked, whether she is a virgin or a widow, to the bridegroom; and after that some grave man presents the bridegroom naked to the bride. We indeed both laughed at this, and condemned it as very indecent. But they, on the other hand, wondered at the folly of the men of all other nations, who, if they are but to buy a horse of a small value, are so cautious that they will see every part of him, and take off both his saddle and all his other tackle, that there may be no secret ulcer hid under any of them; and that yet in the choice of a wife, on which depends the happiness or unhappiness of the rest of his life, a man should venture upon trust, and only see about a hand's-breadth of the face, all the rest of the body being covered, under which there may lie hid what may be contagious, as well as loathsome. All men are not so wise as to choose a woman only for her good qualities; and even wise men consider the body as that which adds not a little to the mind: and it is certain there may be some such deformity covered with the clothes as may totally alienate a man from his wife when it is too late to part with her. If such a thing is discovered after marriage, a man has no remedy but patience. They therefore think it is reasonable that there should be good provision made against such mischievous frauds.

There was so much the more reason for them to make a regulation in this matter, because they are the only people of those parts that neither allow of polygamy, nor of divorces, except in the case of adultery, or insufferable perverseness; for in these cases the Senate dissolves the marriage, and grants the injured person leave to marry again; but the guilty are made infamous, and are never allowed the privilege of a second marriage. None are suffered to put away their wives against their wills, from any great calamity that may have fallen on their persons; for they look on it as the height of cruelty and treachery to abandon either of the married persons when they need most the tender care of their comfort, and that chiefly in the case of old age, which as it carries many diseases along with it, so it is a disease of itself. But it frequently falls out that when a married couple do not well agree, they by mutual consent separate, and find out other persons with whom they hope they may live more happily. Yet this is not done without obtaining leave of the Senate, which never admits of a divorce, but upon a strict inquiry made, both by the senators and their wives, into the grounds upon which it is desired; and even when they are satisfied concerning the reasons of it, they go on but slowly, for they imagine that too great easiness in granting leave for new marriages would very much shake the kindness of married people. They punish severely those that defile the marriage-bed. If both parties are married they are divorced, and the injured persons may marry one another, or whom they please; but the adulterer and the adulteress are condemned to slavery. Yet if either of the injured persons cannot shake off the love of the married person, they may live with them still in that state, but they must follow them to that labour to which the slaves are condemned; and sometimes the repentance of the condemned, together with the unshaken kindness of the innocent and injured person, has prevailed so far with the Prince that he has taken off the sentence; but those that relapse after they are once pardoned are punished with death. . . .

They have but few laws, and such is their constitution that they need not many. They very much condemn other nations, whose laws, together with the commentaries on them, swell up to so many volumes; for they think it an unreasonable thing to oblige men to obey a body of laws that are both of such a bulk, and so dark as not to be read and understood by every one of the subjects.

They have no lawyers among them, for they consider them as a sort of people whose profession it is to disguise matters, and to wrest the laws; and therefore they think it is much better that every man should plead his own cause, and trust it to the judge, as in other places the client trusts it to a counsellor. By this means they both cut off many delays, and find out truth more certainly: for after the parties have laid open the merits of the cause, without those artifices which lawyers are apt to suggest, the judge examines the whole matter, and supports the simplicity of such well-meaning persons, whom otherwise crafty men would be sure to run down: and thus they avoid those evils which appear very remarkably among all those nations that labour under a vast load of laws. Every one of them is skilled in their law, for as it is a very short study, so the plainest meaning of which words are capable is always the sense of their laws. And they argue thus: all laws are promulgated for this end, that every man may know his duty; and therefore the plainest and most obvious sense of the words is that which ought to be put upon them; since a more refined exposition cannot be easily comprehended, and would only serve to make the laws become useless to the greater part of mankind, and especially to those who need most the direction of them: for it is all one, not to make a law at all, or to couch it in such terms that without a quick apprehension, and much study, a man cannot find out the true meaning of it; since the generality of mankind are both so dull, and so much employed in their several trades, that they have neither the leisure nor the capacity requisite for such an inquiry.

Thomas More (1478–1535) was an English statesman who was knighted by Henry VIII for service to the crown but later executed for his refusal to sanction Henry as head of the church in England. He was canonized in 1935.

Source: Thomas More, UTOPIA, in IDEAL COMMONWEALTHS, ed. Henry Morley (London: George Routledge and Sons, 1885), 96–111, 122–28, 129–33, 135–36.

François Rabelais
The Abbey of Theleme

The great French writer François Rabelais presented both a critique of monasticism and the depiction of an ideal life for those primarily interested in pleasure.

Chapter LII. How Gargantua Caused to Be Built for the Monk the Abbey of Theleme

There was left only the monk to provide for, whom Gargantua would have made abbot of Sevillé, but he refused it. He would have given him the abbey of Bourgueil, or of Sanct Plorent, which was better, or both if it pleased him. But the monk gave him a very peremptory answer, that he would never take upon him the charge nor government of monks. "For how shall I be able," said he, "to rule over others, that have not power or command over myself? If you think I have done you, or may here after do you any acceptable service, give me leave to found an abbey after my own mind and fancy." The notion pleased Gargantua very well, who thereupon offered him all the country of Theleme by the river of Loire, till within two leagues of the great forest of Port-huault. The monk then requested Gargantua to institute his religious order contrary to all others. "First then," said Gargantua, "you must not build a wall about your convent, for all other abbeys are strongly walled and mured about." "See," said the monk, "and without cause, where there is mur before and mur behind, there is store of murmur, envy, and mutual conspiracy."

Moreover, seeing there are certain convents in the world, whereof the custom is, if any woman came, I mean chaste and honest women, they immediately sweep the ground which they have trod upon; therefore was it ordained, that if any man or woman, entered into religious orders, should by chance come within this new abbey, all the rooms should be thoroughly washed and cleansed, through which they had passed. And because in all other monasteries and nunneries all is compassed, limited, and regulated by hours, it was decreed, that in this new structure there should be neither clock nor dial, but that, according to the opportunities and incident occasions, all their hours should be disposed of. "For," said Gargantua, "the greatest loss of time that I know, is, to count the hours. What good comes of it? Nor can there be any greater dotage in the world, than for one to guide and direct his courses by the sound of a bell, and not by his own judgment and discretion."

Item, Because at that time they put no women into nunneries, but such as were either purblind, blinkards, lame, crooked, ill-favoured, mis-shapen, fools, senseless, spoiled, or corrupt; nor encloistered any men, but those that were either sickly, subject to defluxions, ill bred louts, simple sots, or peevish trouble houses. "But to the purpose," said the monk; "a woman that is neither fair nor good, to what use serves she?" "To make a nun of," said Gargantua. "Yea," said the monk, "and to make shirts and smocks." Therefore was it ordained, that into this religious order should be admitted no women that were not fair, well featured, and of a sweet disposition; nor men that were not comely, personable, and well conditioned.

Item, because in the convents of women, men come not but underhand, privily, and by stealth, it was therefore enacted, that in this house there shall be no women in case there be not men nor men in case there be not women.

Item, because both men and women that are received into religious orders, after the expiring of their novitiate, or probation year, were constrained and forced perpetually to stay there all the days of their life; it was therefore ordered, that all whatever, men or women, admitted within this abbey, should have full leave to depart with peace and contentment, whensoever it should seem good to them so to do.

Item, for that the religious men and women did ordinarily make three vows, to wit, those of chastity, poverty, and obedience; it was therefore constituted and appointed, that in this convent they might be honorably married, that they might be rich, and live at liberty. In regard of the legitimate time of the persons to be initiated, and years under and above which they were not capable of reception, the women were to be admitted from ten till fifteen, and the men from twelve to eighteen.

Chapter LIII. How the Abbey of the Thelemites Was Built and Endowed

The architecture was in a figure hexagonal, and in such a fashion that in every one of the six corners there was built a great round tower of threescore feet in diameter; and were all of a like form and bigness. Upon the north side ran along the river of Loire, on the bank whereof was situated the tower called Arctic. Going towards the east, there was another, called Calaer; the next following Anatole; the next Mesembrine; the next Hesperia, and the last Criere. Every tower was distant from the other the space of three hundred and twelve paces. The whole edifice was everywhere six stories high, reckoning the cellar under ground for one. The second was arched after the fashion of a basket-handle. The rest were ceiled with pure wainscot, flourished with Flanders fret-work, in the form of the foot of a lamp; and covered above with fine slates, with an indorsement of lead, carrying the antique figures of little flower-baskets, and animals of all sorts, notably well suited to one another, and gilt, together with the gutters, which jetting without the walls, from betwixt the cross bars in a diagonal figure, painted with gold and azure, reached to the very ground, where they ended into great conduit-pipes, which carried all away unto the river from under the house.

This same building was a hundred times more sumptuous and magnificent than ever was Bonnivet, Chambourg, or Chantilly. For there were in it nine thousand, three hundred, and two and thirty chambers; every one whereof had a withdrawing room, a handsome closet, a wardrobe, an oratory, and neat passage, leading into a great and spacious hall. Between every tower, in the midst of the said body of building, there was a pair of winding stairs, where of the steps were part of porphyry, part of Numidian stone, and part of serpentine marble; each of those steps being two and twenty feet in length, and three fingers thick, and the just number of twelve betwixt every rest or landing place. In every resting place were two fair antique arches, where the light came in; and by those they went into a cabinet made even with, and of the breadth of the said winding, and then re-ascending above the roofs of the house ending conically in a pavillion. By that vize or winding, they entered on every side into a great hall, and from the halls into the chambers. From the Arctic tower unto the Criere, were the fair great libraries in Greek, Latin, Hebrew, French, Italian, and Spanish, respectively distributed in their several cantons, according to the diversity of these languages. In the midst there was a wonderful winding-stair, the entry whereof was without the house, in a vault or arch, six fathoms broad. It was made in such symmetry and largeness that six men at arms, with their lances in their rests, might together in a breast ride all up to the very top of all the palace. From the tower Anatole to the Mesembrine were spacious galleries, all colored over and painted with the ancient prowesses, histories, and descriptions of the world. In the midst thereof there was likewise such another ascent and gate, as we said there was on the river side. . . .

Chapter LV. What Manner of Dwelling the Thelemites Had

In the middle of the lower court there was a stately fountain of fair alabaster. Upon the top thereof stood the three Graces, with their cornucopias, or horns of abundance, and did jet out the water at their breasts, mouth, ears, eyes, and other open passages of the body. The inside of the buildings in this lower court, stood upon great pillars of chalcedony stone, and porphyry marble, made archwise, after a goodly antique fashion: within those were spacious galleries, long and large, adorned with curious pictures, the horns of bucks and unicorns; with rhinoceroses, water horses, called hippopotames; the teeth and tusks of elephants, and other things well worth the beholding. The lodging of the ladies took up all from the tower Arctic unto the gate Mesembrine. The men possessed the rest. Before the said lodging of the ladies, that they might have their recreation between the two first towers, on the outside were placed the tilt-yard, the barriers or lists for tournaments, the hippodrome or riding court, theatre or public play-houses, and natatory or place to swim in, with most admirable baths in three stages, situated above one another, well furnished with all necessary accommodations and store of myrtle water. By the river-side was a fine pleasure garden, and in the midst of the glorious labyrinth. Between the two towers were the courts for tennis and the football. Towards the tower Criere stood the orchard, full of all fruit trees, set and ranged in a quincuncial order. At the end of that was the great park, abounding with all sorts of venison. Betwixt the third couple of towers were the butts and marks for shooting with a snap-work gun, an ordinary bow for common archery, or with a cross-bow. The domestic offices were without the tower of Hesperia, of one story high. The stables were beyond the offices, and before them stood the falconry, managed by bird-keepers and falconers, very expert in the art, and it was yearly supplied and furnished by the Candians, Venetians, and Sarmatians with all sorts of most excellent hawks, eagles, gerfalcons, goshawks, sacres, lanners, falcons, sparhawks, merlins, and all other kinds of them; so gentle and perfectly well manned, that flying of themselves sometimes from the castle, for their own disport, they would not fail to catch whatever they encountered. The venery, where the beagles and hounds were kept, was a little farther off drawing towards the park.

All the halls, chambers, and closets, or cabinets, were richly hung with tapestry, and hangings of divers sorts, according to the variety of the seasons of the year. All the pavements and floors were covered with green cloth. The beds were all embroidered. In every back-chamber or withdrawing room, there was a looking glass of pure crystal, set in a frame of fine gold, garnished all about with pearls, and was of such greatness that it would represent to the full the whole lineaments and proportion of the person that stood before it. At the going out of the halls, which belong to the ladies' lodgings, were the perfumers and trimmers, through whose hands the gallants passed when they were to visit the ladies. These sweet artificers did every morning furnish the ladies' chambers with the spirit of roses, orange-flower-water, and angelica; and to each of them gave a little precious casket, vaporing forth the most odoriferous exhalations of the choicest aromatical scents. . . .

Chapter LVII. How the Thelemites Were Governed, and of Their Manner of Living

All their life was spent not in laws, statutes, or rules, but according to their own free will and pleasure. They rose out of their beds when they thought good: they did eat, drink, labour, sleep, when they had a mind to it, and were disposed for it. None did awake them, none did offer to constrain them to eat, drink, nor do any other thing; for so had Gargantua established it. In all their rule and strictest tie of their order, there was but this one clause to be observed—

DO AS THOU WOULDST

Because men that are free, well-born, well-bred, and conversant in honest companies, have naturally an instinct and spur that prompteth them into virtuous actions, and withdraws them from vice, which is called honour. Those same men, when by base subjection and constraint they are brought under and kept down, turn aside from that noble disposition, by which they formerly were inclined to virtue, to shake off that bond of servitude, wherein they are so tyrannously enslaved; for it is agreeable to the nature of man to long after things forbidden, and to desire what is denied us.

By this liberty they entered into a very laudable emulation, to do all of them what they saw did please one. If any of the gallants or ladies should say, "Let us drink," they would all drink. If any one of them said, "Let us play," they all played. If one said, "Let us go a walking into the fields," they went all. If it were to go a hawking, or a hunting, the ladies mounted upon dainty well paced nags, seated in a stately palfrey saddle, carried on their lovely fists miniardly begloved every one of them, either a sparhawk, or a laneret, or a marlin, and the young gallants carried the other kinds of hawks. So nobly were they taught, that there was neither he nor she amongst them, but could read, write, sing, play upon several musical instruments, speak five or six several languages, and compose in them all very quaintly, both in verse and prose. Never were seen so valiant knights, so noble and worthy, so dextrous and skilful both on foot and horseback, more brisk and lively, more nimble and quick, or better handling all manner of weapons, than were there. Never were seen ladies so proper and handsome, so miniard and dainty, less forward, or more ready with their hand, and with their needle, in every honest and free action belonging to that sex, than were there. For this reason, when the time came that any man of the said abbey, either at the request of his parents or for some other cause, had a mind to go out of it, he carried along with him one of the ladies, namely, her whom he had before that chosen for his mistress, and they were married together. And if they had formerly in Theleme lived in good devotion and amity, they did continue therein, and increase it to a greater height in their state of matrimony; and did entertain that mutual love till the very last day of their life, in no less vigour and fervency than at the very day of their wedding.

François Rabelais (1494?–1553?) was a French satirist, physician, and Franciscan monk who later joined the Benedictine order.

Source: François Rabelais, THE LIFE OF GARGANTUA AND THE HEROIC DEEDS OF PANTA-
GRUEL, trans. Thomas Urquhart (London: George Routledge and Sons, 1883), 164–69,
173–74, 178–80.

Michel de Montaigne
Of the Cannibals

**The discovery of the New World led to the presentation of its inhabitants as
noble savages, peoples who, without the benefits of Christianity and civilization, still seemed to be in some ways better than Europeans.**

From what I have heard of that nation [Brazil, 1557], I can see nothing barbarous or uncivilized about it, except that we all call barbarism that which does
not fit in with our usages. And indeed we have no other level of truth and reason but the example and model of the opinions and usages of the country we
live in. There we always see the perfect religion, the perfect government, the
perfect and accomplished manner of doing all things. Those people are wild in
the sense in which we call wild the fruits that Nature has produced by herself
and in her ordinary progress; whereas in truth it is those we have altered artifi-
cially and diverted from the common order, that we should rather call wild. In
the first we still see, in full life and vigor, the genuine and most natural and useful virtues and properties, which we have bastardized in the latter, and only
adapted to please our corrupt taste. And yet in some of the uncultivated fruits
of those countries there is a delicacy of flavor that is excellent even to our taste,
and rivals even our own. It is not reasonable that art should gain the point of
honor over our great and powerful mother Nature. We have so overburdened
the beauty and richness of her works with our inventions, that we have quite
smothered her. And yet, wherever she shines in her purity, she marvellously
puts to shame our vain and trivial efforts,

> Uncared, unmarked the ivy blossoms best;
> Midst desert rocks the ilex clusters still;
> And sweet the wild bird's untaught melody.
> —Propertius

Those nations, then, appear to me so far barbarous in this sense, that their
minds have been formed to a very slight degree, and that they are still very close
to their original simplicity. They are still ruled by the laws of Nature, and very
little corrupted by ours; but they are still in such a state of purity, that I am
sometimes vexed that they were not known earlier, at a time when there were
men who could have appreciated them better than we do.

I am sorry that Lycurgus and Plato had no knowledge of them, for it seems to me that what we have learned by contact with those nations surpasses not only all the beautiful colors in which the poets have depicted the golden age, and all their ingenuity in inventing a happy state of man, but also the conceptions and desires of Philosophy herself. They were incapable of imagining so pure and native a simplicity, as that which we see by experience; nor could they have believed that human society could have been maintained with so little human artifice and solder. This is a nation, I should say to Plato, which has no manner of traffic; no knowledge of letters; no science of numbers; no name of magistrate or statesman; no use for slaves; neither wealth nor poverty; no contracts; no successions; no partitions; no occupation but that of idleness; only a general respect of parents; no clothing; no agriculture; no metals; no use of wine or corn. The very words denoting falsehood, treachery, dissimulation, avarice, envy, detraction, pardon, unheard of. How far removed from this perfection would he find the ideal republic he imagined! Men *newly come from the hands of the gods.* (Seneca).

These manners first by nature taught. (Virgil.)

For the rest, they live in a region with a very agreeable and very temperate climate, so that, according to my witnesses, a sick man is rarely seen; and they assured me that they had never seen any man shaking with palsy, or with dripping eyes, toothless, or bent with age. They are settled along the sea coast, and closed in on the land side by large and high mountains, the land between them and the sea extending for a hundred leagues or thereabouts. They have great abundance of fish and flesh, which bear no resemblance to ours, and they eat them roasted without any other preparation. The first man who brought a horse thither, although he had associated with them on several previous voyages, so horrified them in the riding posture, that they shot him dead with arrows before recognizing him.

Their buildings are very long, capable of holding two or three hundred souls, covered with the bark of tall trees, the strips resting by one end on the ground, and leaning to and supporting one another at the top, after the manner of some of our barns, the coverings of which slope down to the ground and serve as side walls. They have a wood so hard that they can cut with it, of which they make their swords and gridirons to roast their meat. Their beds are made of cotton tissue, suspended from the roof like those in our ships, each one having his own: for the women sleep apart from their husbands.

They rise with the sun and eat immediately after rising, for the whole day: for they have no other meal. They drink nothing with that meal, like some other Eastern peoples of whom Suidas tells us, who drank apart from eating; but they drink several times a day, and to excess. Their drink is made of some root, and is of the color of our claret wines, and they only drink it warm. This beverage will keep only two or three days; it has a slightly pungent taste, is anything but heady, good for the stomach, and laxative for such as are not used to it, but a very pleasant drink for those who are. For bread they use a certain white material resembling preserved coriander. I have tried some of it: it is sweet but rather tasteless.

The whole day is spent in dancing. The younger men hunt animals with bows. Some of the women meanwhile spend their time warming their drink, which is their chief duty. One of the old men, in the morning before they begin to eat, preaches to the whole barnfull of people in common, walking from one end to the other, repeating the same words several times, until he has finished the round (for the buildings are quite a hundred paces in length). He recommends only two things, valor against the enemy and love to their wives. And they never fail to stress this obligation, which forms their refrain, 'that it is they who keep their wine warm and seasoned.'

In several places, among others in my house, may be seen the formation of their beds, of their ropes, their wooden swords and bracelets, with which they cover their wrists in battle, and large canes open at one end, by the sound of which they keep the time and rhythm of their dances. They are close shaven all over, and remove their hair much more neatly than we do, although their razors are only made of wood or stone. They believe the soul to be immortal, and that those who have deserved well of the gods are lodged in that part of the heaven where the sun rises, and those who are damned in the west.

They have some kind of priest and prophet, who very seldom appears among the people, having his dwelling in the mountains. On his arrival there is a great feast and a solemn assembly of several villages (each barn, as I have described it, forms a village, and they are about a French league distant one from the other). This prophet speaks to them in public, exhorting them to virtue and their duty; but their whole ethical science comprises only these two articles: an unfaltering courage in war and affection to their women. This man foretells things to come, and the issue they are to expect from their enterprises; urges them to war, or holds them back; but he does so on the understanding that, where he fails to prophesy correctly, and if things turn out otherwise than he has predicted, he is cut into a thousand pieces if he is caught, and condemned for a false prophet. For that reason he who has once miscalculated is seen no more.

Divination is a gift of God, wherefore to abuse it ought to be regarded as a punishable imposture. Among the Scythians, when the prophets fail to hit the mark, they are laid, shackled hand and foot on a little cart filled with heather and drawn by oxen, on which they were burned. They who take in hand such matters as depend on the conduct of human capacity are to be excused if they do their best. But those others who come and delude us with assurances of an extraordinary faculty that is beyond our ken, should they not be punished when they fail to carry out what they promise, and for the tenacity of their imposture?

They have their wars with the nations beyond their mountains, further back on the mainland, to which they go quite naked, with no other weapons but bows or wooden swords pointed at one end, after the fashion of the tongues of our boar spears. It is marvellous with what obstinacy they fight their battles, which never end but in massacre and bloodshed for of routs and terrors they know not even the meaning. Each man brings back as a trophy the head of the enemy he has slain, and fixes it over the entrance to his dwelling. After treating his prisoner well for a considerable time, and giving him all that hospitality can devise, his captor convokes a great gathering of his acquaintance. He ties a cord to one of his prisoner's arms, holding him at some distance for fear of being hurt, and gives the other arm to be held in the same way by his best friend; and these two, in the presence of the whole assembly, dispatch him with their swords. This done, they roast and eat him in common, and send bits of him to their absent friends. Not, as one might suppose, for nourishment, as the ancient Scythians used to do, but to signify an extreme revenge.

And that it is so, may be seen from this: having perceived that the Portuguese, who had allied themselves with their adversaries, inflicted a different kind of death on their prisoners, which was to bury them up to the waist, shoot the upper part of the bodies full of arrows, and afterwards to hang them; they imagined that these people of another world (seeing that they had sown the knowledge of a great many vices among their neighbors, and were much greater masters than themselves in every kind of wickedness) had some reason for adopting this kind of vengeance, and that it must be more painful than their own; wherefore they began to give up their old method, and followed this one.

I am not so much concerned that we should remark on the horrible barbarity of such acts, as that, whilst rightly judging their errors, we should be so blind to our own. I think there is more barbarity in eating a live than a dead man, in tearing on the rack and torturing the body of a man still full of feeling, in roasting him piecemeal and giving him to be bitten and mangled by dogs and swine (as we have not only read, but seen within fresh memory, not between old enemies, but between neighbours and fellow citizens, and, what is worse, under the cloak of piety and religion), than in roasting and eating him after he is dead. We may therefore well call these people barbarians in respect to the rules of reason, but not in respect to ourselves, who surpass them in every kind of barbarity.

Their warfare is entirely noble and generous, and is as fair and excusable as can be expected in that human disease: their only motive being a zeal for valor.

They do not strive to conquer new territory, for they still enjoy that luxuriance of nature which provides them, without labor and pains, with all necessary things in such abundance, that they have no need to enlarge their borders. They are still in that happy state of not desiring more than their natural needs demand: all that is over and above it is for them superfluity.

They generally call each other, if of the same age, brothers; if younger, children; and the old men are fathers to all the others. These latter leave to their heirs in common the full and undivided possession of their property without any but that pure title that Nature gives to her creatures, by bringing them into the world. If their neighbors cross the mountain to attack them, and gain the victory over them, the acquisition of the victor is the glory and advantage of having proved himself the superior in valor and virtue, for otherwise they have no needs for the spoils of the vanquished; and so they return to their own country, where they have no want of any necessaries, nor even of that great portion, which is to know how to enjoy happily their condition, and be content with it. These do the same in their turn. They ask of their prisoners no other reason but a confession and acknowledgment of being vanquished. . . .

The men there have several wives, and the higher their reputation for valor the greater is the number of their wives. It is a remarkably beautiful feature in their marriages, that the same jealousy that our wives have to keep us from the love and favors of other women, they have to an equal degree to procure it. Being more solicitous for their husbands' honor than for anything else, they use their best endeavors to have as many companions as they can, seeing that that is a proof of their husband's worth. . . .

Michel de Montaigne (1533–1592) was a French essayist.

Source: Michel de Montaigne, "Of the Cannibals," in Famous Utopias of the Renaissance, ed. Frederic White (New York: Hendricks House/Farrar Straus, 1946), 141–50.

FOUR

The Seventeenth Century

c/ɔ

Joseph Hall
Mundus alter et idem

The first utopia published in the seventeenth century, *Mundus alter et idem* (1605) by Joseph Hall (1594–1656) is a burlesque of writers of voyages and of the encyclopedists. It is a general satire on human failings and can be thought of as an allegory, though to today's readers it is primarily entertaining. Hall wrote the *Mundus* and his other satire, *Virgidemiae* (1597–1598), early in life. They attack the same things he attacked in his religious writings—the new and the extreme.

In the *Mundus*, Hall attacks a wide range of human foibles by presenting them in their most exaggerated forms. This is a classic satiric technique, probably borrowed from Lucian, and was used by a variety of seventeenth-century authors, usually with less effect. The names of the provinces suggest, for example, that women talk too much and are scolds, criers, teasers, and shrews, among other unpleasant attributes. In Aphrodysia, our hero is too ugly to interest the women; otherwise, he would have been captured to satisfy their "most unseemly lusts." In Amazonia, on the other hand, he would have been put to work at spinning and weaving since "the women attend to military matters and farming" and "wear the breeches and sport long beards."

In Crapulia, the highest honors are given to gluttons and drunkards; one is supposed to eat and drink as much as possible. In Pamphagonia, a district of Crapulia, the fatter one gets the more one is honored. Some of the laws regarding the more heinous crimes in Pamphagonia make the point well:

1. Eating only once a day shall be a crime.
2. He that carelessly overturns a full dish or goblet shall, while standing upright, devour with the tiniest spoon a dish of broth placed at his ankles.

3. No one shall eat alone, lest by eating privately he violate the laws of the table with impunity; citizens are to eat in the streets or in front of windows opened on all sides.

4. Whoever shall omit a meal by sleeping a whole four hours and thus defraud the deity shall be obliged to eat twice.

5. If one's mouth be full, it shall be satisfactory to answer with one's forefinger.

6. A party found guilty of treason shall perish by starvation; the punishment for a party guilty of a lighter transgression shall be the loss of a tooth.

7. Whatever cook shall prepare food in such a manner that it cannot be eaten shall be bound at the public stake, near which shall be hung the half-raw or half-burned meat until some miserable and starving onlooker shall eat it all up.

8. To belch in any manner shall not only be lawful (as some rulers decreed) but honored as well; whoever shall have belched most manfully, clearly, and powerfully shall be assigned as the leader of the next feast.

9. Whoever holds his breath while his girth is being measured shall automatically be considered unmanageable and be condemned to a day in prison without a meal, put behind bars in such a way that he might gaze upon the rest of the noblemen eating (for some this punishment has been deadly).

10. How much anyone consumes shall be measured weekly at the magistrate's, so that if he eats less than what is prescribed, the penalty that fits the crime shall be imposed.

Joseph Hall was bishop of Exeter (1627–1641) and Norwich (1641–1643) and is best known as a writer of religious works defending episcopacy.

Source: Joseph Hall, Another World and Yet the Same: Bishop Joseph Hall's Mundus alter et idem, ed. and trans. Joseph Millar Wands (New Haven: Yale University Press, 1981), 33–34.

William Shakespeare
The Tempest

The idea of a golden age, which had never really disappeared, played a major role in seventeenth-century utopias. It was most often used to satirize the present by offering an alternative in which nature provided abundantly. Gonzalo's famous speech in *The Tempest* is repeated, with variations, throughout history:

> I' th' commonwealth I would, by contraries,
> Execute all things; for no kind of traffic

Would I admit; no name of magistrate;
Letters should not be known; riches, poverty,
And use of service, none; contract, succession,
Bourn, bound of land, tilth, vineyard, none;
No use of metal, corn, or wine, or oil;
No occupation; all men idle, all;
And women too, but innocent and pure;
No sovereignty; . . .

All things in common nature should produce
Without sweat or endeavour; treason, felony,
Sword, pike, knife, gun, or need of any engine,
Would I not have; but nature should bring forth,
Of its own kind, all foison, all abundance,
To feed my innocent people. . . .

I would with such perfection govern, sir,
To excel the golden age.

William Shakespeare (1564–1616) is considered the greatest English playwright.

Source: William Shakespeare, THE TEMPEST, Act 2, Scene 1

Tommaso Campanella
The City of the Sun

*A Poetical Dialogue between a Grandmaster of the Knights
Hospitallers and a Genoese Sea Captain, His Guest*

Grandmaster. Prithee, now, tell me what happened to you during that voyage?

Captain. I have already told you how I wandered over the whole earth. In the course of my journeying I came to Taprobane, and was compelled to go ashore at a place, where through fear of the inhabitants I remained in a wood. When I stepped out of this I found myself on a large plain immediately under the equator.

Grand. And what befell you here?

Capt. I came upon a large crowd of men and armed women, many of whom did not understand our language, and they conducted me forthwith to the City of the Sun.

Grand. Tell me after what plan this city is built and how it is governed?

Capt. The greater part of the city is built upon a high hill, which rises from an extensive plain, but several of its circles extend for some distance beyond the base of the hill, which is of such size that the diameter of the city is upwards of two miles, so that its circumference becomes about seven. On account of the humped shape of the mountain, however, the diameter of the city is really more than if it were built on a plain.

It is divided into seven rings or huge circles named from the seven planets, and the way from one to the other of these is by four streets and through four gates, that look towards the four points of the compass. Furthermore, it is so built that if the first circle were stormed, it would of necessity entail a double amount of energy to storm the second; still more to storm the third; and in each succeeding case the strength and energy would have to be doubled; so that he who wishes to capture that city must, as it were, storm it seven times. For my own part, however, I think that not even the first wall could be occupied, so thick are the earthworks and so well fortified is it with breastworks, towers, guns and ditches.

When I had been taken through the northern gate (which is shut with an iron door so wrought that it can be raised and let down, and locked in easily and strongly, its projections running into the grooves of the thick posts by a marvellous device), I saw a level space seventy paces wide between the first and second walls. From hence can be seen large palaces all joined to the wall of the second circuit, in such a manner as to appear all one palace. Arches run on a level with the middle height of the palaces, and are continued around the whole ring. There are galleries for promenading upon these arches, which are supported from beneath by thick and well shaped columns, enclosing arcades like peristyles, or cloisters of an abbey.

But the palaces have no entrances from below, except on the inner or concave partition, from which one enters directly to the lower parts of the building. The higher parts, however, are reached by flights of marble steps which lead to galleries for promenading on the inside similar to those on the outside. From these one enters the higher rooms, which are very beautiful, and have windows on the concave and convex partitions. These rooms are divided from one another by richly decorated walls. The convex or outer wall of the ring is about eight spans thick the concave, three; the intermediate walls are one, or perhaps one and a half. Leaving this circle one gets to the second plain, which is nearly three paces narrower than the first. Then the first wall of the second ring is seen adorned above and below with similar galleries for walking, and there is on the inside of it another interior wall enclosing palaces. It has also similar peristyles supported by columns in the lower part, but above are excellent pictures, round the ways into the upper houses. And so on afterwards through similar spaces and double walls, enclosing palaces, and adorned with galleries for walking, extending along their outer side, and supported by columns, till the last circuit is reached, the way being still over a level plain.

But when the two gates, that is to say, those of the outmost and the inmost walls, have been passed, one mounts by means of steps so formed that an ascent is scarcely discernible, since it proceeds in a slanting direction, and the steps succeed one another at almost imperceptible heights. On the top of the hill is a rather spacious plain, and in the midst of this there rises a temple built with wondrous art.

Grand. Tell on, I pray you! Tell on! I am dying to hear more.

Capt. The temple is built in the form of a circle; it is not girt with walls, but stands upon thick columns, beautifully grouped. A very large dome, built with great care in the centre or pole, contains another small vault as it were rising out of it, and in this is a spiracle, which is right over the altar. There is but one altar in the middle of the temple, and this is hedged round by columns. The temple itself is on a space of more than three hundred and fifty paces. Without it, arches measuring about eight paces extend from the heads of these columns outwards, whence other columns rise about three paces from the thick, strong and erect wall. Between these and the former columns there are galleries for walking, with beautiful pavements, and in the recess of the wall, which is adorned with numerous large doors, there are immovable seats, placed as it were between the inside columns, supporting the temple. Portable chairs are not wanting, many and well adorned. Nothing is seen over the altar but a large globe, upon which the heavenly bodies are painted, and another globe upon which there is a representation of the earth. Furthermore, in the vault of the dome there can be discerned representations of all the stars of heaven from the first to the sixth magnitude, with their proper names and power to influence terrestrial things marked in three little verses for each. There are the poles and greater and lesser circles according to the right latitude of the place, but these are not perfect because there is no wall below. They seem, too, to be made in their relation to the globes on the altar. The pavement of the temple is bright with precious stones. Its seven golden lamps hang always burning, and these bear the names of the seven planets.

At the top of the building several small and beautiful cells surround the small dome, and behind the level space above the bands or arches of the exterior and interior columns there are many cells, both small and large, where the priests and religious officers dwell to the number of forty nine.

A revolving flag projects from the smaller dome, and this shows in what quarter the wind is. The flag is marked with figures up to thirty six, and the priests know what sort of year the different kinds of winds bring and what will be the changes of weather on land and sea. Furthermore under the flag a book is always kept written with letters of gold.

Grand. I pray you, worthy hero, explain to me their whole system of government; for I am anxious to hear it.

Capt. The great rule among them is a priest whom they call by the name HOH, though we should call him Metaphysic. He is head over all, in temporal and spiritual matters, and all business and lawsuits are settled by him, as the supreme authority. Three princes of equal power—viz., Pon, Sin and Mor—assist him, and these in our tongue we should call POWER, WISDOM and LOVE. To POWER belongs the care of all matters relating to war and peace. He attends to the military arts, and, next to HOH, he is ruler in every affair of a warlike nature. He governs the military magistrates and the soldiers, and has the management of the munitions, the fortifications, the storming of places, the implements of war, the armories, the smiths and workmen connected with matters of this sort.

But WISDOM is the ruler of the liberal arts, of mechanics, of all sciences with their magistrates and doctors, and of the discipline of the schools. As many doctors as there are are under his control. There is one doctor who is called Astrologus; a second, Cosmographus; a third, Arithmeticus, a fourth, Geometra; a fifth, Historiographus; a sixth, Poeta; a seventh, Logicus; an eighth, Rhetor; a ninth, Grammaticus; a tenth, Medicus; an eleventh, Physiologus; a twelfth, Politicus; a thirteenth, Moralis. They have but one book, which they call Wisdom, and in it all the sciences are written with conciseness and marvellous fluency of expression. This they read to the people after the custom of the Pythagoreans. It is Wisdom who causes the exterior and interior, the higher and lower walls of the city to be adorned with the finest pictures, and to have all the sciences painted upon them in an admirable manner. On the walls of the temple and on the dome, which is let down when the priest gives an address, lest the sounds of his voice, being scattered, should fly away from his audience, there are pictures of stars in their different magnitudes, with the powers and motions of each, expressed separately in three little verses.

On the interior wall of the first circuit all the mathematical figures are conspicuously painted—figures more in number than Archimedes or Euclid discovered, marked symmetrically, and with the explanation of them neatly written and contained each in a little verse. There are definitions and propositions, etc. On the exterior convex wall is first an immense drawing of the whole earth, given at one view. Following upon this, there are tablets setting forth for every separate country the customs both public and private, the laws, the origins and the power of the inhabitants; and the alphabets the different people use can be seen above that of the City of the Sun.

On the inside of the second circuit, that is to say of the second ring of buildings, paintings of all kinds of precious and common stones, of minerals and metals, are seen; and a little piece of the metal itself is also there with an apposite explanation in two small verses for each metal or stone. On the outside are marked all the seas, rivers, lakes and streams which are on the face of the earth; as are also the wines and the oils and the different liquids, with the sources from which the last are extracted, their qualities and strength. There are also vessels built into the wall above the arches, and these are full of liquids from one to three hundred years old, which cure all diseases. Hail and snow, storms and thunder, and whatever else takes place in the air, are represented with suitable figures and little verses. The inhabitants even have the art of representing in stone all the phenomena of the air, such as the wind, rain, thunder, the rainbow, etc.

On the interior of the third circuit all the different families of trees and herbs are depicted, and there is a live specimen of each plant in earthenware vessels placed under the outer partition of the arches. With the specimens there are explanations as to where they were first found, what are their powers and natures, and resemblances to celestial things and to metals: to parts of the human body and to things in the sea, and also as to their uses in medicine, etc. On the exterior wall are all the races of fish, found in rivers, lakes and seas, and their habits and values, and ways of breeding, training and living, the purposes for which they exist in the world, and their uses to man. Further, their resemblances to celestial and terrestrial things, produced both by nature and art, are so given that I was astonished when I saw a fish which was like a bishop, one like a chain, another like a garment, a fourth like a nail, a fifth like a star, and others like images of those things existing among us, the relation in each case being completely manifest. There are sea urchins to be seen, and the purple shell fish and mussels; and whatever the watery world possesses worthy of being known is there fully shown in marvellous characters of painting and drawing.

On the fourth interior wall all the different kinds of birds are painted, with their natures, sizes, customs, colors, manner of living, etc.; and the only real phoenix is possessed by the inhabitants of this city. On the exterior are shown all the races of creeping animals, serpents, dragons and worms; the insects, the flies, gnats, beetles, etc., in their different states, strength, venoms and uses, and a great deal more than you or I can think of.

On the fifth interior they have all the larger animals of the earth, as many in number as would astonish you. We indeed know not the thousandth part of them, for on the exterior wall also a great many of immense size are also portrayed. To be sure, of horses alone, how great a number of breeds there is and how beautiful are the forms there cleverly displayed!

On the sixth interior are painted all the mechanical arts, with the several instruments for each and their manner of use among different nations. Alongside the dignity of such is placed, and their several inventors are named. But on the exterior all the inventors in science, in warfare, and in law are represented. There I saw Moses, Osiris, Jupiter, Mercury, Lycurgus, Pompilius, Pythagoras, Zamolxis, Solon, Charondas, Phoroneus, with very many others. They even have Mahomet, whom nevertheless they hate as a false and sordid legislator. In the most dignified position I saw a representation of Jesus Christ and of the twelve Apostles, whom they consider very worthy and hold to be great. Of the representations of men, I perceived Caesar, Alexander, Pyrrhus and Hannibal in the highest place; and other very renowned heroes in peace and war, especially Roman heroes, were painted in lower positions, under the galleries. And when I asked with astonishment whence they had obtained our history, they told me that among them there was a knowledge of all languages, and that by perseverance they continually send explorers and ambassadors over the whole earth, who learn thoroughly the customs, forces, rule and histories of the nations, bad and good alike. These they apply all to their own republic, and with this they are well pleased. I learnt that cannon and typography were invented by the Chinese before we knew of them. There are magistrates, who announce the meaning of the pictures, and boys are accustomed to learn all the sciences, without toil and as if for pleasure; but in the way of history only until they are ten years old.

Love is foremost in attending to the charge of the race. He sees that men and women are so joined together, that they bring forth the best offspring. Indeed, they laugh at us who exhibit a studious care for our breed of horses and dogs, but neglect the breeding of human beings. Thus the education of the children is under his rule. So also is the medicine that is sold, the sowing and collecting of fruits of the earth and of trees, agriculture, pasturage, the preparations for the months, the cooking arrangements, and whatever has any reference to food, clothing, and the intercourse of the sexes. Love himself is ruler, but there are many male and female magistrates dedicated to these arts.

Metaphysic then with these three rulers manage all the above named matters, and even by himself alone nothing is done; all business is discharged by the four together, but in whatever Metaphysic inclines to the rest are sure to agree.

Grand. Tell me, please, of the magistrates, their services and duties, of the education and mode of living, whether the government is a monarchy, a republic, or an aristocracy.

Capt. This race of men came there from India, flying from the sword of the Magi, a race of plunderers and tyrants who laid waste their country, and they determined to lead a philosophic life in fellowship with one another. Although the community of wives is not instituted among the other inhabitants of their province, among them it is in use after this manner. All things are common with them, and their dispensation is by the authority of the magistrates. Arts and honors and pleasures are common, and are held in such a manner that no one can appropriate anything to himself.

They say that all private property is acquired and improved for the reason that each one of us by himself has his own home and wife and children. From this self love springs. For when we raise a son to riches and dignities, and leave an heir to much wealth, we become either ready to grasp at the property of the state, if in any case fear should be removed for the power which belongs to riches and rank; or avaricious, crafty, and hypocritical, if any one is of slender purse, little strength, and mean ancestry. But when we have taken away self love, there remains only love for the state.

Grand. Under such circumstances no one will be willing to labor, while he expects others to work, on the fruit of whose labors he can live, as Aristotle argues against Plato.

Capt. I do not know how to deal with that argument, but I declare to you that they burn with so great a love for their fatherland, as I could scarcely have believed possible; and indeed with much more than the histories tell us belonged to the Romans, who fell willingly for their country, inasmuch as they have to a greater extent surrendered their private property. I think truly that the friars and monks and clergy of our country, if they were not weakened by love for their kindred and friends, or by the ambition to rise to higher dignities, would be less fond of property, and more imbued with a spirit of charity towards all, as it was in the time of the Apostles, and is now in a great many cases.

Grand. St. Augustine may say that, but I say that among this race of men, friendship is worth nothing; since they have not the chance of conferring mutual benefits on one another.

Capt. Nay, indeed. For it is worth the trouble to see that no one can receive gifts from another. Whatever is necessary they have, they receive it from the community, and the magistrate takes care that no one receives more than he deserves. Yet nothing necessary is denied to any one. Friendship is recognized among them in war, in infirmity, in the art contests, by which means they aid one another mutually by teaching. Sometimes they improve themselves mutually with praises, with conversation, with actions and out of the things they need. All those of the same age call one another brothers. They call over twenty two years of age, fathers; those who are less than twenty two are named sons. Moreover, the magistrates govern well, so that no one in the fraternity can do injury to another.

Grand. And how?

Capt. As many names of virtues as there are amongst us, so many magistrates there are among them. There is a magistrate who is named Magnanimity, another Fortitude, a third Chastity, a fourth Liberality, a fifth Criminal and Civil Justice, a sixth Comfort, a seventh Truth, an eighth Kindness, a ninth Diligence, a tenth Gratitude, an eleventh Cheerfulness, a twelfth Exercise, a thirteenth Sobriety, etc. They are elected to duties of that kind, each one to that duty for excellence in which he is known from boyhood to be most suitable. Wherefore among them neither robbery nor clever murders, nor lewdness, incest, adultery, or other crimes of which we accuse one another, can be found. They accuse themselves of ingratitude and malignity when any one denies a lawful satisfaction to another, of indolence, of sadness, of anger, of scurrility, of slander, and of lying, which curseful thing they thoroughly hate. Accused persons undergoing punishment are deprived of the common table, [the company of women[1]] and other honors, until the judge thinks that they agree with their correction.

Grand. Tell me the manner in which the magistrates are chosen.

Capt. You would not rightly understand this, unless you first learnt their manner of living. That you may know then, men and women wear the same kind of garment, suited for war. The women wear the toga below the knee, but the men above. And both sexes are instructed in all the arts together. When this has been done as a start, and before their third year, the boys learn the language and the alphabet on the walls by walking round them. They have four leaders, and four elders, the first to direct them, the second to teach them, and these are men approved beyond all others. After some time they exercise themselves with gymnastics, running, quoits, and other games, by means of which all their muscles are strengthened alike. Their feet are always bare, and so are their heads as far as the seventh ring. Afterwards they lead them to the offices of the trades, such as shoemaking, cooking, metal-working, carpentry, painting, etc. In order to find out the bent of the genius of each one, after their seventh year, when they have already gone through the mathematics on the walls, they take them to the readings of all the sciences; there are four lectures at each reading, and in the course of four hours the four in their order explain everything.

For some take physical exercise or busy themselves with public services or functions, others apply themselves to reading. Leaving these studies all are devoted to the more abstruse subjects, to mathematics, to medicine, and to other sciences. There is continual debate and studied argument amongst them, and after a time they become magistrates of those sciences or mechanical arts in

---

1. The translation used here (the only one in the public domain) is heavily censored, and words suggesting that those being punished were kept away from women were deleted. No other censoring occurs in the selection used here, but in the text as a whole, almost all references to eugenic policies were deleted. *Ed.*

which they are the most proficient; for every one follows the opinion of his leader and judge, and goes out to the plains to the works of the field, and for the purpose of becoming acquainted with the pasturage of dumb animals. And they consider him the more noble and renowned who has dedicated himself to the study of the most arts and knows how to practise them wisely. Wherefore they laugh at us in that we consider our workmen ignoble, and hold those to be noble who have mastered no pursuit; but live in ease, and are so many slaves given over to their own pleasure and lasciviousness, and thus as it were from a school of vices so many idle and wicked fellows go forth for the ruin of the state.

The rest of the officials, however, are chosen by the four chiefs, Hoh, Pon, Sin and Mor, and by the teachers of that art over which they are fit to preside. And these teachers know well who is most suited for rule. Certain men are proposed by the magistrates in council, they themselves not seeking to become candidates, and he opposes who knows anything against those brought forward for election, or if not, speaks in favor of them. But no one attains to the dignity of Hoh except him who knows the histories of the nations, and their customs and sacrifices and laws, and their form of government, whether a republic or a monarchy. He must also know the names of the lawgivers and the inventors in science, and the laws and the history of the earth and the heavenly bodies. They think it also necessary that he should understand all the mechanical arts, the physical sciences, astrology and mathematics. (Nearly every two days they teach our mechanical art. They are not allowed to overwork themselves, but frequent practice and the paintings render learning easy to them. Not too much care is given to the cultivation of languages, as they have a goodly number of interpreters who are grammarians in the state.) But beyond everything else it is necessary that Hoh should understand metaphysics and theology; that he should know thoroughly the derivations, foundations and demonstrations of all the arts and sciences; the likeness and difference of things; necessity, fate, and the harmonies of the universe; power, wisdom, and the love of things and of God; the stages of life and its symbols; everything relating to the heavens, the earth and the sea; and the ideas of God, as much as mortal man can know of Him. He must also be well read in the Prophets and in astrology. And thus they know long beforehand who will be Hoh. He is not chosen to so great a dignity unless he has attained his thirty fifth year. And this office is perpetual, because it is not known who may be too wise for it or who too skilled in ruling. . . .

Grand. I really wish that you would recount all their public duties, and would distinguish between them, and also that you would tell clearly how they are all taught in common.

Capt. They have dwellings in common and dormitories, and couches and other necessaries. But at the end of every six months they are separated by the masters. Some shall sleep in this ring, some in another; some in the first apartment, and some in the second; and these apartments are marked by means of the alphabet on the lintel. There are occupations, mechanical and theoretical, common to both men and women, with this difference, that the occupations which require more hard work, and walking a long distance, are practised by men, such as plowing, sowing, gathering the fruits, working at the threshing floor, and perchance at the vintage. But it is customary to choose women for milking the cows, and for making cheese. In like manner, they go to the gardens near to the outskirts of the city both for collecting the plants and for cultivating them. In fact, all sedentary and stationary pursuits are practised by the women, such as weaving, spinning, sewing, cutting the hair, shaving, dispensing medicines, and making all kinds of garments. They are, however, excluded from working in wood and the manufacture of arms. If a woman is fit to paint, she is not prevented from doing so; nevertheless, music is given over to the women alone, because they please the more, and of a truth to boys also. But the women have not the practice of the drum and the horn.

And they prepare their feasts and arrange the tables in the following manner. It is the peculiar work of the boys and girls under twenty to wait at the tables. In every ring there are the suitable kitchens, barns, and stores of utensils for eating and drinking, and over every department an old man and an old woman preside. These two have at once the command of those who serve, and the power of chastising, or causing to be chastised, those who are negligent or disobedient; and they also examine and mark each one, both male and female, who excels in his or her duties.

All the young people wait upon the older ones who have passed the age of forty, and in the evening when they go to sleep the master and mistress command that those should be sent to work in the morning, upon whom in succession the duty falls, one or two to separate apartments. The young people, however, wait upon one another, and that alas! with some unwillingness. They have first and second tables, and on both sides there are seats. On one side sit the women, on the other the men; and as in the refectories of the monks, there is no noise. While they are eating, a young man reads a book from a platform, intoning distinctly and sonorously, and often the magistrates question them upon the more important parts of the reading. And truly it is pleasant to observe in what manner these young people, so beautiful and clothed in garments so suitable, attend to them, and to see at the same time so many friends, brothers, sons, fathers and mothers in all their turn living together with so much honesty, propriety and love. So each one is given a napkin, a plate, fish, and a dish of food. It is the duty of the medical officers to tell the cooks what repasts shall be prepared on each day, and what food for the old, what for the young, and what for the sick. The magistrates receive the full grown and fatter portion, and they from their share always distribute something to the boys at the table who have shown themselves more studious in the morning at the lectures and debates concerning wisdom and arms. And this is held to be one of the most distinguished honors. For six days they ordain to sing with music at table. Only a few, however, sing; or there is one voice accompanying the lute and one for each other instrument. And when all alike in service join their hands, nothing is found to be wanting. The old men placed at the head of the cooking business and of the refectories of the servants praise the cleanliness of the streets, the houses, the vessels, the garments, the workshops and the warehouses.

They wear white undergarments to which adheres a covering, which is at once coat and legging, without wrinkles. The borders of the fastenings are furnished with globular buttons, extended round and caught up here and there by chains. The coverings of the legs descend to the shoes and are continued even to the heels. Then they cover their feet with large socks, or as it were half buskins fastened by buckles, over which they wear a half boot, and besides, as I have already said, they are clothed with a toga. And so aptly fitting are the garments, that when the toga is destroyed, the different parts of the whole body are straightway discerned, no part being concealed. They change their clothes for different ones four times in the year, that is when the sun enters respectively the constellations Aries, Cancer, Libra and Capricorn, and according to the circumstances and necessity as decided by the officer of health. The keepers of clothes for the different rings are wont to distribute them, and it is marvellous that they have at the same time as many garments as there is need for, some heavy and some slight, according to the weather. They all use white clothing, and this is washed in each month with lye or soap, as are also the workshops of the lower trades, the kitchens, the pantries, the barns, the store-houses, the armories, the refectories and the baths. Moreover, the clothes are washed at the pillars of the peristyles, and the water is brought down by means of canals which are continued as sewers. In every street of the different rings there are suitable fountains, which send forth their water by means of canals, the water being drawn up from nearly the bottom of the mountain by the sole movement of a cleverly contrived handle. There is water in fountains and in cisterns, whither the rain water collected from the roofs of the houses is brought through pipes full of sand. They wash their bodies often, according as the doctor and master command. All the mechanical arts are practised under the peristyles, but the speculative are carried on above in the walking galleries and ramparts where are the more splendid paintings, but the more sacred ones are taught in the temple. In the halls and wings of the rings there are solar time pieces and bells, and hands by which the hours and seasons are marked off. . . .

Grand. Tell me about their children.

Capt. When their women have brought forth children, they suckle them and rear them in temples set apart for all. They give milk for two years or more as the physician orders. After that time the weaned child is given into the charge of the mistresses, if it is a female, and to the masters, if it is a male. And then with other young children they are pleasantly instructed in the alphabet, and in the knowledge of the pictures, and in running, walking and wrestling; also in the historical drawings, and in languages; and they are adorned with a suitable garment of different colors. After their sixth year they are taught natural science, and then the mechanical sciences. The men who are weak in intellect are sent to farms, and when they have become more proficient some of them are received into the state. And those of the same age and born under the same constellation are especially like one another in strength and in appearance, and hence arises much lasting concord in the state, these men honoring one another with mutual love and help. Names are given to them by Metaphysicus, and that not by chance but designedly, and according to each one's peculiarity, as was the custom among the ancient Romans. Wherefore one is called Beautiful *(Pulcher)*, another the Big-nosed *(Naso)*, another Crooked *(Torvus)*, another Lean *(Macer)*, and so on. But when they have become very skilled in their professions and done any great deed in war or in time of peace, a cognomen from art is given to them, such as Beautiful, the great painter *(Pulcher, Pictor Magnus)*, the golden one *(Aureus)*, the excellent one *(Excellens)*, or the strong *(Strenuus)*; or from their deeds, such as Naso the Brave *(Nason Fortis)*, or the cunning, or the great, or very great conqueror; or from the enemy anyone has overcome, Africanus, Asiaticus, Etruscus; or if any one has overcome Manfred or Tortelius, he is called Macer Manfred or Tortelius, and so on. All these cognomens are added by the higher magistrates, and very often with a crown suitable to the deed or art, and with the flourish of music. For gold and silver is reckoned of little value among them except as material for their vessels and ornaments, which are common to all. . . .

Grand. Now it would be very pleasant to learn with what foods and drinks they are nourished, and in what way and for how long they live.

Capt. Their food consists of flesh, butter, honey, cheese, garden herbs, and vegetables of various kinds. They were unwilling at first to slay animals, because it seemed cruel; but thinking afterwards that it was also cruel to destroy herbs which have a share of sensitive feeling, they saw that they would perish from hunger unless they did an unjustifiable action for the sake of justifiable ones, and so now they all eat meat. Nevertheless, they do not kill willingly useful animals such as oxen and horses. They observe the difference between useful and harmful foods, and for this they employ the science of medicine. They always change their food. First they eat flesh, then fish, then afterwards they go back to flesh, and nature is never incommoded or weakened. The old people use the more digestible kind of food, and take three meals a day, eating only a little. But the general community eat twice, and the boys four times, that they might satisfy nature. The length of their lives is generally one hundred years, but often they reach two hundred.

As regards drinking, they are extremely moderate. Wine is never given to young people until they are ten years old, unless the state of their health demands it. After their tenth year they take it diluted with water, and so do the women, but the old men of fifty and upwards use little or no water. They eat the most healthy things, according to the time of the year.

They think nothing harmful which is brought forth by God, except when there has been abuse by taking too much. And therefore in the summer they feed on fruits, because they are moist and juicy and cool, and counteract the heat and dryness. In the winter they feed on dry articles, and in the autumn they eat grapes, since they are given by God to remove melancholy and sadness; and they also make use of scents to a great degree. In the morning, when they have all risen they comb their hair and wash their faces and hands with cold water. Then they chew thyme or rock parsley or fennel, or rub their hands with these plants. The old men make incense, and with their faces to the east repeat the short prayer which Jesus Christ taught us. After this they go to wait upon the old men, some go to the dance, and others to the duties of the state. Later on they meet at the early lectures, then in the temple, then for bodily exercise. Then for a little while they sit down to rest, and at length they go to dinner. . . .

Tommaso Campanella (1568–1639) was a Dominican monk who was persecuted during the Inquisition and spent many years in prison, where he wrote CITY OF THE SUN.

Source: Tommaso Campanella, "City of the Sun," trans. R. W. Halliday, in IDEAL COMMONWEALTHS, ed. Henry Morley (London: George Routledge and Sons, 1885), 217–29, 231–35, 250–51.

Francis Bacon
New Atlantis

"God bless thee, my son; I will give thee the greatest jewel I have. For I will impart unto thee, for the love of God and men, a relation of the true state of Salomon's House. Son, to make you know the true state of Salomon's House, I will keep this order. First, I will set forth unto you the end of our foundation. Secondly, the preparations and instruments we have for our works. Thirdly, the several employments and functions whereto our fellows are assigned. And fourthly, the ordinances and rites which we observe.

"The end of our foundation is the knowledge of causes, and secret motions of things; and the enlarging of the bounds of human empire, to the effecting of all things possible.

"The preparations and instruments are these. We have large and deep caves of several depths; the deepest are sunk 600 fathoms; and some of them are digged and made under great hills and mountains; so that if you reckon together the depth of the hill, and the depth of the caves, they are, some of them, above three miles deep. For we find that the depth of an hill, and the depth of a cave from the flat, is the same thing; both remote alike from the sun and heaven's beams, and from the open air. These caves we call the lower region. And we use them for all coagulations, indurations, refrigerations, and conservations of bodies. We use them likewise for the imitation of natural mines and the producing also of new artificial metals, by compositions and materials which we use and lay there for many years. We use them also sometimes (which may seem strange) for curing of some diseases, and for prolongation of life, in some hermits that choose to live there, well accommodated of all things necessary, and indeed live very long; by whom also we learn many things.

"We have burials in several earths, where we put divers cements, as the Chinese do their porcelain. But we have them in greater variety, and some of them more fine. We also have great variety of composts and soils, for the making of the earth fruitful.

"We have high towers, the highest about half a mile in height, and some of them likewise set upon high mountains, so that the vantage of the hill with the tower, is in the highest of them three miles at least. And these places we call the upper region, account the air between the high places and the low, as a middle region. We use these towers, according to their several heights and situations, for insulation, refrigeration, conservation, and for the view of divers meteors—as winds, rain, snow, hail; and some of the fiery meteors also. And upon them, in some places, are dwellings of hermits, whom we visit sometimes, and instruct what to observe.

"We have great lakes, both salt and fresh, whereof we have use for the fish and fowl. We use them also for burials of some natural bodies, for we find a difference in things buried in earth, or in air below the earth, and things buried in water. We have also pools, of which some do strain fresh water out of salt, and others by art do turn fresh water into salt. We have also some rocks in the midst of the sea, and some bays upon the shore for some works, wherein is required the air and vapour of the sea. We have likewise violent streams and cataracts, which serve us for many motions; and likewise engines for multiplying and enforcing of winds to set also on divers motions.

"We have also a number of artificial wells and fountains, made in imitation of the natural sources and baths, as tincted upon vitriol, sulphur, steel, brass, lead, nitre, and other minerals; and again, we have little wells for infusions of many things, where the waters take the virtue quicker and better than in vessels or basins. And amongst them we have a water, which we call water of

Paradise, being, by that we do to it, made very sovereign for health and prolongation of life.

"We have also great and spacious houses, where we imitate and demonstrate meteors—as snow, hail, rain, some artificial rains of bodies, and not of water, thunders, lightnings; also generations of bodies in air—as frogs, flies, and divers others.

"We have also certain chambers, which we call chambers of health, where we qualify the air as we think good and proper for the cure of divers diseases, and preservation of health.

"We have also fair and large baths, of several mixtures, for the cure of diseases, and the restoring of man's body from arefaction; and others for the confirming of it in strength of sinews, vital parts, and the very juice and substance of the body.

"We have also large and various orchards and gardens, wherein we do not so much respect beauty as variety of ground and soil, proper for divers trees and herbs, and some very spacious, where trees and berries are set, whereof we make divers kinds of drinks, besides the vineyards. In these we practise likewise all conclusions of grafting, and inoculating, as well of wild-trees as fruit-trees, which produceth many effects. And we make by art, in the same orchards and gardens, trees and flowers, to come earlier or later than their seasons, and to come up and bear more speedily than by their natural course they do. We make them also by art greater much than their nature; and their fruit greater and sweeter, and of differing taste, smell, colour, and figure, from their nature. And many of them we so order, as that they become of medicinal use.

"We have also means to make divers plants rise by mixtures of earths without seeds, and likewise to make divers new plants, differing from the vulgar, and to make one tree or plant turn into another.

"We have also parks, and enclosures of all sorts, of beasts and birds; which we use not only for view or rareness, but likewise for dissections and trials, that thereby may take light what may be wrought upon the body of man. Wherein we find many strange effects: as continuing life in them though divers parts, which you account vital, be perished and taken forth; resuscitating of some that seem dead in appearance, and the like. We try also all poisons, and other medicines upon them, as well of chirurgery [surgery] as physic. By art likewise we make them greater or smaller than their kind is, and contrariwise dwarf them and stay their growth; we make them more fruitful and bearing than their kind is, and contrariwise barren and not generative. Also we make them differ in colour, shape, activity, many ways. We find means to make commixtures and copulations of divers kinds, which have produced many new kinds, and them not barren, as the general opinion is. We make a number of kinds of serpents, worms, flies, fishes of putrefaction, whereof some are advanced (in effect) to be perfect creatures, like beasts or birds, and have sexes, and do propagate. Neither do we this by chance, but we know beforehand of what matter and commixture, what kind of those creatures will arise.

"We have also particular pools where we make trials upon fishes, as we have said before of beasts and birds.

"We have also places for breed and generation of those kinds of worms and flies which are of special use; such as are with you your silkworms and bees.

"I will not hold you long with recounting of our brewhouses, bake-houses, and kitchens, where are made divers drinks, breads, and meats, rare and of special effects. Wines we have of grapes, and drinks of other juice, of fruits, of grains, and of roots, and of mixtures with honey, sugar, manna, and fruits dried and decocted; also of the tears or wounding of trees, and of the pulp of canes. And these drinks are of several ages, some to the age or last of forty years. We have drinks also brewed with several herbs, and roots, and spices; yea, with several fleshes, and white-meats; whereof some of the drinks are such as they are in effect meat and drink both, so that divers, especially in age, do desire to live with them with little or no meat or bread. And above all we strive to have drinks of extreme thin parts, to insinuate into the body, and yet without all biting, sharpness, or fretting; insomuch as some of them put upon the back of your hand, will with a little stay pass through to the palm, and yet taste mild to the mouth. We have also waters, which we ripen in that fashion, as they become nourishing, so that they are indeed excellent drinks, and many will use no other. Bread we have of several grains, roots, and kernels; yea, and some of flesh, and fish, dried; with divers kinds of leavings and seasonings; so that some do extremely move appetites, some do nourish so, as divers do live of them, without any other meat, who live very long. So for meats, we have some of them so beaten, and made tender, and mortified, yet without all corrupting, as a weak heat of the stomach will turn them into good chylus, as well as a strong heat would meat otherwise prepared. We have some meats also and bread, and drinks, which taken by men, enable them to fast long after; and some other, that used make the very flesh of men's bodies sensibly more hard and tough, and their strength far greater than otherwise it would be.

"We have dispensatories or shops of medicines; wherein you may easily think, if we have such variety of plants, and living creatures, more than you have in Europe (for we know what you have), the simples, drugs, and ingredients of medicines must likewise be in so much the greater variety. We have them likewise of divers ages, and long fermentations. And for their preparations, we have not only all manner of exquisite distillations, and separations, and especially by gentle heats, and percolations through divers strainers, yea, and substances; but also exact forms of composition, whereby they incorporate almost as they were natural simples.

"We have also divers mechanical arts, which you have not; and stuffs made by them, as papers, linen, silks, tissues, dainty works of feathers of wonderful lustre, excellent dyes, and many others, and shops likewise as well for such as are not brought into vulgar use amongst us, as for those that are. For you must know, that of the things before recited, many of them are grown into use throughout the kingdom, but yet, if they did flow from our invention, we have of them also for patterns and principals.

"We have also furnaces of great diversities, and that keep great diversity of heats; fierce and quick, strong and constant, soft and mild, blown, quiet, dry, moist, and the like. But above all we have heats, in imitation of the sun's and heavenly bodies' heats, that pass divers inequalities, and as it were orbs, progresses, and returns whereby we produce admirable effects. Besides, we have heats of dungs, and of bellies and maws of living creatures and of their bloods and bodies, and of hays and herbs laid up moist, of lime unquenched, and such like. Instruments also which generate heat only by motion. And farther, places for strong insulations; and again, places under the earth, which by nature or art yield heat. These divers heats we use, as the nature of the operation which we intend requireth.

"We have also perspective-houses, where we make demonstrations of all lights and radiations, and of all colours; and out of things uncoloured and transparent, we can represent unto you all several colours, not in rainbows, as it is in gems and prisms, but of themselves single. We represent also all multiplications of light, which we carry to great distance, and make so sharp, as to discern small points and lines. Also all colourations of light: all delusions and deceits of the sight, in figures, magnitudes, motions, colours; all demonstrations of shadows. We find also divers means, yet unknown to you, of producing of light, originally from divers bodies. We procure means of seeing objects afar off, as in the heaven and remote places; and represent things near as afar off, and things afar off as near; making feigned distances. We have also helps for the sight far above spectacles and glasses in use; we have also glasses and means to see small and minute bodies, perfectly and distinctly; as the shapes and colours of small flies and worms, grains, and flaws in gems which cannot otherwise be seen, observations in urine and blood not otherwise to be seen. We make artificial rainbows, halos, and circles about light. We represent also all manner of reflections, refractions, and multiplications of visual beams of objects.

"We have also precious stones, of all kinds, many of them of great beauty and to you unknown; crystals likewise, and glasses of divers kind; and amongst them some of metals vitrificated, and other materials, besides those of which you make glass. Also a number of fossils, and imperfect minerals, which you have not. Likewise loadstones of prodigious virtue: and other rare stones, both natural and artificial.

"We have also sound-houses, where we practise and demonstrate all sounds and their generation. We have harmony which you have not, of quarter-sounds and lesser slides of sounds. Divers instruments of music likewise to you unknown, some sweeter than any you have; with bells and rings that are dainty and sweet. We represent small sounds as great and deep, likewise great sounds, extenuate and sharp; we make divers tremblings and warblings of sounds, which in their original are entire. We represent and imitate all articulate sounds and letters, and the voices and notes of beasts and birds. We have certain helps, which set to the ear do further the hearing greatly; we have also divers strange and artificial echoes, reflecting the voice many times, and as it were tossing it; and some that give back the voice louder than it came, some shriller and some deeper; yea, some rendering the voice, differing in the letters or articulate sound from that they receive. We have all means to convey sounds in trunks and pipes, in strange lines and distances.

"We have also perfume-houses, wherewith we join also practices of taste. We multiply smells which may seem strange: we imitate smells, making all smells to breathe out of other mixtures than those that give them. We make divers imitations of taste likewise, so that they will deceive any man's taste. And in this house we contain also a confiture-house, where we make all sweetmeats, dry and moist, and divers pleasant wines, milks, broths, and salads, far in greater variety than you have.

"We have also engine-houses, where are prepared engines and instruments for all sorts of motions. There we imitate and practise to make swifter motions than any you have, either out of your muskets or any engine that you have; and to make them and multiply them more easily and with small force, by wheels and other means, and to make them stronger and more violent than yours are, exceeding your greatest cannons and basilisks. We represent also ordnance and instruments of war and engines of all kinds; and likewise new mixture and compositions of gunpowder, wild-fires burning in water and unquenchable, also fire-works of all variety, both for pleasure and use. We imitate also flights of birds; we have some degrees of flying in the air. We have ships and boats for going under water and brooking of seas; also swimming girdles and supporters. We have divers curious clocks and other like motions of return, and some perpetual motions. We imitate also motions of living creatures by images of men, beasts, birds, fishes, and serpents; we have also a great number of other various motions, strange for equality, fineness and subtilty.

"We have also a mathematical-house, where are represented all instruments, as well of geometry as astronomy, exquisitely made.

"We have also houses of deceits of the senses, where we represent all manner of feats of juggling, false apparitions, impostures and illusions, and their fallacies. And surely you will easily believe that we, that have so many things truly natural which induce admiration, could in a world of particulars deceive the senses if we would disguise those things, and labour to make them more miraculous. But we do hate all impostures and lies, insomuch as we have severely forbidden it to all our fellows, under pain of ignominy and fines, that they do not show any natural work or thing adorned or swelling, but only pure as it is, and without affectation of strangeness.

"These are, my son, the riches of Salomon's House.

"For the several employments and offices of our fellows, we have twelve that sail into foreign countries under the names of other nations (for our own we conceal), who bring us the books and abstracts, and patterns of experiments of all other parts. These we call merchants of light.

"We have three that collect the experiments which are in all books. These we call deprepators.

"We have three that collect the experiments of all mechanical arts, and also of liberal sciences, and also of practices which are not brought into arts. These we call mystery-men.

"We have three that try new experiments such as themselves think good. These we call pioneers or miners.

"We have three that draw the experiments of the former four into titles and tables, to give the better light for the drawing of observations and axioms out of them. These we call compilers. We have three that bend themselves, looking into the experiments of their fellows, and cast about how to draw out of them things of use and practice for man's life and knowledge, as well for works as for plain demonstration of causes, means of natural divinations, and the easy and clear discovery of the virtues and parts of bodies. These we call dowry-men or benefactors.

"Then after divers meetings and consults of our number, to consider of the former labours and collections, we have three that take care out of them to direct new experiments, of a higher light, more penetrating into Nature than the former. These we call lamps.

"We have three others that do execute the experiments so directed, and report them. These we call inoculators.

"Lastly, we have three that raise the former discoveries by experiments into greater observations, axioms, and aphorisms. These we call interpreters of Nature.

"We have also, as you must think, novices and apprentices, that the succession of the former employed men do not fail; besides a great number of servants and attendants, men and woman. And this we do also: we have consultations, which of the inventions and experiences which we have discovered shall be published, and which not: and take all an oath of secrecy for the concealing of those which we think fit to keep secret: though some of those we do reveal sometime to the state, and some not.

"For our ordinances and rites, we have two very long and fair galleries: in one of these we place patterns and samples of all manner of the more rare and excellent inventions: in the other we place the statues of all principal inventors. There we have the statue of your Columbus, that discovered the West Indies: also the inventor of ships: your Monk that was the inventor of ordnance and of gunpowder: the inventor of music: the inventor of letters: the inventor of printing: the inventor of observations of astronomy: the inventor of works in metal: the inventor of glass: the inventor of silk of the worm: the inventor of wine: the inventor of corn and bread: the inventor of sugars; and all these by more certain tradition than you have. Then we have divers inventors of our own, of excellent works; which since you have not seen, it were too long to make descriptions of them; and besides, in the right understanding of those descriptions you might easily err. For upon every invention of value we erect a statue to the inventor, and give him a liberal and honourable reward. These statues are some of brass, some of marble and touchstone, some of cedar and other special woods gilt and adorned; some of iron, some of silver, some of gold.

"We have certain hymns and services, which we say daily, of laud and thanks to God for His marvellous works. And forms of prayers, imploring His aid and blessing for the illumination of our labours; and turning them into good and holy uses.

"Lastly, we have circuits or visits, of divers principal cities of the kingdom; where as it cometh to pass we do publish such new profitable inventions as we think good. And we do also declare natural divinations of diseases, plagues, swarms of hurtful creatures, scarcity, tempest, earthquake, great inundations, comets, temperature of the year, and divers other things; and we give counsel thereupon, what the people shall do for the prevention and remedy of them."

And when he had said this, he stood up; and I, as I had been taught, knelt down; and he laid his right hand upon my head, and said, "God bless thee, my son, and God bless this relation which I have made. I give thee leave to publish it, for the good of other nations; for we here are in God's bosom, a land unknown." And so he left me; having assigned a value of about two thousand ducats for a bounty to me and my fellows. For they give great largesses, where they come, upon all occasions.

THE REST WAS NOT PERFECTED

Francis Bacon (1561–1626) was an English philosopher and statesman.

Source: The Works of Francis Bacon, Baron of Verulam, Viscount St. Albans, and Lord High Chancellor of England. 10 vols (London: Printed for W. Baynes and Son, 1824), 2:111–22.

15. Every household shall keep all instruments and tools fit for the tillage of the earth, either for planting, reaping or threshing. Some households, which have many men in them, shall keep ploughs, carts, harrows and such like: other households shall keep spades, pick-axes, pruning hooks and such like, according as every family is furnished with men to work therewith.

And if any master or father of a family be negligent herein, the overseer for that circuit shall admonish him between them two; if he continue negligent, the overseers shall reprove him before all the people: and if he utterly refuse, then the ordering of that family shall be given to another, and he shall be a servant under the task-master till he conform.

16. Every family shall come into the field, with sufficient assistance, at seed-time to plough, dig and plant, and at harvest-time to reap the fruits of the earth and carry them into the store-houses, as the overseers order the work and the number of workmen. And if any refuse to assist in this work, the overseers shall ask the reason; and if it be sickness or any distemper that hinders them, they are freed from such service; if mere idleness keep them back, they are to suffer punishment according to the laws against idleness.

17. If any refuse to learn a trade, or refuse to work in seed-time or harvest, or refuse to be a waiter in store-houses, and yet will feed and clothe himself with other men's labours: the overseers shall first admonish him privately; if he continue idle, he shall be reproved openly before all the people by the overseers; and shall be forbore with a month after this reproof. If he still continues idle, he shall then be whipped, and be let go at liberty for a month longer; if still he continue idle, he shall be delivered into the task-master's hand, who shall set him to work for twelve months, or till he submit to right order. And the reason why every young man shall be trained up in some work or other is to prevent pride and contention; it is for the health of their bodies, it is a pleasure to the mind to be free in labours one with another; and it provides plenty of food and all necessaries for the commonwealth.

18. In every town and city shall be appointed store-houses for flax, wool, leather, cloth and for all such commodities as come from beyond seas, and these shall be called general store-houses; from whence every particular family may fetch some commodities as they want, either for their use in their house, or for to work in their trades; or to carry into the country store-houses.

19. Every particular house and shop in a town or city shall be a particular store-house or shop, as now they be; and these shops shall either be furnished by the particular labour of that family according to the trade that family is of,

or by the labour of other lesser families of the same trade, as all shops in every town are now furnished.

20. The waiters in store-houses shall deliver the goods under their charge, without receiving any money, as they shall receive in their goods without paying any money. . . .

34. All overseers and state officers shall be chosen new every year, to prevent the rise of ambition and covetousness; for the nations have smarted sufficiently by suffering officers to continue long in an office, or to remain in an office by hereditary succession.

35. A man that is of a turbulent spirit, given to quarrelling and provoking words to his neighbour, shall not be chosen any officer while he so continues.

36. All men from twenty years of age upwards shall have freedom of voice to choose officers, unless they be such as lie under the sentence of the law.

37. Such shall be chosen officers as are rational men of moderate conversation, and who have experience in the laws of the commonwealth.

38. All men from forty years of age upwards shall be capable to be chosen state officers, and none younger, unless anyone by his industry and moderate conversation doth move the people to choose him. . . .

56. Every man and woman shall have the free liberty to marry whom they love, if they can obtain the love and liking of that party whom they would marry; and neither birth nor portion shall hinder the match, for we are all of one blood, mankind; and for portion, the common store-houses are every man and maid's portion, as free to one as to another.

57. If any man lie with a maid and beget a child, he shall marry her.

58. If a man lie with a woman forcibly, and she cry out and give no consent; if this be proved by two witnesses, or the man's confession, he shall be put to death, and the woman let go free; it is robbery of a woman's bodily freedom.

59. If any man by violence endeavour to take away another man's wife, the first time of such violent offer he shall be reproved before the congregation by the peace-maker; the second time he shall be made a servant under the task-master for twelve months; and if he forcibly lie with another man's wife, and she cry out, as in the case when a maid is forced, the man shall be put to death.

60. When any man or woman are consented to live together in marriage, they shall acquaint all the overseers in their circuit therewith, and some other neighbours; and being all met together, the man shall declare by his own mouth before them all that he takes that woman to be his wife, and the woman shall say the same, and desire the overseers to be witnesses.

61. No master of a family shall suffer more meat to be dressed at a dinner or supper than what will be spent and eaten by his household or company present, or within such a time after, before it be spoiled. If there be any spoil constantly made in a family of the food of man, the overseer shall reprove the

master for it privately; if that abuse be continued in his family, through his neglect of family government, he shall be openly reproved by the peace-maker before all the people, and ashamed for his folly; the third time he shall be made a servant for twelve months under the task-master, that he may know what it is to get food, and another shall have the oversight of his house for the time.

Gerrard Winstanley (1601?–1683) was the leader of the Diggers, a radical, egalitarian group.

Source: Gerrard Winstanley, THE LAW OF FREEDOM AND OTHER WRITINGS, ed. Christopher Hill (Cambridge: Cambridge University Press, 1983), 379–89.

Margaret Cavendish
The Inventory of Judgements Commonwealth

Margaret Cavendish is currently best known for her other utopia, *The Description of a New World, Called the Blazing World* (1666). The work reprinted here is not available in any other modern edition.

This Commonwealth to be composed of Nobility, Gentry, Burgesses, and Pezants, in which are comprized Souldiery, Merchantry, Artificers, Labourers, Commanders, Officers, Masters, Servants, Magistrates, Divines, Lawyers, &c.

This Commonwealth to be governed by one Head or Governour, as a King, for one Head is sufficient for one Body: for several Heads breed several Opinions, and several Opinions breed Disputations, and Disputations Factions, and Factions breed Wars, and Wars bring Ruin and Desolation: for it is more safe to be governed, though by a Foolish Head, than a Factious Heart.

Item, That this Royal Ruler to swear to the People to be Carefull and Loving, as well as the People swear Duty and Fidelity.

The Contracts betwixt the King and People should be these.

Item, That the Militia be put in the Royal Hand: for since Power lyes in the Militia, the Militia ought to lye in the Kingly Power; for, without Power, Authority and Justice are as Cyphers, which signifie nothing.

For which the King shall contract by Promise and Oath, never to give Honours but to the Meritorious.

Item, That if there should be any Dispute betwixt the Royal Command, and the Publick Subjection, there should be two Men chosen, the one for one side, and the other for the other; these to be approved of, both for their Honesty, Wisdome, and Courage, as neither to fear Power, nor Censure, to be free from Bribes, Self-ends, Passions and Partiality, Experienced and Known Men in the Kingdome, or at least as able as any therein, to decide all Differences, and conclude all Disputes, and present all Grievances to the Royal Power, and return his Will, Pleasure, and Desires to the People: for Great Counsels do rather insnarl all Publick Business, than rectifie Errours, by reason of their Various Opinons, and Humoursome Differences, with their Covetous Byasses, and Popular Ambitions.

Item, That the Royal Ruler shall contract with the People, never to give Honours, either for Favour, or sell them for Gain, but to reward the Meritorious, and grace the Virtuous; which will stop the Mouth of Murmure, temper the Spleen of Malice, clear the Eyes of Spight, and encourage Noble Endeavours.

Item, All those that keep not up the Dignity of their House by the Ceremony of the Titles, shall be dishonoured and degraded, as base, and unworthy thereof, in neglecting the Mark of their own, or their Ancestors Merits.

Item, All those that speak against Honour, or Titles, or give them not the due respect, shall never be created thereunto.

Item, It shall be Death for any Herald at Arms to give Arms for Price, or Favour, but to those are worthy thereof, as those that have purchased them by their Merits.

Item, All those that speak against their Native Country, or tell Defects or Weaknesses, or rail or dishonour their Countrymen, shall be banished therefrom, or thereout.

Item, That the Royal Ruler shall have no particular Favorite, they being for the most part Expensive, Proud, Scornfull, and Mischievous, making difference betwixt the King and People, by fomenting Errours untill they make them seem Crimes, and creating Jealousies, by making doubts of the Peoples Fidelity; and Favorites most commonly tread upon the Necks of the Nobility, and ride upon the Backs of the Gentry, and pick the Purse of the Commonalty, justle Justice out by Bribery, and many times unthrone Royalty through Envy to them, which causeth a hatred to the Prince, for perchance perceiving this Favorite neither to have Worth nor Merit, onely a Flattering tongue, that inchants a Credulous Prince. Therefore a Prince should have no Favorite but Justice, no Privy Counseller but his own Breast, his Intention never to be disclosed but when he puts it into Execution.

Item, This Royal Ruler to have none of those they call their Cabinets, which is a Room filled with all useless curiosities, which seems Effeminate, and is so Expensive, bestowing infinite Sums, almost to the impoverishing of a Kingdome, only to fill a Room with little cut, carved Statues, and Models of Stones and Metals; as also divers Toyes made of Amber, Cornelion, Agats, Chrystals, and divers sorts of Shels, and the like; which Room might be better imployed, and to more use, in placing Famous and Learned Authors Works, as a Library, which the whole Kingdome may draw Knowledge and Understanding from, and the Money imployed to more famous Curiosities than Shels, or the like, As in stately Monuments, which shews a Kingdome in a Flourishing Condition, and gives it a Noble Grace, and makes it a Wonder abroad, and a subject of Discourse amongst Strangers, inviting curious and inquisitive Travellers from all Nations to view the Structures thereof.

Besides, It makes a Prince seem Effeminate, which is a disgrace to the Commonwealth, and Forein Nations will despise it, when they see or hear that the Prince is so mean a Spirit, as to take delight in Toyes, spending their time in looking on Shels, Beads, and Babies. For those of Heroick Spirits take Delight to see their Souldiers in Arms, to view their Fortifications, Forts, and Frontiers, to behold their Stately Architecture, Navigable Rivers, their Safe Havens, Sailing Ships, with their Rich Fraights.

Likewise, They delight in Crowns, Scepters, and Thrones, by which they hold Power, and keep up Authority, making Obedience, Fear, and Subjection; making it their Pastime to hear Sutes, to decide Causes, to give Justice. And their Sports like the old Olympick Games.

After these Contracts between the Sovereign and the People, there follow the Laws and Decrees in the Commonwealth.

As first, concerning the Clergy.

Item, That those that exercise the Divine Function, be not preferred for Learning, but for Life, as being honest in their Parish, or Diocese, not exacting more Tythes than their due; also Exemplary in their Actions, Sober in their Behaviour.

Item, That no Divine shall study Controversy, or at least not to dispute, but to preach according to the Doctrine that is allowed to be believed and followed: for Learned Disputes and Controversies are apt to smother a Lively Faith, and quench out a Flaming Zeal.

Item, That no Sermons shall be preached, by reason they do more harm than goood, troubling the Conscience of the Fearfull, the Heads of the Ignorant, and the Ears of the Wise: But there shall be Prayers said in every Parish-Church once a Day, and the Moral Laws, the Divine Laws, and the National Laws, with their threatning punishments, and promising rewards, shall be read and repeated once a Week.

Item, That no Physician shall be allowed to study more than one Disease, or at least practice the Cure but of one, lest they make by their half-knowledge and understanding, a Confusion in the Body for want of Experience.

Item, That all Sutes shall be heard, pleaded and decided in the space of half a Year.

Item, It shall be Death for any to sell Land that is any waies engaged, or entangled, lest it should ruin the Buyer thereof.

Item, That all Landlords and Freeholders shall be bound to plant Timber for Ships, Hemp for Sails, and Tow for Cordage, if the Land be an Isle.

Item, There shall be a set Stipend for Wages, Fees, Rewards, Sales, or Purchases; also of all Merchandizes, that Cosenages, Briberies, Extortions, and the like, may be eschewed.

Item, That none shall execute the Function of two several Trades, nor being imployed in more than in one Office, lest they should perform none well.

Item, That no Alchymy-Lace, nor Stuffs, no Counterfeit Pearls, Diamonds, and the like, shall be worn, nor sold, unless the Counterfeit be sold at as high a price as the Right, or the Right to be sold at as a low a rate as the Counterfeit; and as different Sexes are distinguished by their Habits, so different Habits should distinguish different Qualities, Professions, and Degrees.

Item, That all degrees of Titles shall be distinguished by their Habits and Ceremonies, as well as by their Arms, Titles, Patents, and Creations.

Item, No Men shall wear Swords in time of Peace but Gentlemen, and in the Wars there shall be some differences of Arms to make distinction.

Item, That no Officer, neither in Martial Command, nor Civil Government, shall be chosen or imployed, but such as have Abilities to execute their Authorities, and able to discharge their Duties.

Item, Rewards shall be as frequent as Punishments, lest Industry should grow careless, and the Flame of Heroick Spirits be quenched out.

Item, None shall make Great Feasts, and Sumptuous Entertainments, but for Forein Persons of Quality, or Strangers that travel to see the Kingdome, where they may see the Plenty, Riches, and Magnificence thereof, that they may not despise it when they return to their own Native Country, but give cause to renown it in their Relations.

Item, All Detracting or Slandering Tongues shall be clipt; and the more the Detraction or Slander is, the greater slices shall be cut therefrom.

Item, That the People shall have set times of Recreation, to ease them from their Labours, and to refresh their Spirits.

Item, That all Noble Youths shall be bred by Experienced Age, to perswade, admonish, and correct by Grave Authority, instructed by Virtuous Examples, taught Honourable Principles, and the practice of Heroick Actions; their onely Playfellows shall be the Muses; the Grave and Sober Companions, the Sciences; the Domestick Servants, and Aquaintance, the profitable and usefull Arts for the Life of Man.

As for the generality of Youth, they shall be bred to Silent Attentions, Sober Demeanors, Humble Obediences, Handsome Customes, and Gracefull Arts: As for the meaner sort of Youth, to Trades of Arts, and Arts of Trades, for the use and benefit of the Commonwealth.

Item, No Children shall speak before their Parents, no Servants before their Masters, no Scholars before their Tutors, no Subject before the Prince, but either to answer to their Questions, to deliver a Message, or to know their will and pleasure, to declare their Grievances, to ask pardon for Faults committed, or to present an humble request in the most humblest manner, unless they command them to discourse freely to them, yet not without a respect to their Presence and Authority.

Item, For the Generality, none shall speak but to ask rational, dutifull, and humble Questions, to request just Demands, to discourse of probable Arguments, to defend Right and Truth, to divulge Virtue, to praise the Meritorious, to pray to Heaven, to ask Mercy, to prove Pity, to pacifie Grief, to asswage Anger, to make an Atonement, and to instruct the Ignorant.

Item, All shall be accounted Wise, that endure patiently, that live peaceably, that spend prudently, that speak sparingly, that judge charitably, that wish honestly, and that obey Authority.

Item, All Men that may live quietly at home, and travel to no purpose, or that neglect their own Affairs to follow the Affairs of other Men, or decide those Mens Quarrels they shall have no thanks for, or live upon hopes of great Fortunes, or high Favours, when they may feed upon present Comfort, and enjoy humble Delights in that Estate and Condition they possess, shall wear a Fools Cap, and a Motly Coat.

Item, That none shall live at a greater Expence than their Estate will allow and maintain.

Item, That all Spendthrifts shall be condemned for Fools, all Gamesters for idle Miscreants, all Drunkards for Madmen; a Bedlam provided for the Drunkards, a Bridewell for Gamesters, and an Hospital with Long-Coats for Spendthrifts.

Item, All Men that beget Children shall strive to provide for them, by their Thrifty Managements, or Industrious Labours.

Item, No Man shall Father a Whores Child, or Children, unless he were sure he were the Father, which few can tell; otherwise it makes a Wise Man seem a Fool, as being facile.

Item, It shall be accounted not only a double Crime, but a Baseness equal to Cowardise, and a disgrace equal to a Cuckold, for a Gentleman to court, or to make love to a Common Whore, who is an Alms-Tub of Corruption; but if a Gentleman must or will have a Whore, let him have one of his own making, and not feed upon Reversions.

Item, That no Husband shall keep a Houshold Friend, lest he should make love to his Wife, and he become a Cuckold thereby.

Item, No married man or Master of a Family, shall kiss or make love to his Maid, nor Serving-men to their Mistrisses, lest they should grow idly Amorous, impertinently Bold, rudely Saucy, neglecting their Duty to their Mistris or Master, through scornful Pride.

Item, In all publike Company all Husbands shall use their Wives with Respect, unless they dishonor themselves with the neglect thereof.

Item, No Husband nor Wife, although but a day married, shall kiss each other in publick, lest it turn the Spectators from a lawfull and wholsome Appetite of Marriage, to a gluttonous Adultery, or weakning the Appetite so much as to cause a Loathing, or an aversion to the Wedlock Bed.

Item, No Wife shall entertain an Admiring Servant, lest their Husbands and her own Reputaton be lost or buried in his admiring Courtships; nor their Hearts to receive and return Love to none but their Husbands, no not Platonick love, for the Conversation of Souls, is a great temptation to Amorous Friendship; indeed the Soul of a Platonick Lover is a Baud to the Body.

Item, That Dancing be commendable as a gracefull Art in Maids or Batchelors, but shall be accounted an Effeminacy for married Men, a May-Game for Old men, and a Wanton Lightnes for Married Women.

Item, That no woman of quality should receive Visits or give Visits, but in publick Meetings, nor have any whisperings or private Conference, that her Actions might have sufficient Witnesse, and her Discourses a generall Audience.

Item, That none shall marry against their own liking or free choice, lest they make their Marriage an excuse for Adultery.

Item, It shall be allowed for Maids to entertain all Honorable, as Matrimonial Suters, untill such time as she hath made choice of one of them to settle her Affections upon; for it is good reason one should take time and observe Humors, before they bind themselves in Wedlock Bonds, for when once bound nothing but Death can part them; but when they are once married, their Ears to be sealed from all Loves pleadings, protestings, Vows making, high praises, and Complementall phrases.

Item, That none shall keep a Mistris above halfe a year, but change, lest she grow more imperious than a Wife made of a Widow.

Item, All Lovers shall be licensed to bragg or speak well of themselves to their Mistris, when they have done no meritorious Actions to speak for them.

Item, All those that have Beauty enough to make a Lover, if they have not wit to keep a Lover, shall be accounted no better than a senseless Statue.

Item, It shall not be, as it is in these Daies, accounted a prise or purchase amongst Ladies, to get either by their Wit or Beauty, admiring Servants, especially if they be of amorous natures; for then Nature drives them to her Beauty or Wit, more than her Beauty or Wit draws them to it.

Item, All those that are proud without a cause, it shall be a sufficient cause to be scorned.

Item, Eloquence shall not be imployed nor pleaded in Amorous Discourses, nor to make Falsehood to appear like Truth; but to dress and adorn Vertue that she may be accepted and entertained by those that will refuse and shun her acquaintance if she be clad in plain Garments.

Item, There shall be none condemn another Language, nor account another to be better, if it be Significant, Copious and Eloquent, such as the English Tongue is.

Item, All passionate Speeches, or Speeches to move passion, shall be expressed in Number.

Item, That all Natural Poets shall be honored with Title, esteemed with Respect, or enriched for the Civilizing of a Nation, more than Contracts, Laws or Punishments, by Soft Numbers, and pleasing Phansies; and also guard, a Kingdom more than Walls or Bulworks, by creating Heroick Spirits with Illustrious Praises, inflaming the Mind with Noble Ambition. . . .

> But I would have this Monarchy I make,
> To have a Judge[1] that will good Counsel take; One that is
>   wise to govern, and to see
> What Faults to mend, and what the Errors be,
> Making the Common-wealth his only Minion
> Striving for to enlarge his own Dominion,
> To love his People, with a tender Care,
> To wink at Frailties which in Nature are,
> And Just to punish Crimes, as hating ill,
> Yet sorry for the Malefactor still;
> Glad to reward, and Virtue to advance
> In real Favours, not in Countenance,
> Not to pay Merits with good Words and Smiles,
> (Dissembling Promises poor Men beguiles)
> Nor yet good Services are done long past,
> (Ungratefull Souls will in Oblivion cast)
> But have the Eye of Memory so clear,
> The least good Service shall to him appear.
> Nor would I have one idly to neglect
> His Peoples Safety, but for to protect
> Their Lives and Goods, with all the care he can,
> And upright Justice to the poorest Man;
> To be a Father to the Common-wealth,
> And a Physician to restore them Health,

---

1. I call the chief Ruler Judge as they did in the old Law or Time.

By purging out the Humours, which are Crimes,
Which Crimes, like corrupt Humours, breed oft-times
Factious Diseases, which without all doubt
Would Ruin bring, if timely not cast out:
No cruell Scarlet Favorite to make,
Nor Pleading, Fauning, Cheating men to take
Into their Bosoms, who, with Gouty Pride
Straight swell so bigg, they must on Shoulders ride,
Or else on Noble Cush'ons they must lye,
To bear them up; but oft the Feathers fly,
If Pride do presse too hard; and oft they take
Some great mens Fames, thinking thereby to make,
In giving Praises high, a Screen to hide
The face of Favour, but the Tail is spide.
Nor such a Judge, as one takes delight
To play at Cards and Dice most of the Night;
Or drink till drunk, then carried to his Bed,
As to a Grave, he seeming like one dead,
When he those watchfull hours, and times should spend
In thinking which way he should Errors mend;
For Commonwealths that ere, and Kingdoms, Realm,
Like Garments, have full many a Stich and Seam:
This Publike Garment oft the Prince must view,
Where it is rent, cause't to be sticht a new,
Or else it soon wears out, in pieces fall,
And though they patch, it will not last at all.
Nor such a Judge, so timorous, lives in fear,
And durst not, without Guards, walk any where,
Which starts at every Noise, or Object see,
If strange and new those Sounds and Objects be;
Suspects the Light, yet Darkness hates like Hell,
And thinks Conspiracy in's sleep doth dwell,
And with this Fear a Tyrant he becomes,
And then he Massacres, and Martyrdoms
All his best Subjects, free from factious strife,
That Loyal are, and wish him longer life,
But scorn to flatter, or applaud his Crimes,
And keep up Right, and Honour in their minds,
Nor are they guilty in Word, Deed, or Thought,
But, by Suspition judg'd, to Slaughter brought;
But all the innocent Blood that they do spill,

Like to a Sea, flows to their Conscience ill;
And every Thought that moves within their Brain,
Appears like Ghosts of Men that they have slain;
And when they dye, into despair they fall,
Or like a Beast or Stone, no Sense at all.
Nor such a Judge that is given to the Spirit,
Or so devout as Heaven he thinks to merit,
Praies Night and Day, or Beads do number ore
Upon cold Stones, *Joves* Altar kneels before,
Unfit in Earthly Government to Reign,
For Praier seldome doth a Kingdome gain,
Nor keeps in safety from an Enemy,
But leaves his People all to Slavery;
For if he praying be, whilst they do Fight,
They'll soon be taken, or be put to flight,
Jove Courage gives to Man, as well as Zeal,
And Prudence for to Rule a Commonweal;
And doing Justice, pleaseth *Jove* far more
Than lazy Praying, idly to implore
His great assistance which he seldom gives,
Unless no hope of Human Help there lives.
Jove gives man Strength, himself for to defend,
Which, if he useth not, may *Jove* offend.
But such faint-hearted Prince, is fitter for
A private life, than Kingdome that's in War;
And fitter to Obey, than to Command,
Or Rule and Reign, in Peace, War, Sea, or Land;
And fitter far it were, whilst he doth live,
That he the Sovereign Power up did give
Unto a Kinsman, or himself did choose
A Wife and Valiant Man, that Power to use
Not but Religious Orders are right meet;
For why, Religion is the Publick Feet
On which the Common-Wealth in safety stands,
And Ceremonies are the Sacred Hands
To Consecrate good Custom, Dutious Zeal,
And make Obedience in a Common-weal.
The Judge I chuse, his Wisdome shall be such,
The whole Worlds Government shall seem not much,
In which of all the Planets there must Reign
I do not care, I tell my Readers plain.

Margaret Cavendish (1624?–1674) was a novelist and poet who, with her husband, was banished from England until the return of the monarchy. She is now recognized as an important early feminist writer.

Source: [Margaret Cavendish], "The Inventory of Judgements Commonwealth, the Author cares not in what World it is established," in THE WORLDS OLIO. WRITTEN BY THE RIGHT HONORABLE, THE LADY MARGARET OF NEWCASTLE (London: J. Martin and J. Allestrye, 1655), 205–19.

James Harrington
The Commonwealth of Oceana

James Harrington's *The Commonwealth of Oceana* (1656) represents the moderate reaction to both the monarchists and the radical democrats of mid-seventeenth-century British political thought. Harrington, who was immensely influential on the framing of the U.S. Constitution, presents a government balanced among the various centers of power in the country.

The third division (unseen hitherto) is into equal and unequal, and this is the main point, especially as to domestic peace and tranquillity; for to make a commonwealth unequal, is to divide it into parties, which sets them at perpetual variance, the one party endeavoring to preserve their eminence and inequality and the other to attain to equality; whence the people of Rome derived their perpetual strife with the nobility and Senate. But in an equal commonwealth there can be no more strife than there can be overbalance in equal weights; wherefore the Commonwealth of Venice, being that which of all others is the most equal in the constitution, is that wherein there never happened any strife between the Senate and the people.

An equal commonwealth is such a one as is equal both in the balance or foundation, and in the superstructure; that is to say, in her agrarian law and in her rotation.

An equal agrarian is a perpetual law, establishing and preserving the balance of dominion by such a distribution, that no one man or number of men, within the compass of the few or aristocracy, can come to overpower the whole people by their possessions in lands.

As the agrarian answers to the foundation, so does rotation to the superstructures.

Equal rotation is equal vicissitude in government, or succession to magistracy conferred for such convenient terms, enjoying equal vacations, as take in the whole body by parts, succeeding others, through the free election or suffrage of the people.

The contrary, whereunto is prolongation of magistracy, which, trashing the wheel of rotation, destroys the life or natural motion of a commonwealth.

The election or suffrage of the people is most free, where it is made or given in such a manner that it can neither oblige nor disoblige another, nor through fear of an enemy, or bashfulness toward a friend, impair a man's liberty.

Wherefore, says Cicero, the tablet or ballot of the people of Rome (who gave their votes by throwing tablets or little pieces of wood secretly into urns marked for the negative or affirmative) was a welcome constitution to the people, as that which, not impairing the assurance of their brows, increased the freedom of their judgment. I have not stood upon a more particular description of this ballot, because that of Venice exemplified in the model is of all others the most perfect.

An equal commonwealth (by that which has been said) is a government established upon an equal agrarian, arising into the superstructures or three orders, the Senate debating and proposing, the people resolving, and the magistracy executing, by an equal rotation through the suffrage of the people given by the ballot. For though rotation may be without the ballot, and the ballot without rotation, yet the ballot not only as to the ensuing model includes both, but is by far the most equal way; for which cause under the name of the ballot I shall hereafter understand both that and rotation too. . . .

But there be those who say (and think it a strong objection) that, let a commonwealth be as equal as you can imagine, two or three men when all is done will govern it; and there is that in it which, notwithstanding the pretended sufficiency of a popular State, amounts to a plain confession of the imbecility of that policy, and of the prerogative of monarchy; forasmuch as popular governments in difficult cases have had recourse to dictatorian power, as in Rome.

To which I answer, that as truth is a spark to which objections are like bellows, so in this respect our commonwealth shines; for the eminence acquired by suffrage of the people in a commonwealth, especially if it be popular and equal, can be ascended by no other steps than the universal acknowledgment of virtue: and where men excel in virtue, the commonwealth is stupid and unjust, if accordingly they do not excel in authority. Wherefore this is both the advantage of virtue, which has her due encouragement, and of the commonwealth, which has her due services. These are the philosophers which Plato would have to be princes, the princes which Solomon would have to be mounted, and their steeds are those of authority, not empire; or, if they be buckled to the chariot of empire, as that of the dictatorian power, like the chariot of the sun, it is glorious for terms and vacations or intervals. And as a commonwealth is a government of laws and not of men, so is this the principality of virtue, and not of man; if that fail or set in one, it rises in another who is created his immediate successor. And this takes away that vanity from under the sun, which is an error proceeding more or less from all other rulers under heaven but an equal commonwealth. . . .

But let a commonwealth be equal or unequal, it must consist, as has been shown by reason and all experience, of the three general orders; that is to say, of the Senate debating and proposing, of the people resolving, and of the magistracy executing. Wherefore I can never wonder enough at Leviathan, who, without any reason or example, will have it that a commonwealth consists of a single person, or of a single assembly; nor can I sufficiently pity those "thousand gentlemen, whose minds, which otherwise would have wavered, he has framed (as is affirmed by himself) in to a conscientious obedience (for so he is pleased to call it) of such a government."

But to finish this part of the discourse, which I intend for as complete an epitome of ancient prudence, and in that of the whole art of politics, as I am able to frame in so short a time:

The two first orders, that is to say, the Senate and the people, are legislative, whereunto answers that part of this science which by politicians is entitled "of laws;" and the third order is executive, to which answers that part of the same science which is styled "of the frame and course of courts or judicatories." A word to each of these will be necessary.

And first for laws: they are either ecclesiastical or civil, such as concern religion or government.

Laws, ecclesiastical, or such as concern religion, according to the universal course of ancient prudence, are in the power of the magistrate; but, according to the common practice of modern prudence, since the papacy, torn out of his hands.

But, as a government pretending to liberty, and yet suppressing liberty of conscience (which, because religion not according to a man's conscience can to him be none at all, is the main) must be a contradiction, so a man that, pleading for the liberty of private conscience, refuses liberty to the national conscience, must be absurd.

A commonwealth is nothing else but the national conscience. And if the conviction of a man's private conscience produces his private religion, the conviction of the national conscience must produce a national religion. Whether this be well reasoned, as also whether these two may stand together, will best be shown by the examples of the ancient commonwealths taken in their order. . . .

To come to civil laws. If they stand one way and the balance another, it is the case of a government which of necessity must be new modelled; wherefore your lawyers, advising you upon the like occasions to fit your government to their laws, are no more to be regarded than your tailor if he should desire you to fit your body to his doublet. There is also danger in the plausible pretence of reforming the law, except the government be first good, in which case it is a good tree, and (trouble not yourselves overmuch) brings not forth evil fruit; otherwise, if the tree be evil, you can never reform the fruit, or if a root that is naught bring forth fruit of this kind that seems to be good, take the more heed, for it is the ranker poison. . . .

The materials of a commonwealth are the people, and the people of Oceana were distributed by casting them into certain divisions, regarding their quality, their age, their wealth, and the places of their residence or habitation, which was done by the ensuing orders.

The first order "distributes the people into freemen or citizens and servants, while such; for if they attain to liberty, that is, to live of themselves, they are freemen or citizens."

This order needs no proof, in regard of the nature of servitude, which is inconsistent with freedom, or participation of government in a commonwealth.

The second order "distributes citizens into youth and elders (such as are from eighteen years of age to thirty, being accounted youth; and such as are of thirty and upward, elders), and establishes that the youth shall be the marching armies, and the elders the standing garrisons of this nation." . . .

The third order "distributes the citizens into horse and foot, by the sense or valuation of their estates; they who have above £100 a year in lands, goods, or moneys, being obliged to be of the horse, and they who have under that sum to be of the foot. But if a man has prodigally wasted and spent his patrimony, he is neither capable of magistracy, office, or suffrage in the commonwealth." . . .

The fourth order "distributes the people according to the places of their habitation, into parishes, hundreds, and tribes."

For except the people be methodically distributed, they cannot be methodically collected; but the being of a commonwealth consists in the methodical collection of the people. . . .

James Harrington (1611–1677) was an English political theorist.

Source: James Harrington, "The Commonwealth of Oceana," in IDEAL COMMONWEALTHS, rev. ed., ed. Henry Morley (New York: Colonial Press, 1901), 204–5, 206–7, 209–10, 211–12, 238–40.

FIVE

The Eighteenth Century

❧

Jonathan Swift
Gulliver's Travels

In the fourth book of Jonathan Swift's _Gulliver's Travels_, "A Voyage to the Country of the Houyhnhnms," Lemuel Gulliver visits a country in which the dominant natives are horses. The other main inhabitants are the brutish, human-shaped Yahoos. _Gulliver's Travels_ gave rise to an entire subgenre of literature, loosely known as Gulliveriana, in which a traveler visits one or more countries inhabited by speaking animals or odd humans.

A Voyage to the Country of the Houyhnhnms

I have related the Substance of several Conversations I had with my Master, during the greatest Part of the Time I had the Honour to be in his Service; but have indeed for Brevity sake omitted much more than is here set down.

When I had answered all his Questions, and his Curiosity seemed to be fully satisfied; he sent for me one Morning early, and commanding me to sit down at some Distance, (an Honour which he had never before conferred upon me) He said, he had been very seriously considering my whole Story, as far as it related both to my self and my Country: That, he looked upon us as a Sort of Animals to whose Share, by what Accident he could not conjecture, some small Pittance of _Reason_ had fallen, whereof we made no other Use than by its Assistance to aggravate our _natural_ Corruptions, and to acquire new ones which Nature had not given us. That, we disarmed our selves of the few Abilities she had bestowed; had been very successful in multiplying our original Wants, and seemed to spend our whole Lives in vain Endeavours to supply them by our own Inventions. That, as to my self, it was manifest I had neither the Strength or Agility of a common _Yahoo;_ that I walked infirmly on my hinder Feet; had

141

found out a Contrivance to make my Claws of no Use or Defence, and to remove the Hair from my Chin, which was intended as a Shelter from the Sun and the Weather. Lastly, That I could neither run with Speed, nor climb Trees like my *Brethren* (as he called them) the *Yahoos* in this Country.

That our Institutions of *Government* were plainly owing to our gross Defects in *Reason*, and by consequence, in *Virtue;* because *Reason* alone is sufficient to govern a *Rational* Creature; which was therefore a Character we had no Pretence to challenge, even from the Account I had given of my own People; although he manifestly perceived, that in order to favour them, I had concealed many Particulars, and often *said the Thing which was not*.[1]

He was the more confirmed in this Opinion, because he observed, that as I agreed in every Feature of my Body with other *Yahoos*, except where it was to my real Disadvantage in point of Strength, Speed and Activity, the Shortness of my Claws, and some other Particulars where Nature had no Part; so, from the Representation I had given him of our Lives, our Manners, and our Actions, he found as near a Resemblance in the Disposition of our Minds. He said, the *Yahoos* were known to hate one another more than they did any different Species of Animals; and the Reason usually assigned, was, the Odiousness of their own Shapes, which all could see in the rest, but not in themselves. He had therefore begun to think it not unwise in us to *cover* our Bodies, and by that Invention, conceal many of our Deformities from each other, which would else be hardly supportable. But, he now found he had been mistaken; and that the Dissentions of those Brutes in his Country were owing to the same Cause with ours, as I had described them. For, if (said he) you throw among five *Yahoos* as much Food as would be sufficient for fifty, they will, instead of eating peaceably, fall together by the Ears, each single one impatient to *have all to it self;* and therefore a Servant was usually employed to stand by while they were feeding abroad, and those kept at home were tied at a Distance from each other. That, if a Cow died of Age or Accident, before a *Houyhnhnm* could secure it for his own *Yahoos,* those in the Neighbourhood would come in Herds to seize it, and then would ensue such a Battle as I had described, with terrible Wounds made by their Claws on both Sides, although they seldom were able to kill one another, for want of such convenient Instruments of Death as we had invented. At other Times the like Battles have been fought between the *Yahoos* of several Neighbourhoods without any visible Cause: Those of one District watching all Opportunities to surprise the next before they are prepared. But if they find their Project hath miscarried, they return home, and for want of Enemies, engage in what I call a *Civil War* among themselves.

---

1. There is no word in the language of the *Houyhnhnms* for lying. *Ed.*

That, in some Fields of his Country, there are certain *shining Stones* of several Colours, whereof the *Yahoos* are violently fond; and when Part of these *Stones* are fixed in the Earth, as it sometimes happeneth, they will dig with their Claws for whole Days to get them out, and carry them away, and hide them by Heaps in their Kennels; but still looking round with great Caution, for fear their Comrades should find out their Treasure. My Master said, he could never discover the Reason of this unnatural Appetite, or how these *Stones* could be of any Use to a *Yahoo;* but now he believed it might proceed from the same Principle of *Avarice,* which I had ascribed to Mankind. That he had once, by way of Experiment, privately removed a Heap of these *Stones* from the Place where one of his *Yahoos* had buried it: Whereupon, the sordid Animal missing his Treasure, by his loud lamenting brought the whole Herd to the Place, there miserably howled, then fell to biting and tearing the rest; began to pine away, would neither eat nor sleep, nor work, till he ordered a Servant privately to convey the *Stones* into the same Hole, and hide them as before; which when his *Yahoo* had found, he presently recovered his Spirits and good Humour; but took Care to remove them to a better hiding Place; and hath ever since been a very serviceable Brute.

My Master further assured me, which I also observed my self; That in the Fields where these *shining Stones* abound, the fiercest and most frequent Battles are fought, occasioned by perpetual Inroads of the neighbouring *Yahoos.*

He said, it was common when two *Yahoos* discovered such a *Stone* in a Field, and were contending which of them should be the Proprietor, a third would take the Advantage, and carry it away from them both; which my Master would needs contend to have some Resemblance with our *Suits at Law;* wherein I thought it for our Credit not to undeceive him; since the Decision he mentioned was much more equitable than many Decrees among us: Because the Plaintiff and Defendant there lost nothing beside the *Stone* they contended for; whereas our *Courts of Equity,* would never have dismissed the Cause while either of them had any thing left.

My Master continuing his Discourse, said, There was nothing that rendered the *Yahoos* more odious, than their undistinguished Appetite to devour every thing that came in their Way, whether Herbs, Roots, Berries, corrupted Flesh of Animals, or all mingled together: And it was peculiar in their Temper, that they were fonder of what they could get by Rapine or Stealth at a greater Distance, than much better Food provided for them at home. If their Prey held out, they would eat till they were ready to burst, after which Nature had pointed out to them a certain Root that gave them a general Evacuation.

There was also another Kind of Root very *juicy,* but something rare and difficult to be found, which the *Yahoos* fought for with much Eagerness, and would suck it with great Delight: It produced the same Effects that Wine hath upon us. It would make them sometimes hug, and sometimes tear one another; they would howl and grin, and chatter, and reel, and tumble, and then fall asleep in the Mud.

I did indeed observe, that the *Yahoos* were the only Animals in this Country subject to any Diseases; which however, were much fewer than Horses have among us, and contracted not by any Treatment they meet with, but by the Nastiness and Greediness of that sordid Brute. Neither has their Language any more than a general Appellation for those Maladies; which is borrowed from the Name of the Beast, and called *Hnea Yahoo,* or the *Yahoo's-Evil;* and the Cure prescribed is a Mixture of *their own Dung* and *Urine,* forcibly put down the *Yahoo's* Throat. This I have since often known to have been taken with Success: And do here freely recommend it to my Countrymen, for the publick Good, as an admirable Specifick against all Diseases produced by Repletion.

As to Learning, Government Arts, Manufactures, and the like; my Master confessed he could find little or no resemblance between the *Yahoos* of that Country and those in ours. For, he only meant to observe what Parity there was in our Natures. He had heard indeed some curious *Houyhnhnms* observe, that in most Herds there was a Sort of ruling *Yahoo,* (as among us there is generally some leading or principal Stag in a Park) who was always more *deformed* in Body, and *mischievous in Disposition,* than any of the rest. That, this Leader had usually a Favourite as *like himself* as he could get, whose Employment was to *lick his Master's Feet and Posteriors, and drive the Female* Yahoos to *his Kennel;* for which he was now and than rewarded with a Piece of Ass's Flesh. This Favourite is hated by the whole Herd; and therefore to protect himself, keeps always near the Person of his *Leader.* He usually continues in Office till a worse can be found; but the very Moment he is discarded, his Successor, at the Head of all the *Yahoos* in that District, Young and Old, Male and Female, come in a Body, and discharge their excrements upon him from Head to Foot. But how far this might be applicable to our *Courts* and *Favourites,* and *Ministers of State,* my Master said I could best determine.

I durst make no Return to this malicious Insinuation, which debased human Understanding below the Sagacity of a common *Hound,* who hath Judgment enough to distinguish and follow the Cry of the *ablest Dog in the Pack,* without being ever mistaken.

My Master told me, there were some Qualities remarkable in the *Yahoos,* which he had not observed me to mention, or at least very slightly, in the Accounts I had given him of human Kind. He said, those Animals, like other Brutes, had their Females in common; but in this they differed, that the *She-Yahoo* would admit the Male, while she was pregnant; and that the Hees would quarrel and fight with the Females as fiercely as with each other. Both which

Practices were such Degrees of infamous Brutality, that no other sensitive Creature ever arrived at.

Another Thing he wondered at in the *Yahoos,* was their strange Disposition to Nastiness and Dirt; whereas there appears to be a natural Love of Cleanliness in all other Animals. As to the two former Accusations, I was glad to let them pass without any Reply, because I had not a Word to offer upon them in Defence of my Species, which otherwise I certainly had done from my own Inclinations. But I could have easily vindicated human Kind from the Imputation of Singularity upon the last Article, if there had been any *Swine* in that Country, (as unluckily for me there were not) which although it may be a *sweeter Quadruped* than a *Yahoo,* cannot I humbly conceive in Justice pretend to more Cleanliness; and so his Honour himself must have owned, if he had seen their filthy Way of feeding, and their Custom of wallowing and sleeping in the Mud.

My Master likewise mentioned another Quality, which his Servants had discovered in several *Yahoos,* and to him was wholly unaccountable. He said, a Fancy would sometimes take a *Yahoo,* to retire into a Corner, to lie down and howl, and groan, and spurn away all that came near him, although he were young and fat, and wanted neither Food nor Water; nor did the Servants imagine what could possibly ail him. And the only Remedy they found was to set him to hard Work, after which he would infallibly come to himself. To this I was silent out of Partiality to my own Kind; yet here I could plainly discover the true Seeds of Spleen, which only seizeth on the *Lazy,* the *Luxurious,* and the *Rich;* who, if they were forced to undergo the *same Regimen,* I would undertake for the Cure.

His Honour had further observed, that a *Female-Yahoo* would often stand behind a Bank or a Bush, to gaze on the young Males passing by, and then appear, and hide, using many antick Gestures and Grimaces; at which time it was observed, that she had a most *offensive Smell;* and when any of the Males advanced, would slowly retire, looking often back, and with a counterfeit Shew of Fear, run off into some convenient Place where she knew the Male would follow her.

At other times, if a Female Stranger came among them, three or four of her own Sex would get about her, and stare and chatter, and grin, and smell her all over; and then turn off with Gestures that seemed to express Contempt and Disdain.

Perhaps my Master might refine a little in these Speculations, which he had drawn from what he observed himself, or had been told by others; However, I could not reflect without some Amazement, and much Sorrow, that the Rudiments of *Lewdness, Coquetry, Censure, and Scandal,* should have Place by Instinct in Womankind.

I expected every Moment, that my Master would accuse the *Yahoos* of those unnatural Appetites in both Sexes, so common among us. But Nature it seems hath not been so expert a Schoolmistress, and these politer Pleasures are entirely the Productions of Art and Reason, on our Side of the Globe.

As I ought to have understood human Nature much better than I supposed it possible for my Master to do, so it was easy to apply the Character he gave of the *Yahoos* to myself and my Countrymen; and I believed I could yet make further Discoveries from my own Observation. I therefore often begged his Honour to let me go among the Herds of *Yahoos* in the Neighbourhood; to which he always very graciously consented, being perfectly convinced that the Hatred I bore those Brutes would never suffer me to be corrupted by them; and his Honour ordered one of his Servants, a strong Sorrel Nag, very honest and good-natured, to be my Guard; without whose Protection I durst not undertake such Adventures. For I have already told the Reader how much I was pestered by those odious Animals upon my first Arrival. I afterwards failed very narrowly three or four times of falling into their Clutches, when I happened to stray at any Distance without my Hanger. And I have Reason to believe, they had some Imagination that I was of their own Species, which I often assisted myself, by stripping up my Sleeves, and strewing my naked Arms and Breast in their Sight, when my Protector was with me: At which times they would approach as near as they durst, and imitate my Actions after the Manner of Monkeys, but ever with great Signs of Hatred; as a tame *Jack Daw* with Cap and Stockings, is always persecuted by the wild ones, when he happens to be got among them.

They are prodigiously nimble from their Infancy; however, I once caught a young Male of three Years old, and endeavoured by all Marks of Tenderness to make it quiet; but the little Imp fell a squalling, and scratching, and biting with such Violence, that I was forced to let it go; and it was high time, for a whole Troop of old ones came about us at the Noise; but finding the Cub was safe, (for away it ran) and my Sorrel Nag being by, they durst not venture near us. I observed the young Animal's Flesh to smell very rank, and the Stink was somewhat between a *Weasel* and a *Fox,* but much more disagreeable. I forgot another Circumstance, (and perhaps I might have the Reader's Pardon, if it were wholly omitted) that while I held the odious Vermin in my Hands, it voided its filthy Excrements of a yellow liquid Substance, all over my Cloaths; but by good Fortune there was a small Brook hard by, where I washed myself as clean as I could; although I durst not come into my Master's Presence, until I were sufficiently aired.

By what I could discover, the *Yahoos* appear to be the most unteachable of all Animals, their Capacities never reaching higher than to draw or carry Burthens. Yet I am of Opinion, this Defect ariseth chiefly from a perverse, restive Disposition. For they are cunning, malicious, treacherous and revengeful. They are strong and hardy, but of a cowardly Spirit, and by Consequence insolent, abject, and cruel. It is observed, that the *Red-haired* of both Sexes are more libidinous and mischievous than the rest, whom yet they much exceed in Strength and Activity.

The *Houyhnhnms* keep the *Yahoos* for present Use in Huts not far from the House; but the rest are sent abroad to certain Fields, where they dig up Roots, eat several Kinds of Herbs, and search about for Carrion, or sometimes catch *Weasels* and *Luhimuhs* (a Sort of *wild Rat*) which they greedily devour. Nature hath taught them to dig deep Holes with their Nails on the Side of a rising Ground, wherein they lie by themselves; only the Kennels of the Females are larger, sufficient to hold two or three Cubs.

They swim from their Infancy like Frogs, and are able to continue long under Water, where they often take Fish, which the Females carry home to their Young. And upon this Occasion, I hope the Reader will pardon my relating an odd Adventure.

Being one Day abroad with my Protector the Sorrel Nag, and the Weather exceeding hot, I entreated him to let me bathe in a River that was near. He consented, and I immediately stripped myself stark naked, and went down softly into the Stream. It happened that a young Female *Yahoo* standing behind a Bank, saw the whole Proceeding; and inflamed by Desire, as the Nag and I conjectured, came running with all Speed, and leaped into the Water within five Yards of the Place where I bathed. I was never in my Life so terribly frighted; the Nag was grazing at some Distance, not suspecting any Harm: She embraced me after a most fulsome Manner; I roared as loud as I could, and the Nag came galloping towards me, whereupon she quitted her Grasp, with the utmost Reluctancy, and leaped upon the opposite Bank, where she stood gazing and howling all the time I was putting on my Cloaths.

This was Matter of Diversion to my Master and his Family, as well as of Mortification to my self. For now I could no longer deny, that I was a real *Yahoo*, in every Limb and Feature, since the Females had a natural Propensity to me as one of their own Species: Neither was the Hair of this Brute of a Red Colour, (which might have been some Excuse for an Appetite a little irregular) but black as a Sloe, and her Countenance did not make an Appearance altogether so hideous as the rest of the Kind; for, I think, she could not be above Eleven Years old.

Having already lived three Years in this Country, the Reader I suppose will expect, that I should, like other Travellers, give him some Account of the Manners and Customs of its Inhabitants, which it was indeed my principal Study to learn.

As these noble *Houyhnhnms* are endowed by Nature with a general Disposition to all Virtues, and have no Conceptions or Ideas of what is evil in a rational

Creature; so their grand Maxim is, to cultivate *Reason,* and to be wholly governed by it. Neither is Reason among them a Point problematical as with us; where Men can argue with Plausibility on both Sides of a Question; but strikes you with immediate Conviction; as it must needs do where it is not mingled, obscured, or discoloured by Passion and Interest. I remember it was with extreme Difficulty that I could bring my Master to understand the Meaning of the Word *Opinion,* or how a Point could be disputable; because *Reason* taught us to affirm or deny only where we are certain; and beyond our Knowledge we cannot do either. So that Controversies, Wranglings, Disputes, and Positiveness in false or dubious Propositions, are Evils unknown among the *Houyhnhnms.* In the like Manner when I used to explain to him our several Systems of *Natural Philosophy,* he would laugh that a Creature pretending to *Reason,* should value itself upon the Knowledge of other Peoples Conjectures, and in Things, where that Knowledge, if it were certain, could be of no Use. Wherein he agreed entirely with the Sentiments of *Socrates,* as *Plato* delivers them; which I mention as the highest Honour I can do that Prince of Philosophers. I have often since reflected what Destruction such a Doctrine would make in the Libraries of *Europe;* and how many Paths to Fame would be then shut up in the Learned World.

Friendship and *Benevolence* are the two principal Virtues among the *Houyhnhnms;* and these not confined to particular Objects, but universal to the whole Race. For, a Stranger from the remotest Part, is equally treated with the nearest Neighbour, and where-ever he goes, looks upon himself as at home. They preserve *Decency* and *Civility* in the highest Degrees, but are altogether ignorant of *Ceremony.* They have no Fondness for their Colts or Foles; but the Care they take in educating them proceedeth entirely from the Dictates of *Reason.* And, I observed my Master to shew the same Affection to his Neighbour's Issue that he had for his own. They will have it that *Nature* teaches them to love the whole Species, and it is *Reason* only that maketh a Distinction of Persons, where there is a superior Degree of Virtue.

When the Matron *Houyhnhnms* have produced one of each Sex, they no longer accompany with their Consorts, except they lose one of their Issue by some Casualty, which very seldom happens: But in such a Case they meet again; or when the like Accident befalls a Person, whose Wife is past bearing, some other Couple bestows on him one of their own Colts, and then go together a second Time, until the Mother be pregnant. This Caution is necessary to prevent the Country from being overburthened with Numbers. But the Race of inferior *Houyhnhnms* bred up to be Servants is not so strictly limited upon this Article; these are allowed to produce three of each Sex, to be Domesticks in the Noble Families.

In their Marriages they are exactly careful to chuse such Colours as will not make any disagreeable Mixture in the Breed. *Strength* is chiefly valued in the Male, and *Comeliness* in the Female; not upon the Account of *Love,* but to preserve the Race from degenerating: For, where a Female happens to excel in *Strength,* a Consort is chosen with regard to *Comeliness.* Courtship, Love, Presents, Joyntures, Settlements, have no Place in their Thoughts; or Terms whereby to express them in their Language. The young Couple meet and are joined, merely because it is the Determination of their Parents and Friends: It is what they see done every Day; and they look upon it as one of the necessary Actions in a reasonable Being. But the Violation of Marriage, or any other Unchastity, was never heard of: And the married Pair pass their Lives with the same Friendship, and mutual Benevolence that they bear to all others of the same Species, who come in their Way; without Jealousy, Fondness, Quarrelling, or Discontent.

In educating the Youth of both Sexes, their Method is admirable, and highly deserveth our Imitation. These are not suffered to taste a Grain of *Oats,* except upon certain Days, till Eighteen Years old; nor *Milk,* but very rarely; and in Summer they graze two Hours in the Morning, and as many in the Evening, which their Parents likewise observe; but the Savants are not allowed above half that Time; and a great Part of the Grass is brought home, which they eat at the most convenient Hours, when they can be best spared from Work.

Temperance, Industry, Exercise and *Cleanliness,* are the Lessons equally enjoyned to the young ones of both Sexes: And my Master thought it monstrous in us to give the Females a different Kind of Education from the Males, except in some Articles of Domestick Management; whereby, as he truly observed, one Half of our Natives were good for nothing but bringing Children into the World: And to trust the Care of their Children to such useless Animals, he said was yet a greater Instance of Brutality.

But the *Houyhnhnms* train up their Youth to Strength, Speed, and Hardiness, by exercising them in running Races up and down steep Hills, or over hard stony Grounds; and when they are all in a Sweat, they are ordered to leap over Head and Ears into a Pond or a River. Four times a Year the Youth of certain Districts meet to shew their Proficiency in Running, and Leaping, and other Feats of Strength or Agility; where the Victor is rewarded with a Song made in his or her Praise. On this Festival the Servants drive a Herd of *Yahoos* into the Field, laden with Hay, and Oats, and Milk for a Repast to the *Houyhnhnms;* after which, these Brutes are immediately driven back again, for fear of being noisome to the Assembly.

Every fourth Year, at the *Vernal Equinox,* there is a Representative Council of the whole Nation, which meets in a Plain about twenty Miles from our House, and continueth about five or six Days. Here they inquire into the State and Condition of the several Districts; whether they abound or be deficient in Hay or Oats, or Cows or *Yahoos?* And where-ever there is any Want (which is but seldom) it is immediately supplied by unanimous Consent and Contribution. Here likewise the Regulation of Children is settled: As for instance, if a *Houy-hnhnm* hath two Males, he changeth one of them with another who hath two Females: And when a Child hath been lost by any Casualty, where the Mother is past Breeding, it is determined what Family in the District shall breed another to supply the Loss. . . .

The *Houyhnhnms* have no Letters, and consequently, their Knowledge is all traditional. But there happening few Events of any Moment among a People so well united, naturally disposed to every Virtue, wholly governed by Reason, and cut off from all Commerce with other Nations; the historical Part is easily preserved without burthening their Memories. I have already observed, that they are subject to no Diseases, and therefore can have no Need of Physicians. However, they have excellent Medicines composed of Herbs, to cure accidental Bruises and Cuts in the Pastern or Frog of the Foot by sharp Stones, as well as other Maims and Hurts in the several Parts of the Body.

They calculate the Year by the Revolution of the Sun and the Moon, but use no Subdivisions into Weeks. They are well enough acquainted with the Motions of those two Luminaries, and understand the Nature of *Eclipses;* and this is the utmost Progress of their *Astronomy.*

In *Poetry* they must be allowed to excel all other Mortals wherein the Justness of their Similes, and the Minuteness, as well as Exactness of their Descriptions, are indeed inimitable. Their Verses abound very much in both of these; and usually contain either some exalted Notions of Friendship and Benevolence, or the Praises of those who were Victors in Races, and other bodily Exercises. Their Buildings, although very rude and simple, are not inconvenient, but well contrived to defend them from all Injuries of Cold and Heat. They have a Kind of Tree, which at Forty Years old loosens in the Root, and falls with the first Storm; it grows very strait, and being pointed like Stakes with a sharp Stone, (for the *Houyhnhnms* know not the Use of Iron) they stick them erect in the Ground about ten Inches asunder, and then weave in Oat-straw, or sometimes Wattles betwixt them. The Roof is made after the same manner, and so are the Doors.

The *Houyhnhnms* use the hollow Part between the Pastern and the Hoof of their Fore-feet, as we do our Hands, and this with greater Dexterity, than I could at first imagine. I have seen a white Mare of our Family thread a Needle (which I lent her on Purpose) with that Joynt. They milk their Cows, reap their Oats, and do all the Work which requires Hands, in the same Manner. They have a Kind of hard Flints, which by grinding against other Stones, they form into Instruments, that serve instead of Wedges, Axes, and Hammers. With Tools made of these Flints, they likewise cut their Hay, and reap their Oats, which there groweth naturally in several Fields: The *Yahoos* draw home the Sheaves in Carriages, and the Servants tread them in certain covered Hutts, to get out the Grain, which is kept in Stores. They make a rude Kind of earthen and wooden Vessels, and bake the former in the Sun.

If they can avoid Casualties, they die only of old Age, and are buried in the obscurest Places that can be found, their Friends and Relations expressing neither Joy nor Grief at their Departure; nor does the dying Person discover the least Regret that he is leaving the World, any more than if he were upon returning home from a Visit to one of his Neighbours: I remember, my Master having once made an Appointment with a Friend and his Family to come to his House upon some Affair of Importance; on the Day fixed, the Mistress and her two Children came very late; she made two Excuses, first for her Husband, who, as she said, happened that very Morning to *Lhnuwnh*. The Word is strongly expressive in their Language, but not easily rendered into *English;* it signifies, *to retire to his first Mother.* Her Excuse for not coming sooner, was, that her Husband dying late in the Morning, she was a good while consulting her Servants about a convenient Place where his Body should be laid; and I observed she behaved herself at our House, as cheerfully as the rest: She died about three Months after.

They live generally to Seventy or Seventy-five Years, very seldom to Fourscore: Some Weeks before their Death they feel a gradual Decay, but without Pain. During this time they are much visited by their Friends, because they cannot go abroad with their usual Ease and Satisfaction. However, about ten Days before their Death, which they seldom fail in computing, they return the Visits that have been made by those who are nearest in the Neighbourhood, being carried in a convenient Sledge drawn by *Yahoos;* which Vehicle they use, not only upon this Occasion, but when they grow old, upon long Journeys, or when they are lamed by any Accident. And therefore when the dying *Houyhnhnms* return those Visits, they take a solemn Leave of their Friends, as if they were going to some remote Part of the Country, where they designed to pass the rest of their Lives.

I know not whether it may be worth observing, that the *Houyhnhnms* have no Word in their Language to express any thing that is *evil,* except what they borrow from the Deformities or ill Qualities of the *Yahoos.* Thus they denote the Folly of a Servant, an Omission of a Child, a Stone that cuts their Feet, a Continuance of foul or unseasonable Weather, and the like, by adding to each the Epithet of *Yahoo.* For Instance, *Hhnm Yahoo, Whnaholm Yahoo, Ynlhmndwihlma Yahoo,* and an ill contrived House, *Ynholmbumrohlnw Yahoo.*

Jonathan Swift (1667–1745) was an Anglo-Irish poet, satirist, and clergyman.

Source: [Jonathan Swift], TRAVELS INTO SEVERAL REMOTE NATIONS OF THE WORLD. IN FOUR PARTS. By Lemuel Gulliver [pseud.]. Volume 3 of WORKS (Dublin: George Faulkner, 1735) 315–52, 356–60. Originally published 1726 and better known as GULLIVER'S TRAVELS.

Louis Sébastien Mercier
Memoirs of the Year Two Thousand Five Hundred

For many years, Louis Sébastien Mercier's *L'an deux mille quatre cent quar-ante* (1771) was thought to be the first literary utopia set in the future. While we now know that it was not the first, it long played an important role in the development of utopian literature. For example, it was the first translation of a utopia to be published in the United States (Philadelphia, 1795).

Chap. IX. The Form of Government.

MAY I ask what is the present form of government? Is it monarchical, demo-cratic, or aristocratic (1)? — "It is neither of them; it is rational, and made for man. Monarchy is no more. Monarchical governments, as you knew, though to little purpose, lose themselves in despotism, as the rivers are lost in the bosom of the ocean; and despotism soon sinks under its own weight (2). This has been all literally accomplished, and never was there a more certain prophecy.

"WHEN we consider the lights that have been acquired, it would doubtless be a disgrace to the human race, to have measured the distance between the sun and the earth, to have weighed the heavenly orbs, and not to have discovered those simple and efficacious laws by which mankind should be governed. It is true, that pride, luxury, and self-interest produce a thousand obstacles; but how glorious is it to discover the means of making those private passions subservient to the general good! The vessel that plows the ocean commands the elements at the same moment that it is obedient to their empire: submissive to a double im-pulse, it incessantly re-acts against them. You there see, perhaps, the most lively image of a state; born up by tempestuous passions, it receives from them its movements, and at the same time resists the storm. "The art of the pilot is all." Your political light was nothing more than a crepuscule; and you wretchedly complained of the Author of nature, at the same time that he had given you both intelligence and strength for government. There only wanted a loud voice to rouse the multitude from their lethargy. If oppression thundered on your heads, you ought to have accused your own weakness only. Liberty and happi-ness appertain to those who dare to seize them. All is revolution in this world;

the most happy of all has had its point of maturity, and we have gathered its fruits (3).

"FREED from oppression, we have taken care not to place all the strength and springs of government, all the rights and attributes of power, in the hands of one man (4). Instructed by the misfortunes of past ages, we are become less imprudent. If Socrates or Marcus Aurelius should again visit the earth, we should not confide to them, an arbitrary power; not from a mistrust, but from a fear of depreciating the sacred character of a free citizen. Is not the law the voice of the general will of the people? And how can we dare to commit so important a deposit to a single man? Has he not his unguarded moments? And, even supposing him to be free from them, shall men resign that liberty which is their most valuable inheritance (5)?

"WE have experienced how contrary an absolute sovereignty is to the true interest of a nation. The art of raising refined tributes, all the powers of that terrible machine progressively multiplied; the embarrasment of the laws, one opposing another; chicanery devouring the possessions of individuals; the cities crowded by privileged tyrants; the venality of offices; ministers and intendants treating the different parts of the kingdom as conquered countries; a subtle hardness of heart that justifies inhumanity; royal officers, who are in no degree responsible to the people, and who insult them, stead of listening to their complaints; such was the effect of that vigilant despotism, which collected every intelligence, to employ it to a bad purpose; not unlike those burning glasses that collect the sun's rays, to destroy such objects as are presented to them. When we passed through France, that fine kingdom, which nature has favoured with her propitious regards, what did we behold? Districts desolated by tax-gatherers; citics become boroughs, and boroughs villages; the people pale and meagre; in a word, beggars instead of inhabitants. All these evils were known; but evident principles were avoided to embrace a system of dissipation (6), and the shadows that were raised, authorised the general depredation.

"CAN you believe it? The revolution was effected without trouble, and by the heroism of one great man. A philosophic prince, worthy of a throne, because he regarded it with indifference; more sollicitous for the happiness of mankind than for the phantom of power, distrusting posterity, and distrusting himself, offered to put the estates of the nation in possession of their ancient prerogative; he was sensible, that in an extensive kingdom there should be an union of the different provinces, in order to its being well governed; as in the human body, beside the general circulation, each part has one that is peculiarly adapted to itself; so each province, while it obeys the general laws, modifies those that are peculiar to it, agreeable to its soil, its position, its commerce and respective interests. Hence all lives, all flourishes. The provinces are no longer devoted to serve the court, and ornament the capital (7). A blind order from the throne, does not carry troubles into those parts where the king's eye has never penetrated. Each province is the guardian of its own security and its own happiness; its principle of life is not far too distant from it; it is within itself, always ready to assist the whole, and to remedy evils that may arise. The present succours are left to those who are intrusted in its welfare, and will not palliate the cure, much less will they rejoice at those incidents that may weaken their country.

"THE abolute sovereignty is now abolished; the chief magistrate preserves the name of king; but he does not foolishly attempt to bear all that burden which oppressed his ancestors. The legislative power of the kingdom is lodged in the states assembled. The administration of affairs, as well political as civil, is assigned to the senate; and the monarch, armed with the sword of justice, watches over the execution of the laws. He proposes every useful establishment. The senate is responsible to the king, and the king and senate are responsible to the states; which are assembled every two years. All is there decided by the majority of voices. The enacting of new laws, the filling of vacant posts, and the redressing of grievances, appertain to them; particular, or unforseen cases are left to the wisdom of the monarch.

"HE is happy (8), and his throne is fixed upon a basis the more solid, as his crown is guaranted by the liberty of the nation (9). Those souls, that would have been but mean, owe their virtue to that eternal source of greatness. The citizen is not separated from the state; he is incorporated with it (10), and, in return, he shows with what zeal he exerts himself, in all that can interest its glory.

"EVERY act published by the senate, explains, in a few words, its origin and its design. We cannot conceive how it was possible in your age, that pretended so much discernment, for magistrates to dare, in their surly pride, to publish dogmatic arrets, like the decrees of the theologians. As if the law was not the public reason, or it was not necessary that the people should be instucted, in order to their more ready obedience. Those ancient magistrates, who called themselves the fathers of their country, must have been ignorant of the great art of persuasion; that art which acts so powerfully, and without labour; or rather, they must have had no fixed point of view, no determinate course, but sometimes riotous and seditious, and sometimes creeping slaves, they flattered or harrassed the throne: by turns wrangling for trifles, and felling the people for a bribe.

"You will readily believe that we have discarded those magistrates, accustomed from their youth to all that insensibility which is necessary coolly to despose of the property, the honour, and lives of their follow citizens. Bold in defence of their meanest privileges, careless of what concerned the public welfare, they sunk at last into a perpetual indolence, and even spared others the trouble of corrupting them. Very different are our magistrates; the title of fathers of their country with which we honour them, they merit in the fullest sense of the term.

"The reins of government are now committed to wise and resolute hands, that pursue a regular plan. The laws reign, and no man is above them; which was a horrid evil in your Gothic government. The general good of the nation is founded on the security of each individual. No one fears man, but the laws; the sovereign himself is sensible that they hang over his head (11). His vigilance renders the senators more attentive to their several duties; the confidence he reposes in them softens their labours, and his authority gives the necessary force and activity to their decisions. Thus the scepter, which oppressed your kings, is light in the hands of our monarch. He is not a victim pompously decorated, and incessantly a sacrifice to the exigencies of the state; he bears that burthen only which is proportioned to the limited strength he has received from nature.

"We have a prince that fears the Almighty, that is pious and just, whose heart is devoted to God and his country, who dreads the divine vengeance, and the censure of posterity, and who regards a good conscience, and a spotless fame, as the highest degree of felicity. It is not so much great talents, or an extensive knowledge, that does good, as the sincere desire of an upright heart that loves it, and wishes to accomplish it. Frequently the boasted genius of a monarch, far from advancing the happiness of a kingdom, is exerted in destroying its liberties.

"We have conciliated what seemed almost incompatible, the good of the nation with that of individuals. They even pretended that the general happiness of a state was necessarily distinct from that of some of its members. We have not espoused that barbarous policy, founded either on an ignorance of just laws, or on a contempt of the poorest, but most useful men in the state. There were cruel and detestable laws that supposed man to be wicked; but we are much disposed to believe that they have only become so since the institution of those laws. Arbitrary power has griped the human heart, and by its irritation has rendered it inflamed and ulcerated.

"Our monarch has every necessary power and opportunity to do good, but is prevented from doing evil. We represent the nation to him always in a favourable light; we display its valour, its fidelity toward its prince, and its hatred of a foreign yoke.

"There are censors who have the right of expelling from about the prince all who are inclined to irreligion, to licentiousness, to falshood, and to that baneful art of covering virtue with ridicule (12). We do not admit amongst us that class of men, who, under the title of nobility (which, to render it completely ridiculous, was venal) crawled about the throne, and would follow no other profession than that of a soldier or a courtier; who lived in idleness, fed their pride with old parchments, and displayed a deplorable spectacle of equal vanity and misery. Your grenadiers shed their blood with as much intrepidity as the most noble among them, without rating it at so high a price. Such a denomination, moreover, in our republic would give offence to the other orders of the state. Our citizens are all equal; the only distinctions we know are those which naturally arise among men from their virtue, their genius, and industry (13).

"BESIDES all those ramparts, those barriers, and precautions used to prevent the monarch from forgetting, in time of public calamities, what he owes to the poor, he observes every year a solemn fast, which continues for three days, during which time he suffers continual hunger and thirst, and sleeps upon the ground. This severe and salutary fast imprints on his heart the most tender commiseration towards the necessitous. Our sovereign, it is true, has no need of this penance to remind him; but it is a law of the state, a sacred law, constanly followed and respected. By the example of our monarch, every man who has any connection with government, makes it his duty to feel what is want; and is from thence more disposed to assist those who are obliged to submit to the imperious and cruel law of extreme necessity (14)."

BUT, I said that these changes must have been long, laborious, and difficult. What efforts you must have made! — The philosopher, with a pleasing smile, replied, "Good is not more difficult than evil. The human passions are frightful obstacles; but when the mind is once convinced of its true interest, the man becomes just and faithful. It seems to me that a single person might govern the world, if the hearts of men were disposed to toleration and equity. Notwithstanding the common inconsequence of those of your age, it was foreseen that reason would one day make a great progress; its effects have become visible, and the happy principles of a wise government have been the first fruits of its reformation." . . .

Chap. XIII. On Commerce.

IT seems, by what you have told me, that France has no longer any colonies in the new world; that each part of America forms a separate kingdom, though united under one spirit of legislation? "We should be highly ridiculous to send our dear fellow citizens two thousand leagues from us. Why should we thus estrange ourselves from our brethren? Our climate is at least as good as that of America. Every necessary production is here common, and by nature excellent. The colonies were to France what a country-house is to a private person: the house in the country; sooner or later, ruins that in town.

"WE have a commerce, but it consists merely in the exchange of superfluities among ourselves. We have prudently banished three natural poisons, of which you made perpetual use; snuff, coffee, and tea. You stuffed your heads with a villanous powder, that deprived you Frenchmen of what little memory you had. You burned your stomach with liquors that destroyed it by encreasing its action. Those nervous disorders so common among you, were owing to the effeminate liquor which carried off the nourishing juice of the animal life. We cultivate an interior commerce only, of which we find the good effects; founded principally on agriculture, it distributes the most necessary aliments; it satisfies the wants of man, but not his pride.

"No man blushes to till his own ground, and to improve it to the highest degree possible. Our monarch himself has several acres which are cultivated under his own eye. We have not among us any of those titled gentry, whose only pursuit was idleness.

"FOREIGN traffic was the real father of that destructive luxury, which produced in its turn, that horrid inequality of fortunes, which caused all the wealth of the nation to pass into a few hands. Because a woman could carry in her ears the patrimony of ten families, the peasant was forced to sell the land of his ancestors, and to fly, with tears, from that soil where he found nought but misery and disgrace: for those insatiable monsters, who had accumulated the gold, even derided the misfortunes of those they had plundered (15). We began by destroying those great companies that absorbed all the fortunes of individuals, annihilated the generous boldness of a nation, and gave as deadly a blow to morality as to the state.

"IT may be very agreeable to sip chocolate, to breathe the odour of spices, to eat sugar and ananas, to drink Barbadoes water, and to be clothed in the gaudy stuffs of India. But are these sensations sufficiently voluptuous to close our eyes against the crowd of unheard of evils that your luxury engendered in the two hemispheres? You violated the most sacred ties of blood and nature on the coast of Guinea. You armed the father against the son, while you pretended to the name of Christians and of men. Blind barbarians! You have been but too well convinced by a fatal experience. A thirst for gold extolled by every heart; amiable moderation banished by avidity; justice and virtue regarded as chimeras; avarice, pale and restless, plowing the waves, and peopling with carcases the depths of the ocean; a whole race of men bought and sold, treated as the vilest animals; kings become merchants, covering the seas with blood for the flag of a frigate: Gold, to conclude, flowing from the mines of Peru like a flaming river, and running into Europe, burned up every where in its course the roots of happiness, and was then forever lost on the eastern world, where superstition buried in the earth, on one side, what avarice had painfully drawn from it, on the other. Behold a faithful picture of the advantages that foreign commerce produced to the world.

"OUR vessels do not make the tour of the globe, to bring back cochineal and indigo. Know you where are our mines? Where is our Peru? In labour and assiduity. All that promotes ease and convenience, that directly tends to assist nature, is cultivated with the greatest care. All that belongs to pomp, to ostentation and vanity, to a puerile desire of an exclusive possession of what is merely the work of fancy, is severely prohibited. We have cast into the sea those deceitful diamonds, those dangerous pearls, and all those whimsical stones that rendered the heart, like them, impenetrable. You thought yourselves highly ingenious in the refinements of luxury, but your pursuits were merely after superfluities, after the shadow of greatness; you were not even voluptuous. Your futile and miserable inventions were confined to a day. You were nothing more than children fond of glaring objects, incapable of satisfying your real wants. Ignorant of the art of happiness, you fatigued yourselves, far from the object of your pursuits, and mistook, at every step, the image for the reality.

"When our vessels leave their harbours, they take not thunder with them, to seize on the vast extent of waters, a fugitive prey that forms a point scarce perceptible to the sight. The echo of the waves bears not to heaven the hideous cries of furious wretches that dispute, at the expence of life itself, a passage over the immense and vacant ocean. We visit distant nations, but instead of the productions of their lands, we bring home the most useful discoveries relative to their legislature, their physical life, and their manners. Our vessels serve to connect our astronomical knowledge; more than three hundred observatories erected on this globe are ready to mark the least alteration that occurs in the heavens. The earth is the post where watches the centinel of the firmament who never sleeps. Astronomy is become an important science, as it proclaims, with a majestic voice, the glory of the Creator, and the dignity of that thinking being who has proceeded from his hands. But now we talk of commerce, let us not forget the most extraordinary kind that ever existed. You ought to be very rich," he said, "for in your youth, doubtless, you placed out money on annuities, especially on survivorships, as did one half of Paris. An invention of wonderful ingenuity was that sort of lottery, where they played at life and death, and the winnings were to go to the longest liver! You should have a most plentiful annuity! They renounced father and mother, brother and sister, all friends and relations, to double their revenue. They made the king their heir, then slept in a profound indolence, and lived only for themselves." — Ah! why do you tell me of these matters? Those rueful edicts that completed our corruption, and dissolved connections, till then held sacred; that barbarous refinement which publicly consecrated self-love, that detached the citizens from each other, and made them solitary and lifeless beings, drew tears from my eyes, when I reflected on the future condition of the state. I saw private fortunes melt away, and the excessive mass of opulence swell by their dissolution; but the fatal blow that was given to morals affected me still more deeply; no longer any connection between hearts that ought to be devoted to each other; they gave to interest a keener sword; interest of itself already so formidable; the sovereign authority laid those barriers at its feet, that it would never have dared to attack of itself. — "Good old man," said my guide, "you have done well to sleep, or you would have seen the annuitants and the state punished for their mutual imprudence. Politics, since that period, has made no such solecism; it does not now ruin, but unite and enrich the citizens."

AUTHOR'S NOTES

1. The genius of a nation does not depend on the atmosphere that surounds it; the climate is not the physical cause of its grandeur or debasement. Force and courage belong to the people of this earth; but the causes that put them in motion and sustain them, are derived from certain circumstances, that are sometimes sudden, sometimes slow in their operations; but, sooner or later, they never fail to arrive. Happy are the people who, by information or by instinct, seize the crisis.

2. Would you know what are the general principles that habitually prevail in the councils of a monarch? Here follows the substance of what is there said, or rather of what is there done. Taxes of every kind should be multiplied, for the prince can never be rich enough, considering that he is to maintain armies and the officers of his household, who ought, by all means, to be extremely magnificent. If the people complain of these loads they do wrong, and must be curbed.

No injustice can be done them, for in reality they have nothing but what the good will of the prince gives them, and which he may take again whenever he shall think fit,—especially if the interest or splendor of his crown require it. Beside, it is notorious, that a people at their ease, and in the midst of plenty, become less laborious, and may become indolent. We should therefore retrench their prosperity that we may add to their submission. The poverty of the subject is forever the strongest rampart of a monarch; and the poorer the individuals are, the more obedient the nation will be. Once taught to submit, they will perform it by habit, which is the most certain method of being obeyed. It is not sufficient that they merely submit, they must be taught to believe; that the spirit of wisdom here presides in the highest perfection, and submit accordingly, without daring to dispute about the decrees that proceed from our infallible knowledge.

If a philosopher should have access to this prince, and advancing to the midst of his council, should say to him, "Take heed how you give credit to these evil counsellors; you are surrounded by the enemies of your family; your grandeur and security are founded less on an arbitrary power, than on the love of your people. If they are unhappy, they will the more ardently wish for a revolution, and will shake either your throne, or that of your children. The people are immortal, but you must pass away. The majesty of the throne resides more in a truly paternal tenderness, than in an unlimited power; that power is violent, and contrary to the order of nature. By being more moderate, you will become more potent. Set an example of justice, and know that it is by morality alone that a prince becomes powerful and respectable."

This philosopher would certainly be taken for an enthusiast, and perhaps they would not even vouchsafe to punish him for his virute.

3. In certain states it is an epoch that becomes necessary; an epoch terrible and bloody, but the signal of liberty. It is of a civil war that I speak. It is what calls forth all the men of exalted genius, some to attack, and others to defend liberty. A civil war displays the most hidden talents. Men of wonderful abilities arise, and appear worthy to command the human race. It is a horid remedy! But in the stupour of a state, when the minds of men are plunged in a deep lethargy, it becomes necessary.

4. A despotic government is nothing more than a league between a sovereign and a small number of favourite subjects, in order to cheat and plunder the rest. In that case the monarch, or he that represents him, divides and destroys society, becomes a separate and central body, that lights up every passion as it lifts, and sets them in motion for its personal interest. He creates justice and injustice, his humour becomes a law, and his favour the measure of public esteem. This system is too violent to be durable. Justice, on the contrary, is a barrier that equally protects the subject and the prince. Liberty alone can form animated citizens, the only citizens, in fact, among rational beings. A king is never powerful but at the head of a free and contented people. The nation once debased, the throne sinks.

5. Liberty begets miracles, it triumphs over nature, it causes harvests to grow upon rocks; it gives a smiling air to the most doleful regions; it enlightens the peasant, and makes him more penetrative than the proud slaves of the most polished court. Other climates, the most finished works of the creation, delivered up to servitude, exhibit nothing but desolated lands, pale and dejected visages, that dare not lift their eyes to heaven. Choose then, man! be happy or miserable; if yet it be in thy power to choose: fear tyranny, detest slavery, arm thyself, live free, or die.

6. An intendant of the province, desirous of giving the * * * * , who was going up to Soissons, an idea of the abundance that reigned in France, caused the fruit-trees of the country round about to be dug up, and planted in the streets of the city, by digging up the pavement. These trees he decorated with garlands of gilt paper. This intendant was, without knowing it, a very great painter.

7. From error and ignorance spring all the evils that oppress humanity. Man is wicked only because he mistakes his true interest. In speculative physics, in astronomy, and mathematics, we may err without any real detriment; but politics will not admit of the least error. There are vices in government more destructive than natural plagues. An error of this kind depopulates and impoverishes a kingdom. If the most severe, the most profound speculation is ever necessary, it is in those public and problematic cases, where reasons of equal weight hold the judgment in equilibrium. Nothing is then more dangerous than the tricks of office; they produce inconceivable errors; and the state is not sensible of its condition till arrived on the brink of ruin. We cannot, therefore, be too clear in the complicated art of government, as the least deviation is a line that constantly recedes as it increases, and produces an immense error. The laws have been hitherto nothing more than palliatives, that have been turned into general remedies; they are, as has been very justly said, the offspring of necessity, and not of philosophy; it belongs to the latter to correct their defects. But what courage, what zeal, what love of humanity

must he have, who, from such a chaos, shall form a regular system! But, at the same time, where is the man that would be more dear to the human race? Let him remember, that it is of all objects the most important; that the happiness of mankind, and consequently their virtues, are therein highly interested.

8. M. d'Alembert [French mathematician and coeditor of the great *Encyclopédie—Ed.*] says, that a king who does his duty is of all men the most miserable; and that he who does it not, is of all others the most to be pitied. But why is the king who does his duty the most miserable? Is it from the multiplicity of his labours? No; a happy labour is a real pleasure. Does he make no account of that inward satisfaction which arises from a consciousness of having promoted the happiness of mankind? Does he not believe that virtue is its own reward? Beloved by all, except the wicked, can the heart of such a king be insensible to pleasure? Who has not felt the satisfaction that results from doing good? The king who does not fulfil his duty is the most to be pitied. Nothing more true, especially if he be sensible to remorse and infamy; if he be not, he is still the more to be pitied. Nothing more just than this last position.

9. It is good in every state, even in a republic, to have a limited chief. It is a sort of spectre that drives away all projects from the mind of the ambitious. Royalty in this case is like a scare-crow in a field, that prevents the birds from feeding upon the corn.

10. They who have said, that in a monarchy, the king is the depositary of the will of the people, have asserted an absurdity. There is, in fact, nothing more ridiculous, than for intelligent beings, like men, to say to one or more, "Will for us," the people have always said to their monarch; "Act for us," after you have clearly understood what is our will.

11. Every government where one man alone is above the laws, and can violate them with impunity, must be iniquitious and unhappy. In vain has a man of genius employed all his talents to make us acquiesce in the principles of an Asiatic government: they offer too great violence to human nature. Behold the proud vessel that plows the ocean, there needs but an imperceptible passage to admit the water, and cause her perdition. So one man that is above the law, may cause those acts of injustice and iniquity to enter a state, which, by an inevitable effect, will hasten its ruin. What matters it whether we perish by one or many? The misfortune is the same. What imports it whether tyranny have a hundred arms, or one only, that extends itself over the whole empire; if it fall on every individual, if it spring out fresh at the very instant it is cut off? Beside, it is not despotism that terrifies and confounds; it is its propagation. The viziers, the pachas, &c. imitate their masters; they devour others while they expect to be devoured. In the government of Europe, their shocks, the simultaneous re-action of their several bodies, affords moments of equilibrium, during which the people breathe; the limits of their respective powers, perpetually disordered, holds the place of liberty; and the phantom is, at least consolatory to those who cannot attain the reality.

12. I am much inclined to believe that sovereigns are almost always the most honest men in their courts. The soul of Narcissus was still more foul than that of Nero.

13. Why cannot the French suffer a republican government? Who in this kingdom is ignorant of the pre-eminence of the noblesse, founded on the institution itself, and confirmed by the custom of many ages? Yet when under the reign of John, the third

estate rose from their abject condition, they took their seat in the assembly of the nation; that haughty and barbarous noblesse beheld it without commotion, associate with the orders of the kingdom, though the times were still filled with prejudices of the police of the fiefs, and the profession of arms. The honour of the French nation, a principle ever active, and superior to the wisest institutions, may therefore one day become the soul of a republic; especially when a taste for philosophy, a knowledge of political laws, and the experience of so many evils, shall have destroyed that levity, that indiscretion which blasts those brilliant qualities that would make the French the first people in the universe; if they would well consider, ripen, and support their projects.

14. In the front of a philosopher's hermitage there was a rich and lofty mountain, favoured with the most benign regards of the sun. It was covered with beautiful pastures, with golden grain, with cedars and aromatic plants. Birds, the most pleasing to the sight, and delicious to the taste, fanned the air in flocks with their wings, and filled it with their harmonious warblings. The bounding deer peopled the woods. Some genial lakes produced in their silver waters the trout, the perch, and dace. Three hundred families were spread over this mountain, and there found a blest abode, in the midst of peace and plenty, and in the bosom of those virtues they constantly practised: each morn and eve they sent their grateful thanks to heaven. But behold the indolent and voluptuous Osman mounts the throne, and all these families are presently ruined, driven from their abodes, and become vagabonds upon the earth. The beauteous mountain was seized by his vizier, a noble robber, who feasted his dogs, his concubines, and his flatterers, with the plunder of the unhappy people. Osman one day losing himself in the chace, met the philosopher, whose hut had escaped that torrent which had swept all else before it. The philosopher recollected the monarch, without his suspecting it: he treated him with a noble courtesy. They talked of the present times. — "Alas! said the sage old man, we knew what pleasure was some ten years since; but now all suffers: extreme poverty has drove the poor from their habitations; wrings their souls, and each day sees them go drooping to the grave, oppressed by extreme misery." — "Pray tell me, said the monarch, what is that misery?" The philosopher sighed, remained silent, and set the prince in the way to his palace.

15. I smile with indignant pity when I see so many fine projects offered for the improvement of agriculture and population, while the taxes continually increasing, rob the people of the sweat of their brow; and the price of corn is augmented by the monopoly of those who have all the money of the kingdom in their hands. Must we forever cry to those proud and obdurate ears, "Give us a full and unbounded liberty of commerce and navigation, and a diminution of taxes." These are the only means of nourishing the people, and preventing that depopulation which we see already begun. But, alas! Patriotism is a contraband virtue. The man who lives for himself alone, who thinks of nought but himself, who is silent, and turns away his eyes for fear of horror, he is the good citizen; they even praise his prudence and moderation. For my own part, I cannot remain silent, I must declare what I have seen. It is into most of the provinces of France that we must go to see the people completely miserable. It is now, in 1770, three winters together that we have seen bread dear. The last year one half of the peasants had need of public charity, and this winter will complete their ruin; for they who have lived till now selling their

effects, have nothing left to sell. These poor people have a patience that makes me admire the force of the laws and of education.

Louis Sébastien Mercier (1740–1814) was a French educator, historian, politician, and dramatist.

Source: [Louis Sébastien Mercier], L'AN DEUX MILLE QUATRE CENT QUARANTE (1771); translated in English as MEMOIRS OF THE YEAR TWO THOUSAND FIVE HUNDRED (London, 1772).

Nicolas-Edmé Restif de la Bretonne
L'andrographe

L'andrographe (1781) explores formal rules for marriage.

On Marriage

Art. XXXIV. All young people of both sexes will be destined to wed, for matrimony is the state for which Nature, religion, and the social laws intended them. Every well-built individual will be obliged to marry, and to this end detailed procedures will be set forth in the following articles.

XXXV. Only in cases of infirmity or deformity will exceptions be made. The sick, whatever their ailments may be, will not be required to marry at all. As for the deformed, if they are vigorous, they will only be prohibited from marrying virgins, but they will nevertheless be able to secure widows of thirty-five and over. Such widows, for their part, will not be able to marry well-formed young men, unless there are too many for the girls, in which case the magistrate will grant a license to the widows to marry the youngest and handsomest of the surplus youths. Deformed men, as a compensation for their handicap, will be favored for all positions where celibacy is a suitable qualification.

XXXVI. In the future the choice of a mate will depend neither on caprice nor interest. The degree of merit of each presentable young man will give him the right to choose among all the girls, as set forth in Article XXX of the First Title. For this purpose, at the four great marriage festivals which will be fixed around the solstices and equinoxes, namely at the St. André, at Carnival, at the St. Jean, and on the ninth of September after harvest, all work will stop for three days throughout the nation. The whole population will assemble to witness the marriages and to participate in the joy of the newly weds. These three days will be preceded by a fortnight of preparation in families that have boys or girls to be married at the approaching festival. Their clothes will be got ready, and they will be given special instruction—the boys, as prescribed in Article XLI below, the girls, in Article LXV of the *Gynographs* regulation. Choosing will take place on the second of the three festival days, the first having been employed by the eligible young people in reading the moral register and in parading before one another. On selection day, all the girls will range themselves in a row or a number of rows in accordance with the locality, and the boys will be lined up separately. The first class will step forth and choose among the girls the ones who please them, in the presence of their parents, who will speak with those of the girls. Then will come the second class, and so on through the sixth, who will choose last. Within the different classes of young men, those who have rather more merit will always take precedence (the drawing of lots, discussed in Article XXX, taking place only among those who are perfectly equal): in each class every lad will have a number beginning with one for the most deserving, and this system will be in force through the last members of class six. Each girl thus publicly chosen will modestly follow her future husband to the altar, where all the boys and girls will be forthwith united in a single general blessing. The parents have but to see to it that the couple related to them by blood pronounce the "yes." In making choices, relative age will be regulated as set forth in Article XXVIII of the *Gynographs,* and other conditions in accordance with Article XXIX of this regulation for girls. Immediately after the benediction, the newly weds will be separated, to be reunited only at intervals and in the manner prescribed by Article XLII. Every wife will have a ring inscribed with the class and rank of her husband.

XXXVII. In the event that a girl chosen by a young man cannot bring herself to receive him as a husband, she will immediately make her opposition known through one of the matrons of the Committee of Ancient Dames established by Article LXXX of the *Gynographs* regulation. Then the reasons for the rejection will be examined in the open, not to determine their validity—there will always be some—but to inflict punishment on the girl if the reasons are to her discredit. In case of doubt, her marriage will be put off until the next festival; in case she is wrong and the reasons advanced are false, she will be cast into the lowest ranks, to be chosen in the future only by members of the class last in merit and good looks; in case she is right, she may that same day be rechosen by one of the substitute young men, who are ten in number, in place of the one whom she has justly rejected. (To the details of Article XII of the *Gynographs* should be added that girls of first merit will be placed in the front row, the more readily to be viewed and selected by the members of class one and class two and other young men of distinction. Note that in girls a degree of beauty, gentleness, or at least amiability must be joined to the virtues appropriate to their sex.)

XXXVIII. Every boy who has some bodily defect will be excluded from the legitimate classes, and different classes of cripples will be constituted, in accordance with their degree of infirmity. (1) Those disabled by accident who can still work will have a choice of marriage or the ecclesiastical state, secular or regular, as with the following class. (2) The lame without any other deformity will form a second class who can be given young girls as wives if they are otherwise vigorous and healthy. (3) The bandy-legged will qualify only for widows. (4) Congenital hunchbacks and deformed men will only obtain women past forty. (5) The deaf and one-eyed will have as wives only rejected girls who have not been chosen at the marriage festivals. (6) The blind will have the ugliest girls who have not been able to find husbands. Selection among the malformed will have as many divisions as among the robust. Priority will be given to those uniting the least deformity with the greatest merit; the rest will be ranked in accordance with the merit which offsets their deformities, until that subject is reached who has the least merit and the greatest deformity. Finally, it should be observed that those whose illness is communicable, such as the scrofulous, the scorbutic, the herpetic, the syphilitic, and so on, will not be able to marry, or will be permitted to marry only women past fifty, who might be willing to expose themselves to the disease. This will apply also to those attacked by epilepsy, consumption, and so on.

XXXIX. The reasons for the rejection of a young man will have to be specific, since the Committee of Elders, who will be treated under Title Five, will have carefully excluded those who might fall under some general cause. Thus, (1) A specific and secret insult to a girl will be a cause of rejection; (2) A secret vice known to the girl; (3) An insult to her father, brother, uncle, male cousin germane, mother, sister, aunt, female cousin germane, teacher of either sex; (4) Mockery of the girl; (5) Refusal to do her a favor; (6) Having on some occasion demonstrably preferred someone else to her. With all these reasons, especially the last, the girl cannot be proved in the right and the boy put off to another festival and even cast into a lower class, unless the offense has been grave in nature.

XL. Even if the reasons are not legitimate, the rejection will be sustained, but then the girl will be punished in accordance with the circumstances. In case of failure to prove frivolous charges, her marriage will merely be postponed to another festival and the boy will no longer be able to choose her. But if the girl falsely made serious accusations, or if she gave illegitimate reasons for rejection such as the following: (1) That he is not handsome; (2) That he has no taste for light amusement, to which people apply the empty term agreeableness; (3) That he is serious and cold; (4) That he made errors when in fact he was right, such as having occasionally voiced correct observations about the real shortcomings of the young lady; (5) That he is too rigidly virtuous; (6) That his family is inferior—in such and similar instances the girl will be demoted to the lower classes, and in (4) and (5) she will be put in the last row. As for the boy who is rejected without cause, he may again choose that very day among all the girls who have not been taken, if there are any left; otherwise, among ten of the following class, who like the boys will always be kept in reserve as a supplement in case of a shortage.

XLI. In addition to the sage counsel which has been given to the young people before marriage, the chief of the Committee of Elders will address them immediately after the celebration that forms part of the festival and he will recapitulate all the earlier instructions, to wit: (1) That marriage is a hallowed state and the act of marriage the most honorable and sacred of nature's mysteries; (2) That consequently one may permit oneself nothing which might profane it either by brutal transports of passion or indecent liberties, obscene speech, and so on; (3) That the delights with which nature accompanies the act of marriage are a beneficence for which thanks are due her; (4) That these delights should persuade a reasonable spirit to bear with resignation the pains attached to the conjugal bond; (5) That since a father's pleasure in the birth of his children is the tenderest that can be experienced, it should make a wife dearer to us and should commit us to bringing up the children well; (6) That the impatience of a husband with his wife, brutality, rage, and so on, are acts at once ferocious and puerile; (7) That for the sake of the children's constitution and the father's health, the taste for carnal pleasure inspired by a wife should cease to exercise the dominion and ardor of a novelty, since this taste might consume the husband's strength and give the fatherland children with weak bodies but violent passions, that is, disproportionate to their strength; (8) That there is among married couples a sort of gentle intimacy founded upon confidence and mutual need, which is preferable even to the tenderest love, since that can only be a detriment to the fulfillment of one's duties because it is too absorbing; (9) That one cannot master the art of inspiring love or prevent it from waning, but one can be adept at winning confidence, fostering mutual dependence, and these virtues are the foundation of happiness; (10) That spouses should be polite to each other, politeness being a kind of amiability which renders us agreeable, for no persons have more need to be agreeable one to another than spouses destined to live together; (11) That consequently they should not be exigent, captious, sensitive; sincerity, amiable candor, frankness should be the soul of their converse; (12) They will be warned that they should enjoy hymen's pleasures only in stealth until the age of 35; (13) That at this age they will be free, as mature men; (14) That it is low, criminal, and reprehensible to give a bad example to youth either by word or indecent action contrary to good morals; (15) That a good example set by one's conduct with one's spouse will be praised and there will be public rewards for those who have particularly distinguished themselves in this respect; (16) That the proper education of children is the principal responsibility of married people, in view of the fact that it serves the general good while accomplishing a private good; (17) That fathers of wicked children will not be esteemed, while good children of wicked parents will be considered doubly meritorious; (18) That the wicked father of a good son will nonetheless be punished and relegated to the last classes of men, as will be specified in Article LV of Title Three of this regulation, but that his good son may obtain his pardon once; (19) That a pusillanimous husband who lets himself in a cowardly manner be dominated, mastered, and led by his wife out of weakness or love will be publicly censured for the first offense; for further offences he will be obliged to appear in the village or city assemblies with a little distaff and a little spindle in his hat; (20) That, on the other hand, every husband who preserves masculine dignity without harshness, who is the guide, protector, noble and upright defender of his spouse, will be lauded if he has these qualities to a notable degree, and in the event of exemplary conduct in this respect, he will be raised to a class above the one in which he stood at the time of his marriage; (21) That distinguished services rendered to the state, sublime moral virtues, an invention useful and rare, a splendid and superb system of bringing up children that has produced excellent results, will likewise raise a citizen in grade and might even elevate him to the level of top man in the top class, in accordance with his deserts; (22) Finally, that a bad husband, quarrelsome, drunk, brutal to the point of striking his wife, will be sequestered from society, confined to the class of the helpless deformed, and treated with terrible severity. Still further instructions might be added according to the time and circumstances.

XLII. The newly weds will see their wives only through the grillwork separating men and women in the common room set aside for meals and public diversions. Each evening the young man will return to his parents' home, and his wife's parents will take their daughter home, where she will live as before her marriage. But she will sleep alone, and if her husband is clever enough to get to her, joy will be with him. However, he will never be encouraged by the parents, who would otherwise be considered blameworthy. Until the age of 35, a husband cannot be seen with his wife anywhere without dishonor and without exposing himself to censure; but anything he does in secret and without being discovered, though the results may betray him, will be praised. And it will be a great achievement to have had several children by one's wife without ever having been caught by the parents or seen alone with one's wife. This virtue carried to the highest point of perfection will result in advancement by a degree to a higher class. And if it is joined to another cause of advancement the husband will be graded one number higher than his equals in merit.

XLIII. Should it happen that a newly wed husband, in defiance of this wise regulation, presumes to behave freely with his wife in accordance with present abuses, he will be deported, that is to say, sent to the colonies until the age of 35, at which time he will be obliged to go back to his country, where he will be placed in the lowest class. His wife will then be returned to him and he will follow the common lot.

XLIV. But if the young husband employs new and clever means to pass happy moments with his wife, he will be praised for it, whatever they are, provided that he uses no violence or firearms, only stratagems either to take the parents of his wife by surprise or to conceal himself from them and remain totally undiscovered. The law provides that in this case the young wife may not elude him or try to make her husband fail. If such a thing should happen, she would be punished as a felon by the Committee of Ancient Dames, even without her husband's filing complaint. There will be instances, however, when the young husbands will be warned by their families that nothing is to be attempted; and mothers especially will be authorized to keep the newly weds under their surveillance on those occasions.

XLV. When brides become pregnant, their husbands will be allowed to see them every day and to spend one or two hours with them under the eyes of the mother and the whole household. For this purpose, mealtimes will be preferred. This indulgence is intended to instill a kind of contentment in the soul of the young wife, who will take care to inform her mother as soon as she believes herself pregnant. Until the pregnancy is confirmed, however, permission will be granted the husband only for a brief interview. Finally, in the last two months, the husband may remain much longer with his wife if his parents or the Elders judge he can do so without neglecting his duties. Otherwise this privilege will not be granted. The bad conduct of husbands or wives will deprive them of this advantage.

XLVI. If, despite all the security which the regulation gives to the conjugal union, it should transpire that a woman commits an essential infidelity, a single eyewitness will suffice to convict her; for even if she has not committed the crime of adultery, an intimacy great enough to arouse suspicion will be enough to render her unworthy of her husband. If it is the husband himself who has seen it, his testimony will be irrefutable. The marriage will be broken, entirely annulled, if there are still no children; and the woman will be confined to outcasts disgraced in the eyes of nature in proportion to her transgression and the degree of its certainty. That is, if there is only one witness and consequently the consummation of the adultery is not completely proved, she will be put in the rank of the least deformed, and as such she might be given in marriage to a deformed young man from among those who can marry girls, as set forth in Article XXXVIII, or to a widower. If there is a clear-cut conviction either on the testimony of her husband or of two or more witnesses, the woman thus justly repudiated will be given to the most deformed blind men, and condemned to serve them and to lead them under pain of prison and flogging in case she fails to conduct herself well or to care for them. It should be noted that the guilty will always be sent to a different region, to places known only to the chief of the Committee of Elders, so that the deformed who marry them will be ignorant of their particular crime and will not be able to reproach them with it. For there are still other crimes for which girls will be cast into the deformed classes, such as indiscretion, indolence, inveterate slovenliness, base malice, habitual calumny, and so on. (This should serve as a supplement to Article XIX of the *Gynographs*.) When women are unfaithful after they have had children, the marriage will not be dissolved. If the charge is not completely proved, they will be deprived of the right to bring up their daughters. If the crime is certain, they will be treated as prescribed in Article XLIII of the *Gynographs*.

If it is the man who is unfaithful, it will be ascertained whether his partner was a girl or a widow or a deformed person or a guilty woman assimilated to the deformed. Then the circumstances will be examined to see whether the act occurred after he had long been unable to approach his wife or whether he lacked this excuse in his favor. And a decision will be made accordingly, to wit: (1) If it is a well-formed girl and one without reproach whom he has thus dishonored, he will not be obliged to pay damages; under the system of equal wealth established by this regulation such penalties could not be inflicted, and even under the present system they should not be imposed since they would hurt the family of the seducer, which is not guilty. But the seducer's punishment will be personal and will consist throughout his whole life of not being able to pass before the girl or her parents without falling on his knees and asking their pardon, even if he should meet them ten times a day. He would be forbidden to reply to anything they might say to him, or to complain, save to the Committee of Elders to put bounds to the matter on its own initiative. (2) If the man has seduced a married woman, the marriage of the adulterer will be broken if he has no children and his wife demands it. She will remain free to marry again anyone permitted by law to marry widows. But the two adulterers will not be able to marry each other under any circumstances. The woman will be consecrated to the blind, deformed ones, and the man obliged to take the hand of any blind girl who would condescend to receive him, with the injunction that he must treat her well, and so on. (3) If the husband has been adulterous with a widow, the marriage will not be dissolved, but the guilty one will be publicly stigmatized by the Committee and will be barred from amusements at the four marriage festivals. Instead of giving themselves over to pleasures like the rest on those days, the guilty of every description, especially the last group, will do the heavy work, will carry water, help in the kitchen, and so on. In case of repeated offenses, they will be condemned for life (see Article LXII on crimes and LXVIII on cooks under the following Title). (4) If the husband has forgotten his duty with a deformed person, he will only be subject to a reprimand and condemned to do the lighter work during the four festivals. (5) Finally, if it was with a guilty one assimilated to the deformed, the marriage would be dissolved if there were no children and the wife demanded it. And the husband condemned in the same sentence as the criminal woman would be obliged to marry her, the adultery in this case destroying the marriage as is written in the Gospel. (6) In conclusion, it should be observed that if the man has fornicated with women of the last three classes at a time when he was forced to abstain from his own wife, either because of her illness or absence, the punishment will be incomparably lighter and of the easiest kind, such as a reprimand and the least onerous service at the marriage festivals. If, of course, the laws of the several countries are absolutely opposed to the dissolution of the marriage bonds, it could be omitted.

Nicolas-Edmé Restif de la Bretonne (1734–1806) was a prolific writer who published over three hundred volumes.

Source: Reprinted with the permission of The Free Press, a Division of Simon & Schuster from FRENCH UTOPIAS: AN ANTHOLOGY OF IDEAL SOCIETIES, edited and translated by Frank E. and Fritzie P. Manuel. Copyright © 1966 by The Free Press.

William Godwin
Enquiry Concerning Political Justice

Of the Future of Political Societies

Government can have no more than two legitimate purposes, the suppression of injustice against individuals within the community, and the common defence against external invasion. The first of these purposes, which alone can have an uninterrupted claim upon us, is sufficiently answered by an association, of such an extent, as to afford room for the institution of a jury to decide upon the offences of individuals within the community, and upon the questions and controversies respecting property which may chance to arise. It might be easy indeed for an offender to escape from the limits of so petty a jurisdiction; and it might seem necessary, at first, that the neighbouring parishes,[1] or jurisdictions, should be governed in a similar manner, or at least should be willing, whatever was their form of government, to co-operate with us in the removal or reformation of an offender whose present habits were alike injurious to us

---

1. The word parish is here used without regard to its origin, and merely in consideration of its being a word descriptive of a certain small portion of territory, whether in population or extent which custom has rendered familiar to us.

and to them. But there will be no need of any express compact, and still less of any common centre of authority, for this purpose. General justice, and mutual interest, are found more capable of binding men than signatures and seals. In the meantime all necessity for causing the punishment of the crime, to pursue the criminal would soon, at least, cease if it ever existed. The motives to offence would become rare: its aggravations few: and rigour superfluous. The principal object of punishment is restraint upon a dangerous member of the community; and the end of this restraint would be answered by the general inspection that is exercised by the members of a limited circle over the conduct of each other, and by the gravity and good sense that would characterize the censures of men, from whom all mystery and empiricism were banished. No individual would be hardy enough in the cause of vice to defy the general consent of sober judgement that would surround him. It would carry despair to his mind or, which is better, it would carry conviction. He would be obliged by a force not less irresistible than whips and chains, to reform his conduct.

In this sketch is contained the rude outline of political government. Controversies between parish and parish would be, in an eminent degree, unreasonable, since, if any question arose, about limits, for example, the obvious principles of convenience could scarcely fail to teach us to what district any portion of land should belong. No association of men, so long as they adhered to the principles of reason, could possibly have an interest in extending their territory. If we would produce attachment in our associates, we can adopt no surer method than that of practising the dictates of equity and moderation; and, if this failed in any instance, it could only fail with him who, to whatever society he belonged, would prove an unworthy member. The duty of any society to punish offenders is not dependent upon the hypothetical consent of the offender to be punished, but upon the duty of necessary defence.

But however irrational might be the controversy of parish with parish in such a state of society, it would not be the less possible. For such extraordinary emergencies therefore, provision ought to be made. These emergencies are similar in their nature to those of foreign invasion. They can only be provided against by the concert of several districts declaring and, if needful, enforcing the dictates of justice.

One of the most obvious remarks that suggests itself upon these two cases, of hostility between district and district, and of foreign invasion which the interest of all calls upon them jointly to repel, is that it is their nature to be only of occasional recurrence, and that therefore the provisions to be made respecting them need not be, in the strictest sense, of perpetual operation. . . .

It is a curious subject to enquire into the due medium between individuality and concert. On the one hand, it is to be observed that human beings are formed for society. Without society, we shall probably be deprived of the most eminent enjoyments of which our nature is susceptible. In society, no man possessing the genuine marks of a man can stand alone. Our opinions, our tempers and our habits are modified by those of each other. This is by no means the mere operation of arguments and persuasives; it occurs in that insensible and gradual way which no resolution can enable us wholly to counteract. He that would attempt to counteract it by insulating himself will fall into a worse error than that which he seeks to avoid. He will divest himself of the character of a man, and be incapable of judging his fellow men, or of reasoning upon human affairs.

On the other hand, individuality is of the very essence of intellectual excellence. He that resigns himself wholly to sympathy and imitation can possess little of mental strength or accuracy. The system of his life is a species of sensual dereliction. He is like a captive in the garden of Armida; he may revel in the midst of a thousand delights; but he is incapable of the enterprise of a hero, or the severity of a philosopher. He lives forgetting and forgot. He has deserted his station in human society. Mankind cannot be benefited by him. He neither animates them to exertion, nor leads them forward to unexpected improvement. When his country or his species call for him, he is not found in his rank. They can owe him no obligations; and, if one spark of a generous spirit remain within him, he will view his proceedings with no complacency. The truly venerable, and the truly happy, must have the fortitude to maintain his individuality. If he indulge in the gratifications, and cultivate the feelings of man, he must at the same time be strenuous in following the train of his disquisitions, and exercising the powers of his understanding.

The objectors of a former chapter [Chapter V] were partly in the right when they spoke of the endless variety of mind. It would be absurd to say that we are not capable of truth, of evidence and agreement. In these respects, so far as mind is in a state of progressive improvement, we are perpetually coming nearer to each other. But there are subjects about which we shall continually differ, and ought to differ. The ideas, associations and circumstances of each man are properly his own; and it is a pernicious system that would lead us to require all men, however different their circumstances, to act by a precise general rule. Add to this that, by the doctrine of progressive improvement, we shall always be erroneous, though we shall every day become less erroneous. The proper method for hastening the decline of error, and producing uniformity of judgement, is not by brute force, by laws, or by imitation; but, on the contrary, by exciting every man to think for himself.

From these principles it appears that everything that is usually understood by the term co-operation is, in some degree, an evil. A man in solitude is obliged to sacrifice or postpone the execution of his best thoughts, in compliance with his necessities, or his frailties. How many admirable designs have perished in the conception, by means of this circumstance? It is still worse when a man is also obliged to consult the convenience of others. If I be expected to eat or to work in conjunction with my neighbour, it must either be at a time most convenient to me, or to him, or to neither of us. We cannot be reduced to a clockwork uniformity. . . .

Whether, by the nature of things, co-operation of some sort will always be necessary is a question we are scarcely competent to decide. At present, to pull down a tree, to cut a canal, to navigate a vessel, require the labour of many. Will they always require the labour of many? When we recollect the complicated machines of human contrivance, various sorts of mills, of weaving engines, steam engines, are we not astonished at the compendium of labour they produce? Who shall say where this species of improvement must stop? At present, such inventions alarm the labouring part of the community; and they may be productive of temporary distress, though they conduce, in the sequel, to the most important interests of the multitude. But, in a state of equal labour, their utility will be liable to no dispute. Hereafter it is by no means clear that the most extensive operations will not be within the reach of one man; or, to make use of a familiar instance, that a plough may not be turned into a field, and perform its office without the need of superintendence. It was in this sense that the celebrated [Benjamin] Franklin conjectured that 'mind would one day become omnipotent over matter'.

The conclusion of the progress which has here been sketched is something like a final close to the necessity of manual labour. It may be instructive in such cases to observe how the sublime geniuses of former times anticipated what seems likely to be the future improvement of mankind. It was one of the laws of Lycurgus that no Spartan should be employed in manual labour. For this purpose, under his system, it was necessary that they should be plentifully supplied with slaves devoted to drudgery. Matter, or, to speak more accurately, the certain and unintermitting laws of the universe, will be the Helots [slaves] of the period we are contemplating. . . .

The subject of cohabitation is particularly interesting as it includes in it the subject of marriage. It will therefore be proper to pursue the enquiry in greater detail. The evil of marriage, as it is practised in European countries, extends further than we have yet described. The method is for a thoughtless and romantic youth of each sex to come together, to see each other, for a few times and under circumstances full of delusion, and then to vow eternal attachment. What is the consequence of this? In almost every instance they find themselves deceived. They are reduced to make the best of an irretrievable mistake. They are led to conceive it their wisest policy to shut their eyes upon realities, happy, if, by any perversion of intellect, they can persuade themselves that they were right in their first crude opinion of each other. Thus the institution of marriage is made a system of fraud; and men who carefully mislead their judgements in the daily affair of their life must be expected to have a crippled judgement in every other concern.

Add to this that marriage, as now understood, is a monopoly, and the worst of monopolies. So long as two human beings are forbidden, by positive institution, to follow the dictates of their own mind, prejudice will be alive and vigorous. So long as I seek, by despotic and artificial means, to maintain my possession of a woman, I am guilty of the most odious selfishness. Over this imaginary prize, men watch with perpetual jealousy; and one man finds his desire, and his capacity to circumvent, as much excited as the other is excited to traverse his projects, and frustrate his hopes. As long as this state of society continues, philanthropy will be crossed and checked in a thousand ways, and the still augmenting stream of abuse will continue to flow.

The abolition of the present system of marriage appears to involve no evils. We are apt to represent that abolition to ourselves as the harbinger of brutal lust and depravity. But it really happens, in this, as in other cases, that the positive laws which are made to restrain our vices irritate and multiply them. Not to say that the same sentiments of justice and happiness which, in a state of equality, would destroy our relish for expensive gratifications might be expected to decrease our inordinate appetites of every kind, and to lead us universally to prefer the pleasures of intellect to the pleasures of sense.

It is a question of some moment whether the intercourse of the sexes, in a reasonable state of society would be promiscuous, or whether each man would select for himself a partner to whom he will adhere as long as that adherence shall continue to be the choice of both parties. Probability seems to be greatly in favour of the latter. Perhaps this side of the alternative is most favourable to population. Perhaps it would suggest itself in preference to the man who would wish to maintain the several propensities of his frame, in the order due to their relative importance, and to prevent a merely sensual appetite from engrossing excessive attention. It is scarcely to be imagined that this commerce, in any state of society, will be stripped of its adjuncts, and that men will as willingly hold it with a woman whose personal and mental qualities they disapprove as with one of a different description. But it is the nature of the human mind to persist, for a certain length of time, in its opinion or choice. The parties therefore, having acted upon selection, are not likely to forget this selection when the interview is over. Friendship, if by friendship we understand that affection for an individual which is measured singly by what we know of his worth, is one of the most exquisite gratifications, perhaps one of the most improving exercises, of a rational mind. Friendship therefore may be expected to come in aid of the sexual intercourse, to refine its grossness, and increase its delight. All these arguments are calculated to determine our judgement in favour of marriage as a salutary and respectable institution, but not of that species of marriage in which there is no room for repentance and to which liberty and hope are equally strangers.

Admitting these principles therefore as the basis of the sexual commerce, what opinion ought we to form respecting infidelity to this attachment? Certainly no ties ought to be imposed upon either party, preventing them from quitting the attachment, whenever their judgement directs them to quit it. With respect to such infidelities as are compatible with an intention to adhere to it, the point of principal importance is a determination to have recourse to no species of disguise. In ordinary cases, and where the periods of absence are of no long duration, it would seem that any inconstancy would reflect some portion of discredit on the person that practised it. It would argue that the person's propensities were not under that kind of subordination which virtue and self-government appear to prescribe. But inconstancy, like any other temporary dereliction, would not be found incompatible with a character of uncommon excellence. What, at present, renders it, in many instances, peculiarly loathsome is its being practised in a clandestine manner. It leads to a train of falsehood and a concerted hypocrisy, than which there is scarcely anything that more eminently depraves and degrades the human mind.

William Godwin (1756–1836) was the earliest British anarchist theorist.

Source: William Godwin, ENQUIRY CONCERNING POLITICAL JUSTICE. 3d. ed. (London, 1798).

Timothy Dwight
Greenfield Hill

In the final section of Timothy Dwight's poem *Greenfield Hill* (1794), God and humankind have combined to produce eutopia in America under God's guidance. His eutopia presents the town where he was pastor—Greenfield Hill, Connecticut—in the future, but it is really a vision of the future of the United States revealed by the "Genius of the Sound." The vision that Dwight presents in his rather overblown poetry shows the future United States as the place where law, education, and a system of equal property have enabled all people to become truly free.

> Here first th' enduring reign of Peace be known:
> The voice of scepter'd Law wide realms obey,
> And choice erect, and freeman hail, and sway:
> The sun of knowledge light the general mind,
> And cheer, through every class, oppres'd mankind;

Here Truth, and Virtue, doom'd no more to roam,
Pilgrims in eastern climes, shall find their home;
Age after age, exalt their glory higher,
That light the soul, and this the life inspire;
And Man once more, self-ruin'd Phoenix, rise,
On wings of Eden, to his native skies. . . .

Through the whole realm, behold convenient farms
Fed by small herds, and gay with cultur'd charms;
To sons, in equal portions, handed down. . . .

See the wide realm in equal shares possess'd!
How few the rich, or poor! how many bless'd!
O happy state! the state, by Heaven design'd
To rein, protect, employ, and bless mankind.

Timothy Dwight (1752–1817), a Congregational minister, president of Yale (1795–1817), and the grandson of Jonathan Edwards, was an important figure in the intellectual life of New England after the Revolution.

Source: Timothy Dwight, "Part VII. The Vision," in his GREENFIELD HILL: A POEM IN SEVEN PARTS (New York: Printed by Childs and Swaine, 1794), 151, 153, 155.

Antoine-Nicolas de Condorcet
Sketch for a Historical Picture of the Progress of the Human Mind

The Tenth Stage

The future progress of the human mind

IF MAN CAN, with almost complete assurance, predict phenomena when he knows their laws, and if, even when he does not, he can still, with great expectation of success, forecast the future on the basis of his experience of the past, why, then, should it be regarded as a fantastic undertaking to sketch, with some pretence to truth, the future destiny of man on the basis of his history? The sole foundation for belief in the natural sciences is this idea, that the general laws directing the phenomena of the universe, known or unknown, are necessary and constant. Why should this principle be any less true for the development of the intellectual and moral faculties of man than for the other operations of nature? Since beliefs founded on past experience of like conditions provide the only rule of conduct for the wisest of men, why should the philosopher be forbidden to base his conjectures on these same foundations, so long as he does not attribute to them a certainty superior to that warranted by the number, the constancy, and the accuracy of his observations?

Our hopes for the future condition of the human race can be subsumed under three important heads: the abolition of inequality between nations, the progress of equality within each nation, and the true perfection of mankind. . . .

The time will . . . come when the sun will shine only on free men who know no other master but their reason; when tyrants and slaves, priests and their stupid or hypocritical instruments will exist only in works of history and on the stage; and when we shall think of them only to pity their victims and their dupes; to maintain ourselves in a state of vigilance by thinking on their excesses; and to learn how to recognize and so to destroy, by force of reason, the first seeds of tyranny and superstition, should they ever dare to reappear amongst us.

In looking at the history of societies we shall have had occasion to observe that there is often a great difference between the rights that the law allows its citizens and the rights that they actually enjoy, and, again, between the equality established by political codes and that which in fact exists amongst individuals: and we shall have noticed that these differences were one of the principal causes of the destruction of freedom in the Ancient republics, of the storms that troubled them, and of the weakness that delivered them over to foreign tyrants.

These differences have three main causes: inequality in wealth; inequality in status between the man whose means of subsistence are hereditary and the man whose means are dependent on the length of his life, or, rather, on that part of his life in which he is capable of work; and, finally, inequality in education. . . .

It is easy to prove that wealth has a natural tendency to equality, and that any excessive disproportion could not exist or at least would rapidly disappear if civil laws did not provide artificial ways of perpetuating and uniting fortunes; if free trade and industry were allowed to remove the advantages that accrued wealth derives from any restrictive law or fiscal privilege; if taxes on covenants, the restrictions placed on their free employment, their subjection to tiresome formalities and the uncertainty and inevitable expense involved in implementing them did not hamper the activity of the poor man and swallow up his meagre capital; if the administration of the country did not afford some men ways of making their fortune that were closed to other citizens; if prejudice and avarice, so common in old age, did not preside over the making of marriages; and if, in a society enjoying simpler manners and more sensible institutions, wealth ceased to be a means of satisfying vanity and ambition, and if the equally misguided notions of austerity, which condemn spending money in the cultivation of the more delicate pleasures, no longer insisted on the hoarding of all one's earnings. . . .

We shall point out how it can be in great part eradicated by guaranteeing people in old age a means of livelihood produced partly by their own savings and partly by the savings of others who make the same outlay, but who die before they need to reap the reward; or, again, on the same principle of compensation. by securing for widows and orphans an income which is the same and costs the same for those families which suffer an early loss and for those which suffer it later; or again by providing all children with the capital necessary for the full use of their labour, available at the age when they start work and found a family, a capital which increases at the expense of those whom premature death prevents from reaching this age. It is to the application of the calculus to the probabilities of life and the investment of money that we owe the idea of these methods which have already been successful, although they have not been applied in a sufficiently comprehensive and exhaustive fashion to render them really useful, not merely to a few individuals, but to society as a whole, by making it possible to prevent those periodic disasters which strike at so many families and which are such a recurrent source of misery and suffering. . . .

The degree of equality in education that we can reasonably hope to attain, but that should be adequate, is that which excludes all dependence, either forced or voluntary. We shall show how this condition can be easily attained in the present state of human knowledge even by those who can study only for a small number of years in childhood, and then during the rest of their life in their few hours of leisure. We shall prove that, by a suitable choice of syllabus and of methods of education, we can teach the citizen everything that he needs to know in order to be able to manage his household, administer his affairs and employ his labour and his faculties in freedom; to know his rights and to be able to exercise them; to be acquainted with his duties and fulfil them satisfactorily; to judge his own and other men's actions according to his own lights and to be a stranger to none of the high and delicate feelings which honour human nature; not to be in a state of blind dependence upon those to whom he must entrust his affairs or the exercise of his rights; to be in a proper condition to choose and supervise them; to be no longer the dupe of those popular errors which torment man with superstitious fears and chimerical hopes; to defend himself against prejudice by the strength of his reason alone; and, finally, to escape the deceits of charlatans who would lay snares for his fortune, his health, his freedom of thought and his conscience under the pretext of granting him health, wealth and salvation.

From such time onwards the inhabitants of a single country will no longer be distinguished by their use of a crude or refined language; they will be able to govern themselves according to their own knowledge; they will no longer be limited to a mechanical knowledge of the procedures of the arts or of professional routine: they will no longer depend for every trivial piece of business, every insignificant matter of instruction on clever men who rule over them in virtue of their necessary superiority; and so they will attain a real equality since differences in enlightenment or talent can no longer raise a barrier between men who understand each other's feelings, ideas and language, some of whom may wish to be taught by others but, to do so, will have no need to be controlled by them, or who may wish to confide the care of government to the ablest of their number but will not be compelled to yield them absolute power in a spirit of blind confidence. . . .

Among the causes of the progress of the human mind that are of the utmost importance to the general happiness, we must number the complete annihilation of the prejudices that have brought about an inequality of rights between the sexes, an inequality fatal even to the party in whose favour it works. It is vain for us to look for a justification of this principle in any differences of physical organization, intellect or moral sensibility between men and women. This inequality has its origin solely in an abuse of strength, and all the later sophistical attempts that have been made to excuse it are vain.

We shall show how the abolition of customs authorized, laws dictated by this prejudice, would add to the happiness of family life, would encourage the practice of the domestic virtues on which all other virtues are based, how it would favour the progress of education, and how, above all, it would bring about its wider diffusion; for not only would education be extended to women as well as to men, but it can only really be taken proper advantage of when it has the support and encouragement of the mothers of the family. . . .

A universal language is that which expresses by signs either real objects themselves, or well-defined collections composed of simple and general ideas, which are found to be the same or may arise in a similar form in the minds of all men, or the general relations holding between these ideas, the operations of the human mind, or the operations peculiar to the individual sciences, or the procedures of the arts. So people who become acquainted with these signs, the ways to combine them and the rules for forming them will understand what is written in this language and will be able to read it as easily as their own language. . . .

All the causes that contribute to the perfection of the human race, all the means that ensure it must by their very nature exercise a perpetual influence and always increase their sphere of action. The proofs of this we have given and in the great work they will derive additional force from elaboration. We may conclude then that the perfectibility of man is indefinite. . . .

Antoine-Nicolas de Condorcet (1743–1794) was a French mathematician and social theorist.

Source: Antoine-Nicolas de Condorcet, SKETCH FOR A HISTORICAL PICTURE OF THE PROGRESS OF THE HUMAN MIND, trans. June Barraclough (New York: Noonday Press, 1955), 173, 179, 180, 181, 182–83, 193, 197–98, 199.

Thomas Spence
The Constitution of Spensonia

Declaration

The Spensonian people, convinced that forgetfulness and contempt for the natural rights of man are the only cause of the crimes and misfortunes of the world, have resolved to expose in a declaration their sacred and inalienable rights in order that all citizens being always able to compare the acts of the government, with the ends of every social institution, may never suffer themselves to be oppressed and degraded by tyranny; and that the people may always have before their eyes the basis of their liberty and happiness; the magistrates, the rule of their conduct and duty; and legislators, the object of their mission,

They acknowledge therefore and proclaim in the presence of the Supreme Being, the following declaration of the rights of man and citizens:

1. The end of society is common happiness. Government is instituted to secure to man the enjoyment of his natural and imprescriptible rights.

2. These rights are equality, liberty, safety, and property, natural and acquired.

3. All men are equal by nature and before the law, and have a continual and inalienable property in the earth, and its natural productions.

4. The law is the free and solemn expression of the general will. It ought to be the same for all, whether it protects or punishes. It cannot order but what is just and useful to society. It cannot forbid but what is hurtful.

5. Social laws, therefore, can never proscribe natural rights. And every man, woman, and child still retain from the day of their birth to the day of their death their primogenial right to the soil of their respective parishes.

6. Thus, after a parish, out of its rents, has remitted to the state and county its legal quota towards their expenses, and provided for defraying its own proper contingencies, the remainder of the rents is the indisputable joint property of all the men, women, and children having settlement in the parish, and ought to be equally divided among them. . . .

Of the Commonwealth.
Of the State of Citizens

4. Every man or woman born or otherwise having acquired a settlement in a parish of Spensonia and of the age of twenty-one years complete; is admitted to the exercise of the rights of a Spensonian citizen, as far as their sex will allow.

5. Female citizens have the same right of suffrage in their respective parishes as the men: because they have equal property in the country and are equally

subject to the laws and, indeed, they are in every respect, as well on their own account as on account of their children, as deeply interested in every public transaction. But in consideration of the delicacy of their sex, they are exempted from, and are ineligible to, all public employments.

6. Every man, woman, and child, whether born in wedlock or not (for nature and justice know nothing of illegitimacy), is entitled quarterly to an equal share of the rents of the parish where they have settlement. But the public aide to the state, and the county, must first be deducted and the expenses of the parish provided for.

Thomas Spence (1750–1814) was an English radical agitator, bookseller, printer, and pamphleteer.

Source: T[homas] Spence, CONSTITUTION OF SPENSONIA. (London: Author, 1803). This is the third edition of a book originally published as THE CONSTITUTION OF A PERFECT COMMONWEALTH. BEING THE FRENCH CONSTITUTION OF 1793. AMENDED, AND RENDERED ENTIRELY CONFORMABLE TO THE WHOLE RIGHTS OF MAN. (London: Author, 1798). The second edition was published as THE CONSTITUTION OF SPENSONIA A COUNTRY IN FAIRYLAND SITUATED BETWEEN UTOPIA AND OCEANA BROUGHT FROM THENCE BY CAPTAIN SWALLOW (I.E. THOMAS SPENCE) (London: Author, 1801).

SIX

The Nineteenth Century

ev

Communal Societies as Utopias

SHAKERS

The most important group of intentional communities in the United States was established by the Shakers, or the United Society of Believers in Christ's Second Appearing. The Shakers (Shaking Quakers) originated in the English midlands (Bolton, north of Manchester) in the 1750s. The central figure in the early development of the Shaker movement was Ann Lee (originally Lees, 1736–1784), later known as Mother Ann, who became leader of the group after having been jailed in Manchester in 1772 and 1773 for violating the Sabbath. She taught that sexual intercourse was the cause of all human suffering and, hence, preached celibacy. Her personal basis for this belief was the death in infancy of all four of her children.

Ann Lee came to the United States in 1774 with a number of followers. She preached throughout upstate New York and New England, leading revivals and converting many people. After her death, the Shakers were brought together to lead a communal, withdrawn life by Joseph Meachem (1741–1796). He appointed Lucy Wright (1760–1821) to head the Shaker sisters, thereby establishing a system of equal, dual authority.

The most fundamental theological propositions put forth by the Shakers concerned the dual nature of God. On this earth, God's duality was represented by Christ and Mother Ann. This dual pattern pervaded Shaker life. Another important Shaker tenet was order; in the political sphere, they sought to establish an egalitarian order.

Frederick William Evans
The Shaker Compendium

The Ministry who are the central executive of the whole order, consists of two brethren and two sisters, and every regularly organized community or family in a society has two elder brethren and two elder sisters, who have charge of the spiritual affairs; also, two deacons and two deaconesses, who have the care of the temporalities. All other positions of care and trust are filled after the dual order. Yet each sex continues in its own appropriate sphere of action in all respects, there being a proper subordination, deference, and respect of the female to the male, in his order, and of the male to the female, in her order.

Frederick William Evans (1808–1893) was a reformer and a Shaker elder.

Source: F[rederick] W[illiam] Evans, SHAKER COMPENDIUM OF THE ORIGINS, HISTORY, PRINCIPLES, RULES AND REGULATIONS, GOVERNMENT, AND DOCTRINES OF THE UNITED SOCIETY OF BELIEVERS IN CHRIST'S SECOND APPEARING. WITH BIOGRAPHIES OF ANN LEE, WILLIAM LEE, JAS. WHITTAKER, J. HOCKNELL, J. MEACHAM, AND LUCY WRIGHT (1859; reprint, New York: Burt Franklin, 1972), 54.

The Millenial Laws

The Millennial Laws, the Shakers' code of behavior, were designed to maintain the communities' internal cohesion and separation from the rest of the world.

1. Those called as Deacons or Trustees, shall stand as stewards in the house of God, and their dwelling place should be at the outer court.

2. It is the duty of the Deacons and Deaconesses or Trustees, to see to the domestic concerns of the family in which they reside, and to perform all business transactions, either with the world, or with believers in other families or societies. All trade and traffic, buying and selling, changing and swapping, must be done by them or by their immediate knowledge and consent.

3. No new fashions in manufacture, clothing, or wares of any kind, may be introduced among Believers, without the sanction of the Ministry, thro' the medium of the Elders of each family thereof.

4. All monies, book accounts, deeds, bonds, notes, etc., which belong to the family, must be kept at the office, unless some other suitable place be provided therefore, by the proper authorities. Exceptions with regard to spending money are sometimes necessary, which must always be directed by the Elders, in union with the Ministry.

5. The Deacons or Trustees should keep all their accounts booked down, regular and exact, and as far as possible avoid controversies with the world.

6. Believers must not run in debt to the world.

7. The purchases of needful articles that appear substantial and good, and suitable for Believers to use, should not be neglected to purchase those which are needlessly adorned, even if they are a little cheaper.

8. Neither Trustees, nor anyone in their employ should be gone from home among the world, on trading business, more than four weeks, at one and the same time.

9. Three brethren who shall be appointed by the Ministry, two of which if consistent, should be Deacons or Trustees, are sufficient to go to the great and wicked cities to trade for any one family.

10. Believers should have no connection in trade or barter with those who have turned their backs to the way of God. Neither should they sojourn with them at night, nor keep company with them in the day, if possibly consistent to avoid it. But if it be necessary to hold conversation with them, do it in such a manner, that when you return home, you can give a correct account of it to your Elders, which should always be done.

11. When you resort to taverns and to public places, you shall not in any wise blend and gather with the wicked, by uniting in unnecessary conversation, jesting and joking, talking upon politics with them, or disputing or enquiring into things which will serve to draw your sense from the pure way of God.

14. Members employed by the Deacons or Trustees to do business at home or abroad, must render a full and explicit account to them, of all their transactions and expenditures, when such duties are performed, specifying particularly every article for which such expenses were made.

16. When two or more are out together, they should as far as possibly consistent, all eat at one tavern, and lodge in one room, and when you walk in the streets, you should keep so close together that there would not be room for even as much as a dog to run between you and your companion.

17. Those who go out on business for the Deacons or Trustees, have no more right to buy, sell, barter or trade in any way, than any other member in the family, save by the authority of those who send them.

18. It is contrary to good order for any persons except the Ministry and Elders, to have correspondence with the Deacons or Trustees, relative to their official lot and calling, such as their bargains and contracts in general, except in cases wherein they are by them employed to do business, in union with the Elders, and in such a manner as the nature of the case may require. But it is reasonable and consistent for members to know the market prices of articles bought or sold, as groceries, dry goods, provisions, hard ware and other wares if they desire to. But it should be understood that the Deacons are under no ob-

ligation to tell common members just what they paid for articles sold; but they should be free to tell the market prices.

19. The order of God forbids that Believers should lend money upon usury (or interest) to their brethren of the household of faith, neither should Believers accept interest (or usury) from their brethren, should it be offered.

24. A supply of such small tools and articles as sisters need, which brethren make, should be made by order of the Deacons, and delivered to the Deaconesses, to whom the sisters should apply for the same, when desired.

25. If sisters desire tools, conveniences, or articles of manufacture which come in the brethren's line of business, and which it would require much time to make, they must apply to the Deaconesses, but if it be small chores, they may apply to either Deacons or Deaconesses for the same.

26. When brethren need help of the sisters in their line of business, that will require much time, they must make application to the Deacons, but if it be small chores, they may apply to either Deacons or Deaconesses, as the case may require.

27. No work done in the family for sale, shall go out of the family save by the knowledge and direction of the Deacons & Deaconesses, except in some uncommon emergency, and then a correct account should be rendered as soon as may be.

Source: "The Millennial Laws," in Edward Deming Andrews, THE PEOPLE CALLED SHAKERS: A SEARCH FOR THE PERFECT SOCIETY, new enlarged ed. (Cambridge: Harvard University Press, 1963), 256–60.

Shaker Covenant

The Shaker economic system was based on community property. The following excerpts from the Shaker covenant at the Pleasant Hill community in Kentucky illustrate the legal form Shaker communalism took.

Art. 6.—We further consent and agree, that it is and shall be the special duty of the Deacons and Trustees . . . to have the immediate charge and oversight of all and singular the property, estate, and interest dedicated, devoted, and given up as aforesaid; and it shall be the duty of the said Deacons or Trustees to appropriate, use, and improve the said united interest, for the benefit of the Church, for the relief of the poor, and for such other charitable and religious purposes as the Gospel may require, and as the said Deacons or Trustees in their wisdom shall see fit.

Provided nevertheless, that all the transactions of the said Deacons or Trustees, in their care, management, and disposal of the foresaid interests, shall be for the benefit and privilege and on behalf of the Church, (to which the said Deacons and Trustees are and shall be held responsible,) and not for any personal or private interests, object or purpose whatever.

Art. 8. . . . we do by virtue of this convenant solemnly and conscientiously, jointly and individually, for ourselves, our heirs, and assigns, promise and declare, in the presence of God and of each other, and to all men, that we will never hereafter, either directly or indirectly, make nor require any account of any interests, property, labour, or service, which has been or may be devoted by us or any of us to the purpose before said, nor bring any charge of debt or damage, nor hold any demand whatever against the Church, nor against any member or members thereof, on account of any property or services given, rendered, devoted, or consecrated to the aforesaid sacred or charitable purposes.

Source: John Finch, "Notes of Travel in the United States, Letter IV," in THE NEW MORAL WORLD, 3d series, no. 5 (February 3, 1844): 249.

AMANA, OR THE COMMUNITY OF TRUE INSPIRATION

One of the most economically successful communities was the German pietist commune Amana. Known today for the manufacture of appliances, Amana was first established as the Ebenezer Society in New York State, just east of Buffalo. As Buffalo expanded, the leaders decided to move west; therefore, after thirteen years in upstate New York (1842–1855), Amana moved to Iowa, where it continued as a community until 1932. In Iowa seven villages were established, all of which still exist and attract large numbers of tourists.

The Community of True Inspiration traces its origin to 1714 and the teachings of Eberhard Ludwig Gruber (d. 1728) and Johann Friedrich Rock (1678?–1749). It was led by Christian Metz (1793–1867) and Barbara Heinemann (1795–1883), who believed they were inspired by God to lead the sect and that they continued to receive direct messages from God. The theological basis and social cohesion of the society rested on such continuing revelations—true inspiration. These revelations ranged from the very general to those dealing with specific questions of daily life.

The Twenty-One Rules for the Examination of Our Daily Lives

I. Obey, without reasoning, God, and through God your superiors.
II. Study quiet, or serenity, within and without.

III. Within, to rule and master your thoughts.

IV. Without, to avoid all unnecessary words, and still to study silence and quiet.

V. Abandon self, with all its desires, knowledge and power.

VI. Do not criticize others, either for good or evil, neither to judge nor to imitate them; therefore contain yourself, remain at home, in the house and in your heart.

VII. Do not disturb your serenity or peace of mind—hence neither desire nor grieve.

VIII. Live in love and pity toward your neighbor, and indulge neither anger nor impatience in your spirit.

XI. Be honest, sincere, and avoid all deceit and even secretiveness.

X. Count every word, thought, and work as done in the immediate presence of God, in sleeping and waking, eating, drinking, etc., and give Him at once an account of it, to see if all is done in His fear and love.

XI. Be in all things sober, without levity or laughter; and without vain and idle words, works or thoughts; much less heedless or idle.

XII. Never think or speak of God without the deepest reverence, fear, and love, and therefore deal reverently with all spiritual things.

XIII. Bear all inner and outward suffering in silence, complaining only to God; and accept all from Him in deepest reverence and obedience.

XIV. Notice carefully all that God permits to happen to you in your inner and outward life, in order that you may not fail to comprehend His will and to be led by it.

XV. Have nothing to do with unholy and particularly with needless business affairs.

XVI. Have no intercourse with worldly-minded men; never seek their society; speak little with them, and never without need; and then without fear and trembling.

XVII. Therefore, what you have to do with such men do in haste; do not waste time in public places and worldly society, that you be not tempted and led away.

XVIII. Fly from the society of women-kind as much as possible, as a very highly dangerous magnet and magical fire.

XIX. Avoid obeisance and the fear of men; these are dangerous ways.

XX. Dinners, weddings, feasts, avoid entirely; at the best there is sin.

XXI. Constantly practice abstinence and temperance, so that you may be as wakeful after eating as before.

The general tendency of these rules is clear: withdrawal or separation from the world and its temptations, which is precisely what the people of Amana did.

They established their communities so that they could live a simple life unburdened by the world. Their Constitution reflects this attitude.

Article I

The foundation of our civil organization is and shall remain forever God, the Lord, and the faith, which He worked in us according to His free grace and mercy, and which is founded upon (1) the word of God as revealed in the old and new testament; (2) the testimony of Jesus through the Spirit of Prophecy; (3) the hidden spirit of grace and chastisement.

The purpose of our association as a religious Society is therefore no worldly or selfish one, but the purpose of the love of God in His vocation of grace received by us, to serve Him in the bond of union, inwardly and outwardly, according to His laws and His requirements in our own consciences, and thus to work out the salvation of our souls, through the redeeming grace of Jesus Christ, in self-denial, in the obedience to our faith, and in the demonstration of our faithfulness in the inward and outward service of the Community by the power of grace which God presents us with.

And to fulfill this duty we do hereby covenant and promise collectively and each to the other by the acceptance and signing of this present Constitution.

Article II

In this bond of union tied by God amongst ourselves, it is our unanimous will and resolution that the land purchased here and that may hereafter be purchased shall be and remain a common estate and property, with all improvements thereupon and all appurtenances thereto, as also with all the labor, cares, troubles and burdens, of which each member shall bear his allotted share with a willing heart.

Article III

Agriculture and the raising of cattle and other domestic animals, in connection with some manufactures and trades shall under the blessing of God form the means of sustenance for this Society. Out of the income of the land and the other branches of industry the common expenses of the Society shall be defrayed.

The surplus, if any, shall from time to time be applied to the improvement of the common estate of the Society, to the building and maintaining of meeting and school houses, printing establishments, to the support and care of the old, sick and infirm members of the Society, to the founding of a business and safety fund, and to benevolent purposes in general.

Article IV

The control and management of all the affairs of this Society shall be vested in a Board of Trustees consisting of thirteen members, to be annually elected out of the number of Elders in the Community, by the members of the Society entitled to vote. The time, place, and manner of holding all elections for officers in this corporation and the qualifications of voters shall be regulated by by-laws to be adopted by the Community.

In the Trustees, so elected, we the undersigned members do hereby vest all the powers, rights of action and privileges granted to corporations by the laws of this State, and also all requisite power and authority to arrange, control, and manage, in brotherly concurrence according to our order of grace, or by a majority of votes, all the affairs and concerns of this corporation whatsoever; to receive new members under this Constitution; to assign to the members their work, labor and employment; to fix the amounts of the yearly allowances for the support of the members; to exclude, order away, and remove such members who are unruly and resisting, and who will not mend themselves after repeated admonition; to settle and liquidate the accounts of those members withdrawing from the Society, either by their own choice or by expulsion; to receive and to administrate all the active and passive property of the Society; to keep books and accounts of everything; to buy and to sell; to make, fulfill, and revoke contracts, to carry on agriculture, the rearing of cattle, manufactures, mills and trades of any kind, to erect buildings, to improve and take down the same; to make inventories; to appoint attorneys, agents, and managers; to borrow, lend and safely invest funds and money; also in the corporate name of the Society, or in the name of the Trustees, or of any member thereof to ask, demand, levy recover and receive all kinds of goods, moneys, principal and interest, effects, debts, demands, inheritances and legacies, wheresoever and whatsoever; to receive, execute and deliver all deeds, mortgages, notes, powers of attorney, receipts, and all other documents and accounts whatsoever; and to do, transact and carry out all needful, beneficial, legal, proper, just and equitable acts, matters and things in general of all and every kind whatsoever, all for and in the name, behalf and benefit of this corporation.

In the event however of matters of great importance and responsibility it shall be the duty of the Trustees to hold special meetings and to decide therein either by unanimous concurrence or by a majority of votes whether or not such matters shall be submitted for counsel and decision by vote to all the Elders of the Community and to the members entitled to vote.

Every member of this Society is, besides the free board and dwelling, and the support and care secured to him in old age, sickness and infirmity, further entitled out of the common fund to an annual sum of maintenance for him or herself, children and relatives in the Society; and these annual allowances shall be fixed by the Trustees for each member single or in families, according to justice and equity, and shall be from time to time revised and fixed anew, in accordance with a list to be kept thereof.

Source: Bertha M. H. Shambaugh, Amana That Was and Amana That Is (Iowa City: State Historical Association of Iowa, 1932), 243–44, 284–86, 288.

Oneida

The most infamous intentional community, religious or secular, of the nineteenth century, has to be Oneida. The practice of what they called "complex marriage" has fascinated the popular press for over a century. The fact that Oneida was one of the most successful communities economically (the modern manifestation is Oneida Silverplate) and socially gets lost in the concern over the community's communal sexual relations.

The basis of the Oneida Community was the teaching of John Humphrey Noyes (1811–1886), who preached Christian perfectionism. According to Noyes, the Second Coming of Christ had already occurred and the human race was therefore capable of something approaching perfection. Noyes did not preach that the members of the Oneida community were perfect, only that they were closer to the true Christianity of the Bible than the world around them.

In 1841 a group of his followers formed the Putney Society in Vermont. As a result of a prosecution brought for adultery based on the practice of the community, Noyes fled to New York in 1847. In 1848 he and his followers established a community in Oneida, New York. It lasted until 1881 and had branches in Wallingford, Connecticut, New York City, and elsewhere.

Complex marriage meant that everyone in the community was married to everyone else. All men and women were expected to have sexual relations, and did. The basis for complex marriage was Noyes's belief that the Pauline passage about there being no marriage in heaven meant that there should be no marriage on earth, but that no marriage did not mean no sex. The Shakers had drawn the opposite conclusion. But sex meant children; not only could the community not afford children in the early years, the women were not enthusiastic about a regime that would have kept them pregnant most of the time.

Noyes developed a distinction between amative and propagative love. Propagative love was sexual intercourse for the purpose of having children; amative love was sexual intercourse for the purpose of expressing love. The difference was what Noyes called "male continence" (coitus interruptus), in which the male partner avoided ejaculation. Noyes argued that not only did this keep them from producing unwanted children, but it also taught the male considerable self-control. The system worked very well.

Later, when the community could afford children, they undertook a eugenic experiment they called stirpiculture. If they were to have children, they decided it made sense to have the best children possible. The best, in this case, meant that the parents would be drawn from the spiritually most advanced members of the community. A community board decided who should have children, and Noyes fathered many of them.

The community practiced a system called Mutual Criticism as a means of defusing tension. It worked as follows:

System of Criticism

The mode of proceeding was this: any person wishing to be a criticized offered himself for this purpose at a meeting of the Association. His character then became the subject of special scrutiny by all the members of the Association, till the next meeting, when his trial took place. On the presentation of his case, each member in turn was called on to specify as far and as frankly as possible, everything objectionable in his character and conduct. In this way the person criticized had the advantage of a many-sided mirror in viewing himself, or perhaps it may be said, was placed in the focus of a spiritual lens composed of all the judgments in the Association. It very rarely happened that any complaint of injustice was made by the subject of the operation, and generally he received his chastening with fortitude, submission, and even gratitude, declaring that he felt himself relieved and purified by the process. Among the various objectionable features of the character under criticism, some one or two of the most prominent would usually elicit censure from the whole circle, and the judgment on these points would thus have the force of a unanimous verdict. Any soreness which might result from the operation was removed at the succeeding meeting by giving the patient a round of commendations. This system of open and kindly criticism (a sort of reversed substitute for tea-party back-biting in the world) became so attractive by its manifest good results, that every member of the Putney Association submitted to it in the course of the winter of 1846–7; and to this may be attributed much of the accelerated improvement which marked that period of their history. Instead of offences, abounding love and good works followed the letting loose of judgment.

This system was introduced to some extent at Oneida, but the number of members was so large, and their acquaintance with each other in many cases so limited, that it was found necessary to change the mode of proceeding, in order to make criticism lively and effective. Instead of subjecting volunteers for criticism to the scrutiny of the assembly, the Association appointed four of its most spiritual and discerning judges to criticize in course all the members. The critics themselves were first criticized by Mr. Noyes, and then gave themselves to their work, from day to day for three weeks, till they had passed judgment on every character in the Association. The method was first to ascertain as much as possible about the character of the individual about to be criticized, by inquiring among his associates, and then after discussing his character among themselves, to invite him to an interview, plainly tell him his faults, converse with him freely about his whole character, and give him their best advice.

Source: FIRST ANNUAL REPORT OF THE ONEIDA ASSOCIATION: EXHIBITING ITS HISTORY, PRINCIPLES, AND TRANSACTIONS TO JANUARY 1, 1849. PUBLISHED BY ORDER OF THE ASSOCIATION (Oneida Reserve: Leonard & Co., 1850).

Charles Fourier
Selections Describing the Phalanstery

Charles Fourier's writings were among the most influential of any of the utopian socialists. A number of communities in the United States, Brook Farm being the best known, followed Fourier's general ideas, although none of them came close to the size he believed was necessary for a successful community.

THE announcement does, I acknowledge, sound very improbable, of a method for combining three hundred families unequal in fortune, and rewarding each person,—man, woman, child—according to the three properties, *capital, labour, talent.* More than one reader will credit himself with humour when he remarks: "Let the author try to associate but three families, to reconcile three households in the same dwelling to social union, to arrangements of purchases and expenses, to perfect harmony in passions, character, and authority; when he shall have succeeded in reconciling three mistresses of associated households, we shall believe that he can succeed with thirty and with three hundred."

I have already replied to an argument which it is well to reproduce (for repetition will frequently be necessary here); I have observed *that as economy can spring only from large combinations, God had to create a social theory applicable to large masses and not to three or four families.*

An objection seemingly more reasonable, and which needs to be refuted more than once, is that of social discords. How conciliate the passions, the conflicting interests, the incompatible characters,—in short, the innumerable disparities which engender so much discord?

It may easily have been surmised that I shall make use of a lever entirely unknown, and whose properties cannot be judged until I shall have explained them. The passional contrasted Series draws its nourishment solely from those disparities which bewilder civilised policy; it acts like the husbandman who from a mass of filth draws the germs of abundance; the refuse, the dirt, and impure matter which would serve only to defile and infect our dwellings, are for him the sources of wealth.

If social experiments have miscarried, it is because some fatality has impelled all speculators to work with bodies of poor people whom they subjected to a *monastic-industrial* discipline, chief obstacle to the working of the series. Here, as in everything else, it is ever SIMPLISM (*simplisme*) which misleads the civilised, obstinately sticking to experiments with combinations of the poor; they cannot elevate themselves to the conception of a trial with combinations of the rich. They are veritable Lemning rats (migrating rats of Lapland), preferring drowning in a pond to deviating from the route which they have decided upon.

It is necessary for a company of 1,530 to 1,600 persons to have a stretch of land comprising a good square league. . . .

The land should be provided with a fine stream of water; it should be intersected by hills, and adapted to varied cultivation; it should be contiguous to a forest, and not far removed from a large city, but sufficiently so to escape intruders.

The experimental Phalanx standing alone, and without the support of neighbouring phalanxes, will, in consequence of this isolation, have so many gaps in attraction, and so many passional calms to dread in its workings, that it will be necessary to provide it with the aid of a good location fitted for a variety of functions. A flat country such as Antwerp, Leipsic, Orleans, would be totally unsuitable, and would cause many Series to fail, owing to the uniformity of the land surface. It will, therefore, be necessary to select a diversified region, like the surroundings of Lausanne, or, at the very least, a fine valley provided with a stream of water and a forest, like the valley of Brussels or of Halle. A fine location near Paris would be the stretch of country lying between Poissy and Confleurs, Poissy and Menlan.

A company will be collected consisting of from 1,500 to 1,600 persons of graduated degrees of fortune, age, character, of theoretical and practical knowledge; care will be taken to secure the greatest amount of variety possible, for the greater the number of variations either in the passions or the faculties of the members, the easier will it be to make them harmonise in a short space of time.

In this district devoted to experiment, there ought to be combined every species of practicable cultivation, including that in conservatories and hot-houses; in addition, there ought to be at least three accessory factories, to be used in winter and on rainy days; furthermore, various practical branches of science and the arts, independent of the schools.

Above all, it will be necessary to fix the valuation of the capital invested in shares; lands, materials, flocks, implements, etc. This point ought, it seems, to be among the first to receive attention; I think it best to dismiss it here. I shall limit myself to remarking that all these investments in transferable shares and stock-coupons will be represented.

A great difficulty to be overcome in the experimental Phalanx will be the formation of the ties of high mechanism or collective bonds of the Series, before the close of the first season. It will be necessary to accomplish the passional union of the mass of the members; to lead them to collective and individual devotion to the maintenance of the Phalanx, and, especially, to perfect harmony regarding the division of the profits, according to the three factors, *Capital, Labour, Talent.* . . .

We shall see in the chapter on hiatuses of attraction, that the first Phalanx will, in consequence of its social isolation and other impediments inherent to the experimental canton, have twelve special obstacles to overcome, obstacles which the Phalanxes subsequently founded would not have to contend with. That is why it is so important that the experimental canton should have the assistance coming from field-work prolonged eight or nine months, like that in Naples and Lisbon.

As for the selection to be made among the candidates, rich and poor, various qualities which are accounted vicious or useless in civilisation should be looked for; such are:

A good ear for music.
Good manners of families.
Aptitude for the fine arts.

And various rules which are contrary to philosophic ideas should be followed.

To prefer families having few children.
To have one-third of the organisation consist of celibates.
To seek characters regarded as peculiar.
To establish a graduated scale respecting age, fortune, knowledge.

In view of the necessity of uniform education and fusion of the classes among children, I have advised, what I now reiterate, the selection, for the experimental Phalanx, of well-bred families, particularly in the lower class, since it will be necessary to have that class mingle in labour with the rich, and to make the latter find a charm in this amalgamation. That charm will be greatly dependent upon the good breeding of the inferiors; that is why the people in the environs of Paris, Blois, and Tours will be very suitable for the trial, provided, of course, that a proper selection is made.

Let us proceed with the details of composition.

At least seven-eighths of the members ought to be cultivators and manufacturers; the remainder will consist of capitalists, scholars, and artists.

The Phalanx would be badly graded and difficult to balance, if among its capitalists there were several having 100,000 francs, several 50,000 francs, without intermediate fortunes. In such a case it would be necessary to seek to procure intermediate fortunes of 60,000, 70,000, 80,000, 90,000 francs. The Phalanx best graduated in every respect raises social harmony and profits to the highest degree. . . .

The edifice occupied by a Phalanx does not in any way resemble our constructions, whether of the city or country; and none of our buildings could be used to establish a large Harmony of 1,600 persons,—not even a great palace like Versailles, nor a great monastery like the Escurial. If, for the purposes of experiment, only an inconsiderable Harmony of 200 or 300 members, or a *hongrée* of 400 members is organised, a monastery or a palace (Meudon) could be used for it.

The lodgings, plantations, and stables of a Society conducted on the plan of Series of groups, must differ vastly from our villages and country towns, which are intended for families having no social connection, and which act in a perverse manner; in place of that class of little houses which rival each other in filth and ungainliness in our little towns, a Phalanx constructs an edifice for itself which is as regular as the ground permits: here is a sketch of distribution for a location favourable to development.

The central part of the Palace or Phalanstery ought to be appropriated to peaceful uses, and contain the dining-halls, halls for finance, libraries, study, etc. In this central portion are located the place of worship, the *tour d'ordre,* the telegraph, the post-office boxes, the chimes for ceremonials, the observatory, the winter court adorned with resinous plants, and situated in the rear of the parade-court.

One of the wings ought to combine all the noisy workshops, such as the carpenter-shop, the forge, all hammer-work; it ought to contain also all the industrial gatherings of children, who are generally very noisy in industry and even in music. This combination will obviate a great annoyance of our civilised cities, where we find some man working with a hammer in every street, some dealer in iron or tyro on the clarionet, who shatter the tympanum of fifty families in the vicinity.

The other wing ought to contain the caravansary with its ballrooms and its halls appropriated to intercourse with outsiders, so that these may not encumber the central portion of the palace and embarrass the domestic relations of the Phalanx.

The Phalanstery, or edifice of the experimental Phalanx, ought to be constructed of inexpensive material,—wood, brick, etc., because, I repeat, it would be impossible in that first attempt to determine precisely the dimensions suitable either for each individual seristery, the portion designed for the public relations of the series, or for the various workshops, storerooms, stables, etc. . . .

The most poverty-stricken of the Harmonians, a man who hasn't a farthing, gets into a vehicle in a portico well heated and inclosed; he goes from the Palace to the stables through paved and gravelled underground passages; he passes from his dwelling to the public halls and the workshops through galleried streets which are heated in winter and ventilated in summer. In Harmony one can pass through the workshops, stables, shops, ball-rooms, banquet and assembly-halls, etc., in January, without knowing whether it is rainy or windy, hot or cold; and the details which I shall give upon this subject authorise me to say that if the civilised after 3,000 years of research have not yet learned how to house themselves, it is little surprising that they have not yet learned to direct and harmonise their passions. When one fails in the pettiest material calculations, one may well fail in the great calculations concerning the passions. . . .

The galleried street, or continued Peristyle, is located in the second story. It is not adaptable to the ground floor, which must have openings at various points to admit of archways for vehicles.

Those who have seen the gallery of the Louvre, or *Musée de Paris*, may consider it as a model of the galleried street of Harmony—which will likewise have a floor and be placed in the second story—save the difference in the openings and in height. . . .

One is dazzled by lingering a few moments over a picture of the enormous benefits which would be derived from the union of 300 households, in a single edifice, where they would find apartments at various prices, covered ways from part to part, tables of different classes, varied kinds of occupation—in short, everything that tends to shorten and facilitate labour and to render it attractive. . . .

Combined administration gives rise to a multitude of economies as to doings which we consider productive; for example,—three hundred families of an agricultural village send to the markets, not once, but twenty times in the course of a year. The peasant delights in loitering about in the market-places and taverns; though he have nothing but a bushel of beans, he spends an entire day in the city. And for the three hundred families, this constitutes an average loss of 6,000 days of labour, not including the cost of transportation, which is twenty times greater than in association, which sells all its commodities in large quantities, since, in that order, purchases are made only for Phalanxes numbering about 1,500 individuals.

While economising in the complication of sales—the abuse of sending three hundred persons to the markets instead of one, conducting three hundred negotiations instead of one,—economy is at the same time effected in the complication of labour. If a canton sells 3,000 quintals of wheat to three other cantons, the work of grinding and baking will not extend to nine hundred householders, but only to three. Thus, after saving 99 per cent. in distributive labour in the sales, this saving will be repeated in the labour and management of the consumer. There will, therefore, be a double saving of 99 per cent.: and how many more of a similar kind will occur!

Let us observe, in this connection that associative economy is almost always of a composite order; like that which to the saving of expense to the vendor adds, by way of counter-stroke, the saving of expense to the consumer. . . .

There is nothing in which economy is recognised as more urgently needed than in fuel; this economy assumes vast proportions in the associative state; a Phalanx has only five kitchens in place of three hundred; namely:

The administrative, or extra;
The first, second, and third classes.
The provision for animals.
The whole can be supplied by three great fires, which, compared to the
   300 fires of a village, brings the economy in fuel to nine-tenths.

It will be no less enormous in shop fires: it will be seen in the treatise upon the passionate Series, that their groups, whether in their relations in domestic or in manufacturing industry, their relations in pleasure, balls, etc., always operate in large companies and in connecting halls or *Seristeries,* furnished with steam-stoves which it is necessary to heat only three hours for the twenty-four. Individual fires are very rare, except in the coldest part of winter, each one as a rule seldom returning to his quarters before the hour of retiring, when he contents himself with a little brasier while undressing.

Moreover, the cold is not felt in the interior of the phalanstery; every portion of the main buildings is provided with covered galleries, by means of which one can communicate with all parts, sheltered from the inclemencies of the weather. People can go to the workshops, the dining-halls, to balls and assemblies without needing furs or boots, without exposing themselves to colds or inflammations. The closed communication extends even from the phalanstery to the stables, by underground gravelled passages or by galleries supported upon columns at the level of the second floor.

I have just passed in review some of the associative savings: a successive examination of these shows them to amount always to three-fourths or nine-tenths, and frequently to ninety-nine hundredths. We have found it so in the case of the markets, the sale and purchase of commodities; even in petty concerns which one does not to-day deign to take into account, and which assume great importance when the saving amounts to ninety-nine in a hundred, or even to forty-nine in fifty, like that of the milk-women. If a village is situated near a city, we find that the three hundred families will sometimes send a hundred milk-women with a hundred cans of milk, the sale and transportation of which cause these women to lose a hundred mornings. I have observed that they can be replaced by a small cart drawn by an ass, and driven by a woman; a gain of forty-nine fiftieths. The saving is doubled when we consider that the woman, distributing in two or three great establishments (called progressive households, which will constitute the associative *régime* of the cities), will return home in half the time which it would have taken the hundred women: this is a real gain of ninety-nine per cent., in time and in people.

The instances of saving I have just cited all relate to activities already known and practised; we might enumerate a host of others which turn upon activities to be dispensed with: I shall term them *negative* savings,—in contradistinction to the preceding, which are *positive,* or diminution of labour without abolishment of the service.

Let us define some kind of labour to be dispensed with, or negative gain of Association: there is one that assumes vast proportions, and that is, the precautions against theft.

The danger of theft obliges three hundred families of a village, or at least the hundred in easiest circumstances, to make an unproductive outlay in enclosure—walls, barricades, fastenings, landmarks, dogs, ditches, day and night watchmen, and other means of defence against thieves. These useless and expensive devices will be done away with in Association, which possesses the property of preventing larceny, and dispensing with all precautions against danger. We shall see this farther on.

Under associative conditions, it would be impossible for the thief to reap any profit from the thing stolen, excepting in the case of money;—but a people who live in ease and are imbued with sentiments of honour do not even conceive any projects for stealing. It will be shown that children, so essentially robbers of fruit, would not, in the associative state, take an apple off a tree. . . .

In work, as in pleasure, variety is evidently the desire of nature. Any enjoyment prolonged, without interruption, beyond two hours, conduces to satiety, to abuse, blunts our faculties, and exhausts pleasure. A repast of four hours will not pass off without excess; an opera of four hours will end by cloying the spectator. Periodical variety is a necessity of the body and of the soul, a necessity in all nature; even the soil requires alteration of seeds, and seed alteration of soil. The stomach will soon reject the best dish if it be offered every day, and the soul will be blunted in the exercise of any virtue if it be not relieved by some other virtue.

If there is need of variety in pleasure after indulging in it for two hours, so much the more does labour require this diversity, which is continual in the associative state, and is guaranteed to the poor as well as the rich.

The chief source of light-heartedness among Harmonians is the frequent change of sessions. Life is a perpetual torment to our workmen, who are obliged to spend twelve, and frequently fifteen, consecutive hours in some tedious labour. Even ministers are not exempt; we find some of them complain of having passed an entire day in the stupefying task of affixing signatures to thousands of official vouchers. Such wearisome duties are unknown in the associative order; the Harmonians, who devote an hour, an hour and a half, or at most two hours, to the different sessions, and who, in these short sessions, are sustained by cabalistic impulses and by friendly union with selected associates, cannot fail to bring and to find cheerfulness everywhere.

Charles Fourier (1772–1837) was one of the nineteenth-century utopian socialists who proposed community settlements as a means of bringing about a better society.

Source: SELECTIONS FROM THE WORKS OF CHARLES FOURIER, ed. Ch[arles] Gide, trans. Julia Franklin (London: Swan Sonnenschein, 1901), 137–154, 167–168.

AMERICAN FOURIERISM

Charles Fourier's ideas were communicated to the American public by Albert Brisbane (1809–1890) and Horace Greeley (1811–1872), a prominent journalist, newspaper editor, and politician. Fourierist groups sprang up in many places, as did communes loosely based on Fourier's ideas. None of these communes came close to realizing the plan Fourier outlined, but they all assumed that they could reach those goals in the near future.

The most striking difference between the Fourieristic phalanx and the plans put forth for most other communities was that Fourier rejected community property and proposed a joint-stock partnership instead. According to Fourier, each person who joined the community would, if possible, purchase some stock. He also relied on finding some wealthy people who might not want to join the community at the outset but would be willing to provide the risk capital to start a phalanx on the assumption that they would make a profit. Members would be paid for their work and would pay for their board and lodging; they would also accumulate stock in the enterprise.

Albert Brisbane
Association

All lands, machinery, implements, furniture, or other objects brought by members into the Association, are appraised at their cash value, and represented, as well as the moneyed capital paid in, by transferable shares, which are secured upon the personal and real Estate of the Association—that is, upon its domain, edifices, flocks, manufactories, etc. The Council transfers to each person the value in shares of the objects which he has furnished. A person may be a member without being a stockholder, or a stockholder without being a member.

The annual profits of the association are, after the inventory is taken, divided into three unequal portions, and paid as follows:

Seven-twelfths to LABOR.
Three-twelfths to CAPITAL.
Two-twelfths to practical and theoretical KNOWLEDGE—or to SKILL.

The Council, which has charge of the financial department, advances to those members who do not possess any capital or fixed property, food, clothing and lodging for a year. No risk is run in making this advance, for it is known that the product of the labor, which each individual will perform by ATTRACTION or PLEASURE, will exceed in amount the advances made to him; and that the Association, on balancing its accounts at the yearly settlement, will be debtor to the members to whom it made the advance of a MINIMUM.

This Minimum, or sufficiency of worldly goods, will comprise:

Meals at the table of the first price.
A decent dress, and working costumes; besides all implements necessary to their industrial occupations.
A room and bed-room for each individual, and admission to the public halls and saloons, and to all places of amusement.

Brisbane also describes the main building of the phalanx and, in doing so, comments on the social relations.

The square or oblong form should be avoided, as it is both monotonous and heavy. The centre of the Edifice should be the most striking and elegant part of the building, and would be reserved for public purposes and uses.

From the centre, the Wings would project at right angles, and the sub-wings would fall off to the right and left from the main wings. The projecting wings and centre would form a spacious area or square, where large assemblages could be held and celebrations take place.

To avoid giving too great an extension to the building it should be three stories high, and rest upon a spacious basement. In the basement would be located the kitchens, storerooms, some workshops and public halls, etc.

The centre of the Edifice will be reserved, as we said, for public purposes; it will contain the Dining-Halls, Council-Rooms, Library, Reading-Rooms, Lecture-Rooms, Saloons for social unions and the Exchange. An Association, however small, must have its Exchange, where the members can meet to discuss their industrial interests, concert meetings of the groups and series, and transact a variety of business.

From the centre of the Edifice will rise a tower which will overlook the Domain, and communicate, by signals and other means, with all parts of it. A large and opulent Association would have an Observatory, which would be placed in this tower.

The Church would be a separate building in order to give it size; it should be situated near the main Edifice and communicate with it by a covered corridor. In a small Association, the Church could incorporated in the main building.

The Manufactories and Workshops or in the language of Association, the Halls of Industry, would be located in one of the extreme wings. In a small Association, they might be situated in a separate building, as the wings would not be distant enough from the centre to prevent the noise from incommoding the inhabitants.

The public Halls would be distinct in their appropriations for different purposes; they would, with a few exceptions, consist of a number of contiguous saloons, so as to admit of subdivisions in all social unions, meetings, etc. A ball or banquet forms at present but one assemblage, without subdivisions; this confusion will not take place in Association; there would not be, to choose the mode of eating as an example, one vast hall, where all the members, old and young, would dine together; on the contrary, a large Association would have several public banquet halls.

One for persons extremely advanced in age.
Two for children.
Two for tables of the second or middle price.
One for table of the third or higher price.

These different prices are established to suit different tastes, degrees of fortune and the desire of economy; variety is a source of concord, when people possess full liberty to choose and the means of doing so.

In a small Association, three dining-halls would be sufficient: one for children, and two for tables at different prices; this degree of variety at least should be observed. Adjoining the public saloons, small dining-rooms should be fitted up, where parties or groups could eat apart from the large tables. It will happen daily that parties of friends will wish to dine by themselves: they can do so in these rooms, where they will be served in the same manner and at the same price as at the large tables. It will be very little additional trouble to serve meals in them, and as such a distribution of dining halls will promote greatly freedom of choice, and add to individual liberty and comfort, it should not be neglected. People can, if they wish, dine also in their private apartments by paying a small extra charge.

Albert Brisbane (1809–1890) was the primary American advocate of Fourierism.

Source: Albert Brisbane, Association; or, A Concise Exposition of the Practical Part of Fourier's Social Science (New York: Greeley & McElrath, 1843; reprint, New York: AMS Press, 1975), 20, 32.

Charles Henri de Saint-Simon
Sketch of a New Political System

Sixth Letter

I shall show what course the House of Commons (composed, as I said in the previous letter, of the industrial chiefs) should have followed. In order to explain myself more resolutely and more quickly, I shall allow the House itself to speak:

'A first Chamber will be formed and called the Chamber of *Invention*.

'This Chamber will consist of three hundred members, and will be divided into three sections which may meet separately but whose work will only be official when they deliberate together.

'Each section will be able to call a joint meeting of the three sections.

'The first section will consist of two hundred civil engineers; the second of fifty poets and other literary inventors; and the third of twenty-five painters, fifteen sculptors and architects, and ten musicians.

'This Chamber will apply itself to the following tasks:

'At the end of the first year of its formation it will present a project for public works to be undertaken in order to increase France's wealth and improve the condition of its inhabitants in every useful and pleasing respect. Then, each year it will give its advice on additions to be made to its original project and on ways in which it thinks it might be improved.

'Drainage, land clearance, road building, the opening up of canals will be considered the most important part of this project. The roads and canals to be built should not be conceived only as a means of facilitating transport; their construction should be planned so as to make them as pleasant as possible for travellers (1).

'This Chamber will present another report providing a project for public festivals.

'These festivals will be of two kinds: festivals of *hope* and festivals of *remembrance*.

'These festivals will be celebrated successively in the capital and chief towns of the departments and cantons, so that capable orators (who will never be very numerous) may spread the benefits of their eloquence.

'In the festivals of *hope* the orators will explain to the people the plans for public works approved by Parliament, and they will encourage the citizens to work with energy, by showing them how their condition will improve once the plans are executed.

'In the festivals dedicated to *remembrance* it will be the task of the orators to show the people how their present position is better than that of their ancestors.

'The nucleus of the Chamber of Invention will consist of:

'The eighty-six chief engineers for bridges and roads in the departments;
'The forty members of the French Academy;
'The painters, sculptors, and musicians in the Institute.

'Each member of this Chamber will enjoy an annual salary of 10,000 francs.

'Every year a sum of twelve millions will be placed at the disposal of this Chamber to be employed to promote the inventions it considers useful. The first section will dispose of eight millions, and the other two sections will have two millions each.

'The nucleus will itself arrange for the rest of the seats in the Chamber to be filled.

'The Chamber will constitute itself, that is, it will determine who may vote and who may stand for election. Its members may not be elected for more than five years, but they will be eligible for re-election indefinitely, and the Chamber may adopt whatever method of substitution it chooses.

'This Chamber may have one hundred national and fifty foreign associate members. The associates will have the right to sit in the Chamber, and will have a consultative vote.

'A second chamber will be formed with the name Chamber of *Examination*.

'This Chamber will consist of three hundred members: one hundred physicists working on the physics of organic bodies, one hundred working on the physics of inorganic bodies, and one hundred mathematicians.

'This Chamber will be given three tasks:

'It will examine all the projects presented by the first Chamber, and will give its detailed and reasoned opinion on each of them.

'It will draw up a project for general public education, which will be divided into three grades of teaching, for citizens of three different levels of wealth. Its aim will be to ensure that young people are as capable as possible of conceiving, directing, and carrying out useful work.

'As every citizen is at perfect liberty to practise whatever religion he chooses, and may consequently bring up his children in the one he prefers, on no account should there be any question of religion in the Chamber's education project. When the project has been approved by the other two Chambers, the Chamber of Examination will be responsible for its execution and will continue to supervise public education.

'The third task involving this Chamber should be a project for public festivals of the following kind: men's festivals, women's festivals, boys' festivals, girls' festivals, fathers' and mothers' festivals, children's festivals, managers' festivals, workers' festivals. In each of these festivals orators nominated by the Chamber of Examination will make speeches on the social duties of those in whose honour the festival is being celebrated.

'Each member of this Chamber will enjoy an annual salary of 10,000 francs.

'Every year a sum of twenty-five millions will be placed at the disposal of this Chamber, to be employed on the expenditure required by public schools and on ways of hastening the progress of the physical and mathematical sciences.

'The Chamber of *Examination* will be constituted according to the same conditions as the Chamber of *Invention*.

'The Class of Physical and Mathematical Sciences at the Institute will provide the nucleus of this Chamber.

'The Chamber of Examination may have one hundred national and fifty foreign associate members, who will have consultative votes.

'The House of Commons will be reconstituted once the first two Chambers have been formed. It will then assume the name Chamber of Execution.

'This Chamber will take care that in its new composition every branch of industry is represented, and that each branch has a number of deputies proportionate to its importance.

'The members of the Chamber of Execution will not have any salary, since they should all be rich, being chosen from the most important heads of industrial houses.

'The Chamber of Execution will supervise the execution of all approved projects. It alone will be responsible for the imposition and collection of taxes.

'The three Chambers will together form the new Parliament, which will be invested with sovereign power, constitutional as well as legislative.

'Each of the three Chambers will have the right to summon Parliament.

'The Chamber of Execution will be able to direct the attention of the other two Chambers to those subjects it considers suitable.

'Thus, every project will be presented by the first Chamber, examined by the second, and will only be definitely adopted by the third.

'If a project presented by the first Chamber is ever rejected by the second, in order to save time it will be sent back to the first without being considered by the third.'

Now, my dear fellow countrymen, I shall tell you the first three things the new Parliament should have done. I shall speak in its name, in the same way that I have just expressed myself in the name of the House of Commons.

'All Frenchmen (and jurists in particular) will be invited to propose a new system of civil laws and a new system of criminal laws in conformity with the new political system. Property should be reconstituted and founded on a basis which will render it most favourable to production.

'All projects presented to Parliament will be published at the nation's expense. Parliament will choose the best projects for civil and criminal codes. It will give an important reward to their authors, and will admit them to the Chambers when their codes are discussed, giving them a consultative vote in this discussion.

'All Frenchmen (and military engineers in particular) will be invited to present a project for the general defence of the territory. This project should be conceived so as to require the smallest possible number of standing troops. The authors of these works should not lose sight of the fact that all means employed for the defence of our territory will become useless and will have to be abandoned as soon as neighbouring peoples adopt the same political system as the French nation.

'A national reward will be given to the author of the plan which is preferred.

'A loan of two thousand millions will be contracted with a sinking fund, to indemnify those persons with financial interests damaged by the establishment of the new political system.

'A national reward will be given to the author of the work which best fulfils the following three conditions:

'1. It must prove the superiority of the new political system over the old.
'2. It must establish the best method of allocating the indemnity of two thousand millions granted to those whose interests are damaged by the establishment of the new system.
'3. It must show that the sum of two thousand millions granted as indemnity to persons interested in opposing the establishment of the new system is extremely insignificant compared with the advantages that the peaceful establishment of the liberal regime will secure for the nation.'

There, my dear fellow countrymen, is the first survey of what I think we should have done, what we must do.

AUTHOR'S NOTE

1. Fifty thousand acres of land (more, if it is thought right) will be chosen from the most picturesque sites crossed by roads or canals. This ground will be authorised for use as resting-places for travellers and holiday resorts for the inhabitants of the neighbourhood.

Each of these gardens will contain a museum of both natural and industrial products of the surrounding districts. They will also include dwellings for artists who want to stop there, and a certain number of musicians will always be maintained there to inspire the inhabitants of the canton with that passion whose development is necessary for the greatest good of the nation.

The whole of French soil should be turned into a superb English park, adorned with all that the fine arts can add to the beauties of nature. For a long time luxury has been concentrated in the palaces of kings, the residences of princes, the mansions and châteaux of a few powerful men. This concentration is most detrimental to the general interests of society, because it tends to establish two different grades of civilisation, one for persons whose intelligence is developed through habitual viewing of productions of the fine arts, and one for men whose imaginative faculties undergo no development, since the material work in which they are exclusively engaged does not stimulate their intelligence.

Present circumstances favour making luxury national. Luxury will become useful and moral when it is enjoyed by the whole nation. The honour and advantage of employing directly, in political arrangements, the progress of the exact sciences and of the fine arts since the brilliant age of their regeneration, have been reserved for our century.

Charles Henri Saint-Simon (1760–1825) was a French utopian socialist.

Source: HENRI SAINT-SIMON (1760–1825): SELECTED WRITINGS ON SCIENCE, INDUSTRY AND SOCIAL ORGANISATION, ed. and trans. Keith Taylor (London: Croom Helm, 1975), 202–6.

John Adolphus Etzler

The Paradise within Reach of All Men, without Labour, by Powers of Nature and Machinery.

More than any other early socialist, J. A. Etzler believed that technology would bring plenty and equality, and himself invented a self-propelled plow and a wave-powered boat.

I promise to show the means for creating a paradise within ten years, where every thing desirable for human life may be had for every man in superabundance, without labor, without pay; where the whole face of nature is changed into the most beautiful form of which it is capable; where man may live in the most magnificent palaces, in all imaginable refinements of luxury, in the most delightful gardens; where he may accomplish, without his labor, in one year more than hitherto could be done in thousands of years; he may level mountains, sink valleys, create lakes, drain lakes and swamps, intersect everywhere the land with beautiful canals, with roads for transporting heavy loads of many thousand tuns, and for travelling 1000 miles in 24 hours; he may cover the ocean with floating islands moveable in any desired direction with immense power and celerity, in perfect security and in all comforts and luxury, bearing gardens, palaces, with thousands of families, provided with rivulets of sweet water; he may explore the interior of the globe, travel from pole to pole in a fortnight; he may provide himself with means unheard of yet, for increasing his knowledge of the world, and so his intelligence, he may lead a life of continual happiness, of enjoyments unknown yet, he may free himself from almost all the evils that afflict mankind, except death, and even put death far beyond the common period of human life, and finally render it less afflicting: mankind may thus live in, and enjoy a new world far superior to our present, and raise themselves to a far higher scale of beings.

John Adolphus Etzler (?1796–1860) was a German-American socialist and inventor and technologically the most innovative of the early socialist writers.

Source: John Adolphus Etzler, THE PARADISE WITHIN REACH OF ALL MEN, WITHOUT LABOUR, BY POWERS OF NATURE AND MACHINERY, 2 parts (Pittsburgh: Etzler and Reinhold, 1833), 1–2.

Robert Owen
The Book of the New Moral World

Chapter VII

'On the new classification of society, according to age and experience, and the eternal laws of humanity.'

As all men are born ignorant and inexperienced, and must receive their knowledge either from the instincts of their nature, which are given to them at their birth, or from surrounding external objects, animate and inanimate, which they do not create; all, by nature, have equal rights. Neither can it be justly said, that anything formed without its knowledge can have more merit or demerit from being what it is, than another. All men partake of the same general qualities of human nature, in such proportions, and under such combinations as are given to them by the Power which gives to them, and all things, their existence.

The distinctions of class and station are artificial, and have been conceived and adopted by men, while they were ignorant, inexperienced, and irrational. The errors and evils of this classification have been stated in previous parts of this book, and it is now proposed to introduce measures, gradually to supersede them by the natural and rational divisions, into which, experience will prove, it will be greatly for the interest and happiness of all, that society should resolve itself. It may be stated as a first principle of justice, that, 'NO MAN HAS A RIGHT TO REQUIRE ANOTHER MAN TO DO FOR HIM, WHAT HE WILL NOT DO FOR THAT MAN; OR, IN OTHER WORDS ALL MEN, BY NATURE, HAVE EQUAL RIGHTS.

The natural and rational classification of society, when adopted, will for ever preserve those rights inviolate; and it is, beyond all estimate, for the interest and happiness of the human race, that this classification should be universally adopted, for it will calm the evil passions, terminate every contest, private and public, individual and national, and introduce order and wisdom, instead of chaos and irrationality, into all the affairs of mankind.

The futile, petty disputes between men and nations, about matters of no real interest to the well-being of society, would cease; a new spirit of equity, justice, charity, and kindness, would be created, and pervade the population of the world; more, for the permanent well-doing and happiness of mankind, would be effected in one year, than can be accomplished, under the existing classification of society in a century, or, indeed, within any given period of time.

The natural and rational classification of the human race, is the classification of age—each division of age having the occupations to perform, for which each age is best adapted by nature.

By this classification, the causes of the evils with which the human race is now afflicted, will be permanently removed: and whatever is to be done will be effected in a superior manner, willingly, cheerfully, and with high gratification to every one.

There will be no occupation requisite to be performed by one, which will not be equally performed by all; and by all under this system, far more willingly than any of the general affairs of life are now performed by any class, from the sovereign to the pauper. In the present irrational state of the human mind, and human affairs, no one can form a true conception of what individuals may be trained and educated to acquire and accomplish at their various periods of life.

Because it is yet unknown what are the capabilities of human nature when it shall not be forced to imbibe error and falsehood from its birth;—when it shall not be daily trained in most injurious habits and artificial manners;—when it shall be taught truth only, by every word, look, and action of all around it;—when it shall be educated to acquire the best habits for its own happiness, and the well-being of society;—when it shall attain the individual self-sustaining manners, which, by such training, will naturally arise, and ensure pleasure, by its variety, to all;—when it shall possess the valuable knowledge which by such training and education will be given to it;—and when it shall acquire the facilities in the practice of the operations of society, in which, as it advances in life, it will be instructed.

It may be, however, confidently stated, that each individual thus trained, educated, and placed, would acquire far more valuable knowledge and power and accomplish more, and in a superior manner, than great numbers of the human race can acquire or accomplish, under the training, education, and classification of the existing system, founded on, and emanating from, the absurd notions of man's free-will in forming his own convictions, feelings, and general character.

It is, however, somewhat difficult, previous to additional experience, to decide, very accurately, what should be the precise permanent divisions of human life, to form the best classification. But there is now sufficient knowledge for present purposes; and experience will afford more, as soon as it shall be required.

Probably, periods of five years, up to thirty, will afford a useful classification, and each class to be occupied as follows:

First class,—from birth, to the end of the fifth year. To be so placed, trained, and educated, as that they may be in a proper temperature for their age; fed with the most wholesome food; lightly and loosely clothed; regularly and duly exercised in a pure atmosphere; also that their dispositions may be formed to have their greatest pleasure in attending to, and promoting, the happiness of all who may be around them; that they may acquire an accurate knowledge, as far as their young capacities will easily admit, of the objects which they see and can handle, and that no false impression be made on any of their senses by those around them refusing a simple explanation to any of their questions; that they may have no knowledge of individual punishment or reward, nor be discouraged from always freely expressing their thoughts and feelings; that they may be taught, as early as their minds can receive it, that the thoughts and feelings of others are, like their own, instincts of human nature, which they are compelled to have; and thus, may acquire in infancy the rudiments of charity and affection for all; that they may have no fear, but full and implicit confidence in every one around them; and that the universal selfish or individual feeling of our animal existence may be so directed, as to derive its chief gratification from contributing to the pleasure and happiness of others.

By these measures a solid foundation will be laid for healthy and consistent minds, good habits, superior natural manners, fine dispositions, and some useful knowledge. By these means, they will be so well prepared before they leave this class, that, for their age, they will think, speak, and act rationally. They will be, therefore, at the end of this period, in many respects in advance of the average of human beings, as they are now taught and placed, at any time of their lives, for these are so instructed as to be prevented from becoming rational at any time of their lives.

It is true, that at this age they will not be equal to the men of the old world in physical strength, or in the number of sensations which they have experienced, or impressions received; they will, however, for their age, have more sound health, and be more active; they will have superior dispositions, habits, manners, and morals; they will have fewer *notions* and *fancies*, but they will have a greater number of *true* ideas. These true ideas being, of course, all consistent with each other, and in accordance with every known fact, will be of far more advantage to the individuals, than the matured minds of the old world, in the majority of which, there are but few true ideas, among many false notions. These false notions destroy the value of the few true ideas which the individuals may have acquired; for the few true ideas, thus mixed with many errors, tend only the more to perplex their reasoning faculties, and to confound their judgment.

The first class being prepared by this new rational nursing and infant training, will leave the nursery and infant school, to be removed into the appropriate arrangements for the second class; which class will consist of children from five to ten years complete. This class will be lodged, fed, and clothed, upon the same general principles as the first class, making only the difference which their age requires; but now, their exercises will consist in that which will be permanently useful. According to their strength and capacities they will acquire a practice in some of the lighter operations in the business of life; operations which may easily be made to afford them far more pleasure and gratification than can be derived from the useless toys of the old world. Their knowledge will be now chiefly acquired from personal inspection of objects, and familiar conversation with those more experienced than themselves. By this plan being judiciously pursued under rational arrangements properly adapted for the purpose, these children will, in two years, become willing, intelligent assistants in the domestic arrangements and gardens, for some hours in the day, according to their strength. Continuing this mode of education, these children from seven to ten will become efficient operators in whatever their physical strength will enable them easily to accomplish; and whatever they do they will perform as a matter of amusement and for exercise with their equally intelligent and delightful companions. These exercises they will pursue under the immediate directions of the juniors of the third class, for it is anticipated that the young persons twelve years of age, and under, will, with the greatest pleasure and advantage to themselves and society, when, thus rationally trained and placed, perform all the domestic operations of their own immediate association or family, and perform them in a very superior manner.

They will also assist to keep the gardens and pleasure-grounds of the family in the highest order, for the rational enjoyment of themselves, their own immediate association, and also of those numerous superior friends who will visit them from other similar family establishments.

When these children shall be advanced to the age for leaving the second class, they will have their characters so formed physically, intellectually, morally, and practically, that they can no longer be compared with any of the irrational characters which have been formed under the old system of man's free agency. At ten they will be well-trained rational beings, superior in mind, manner, dispositions, feelings, and conduct to any who have yet lived, and their deficiency in physical strength will be amply supplied by the superior mechanical and chemical powers which will be contrived and arranged to be ready for them to direct when they enter the next class. These new operations will be to them a continual source of instruction and amusement, and to which they will look forward with the delight experienced by the acquisition of new important attainments.

The members of the second class, when they shall have completed their tenth year, will enter the third class, which will consist of those from ten to fifteen years complete. This class will be engaged the first two years, that is, from ten to twelve, in directing and assisting those in the second class from seven to ten in their domestic exercises in the house, gardens, and pleasure-grounds, and from twelve to fifteen they will be engaged in acquiring a knowledge of the principles and practices of the more advanced useful arts of life, a knowledge by which they will be enabled to assist in producing the greatest amount of the most valuable wealth, in the shortest time, with the most pleasure to themselves and advantage to society. This will include all the productions required from the soil; from mines, from fisheries, the arts of manufacturing food, to keep and prepare it in the best manner for daily use; the art of working up materials to prepare them for garments, buildings, furniture, machinery, instruments, and implements for all purposes; and to produce, prepare, and execute whatever society requires, in the best manner that the concentrated wisdom and capital of society can direct. In all these operations the members of this class, from twelve to fifteen years, will daily assist for as many hours as will not injure their physical strength, mental powers, or moral feelings; and with their previous training, with the daily superior instruction and aid which they will receive from the members of the class immediately above them, they will perform all that will be necessary for them to do, with no more exercise than their physical and mental health will require to keep them in the best state of body and mind. In these five years, also, they will make a great advance in the knowledge of all the sciences, for they will be surrounded with every facility for acquiring accurately the most valuable knowledge in the shortest time; facilities such as will open more than a 'royal road' to the acquisition of all knowledge attainable by man, with the aid of all the facts yet discovered. This will be a period of great progress and consequent interest to this new race, thus trained to become, for the first time in human history, intelligent rational beings. They will now be well prepared to enter the fourth class, which will be formed of those from fifteen to twenty years complete.

This class will enter upon a most interesting period of human life. Within its duration its members will become men and women of a new race, physically, intellectually, and morally; beings far superior to any yet known to have lived upon the earth; their thoughts and feelings will have been formed in public without secrecy of any kind; for as they passed through the previous divisions, they would naturally make known to each other, in all simplicity, their undisguised thoughts and feelings. By this rational conduct, the particular feelings of affection or otherwise which they were obliged to entertain for each other will be accurately known to all. Thus will it be ascertained who by nature are compelled to have the strongest attachment for each other; and these will naturally unite and associate together, under such wise and well-prepared arrangements, made by the most experienced in the society, as shall be the best devised to insure to the individuals uniting the greatest amount of permanent happiness, with the least alloy to themselves and injury to society.

Under this classification and consequent arrangement of society, every individual will be trained and educated to have all his faculties and powers cultivated in the most superior manner known; cultivated, too, under a new combination of external objects, purposely formed to bring into constant exercise the best and most lovely qualities only of human nature. Each one will be, thus, well educated, physically, intellectually, morally, and practically. Under this classification and consequent arrangement of these associated families, wealth, unrestrained in its production by any of the artificial absurdities now so common in all countries, will be most easily produced in superfluity; and all will be secured in a full supply of the best of it, for all purposes that may be required. They will, therefore, all be equal in their education and condition, and no artificial distinction, or any distinction but that of age, will ever be known among them.

There will be, then, no motive or inducement for any parties to unite except from pure affection, arising from the most unreserved knowledge of each other's character, in all respects, as far as it can be known before the union takes place. There will be no artificial obstacles in the way of the permanent happy union of the sexes; for, under the arrangements of this new state of human existence, the affections will receive every aid which can be devised to induce them to be permanent; and under these arrangements, there can be no doubt that, as the parties will be placed as far as possible in the condition of lovers during their lives, the affections will be far more durable, and produce far more pleasure and enjoyment to the parties, and far less injury to society than has ever yet been experienced under any of the varied arrangements which have emanated from the imagined free-will agency of the human race.

If, however, these superior arrangements to produce happiness between the sexes should fail in some partial instances, which it is possible may yet occur, measures will be introduced, by which, without any severance of friendship between the parties, a separation may be made, the least injurious to them and the most beneficial to the interests of society.

No immorality can exceed that which is sure to arise from society interfering by human laws with natural affections, or from compelling individuals to live continually together, when they have been made, by the laws of their nature, to lose their affections for each other, and especially when they have been made to entertain them strongly for another. How much dreadful misery has been inflicted upon the human race, through all past ages, from this single error! How much demoralization! How many murders! How much secret unspeakable suffering, especially to the female sex! How many evils are experienced over the world at this moment, arising from this single error of the imaginary free-will system, by which men have been so long, so ignorantly, and so miserably governed!

This portion of the subject, to do it full justice, as it has been hitherto involved in so much error and mystery, would require a much more extended development; but this limited view must suffice, as this subject is more fully explained in other parts of this book.

This fourth class will be still more active and general producers of the various kinds of wealth required by society, as well as the kind and intelligent instructors of the senior members of the third class, to enable these senior members to acquire the knowledge which has been previously taught to themselves, when members of the third class. It is not improbable that these four classes, under such simplified arrangements in all the departments of life as may be made, will be sufficient, aided in all ways by the new powers derived from mechanism and chemistry, to produce a surplus of all the wealth which a rational and superior race of beings can require; but to remove all doubt respecting this part of the subject, and to make the business of life a pleasure to all, another class of producers of wealth and instructors in knowledge shall be added, and they will form the

Fifth Class, which class will consist of those from twenty to twenty-five years complete.

This will form the highest and most experienced class of producers and instructors; and beyond the age of this class, none need be required to produce or instruct, except for their own pleasure and gratification. This fifth class will be the superiors and directors in each branch of production and of education. They will perform in a very superior manner, that which is now most defectively done by the principle proprietors and active directing partners of large producing establishments, and by the professors of universities. The great business of human life is, first, to produce abundance of the most valuable wealth for the use and enjoyment of all; and secondly, to educate all to well use and properly enjoy their wealth after it has been produced.

We have now most amply provided for the production of the wealth, and also for the formation of a superior character, to use and enjoy it in the most advantageous or rational manner by the five classes of producers and instructors which have been described.

The *Sixth Class* will consist of those from twenty-five to thirty years of age complete.

The business of this class will be to preserve the wealth produced by the previous classes, in order that no waste may arise, and that all kinds of it may be kept in the best condition, and used, when in the most perfect state, for the beneficial enjoyment of all parties. They will also have to direct the distribution of it as it may be required from the stores, for the daily use of the family. Under the arrangements which may be, and no doubt will be, formed for these purposes, two hours each day will be more than sufficient to execute the regular business of this class in a very superior manner. Some part of the remainder of the day will most likely feel the greatest pleasure in occupying with visits to various parts of their beautiful and interesting establishment, to see how every process is advancing; with each of which, by their previous training, they will be familiar, and now, at their leisure, they may consider whether any improvement can be made in them for the general benefit.

Another portion of the day they will probably devote to their most favourite studies; whether in the fine arts, in the sciences, in trying experiments, in reading, or conversation, or in making excursions to the neighbouring establishments, to give or to receive information, or to make visits of friendship. This will be the prime period for the more active enjoyments of life, and all will be by this calculation most amply enabled to enjoy them. They will have high health, physical and mental; they will have a constant flow of good spirits; they will, by this period, have secured a greater breadth and depth of the most varied useful knowledge in principle and practice than any human beings have ever yet attained; they will also be familiar with those acquirements which, in addition to their attainments in that which is useful in principle and practice, will render them delightful companions to each other, and to all with whom they may come into communication. And they will be thus preparing themselves to become fit members of the class immediately in advance of them, that is, the

Seventh Class. This will consist of all the members of the family from thirty to forty years, inclusive.

The business of this class will be to govern the home department, in such manner as to preserve the establishment in peace, charity and affection; or, in other words, to prevent the existence of any causes which may disturb the harmony of the proceedings. And this result will be most easily effected for the following reasons:

First, because they will know what their own nature really is, and that the convictions and feelings of the individuals are not created by their will, but that they are instincts of their nature, which they must possess and retain, until some new motive or cause shall effect a change in them.

Secondly, because in consequence of this knowledge, all in the establishment will be rational in their thoughts, feelings, and conduct; there will, therefore, be no anger, ill-will, bad temper, inferior or evil passions, uncharitableness, or unkindness.

Thirdly, because no one will find fault with another for his physical, intellectual, or moral nature, or acquired character as all will know how these have been formed; but all will, of necessity, feel a deep interest in doing whatever may be in their power, by kindness directed by judgment, to improve these qualities in every individual.

Fourthly, because there will be no poverty, fear of poverty, or want of any kind.

Fifthly, because there will be no disagreeable objects within or around the establishment to annoy or to produce any injurious or unpleasant effect upon any one.

Sixthly, because according to age, there will be a perfect equality in their education, condition, occupations, and enjoyments.

Seventhly, because by their training, mode of life, and the superior arrangements, in accordance with and congenial to their nature, and by which they will be continually influenced and governed, they will very generally, if not always, enjoy sound health and good spirits.

Eighthly, because there will be no motive to engender ambition, jealousy, or revenge.

Ninthly, because there will be no secrecy or hypocrisy of any kind.

Tenthly, because there will be no buying or selling for a monied profit.

Eleventhly, because there will be no money, the cause now of so much oppression and injustice.

Twelfthly, because there will be no religious or injurious mental perplexities or estranged feelings, on account of religious or other differences of opinion.

Thirteenthly, because there will be no pecuniary anxieties, for wealth of superior qualities will everywhere superabound.

Fourteenthly, because there will be no disappointment of the affections, both sexes rationally and naturally enjoying the rights of their nature at the period designed by nature, and most beneficially to ensure to all virtue and happiness.

Fifteenthly, and lastly, because every one will know that permanent arrangements have been purposely devised and executed to ensure impartial justice to every one, by each being so placed, trained, and educated from birth to maturity, that he will be, as he advances in age, secure of experiencing all the advantages and enjoyments which the accumulated wisdom of his predecessors knows how to give to the faculties and powers which he derived from nature.

This class of domestic governors, will, naturally, for order and convenience, divide themselves into sub-committees, each of which sub-committees will more immediately superintend or govern some one of the departments, which will be divided between them, in the best manner their experience shall direct.

In this manner, the whole business and affairs of each association will be governed without jealousy or contest. And, as each establishment will always be kept in high order, and as no cause which can create disputes or differences will be permitted to remain, there can be little to govern in families thus made rational; every member of them being, from their birth, placed within rational arrangements, and surrounded solely by rational external objects.

By these arrangements and classifications, every one will know, at an early age, that, at the proper period of life, he will have, without contest, his fair, full share of the government of society.

But final decision upon every doubtful point of practice must rest somewhere, and it is, perhaps, most natural, that this power should be vested in the oldest member of this class, who will possess this precedence for a short time only, because he will soon be superseded by the next senior member of this class, and he will become a junior member of the

Eighth Class, which will consist of those from forty to sixty years complete.

After providing for the production of wealth, for its preservation and distribution; for the training, education, and formation of character from birth to maturity, and for the internal government of each establishment: it is necessary to make arrangements to connect each large family or nucleus establishment with all other family establishments founded on the same principles; or to form what may not be improperly called the external or foreign arrangements.

The eighth class will have charge of this department; a department so important to place under the direction of the best-informed and most experienced, yet active members of society. The individuals from forty to sixty years of age will be so informed and experienced as a class, after they shall regularly have passed through the seven previous classes. Their business will be to receive and attend to visitors from other establishments, to correspond with other establishments, to visit, and to arrange the general business of the public roads, conveyances, and exchanges of surplus produce; inventions, improvements, and discoveries, in order that the population of every district may freely partake of the benefits to be derived from the concentrated knowledge and acquirements of the world; and that no part may remain in an ignorant or barbarous state. For by these means a new power of invention and discovery will be opened to mankind, many millions of times more efficient than that which has ever yet been in action, and more will be accomplished by it for the advance of the improvement and happiness of the human race, in one year, than can be attained under this old, ignorant, wretched, and irrational system, in any given period.

The members of this class will circumscribe the world in their travels, giving and receiving in their course the most valuable knowledge, and continually interchanging acts of friendship and kindness with all with whom they come into communication. Their wants, wherever they may go, among these new family associations, will be most amply supplied, for there will be everywhere among them, a large superfluity of every kind of useful or desirable wealth. The most varied and delightful sensations appertaining to human nature, when the physical, intellectual, and moral powers and faculties shall be called forth in their due order and proportions, and cultivated in the superior manner previously described, will be continually called into action; and this period of human life will be one of high utility and enjoyment. For the earth will not be the wild, barren, waste, swamp, or forest, which, with some exceptions, it ever has been and yet is; the united effort of a well-trained world will speedily change it into a well-drained, highly-cultivated, and beautiful pleasure scene, which, by its endless variety, will afford health and enjoyment to all, to a degree such as the human mind in its present degraded and confined state, has not the capacity to imagine. For the human faculties have been cultivated to have a perception of regions of torment, but never of those of happiness; the hitherto fancied heaven of irrational man, would be a state of stupid, monotonous existence, most unsatisfactory to an intelligent, rational being.

By these arrangements, being carried out to the extent intended, the whole human race, from the age of forty, will be, in reality, more truly sovereigns of the world, than any one is now sovereign of an empire or kingdom. These superior rational beings will have all the productions of the earth, which they can use or enjoy much more effectually at their control than any sovereign can now command them. These men of the new classification will all be well trained, and properly prepared, to make the best use of wealth, and to obtain its highest permanent enjoyment, without making abuse of any part of it. And these high enjoyments will be yet enhanced to these men, by the knowledge that they are not depriving a single human being of similar privileges and advantages; but, on the contrary, that each one of their fellow-men will derive additional gratification from witnessing, or knowing, that this control over all the enjoyments which the world in its most highly cultivated or best state can afford, is thus possessed by so many of their fellow-men justly and advantageously for all other classes, and which privileges and advantages all these classes will also, at the proper period of life, equally enjoy.

There is, however, one apparently insurmountable difficulty to be overcome, before the great change in human affairs can be accomplished; one that appears too deep-rooted, too widely spread over all quarters of the world, and too gigantic in its power for mortal man to attempt to contend against. This is the power of PREJUDICE, forced into the minds and upon the habits of all men, by their local position;—a position which inflicts upon them their geographical language, religion, manners, habits, associations of ideas, and conduct, and thus compels all men, without exception, instead of being trained to become rational beings, to acquire the character of irrational animals, to the deep injury of all the inhabitants of the earth. How is this universal evil to be fairly met and overcome, without creating misery by the conflict, to all these localized animals? Mortal man, by any power which in ordinary language he can call his own, would never think of attempting that which now appears to all men of the old world most wild and visionary, nay, not to be exceeded in folly or insanity by any of the most extravagant or mad enterprises ever undertaken by man in his most rude and irrational state. Well, then, what earthly power can be brought to this mighty conflict against localized irrational man; to obtain the victory over him for intelligent rational man; that the human being may no longer remain, or his offspring be forced to become, the mere geographical creatures of local impressions, producing and reproducing continually, local errors and associations of ideas, destructive of real knowledge, of virtue, and of happiness? Evidently most vain would it be for any mere earthly power to enter upon this more than mortal conflict. A new and divine weapon must be obtained from that source whence man has derived his organization and his mental faculties; a weapon of such might and power as shall, when daily wielded, and with certain aim directed, sever the gordian knot of human ignorance and prejudice so effectually, that it shall never more be the cause of inflicting error and misery on man.

But where is this divine weapon to be found? or, when found, who will have the temerity to wield it, and commence the conflict to destroy the localized animal of prejudice, give victory to rational man, and place him, secure for ever, upon the throne of reason, supported by charity and affection, and thus sustained, enable him to govern the world in peace, with ever increasing prosperity!

Rejoice, all ye who have so long desired to see the period arrive, when all of the human race shall become wise, and good, and happy, for this weapon of mighty power has been discovered!—its name is TRUTH! Its sharpness and brilliancy, now that it is, *for the first time*, fully unsheathed to open view, no mortal can withstand. It is a weapon derived direct from the Supreme Power of the Universe—the source whence alone, Truth has ever been obtained, or can ever emanate. Yet who shall wield this divine weapon? who, among the sons of men, have been trained from their youth upwards, to practise with it? who will now dare firmly to grasp it, and boldly go forth to battle against the accumulated prejudices of ages, and cry 'VICTORY OR DEATH?'

My Friends, fear not. The appointed hour is come. The victory is near at hand. It is already secured—there is a little band—insignificant in number, but they have shielded themselves in impenetrable armour—have cast all worldly consequences far away; lovers and worshippers of Truth, without admixture of error, they have no fear of man, or of what man can do against them. Already have they practised with this divine weapon, and are familiar with its use. They have firmly grasped it; they have gone forth; they have entered upon the conflict; and they return not until ignorance, falsehood, superstition, sin, and misery, shall be banished from the abodes of the human race; and peace and charity, reason, truth and justice, love, and happiness, shall reign triumphant, and for ever, over the whole family of man, wherever man shall exist; and slavery, and servitude, and oppression, or evil of any kind, among the sons of men, shall be known no more!

Robert Owen (1771–1858) was a British utopian socialist who founded the New Harmony community in Indiana.

Source: Robert Owen, THE BOOK OF THE NEW MORAL WORLD, part 5 (London, 1844), 286–97.

Étienne Cabet
Voyage to Icaria

Étienne Cabet's *Voyage en Icarie* brought about a major political movement in France, mostly among artisans and small shopkeepers, first to reform France through the electoral system and then to establish a community in the United States. The move to the United States split the Icarians, who had developed a strong electoral position in France but failed to win the presidency in the 1848 elections. Cabet and his followers established communities in Texas, Illinois,

Iowa, and California, in that order. These communities were fairly successful but came to an end in the late 1890s.

Being profoundly convinced by experience that there can be no happiness without association and equality, the Icarians form together a SOCIETY founded on the basis of the most perfect EQUALITY. All of them are *associates and citizens, having equal rights and duties*; they all share equally the *responsibilities* and the *advantages* of the association; they all form a single FAMILY, whose members are united by the bonds of FRATERNITY.

We are therefore a *People* or a nation of brothers; and all our laws must aim at establishing the most absolute equality among us, in all cases where this equality is not materially impossible. . . .

In the same way as we form a single society, one people and one family, our land, with its underground mines and external construction, forms a single estate, which is our social property.

All the personal property of the associates, with all the products of the land and industry, form a single social CAPITAL.

This social property and capital belong indivisibly to the People, who work and exploit them in common, who administer them directly or through delegates, and then share equally all the products. . . .

All the Icarians are associated and equal, all must exercise a trade and work the same number of hours; but they employ all their intelligence to find every possible means of reducing the number of hours of work and rendering it agreeable and without danger.

All the instruments of work and raw materials are provided by the social capital, and all the products of the land and of industry are deposited in public storehouses.

We are all equally provided with food, clothes, a house and furniture out of the social capital, according to the sex, age and other circumstances fixed by law.

Thus, it is the Republic or Community which alone is the owner of everything, which organises its workers, and causes its factories and storehouses to be built, which sees that the land is tilled, that houses are built, and that all the objects necessary for feeding, clothing and housing each family and each citizen are provided.

EDUCATION being considered the basis and foundation of society, the Republic provides it equally for each one of its children as it provides them equally with nourishment. All receive the same elementary education and a specialised instruction suited to their particular profession; this education aims at forming good workers, good parents, good citizens and true men. . . .

As we are all associates and citizens, possessing equal rights, we all have the right to vote and to be elected and are all members of the People and of the popular guard.

United, we compose the NATION or rather the PEOPLE, for in Icaria the People includes all the inhabitants without exception.

Needless to say, the People is SOVEREIGN, and to it alone belong, together with SOVEREIGNTY, the power to draw up its own social contract, its constitution and its laws; it is inconceivable to us that a single individual, or a family, or a class could have the absurd pretension to be our master.

The People, having the sovereign power has the right to regulate, by its constitutions and its laws, everything concerning its person, actions, property, food, clothing, houses, education, work and even its pleasures.

If the Icarian People could be assembled altogether, easily and frequently, in a hall or a valley, it could exercise its sovereignty and draw up its own constitution and laws. As it is a material impossibility to assemble in this manner, it DELEGATES the powers which it cannot exercise directly and reserves all the others for itself. It delegates to a POPULAR ASSEMBLY the power to prepare its constitution and laws, and to an EXECUTIVE the power to see that they are carried out; but it reserves the right to elect all its representatives and all the members of the executive, to approve or reject their proposals and their actions, to administer justice, to maintain order and public peace.

All public functionaries are therefore the representatives of the People, all have been elected temporarily, and are responsible to the People and subject to recall; in order to prevent the ambitious accumulation of offices, the legislative and executive functions are incompatible.

The popular REPRESENTATION is composed of 2,000 deputies who deliberate in common in a single chamber. It is *permanent*, always or nearly always assembled, and half its members are renewed each year. Its most important laws are, like the institution, submitted to the ratification of the People.

The EXECUTIVE is composed of a President and fifteen other members, half of whom can be changed every year; it is completely subordinated to the popular Representation.

The people exercises its rights through its *assemblies* where the elections, deliberations and judgements are also carried out.

In order to render the exercise of the People's rights easier, the country is divided into a hundred small Provinces, subdivided into 1,000 Communes of approximately the same size and population.

You know that each *Provincial* town is at the centre of its province, every *Communal* town at the centre of its commune, and everything is arranged in such a manner that all attend the popular assembles regularly.

While all the Communes and all the Provinces deal with matters of general and national interest through their representatives, each Province and each Commune deals more particularly with matters related to their communal and provincial interests. In this way no question can be neglected.

Divided into 2,000 communal assemblies the People thus takes part in the discussion of its laws, either after or before the deliberations of its own Representatives.

To ensure that the People is able to discuss with a perfect knowledge of the question, everything is carried out in the full light of Publicity, all the facts are recorded by a department of *Statistics*, and everything is published in the popular *Journal* which is distributed to all citizens.

In order to make sure that every question is exhaustively treated, the popular Representation and every communal assembly, that it to say, the whole People, is divided into fifteen great principal Committees dealing with *the constitution, education, agriculture, industry, food, clothing, housing, furnishing, statistics, etc.* Each great Committee therefore comprises a fifteenth of the mass of the citizens; and all the intelligence of a People of men well brought up and well educated is continually applied to discovering and putting into practice all possible ameliorations and improvements.

Our political organisation is therefore a democratic REPUBLIC or even an almost pure DEMOCRACY. . . .

The unanimous will of the people is always to create political and social equality, the equality of happiness and rights, universal and absolute equality: education, food, clothing, houses and furniture, work and pleasure, rights of election, eligibility and deliberations are the same for all of us, our provinces, our communes, our towns, our villages, our farms and our houses are, as far as possible, similar. Everywhere, in a word, you will find equality and happiness. . . .

Eugene's Letter to His Brother

"O my dear Camille, how broken-hearted I feel when I think of France and see the happiness enjoyed by the people of Icaria! You will be able to judge for yourself in learning of their institutions concerning FOOD and *clothes.*

Food

"Concerning this first need of man, like all the others, everything in our unfortunate country is abandoned to chance and to monstrous abuses. Here, on the contrary, everything is regulated according to the most enlightened reason and the most generous care.

"Imagine first, my dear brother, that everything concerning food has been regulated by the *law*. It is the law which accepts or rejects any type of nourishment.

"A *committee* of scientists, set up by the national representatives, with the aid of all the citizens, has made a *list* of all known foods, indicating which are good and which are bad, and the respective qualities of each of them.

"They have done more than that: among the good ones they have indicated which are necessary, useful and agreeable, and they have had this list printed in several volumes and each family possesses a copy.

"They have done still more; they have indicated the most suitable ways of preparing each food, and each family has also a *Cookery Guide*.

"Once the list of good foods had been agreed upon, the Republic undertook the task to have them produced by its agricultural labourers and workers, and distributed them to the families; and as none is able to get any food other than that which is distributed, you will realise that no-one can eat anything which the Republic does not approve.

"The Republic sees first that what is necessary is produced, then what is useful, and finally, in as great a measure as possible, what is agreeable.

"The Republic gives an equal share to everybody, in such a manner that each citizen will receive the same quantity of certain food if there is enough for everyone, and that everyone will receive it in turn if there is only enough, each year or each day, for a section of the population.

"Everyone has therefore an equal share of all foods without distinction, from those which we consider most plain to the most delicate; and the whole population of Icaria is nourished not only as well, but even better, than the richest people in other countries. . . .

"The Committee which I have mentioned before has also discussed and indicated the number of *meals*, the time at which they should be eaten, how long they should last, the number of courses, their nature and the order in which they should be served, varying them continuously, not only according to the seasons and the months but also according to the days, with the result that every meal of the week is different from the other.

"At six o'clock in the morning, before they begin work, all the workers, that is to say all the citizens, eat a very simple breakfast in common at their workshops, prepared and served by the factory restaurant.

"At nine o'clock, they have a luncheon in the workshop, while their wives and their children take theirs at home.

"At two o'clock, all the inhabitants of the same street eat together, in their *republican restaurant*, a dinner prepared by one of the *caterers* of the Republic.

"And every evening between nine and ten, each family has, in its own home, a supper prepared by the women of the household.

"At all these meals, the first TOAST is *to the glory of the good Icar, benefactor of the workers*, BENEFACTOR OF THE FAMILIES, BENEFACTOR OF THE CITIZENS.

"The supper consists mostly of fruits, cakes and sweets. But the *common dinner*, which is taken in superb halls elegantly decorated, and which contain from a thousand to two thousand people, surpasses by its magnificence anything you may be able to imagine. The best restaurants and cafés of Paris are nothing, in my opinion, compared with the restaurants of the Republic. You may not believe me when I tell you that, apart from the abundance and the delicacy of the meals, apart from the decorations with flowers and many other things, a delicious music charms the ear while the sense of smell enjoys delicious perfumes.

"When the young people get married, they do not need to spend their dowry in a bad marriage feast and ruin in advance their future children; the dinners which the husband finds in the wife's restaurant, the wife in the husband's, and the two families in the home of each other, replace the most beautiful dinners of other countries.

"And yet you must realise that these common meals present a great economy compared with separate meals and can therefore afford better fare.

"You will also realise that this community of meals among workers and neighbours has other great advantages, particularly that of inducing the masses to fraternise and also to simplify the housework for women. . . .

"You may like to know how the *distribution* of the food is carried out: nothing is more simple: but again you must admire!

Distribution of Food

"You know firstly that the Republic is the sole grower and producer of all food and that it gathers and stores it in its innumerable and immense storehouses.

"You can easily imagine communal *cellars* like those of Paris and London, great storehouses for flour, bread, meat, fish, vegetables, fruit, etc.

"Each republican storehouse has, like any of our bakers or butchers, the *list* of restaurants, workshops, schools, hospitals and families which it must supply, and the quantity which must be sent to each of them.

"In the storehouse are to be found the employees, utensils, means of transport, and extremely ingenious instruments necessary to the distribution of food.

"Everything having been *prepared in advance* in the storehouse, the provisions for the year, the month or the week and the daily provisions are delivered to the homes in the district served by the storehouse.

"The distribution of these is organised in a charming way. I will not tell you of the perfect cleanliness which reigns everywhere as a matter of course, but I will not fail to tell you that each storehouse has a *basket,* a jug, a measure for each family marked with the number of its house and holding its provision of bread, milk, etc; and all these containers are *double,* so that when the full one has been delivered, the empty one can be brought back. Each house has, at its entrance, an *alcove* in which the delivery man finds the empty container and re-places it by a full one. In this way, the delivery, being always made at the same time, and announced by a particular sound, is carried out without disturbing the family and with no loss of time for the delivery man.

"You can understand, my dear friend, what an economy of time and what advantages this system of mass distribution possesses.

"Besides, everything is perfect in this happy country, inhabited by men who deserve the title of *men,* since, even in the smallest things they always make full use of that sublime reason which Providence has given them for their own hap-piness.

Clothes

"As with food, so it is with the law which regulates everything connected with clothes. A committee has consulted everyone, has examined the clothes worn in every country, has made a *list* of them with their shapes and colours (a mag-nificent book which every family possesses), has indicated which should be adopted and which must be avoided, and has classified them according to their necessity, utility and pleasure.

"Everything that was extravagant and tasteless, has been carefully banned . . . not a single shoe or head-dress is manufactured without being first discussed and adopted according to a model-plan.

"Everyone possesses the same clothes, so that there is no room either for envy or coquettishness. And yet one should not think that *uniformity* here is not without *variety;* for, on the contrary, it is in the clothes that variety combines most happily with the advantages of uniformity. Not only are the two sexes dressed differently, but each of them changes clothes frequently, according to age and condition, for the differences in clothes always indicate the circum-stances and position of the person. Childhood and youth, adolescence and ma-turity, the condition of celibacy or marriage, or widowhood or re-marriage, the various professions and functions are all indicated by the clothes. All the indi-viduals belonging to the same condition wear the same *uniform;* but a thousand various uniforms correspond to a thousand various conditions.

"And the difference between these uniforms consists sometimes in the dif-ference between materials and colours, sometimes in the shape or a distinctive sign.

"Consider also that if the material and the shape is the same for all girls of the same age, the colour varies according to their tastes or their suitability, a certain colour being more fitting for blondes and another for brunettes.

"Consider also that the same person has a simple and comfortable suit of clothes for *work* and another for the *home*, an elegant *drawing room* suit and another for *public meetings*, and a magnificent one for the *feasts* and *ceremonies*, all of them being different. In such a way the variety in costumes is almost infinite.

"The shape of each garment has been fixed in such a manner that it can be manufactured in the most easy, rapid and economic way possible.

"Practically all the clothes, hats and shoes are *elastic*, in such a way that they can suit people of different sizes.

"They are nearly all done by *machine*, either entirely or in part and the workers have little to do to finish them.

"Nearly all clothes are made in four or five different sizes so that the workers never need to take measurements beforehand.

"All the clothes are therefore manufactured in enormous quantities, like the materials, and often at the same time; they are afterwards deposited in immense storehouses where everyone is always sure to find immediately all the objects which he needs and which are due to him according to the law.

"I have been talking to you of the *women*: O my dear Camille, how you would love these Icarians, you so courteous and so full of passion, as I am, for this master-piece of the Creator, if you saw how they surround women with attention, respect and homages, how they concentrate all their thoughts, their solicitude and their happiness upon them, how they constantly endeavour to please them and make them happy, how they do all they can to make them more beautiful, though they are already so beautiful naturally, in order to have more pleasure in adoring them! Happy women! Happy men! Happy Icaria! Unhappy France!" . . .

The factory given over to clock-making occupies a building of one thousand square feet and has three storeys supported by iron columns which replace the thickest walls and in this manner each floor is composed of a single room perfectly lighted.

On the ground floor there are bulky and heavy machines used for cutting the metal and rough casting the parts. The workers are on the top floor, and are divided in as many groups as there are parts, to be manufactured, and each of them always manufactures the same parts. There is so much order and discipline that they look like an army!

One of the workers explains how this "small army" carries out the work:

"We arrive at quarter to six in the morning and leave our clothes in the cloakroom and put on our working-clothes. At six o'clock sharp we begin work as the bell sounds. At nine o'clock we go down to the refectory and have our meal in silence while one of us reads the morning paper aloud. At one o'clock the work ends and when everything is tidied up and cleaned, we go down to the cloak-room where we find everything we need to wash and where we take our outdoor clothes to go to dinner with our families and spend the rest of the day as we think fit.

"During our work we observe the most rigorous silence for two hours, but for another two hours we can talk with our neighbours and the rest of the time we all sing for ourselves or for those who may listen and we often sing together."

Étienne Cabet (1788–1856) was a French utopian socialist of the mid-nineteenth century. He and many of his followers immigrated to the United states and established communities based on his ideas.

Source: Étienne Cabet, VOYAGE EN ICARIE, trans. from the first edition of 1839 by Marie Louise Berneri in her JOURNEY THROUGH UTOPIA (London: Routledge & Kegan Paul, 1950), 224–35.

Karl Marx and Friedrich Engels
The Communist Manifesto

We have seen above that the first step in the revolution by the working class is to raise the proletariat to the position of ruling class, to establish democracy.

The proletariat will use its political supremacy to wrest by degrees all capital from the bourgeoisie, to centralize all instruments of production in the hands of the state, i.e., of the proletariat organized as the ruling class, and to increase the total of productive forces as rapidly as possible.

Of course, in the beginning this cannot be effected except by means of despotic inroads on the rights of property and on the conditions of bourgeois production; by means of measures, therefore, which appear economically insufficient and untenable, but which, in the course of the movement outstrip themselves, necessitate further inroads upon the old social order, and are unavoidable as a means of entirely revolutionizing the mode of production.

These measures will, of course, be different in different countries.

Nevertheless, in the most advanced countries the following will be pretty generally applicable:

1. Abolition of property in land and application of all rents of land to public purposes.
2. A heavy progressive or graduated income tax.

3. Abolition of all right of inheritance.
4. Confiscation of the property of all emigrants and rebels.
5. Centralization of credit in the hands of the state by means of a national bank with state capital and an exclusive monopoly.
6. Centralization of the means of communication and transport in the hands of the state.
7. Extension of factories and instruments of production owned by the state; the bringing into cultivation of waste lands, and the improvement of the soil generally in accordance with a common plan.
8. Equal obligation of all to work. Establishment of industrial armies, especially for agriculture.
9. Combination of agriculture with manufacturing industries; gradual abolition of the distinction between town and country by a more equable distribution of the population over the country.
10. Free education for all children in public schools. Abolition of child factory labour in its present form. Combination of education with industrial production, etc.

When in the course of development class distinctions have disappeared and all production has been concentrated in the hands of a vast association of the whole nation, the public power will lose its political character. Political power, properly so called, is merely the organized power of one class for oppressing another. If the proletariat during its contest with the bourgeoisie is compelled by the force of circumstances to organize itself as a class; if by means of a revolution it makes itself the ruling class and, as such, sweeps away by force the old conditions of production, then it will, along with these conditions, have swept away the conditions for the existence of class antagonisms and of classes generally, and will thereby have abolished its own supremacy as a class.

In place of the old bourgeois society, with its classes and class antagonisms, we shall have an association in which the free development of each is the condition for the free development of all.

Karl Marx (1818–1883) was a German philosopher, social and economic theorist, and the founder of Communism.

Friedrich Engels (1820–1895) was a German philosopher and friend and coauthor of Karl Marx.

Source: Karl Marx and Friedrich Engels, THE COMMUNIST MANIFESTO, trans. Samuel Moore (London: International Publishers, 1886; reprinted, London: Martin Lawrence, 1933), 31–32.

Samuel Butler
Erewhon

Although it spawned a few imitators, Samuel Butler's *Erewhon* (1872) is almost unique in utopian literature. *Erewhon* and its sequel *Erewhon Revisited* (1901) are utopian satires. It is impossible to tell from reading either work what Butler's position is. Every time you think you have understood, he twists it around to make you wonder. The best-known example is his discussion of criminals, whom he describes as simply sick and in need of treatment. It is easy to conclude that he is taking a fairly common position that criminals will respond to rehabilitation. But then we discover that in Erewhon people who are sick are thrown in jail as dangerous to society.

Chapter XXI. The Colleges of Unreason

AFTER supper Mr. Thims told me a good deal about the system of education which is here practiced. I already knew a part of what I heard, but much was new to me, and I obtained a better idea of the Erewhonian position than I had done hitherto: nevertheless there were parts of the scheme of which I could not comprehend the fitness, although I fully admit that this inability was probably the result of my having been trained so very differently and to my being then much out of sorts.

The main feature in their system is the prominence which they give to a study which I can only translate by the word "hypothetics." They argue thus— that to teach a boy merely the nature of the things which exist in the world around him, and about which he will have to be conversant during his whole life, would be giving him but a narrow and shallow conception of the universe, which it is urged might contain all manner of things which are not now to be found therein. To open his eyes to these possibilities, and so to prepare him for all sorts of emergencies, is the object of this system of hypothetics. To imagine a set of utterly strange and impossible contingencies, and require the youths to give intelligent answers to the questions that arise therefrom, is reckoned the fittest conceivable way of preparing them for the actual conduct of their affairs in after life. . . .

The arguments in favor of the deliberate development of the unreasoning faculties were . . . cogent. But here they depart from the principles on which they justify their study of hypothetics; for they base the importance which they assign to hypothetics upon the fact of their being a preparation for the extraordinary, while their study of Unreason rests upon its developing those faculties which are required for the daily conduct of affairs. Hence their professorships of Inconsistency and Evasion, in both of which studies the youths are examined before being allowed to proceed to their degree in hypothetics. The more earnest and conscientious students attain to a proficiency in these subjects which is quite surprising; there is hardly any inconsistency so glaring but they soon learn to defend it, or injunction so clear that they cannot find some pretext for disregarding it.

Life, they urge, would be intolerable if men were to be guided in all they did by reason and reason only. Reason betrays men into the drawing of hard and fast lines, and to the defining by language—language being like the sun, which rears and then scorches. Extremes are alone logical, but they are always absurd; the mean is illogical, but an illogical mean is better than the sheer absurdity of an extreme. There are no follies and no unreasonableness so great as those which can apparently be irrefragably defended by reason itself, and there is hardly an error into which men may not easily be led if they base their conduct upon reason only.

Reason might very possibly abolish the double currency; it might even attack the personality of Hope and Justice. Besides, people have such a strong natural bias towards it that they will seek it for themselves and act upon it quite as much as or more than is good for them: there is no need of encouraging reason. With unreason the case is different. She is the natural complement of reason, without whose existence reason itself were non-existent.

If, then, reason would be non-existent were there no such thing as unreason, surely it follows that the more unreason there is, the more reason there must be also? Hence the necessity for the development of unreason, even in the interests of reason herself. The Professors of Unreason deny that they undervalue reason: none can be more convinced than they are, that if the double currency cannot be rigorously deduced as a necessary consequence of human reason, the double currency should cease forthwith; but they say that it must be deduced from no narrow and exclusive view of reason which should deprive that admirable faculty of the one-half of its own existence. Unreason is a part of reason; it must therefore be allowed its full share in stating the initial conditions.

Chapter XXII. The Colleges of Unreason—continued

OF genius they make no account, for they say that every one is a genius, more or less. No one is so physically sound that no part of him will be even a little unsound, and no one is so diseased but that some part of him will be healthy— so no man is so mentally and morally sound, but that he will be in part both mad and wicked; and no man is so mad and wicked but he will be sensible and honorable in part. In like manner there is no genius who is not also a fool, and no fool who is not also a genius.

When I talked about originality and genius to some gentlemen whom I met at a supper party given by Mr. Thims in my honor, and said that original thought ought to be encouraged, I had to eat my words at once. Their view evidently was that genius was like offences—needs must that it come, but woe unto that man through whom it comes. A man's business, they hold, is to think as his neighbors do, for Heaven help him if he thinks good what they count bad. And really it is hard to see how the Erewhonian theory differs from our own, for the word "idiot" only means a person who forms his opinions for himself.

The venerable Professor of Worldly Wisdom, a man verging on eighty but still hale, spoke to me very seriously on this subject in consequence of the few words that I had imprudently let fall in defense of genius. He was one of those who carried most weight in the university, and had the reputation of having done more perhaps than any other living man to suppress any kind of originality.

"It is not our business," he said, "to help students to think for themselves. Surely this is the very last thing which one who wishes them well should encourage them to do. Our duty is to ensure that they shall think as we do, or at any rate, as we hold it expedient to say we do." In some respects, however, he was thought to hold somewhat radical opinions, for he was President of the Society for the Suppression of Useless Knowledge, and for the Completer Obliteration of the Past.

As regards the tests that a youth must pass before he can get a degree, I found that they have no class lists, and discourage anything like competition among the students; this, indeed, they regard as self-seeking and unneighborly. The examinations are conducted by way of papers written by the candidate on set subjects, some of which are known to him beforehand, while others are devised with a view of testing his general capacity and *savoir faire*.

My friend the Professor of Worldly Wisdom was the terror of the greater number of students; and, so far as I could judge, he very well might be, for he had taken his Professorship more seriously than any of the other Professors had done. I heard of his having plucked one poor fellow for want of sufficient vagueness in his saving clauses paper. Another was sent down for having written an article on a scientific subject without having made free enough use of the words "carefully," "patiently," and "earnestly." One man was refused a degree for being too often and too seriously in the right, while a few days before I came a whole batch had been plucked for insufficient distrust of printed matter.

About this there was just then rather a ferment, for it seems that the Professor had written an article in the leading university magazine, which was well known to be by him, and which abounded in all sorts of plausible blunders. He then set a paper which afforded the examinees an opportunity of repeating these blunders—which, believing the article to be by their own examiner, they of course did. The Professor plucked every single one of them, but his action was considered to have been not quite handsome.

I told them of Homer's noble line to the effect that a man should strive ever to be foremost and in all things to outvie his peers; but they said that no wonder the countries in which such a detestable maxim was held in admiration were always flying at one another's throats.

"Why," asked one Professor, "should a man want to be better than his neighbors? Let him be thankful if he is no worse."

I ventured feebly to say that I did not see how progress could be made in any art or science, or indeed in anything at all, without more or less self-seeking, and hence unamiability.

"Of course it cannot," said the Professor, "and therefore we object to progress."

After which there was no more to be said. Later on, however, a young Professor took me aside and said he did not think I quite understood their views about progress.

"We like progress," he said, "but it must commend itself to the common sense of the people. If a man gets to know more than his neighbors he should keep his knowledge to himself till he has sounded them, and seen whether they agree, or are likely to agree with him. He said it was as immoral to be too far in front of one's own age, as to lag too far behind it. If a man can carry his neighbors with him, he may say what he likes; but if not, what insult can be more gratuitous than the telling them what they do not want to know? A man should remember that intellectual over-indulgence is one of the most insidious and disgraceful forms that excess can take. Granted that every one should exceed more or less, inasmuch as absolutely perfect sanity would drive any man mad the moment he reached it, but . . ."

He was now warming to his subject and I was beginning to wonder how I should get rid of him, when the party broke up, and though I promised to call on him before I left, I was unfortunately prevented from doing so. . . .

Nothing surprised me more than to see the occasional flashes of common sense with which one branch of study or another was lit up, while not a single ray fell upon so many others. I was particularly struck with this on strolling into the Art School of the University. Here I found that the course of study was divided into two branches—the practical and the commercial—no student being permitted to continue his studies in the actual practice of the art he had taken up, unless he made equal progress in its commercial history.

Thus those who were studying painting were examined at frequent intervals in the prices which all the leading pictures of the last fifty or a hundred years had realized, and in the fluctuations in their values when (as often happened) they had been sold and resold three or four times. The artist, they contend, is a dealer in pictures, and it is as important for him to learn how to adapt his wares to the market, and to know approximately what kind of a picture will fetch how much, as it is for him to be able to paint the picture. This, I suppose, is what the French mean by laying so much stress upon "values."

As regards the city itself, the more I saw the more enchanted I became. I dare not trust myself with any description of the exquisite beauty of the different colleges, and their walks and gardens. Truly in these things alone there must be a hallowing and refining influence which is in itself half an education, and which no amount of error can wholly spoil. I was introduced to many of the Professors, who showed me every hospitality and kindness; nevertheless I could hardly avoid a sort of suspicion that some of those whom I was taken to see had been so long engrossed in their own study of hypothetics that they had become the exact antitheses of the Athenians in the days of St. Paul; for whereas the Athenians spent their lives in nothing save to see and to hear some new thing, there were some here who seemed to devote themselves to the avoidance of every opinion with which they were not perfectly familiar, and regarded their own brains as a sort of sanctuary, to which if an opinion had once resorted, none other was to attack it.

I should warn the reader, however, that I was rarely sure what the men whom I met while staying with Mr. Thims really meant; for there was no getting anything out of them if they scented even a suspicion that they might be what they call "giving themselves away." As there is hardly any subject on which this suspicion cannot arise, I found it difficult to get definite opinions from any of them, except on such subjects as the weather, eating and drinking, holiday excursions, or games of skill.

If they cannot wriggle out of expressing an opinion of some sort, they will commonly retail those of some one who has already written upon the subject, and conclude by saying that though they quite admit that there is an element of truth in what the writer has said, there are many points on which they are unable to agree with him. Which these points were, I invariably found myself unable to determine; indeed, it seemed to be counted the perfection of scholarship and good breeding among them not to have—much less to express—an opinion on any subject on which it might prove later that they had been mistaken. The art of sitting gracefully on a fence has never, I should think, been brought to greater perfection than at the Erewhonian Colleges of Unreason.

Even when, wriggle as they may, they find themselves pinned down to some expression of definite opinion, as often as not they will argue in support of what they perfectly well know to be untrue. I repeatedly met with reviews and articles even in their best journals, between the lines of which I had little difficulty in detecting a sense exactly contrary to the one ostensibly put forward. So well is this understood, that a man must be a mere tyro in the arts of Erewhonian polite society, unless he instinctively suspects a hidden "yea" in every "nay" that meets him. Granted that it comes to much the same in the end, for it does not matter whether "yea" is called "yea" or "nay," so long as it is understood which it is to be; but our own more direct way of calling a spade a spade, rather than a rake, with the intention that every one should understand it as a spade, seems more satisfactory. On the other hand, the Erewhonian system lends itself better to the suppression of that downrightness which it seems the express aim of Erewhonian philosophy to discountenance.

However this may be, the fear-of-giving-themselves-away disease was fatal to the intelligence of those infected by it, and almost every one at the Colleges of Unreason had caught it to a greater or less degree. After a few years atrophy of the opinions invariably supervened, and the sufferer became stone dead to everything except the more superficial aspects of those material objects with which he came most in contact. The expression on the faces of these people was repellent; they did not, however, seem particularly unhappy, for they none of them had the faintest idea that they were in reality more dead than alive. No cure for this disgusting fear-of-giving-themselves-away disease has yet been discovered.

It was during my stay in City of the Colleges of Unreason—a city whose Erewhonian name is so cacophonous that I refrain from giving it—that I learned the particulars of the revolution which had ended in the destruction of so many of the mechanical inventions which were formerly in common use. . . .

Chapter XXIII. The Book of the Machines

THE writer commences:—"There was a time, when the earth was to all appearance utterly destitute both of animal and vegetable life, and when according to the opinion of our best philosophers it was simply a hot round ball with a crust gradually cooling. Now if a human being had existed while the earth was in this state and had been allowed to see it as though it were some other world with which he had no concern, and if at the same time he were entirely ignorant of all physical science, would he not have pronounced it impossible that creatures possessed of anything like consciousness should be evolved from the seeming cinder which he was beholding? Would he not have denied that it contained any potentiality of consciousness? Yet in the course of time consciousness came. Is it not possible then that there may be even yet new channels dug out for consciousness, though we can detect no signs of them at present?

"Again. Consciousness, in anything like the present acceptation of the term, having been once a new thing—a thing, as far as we can see, subsequent even to an individual center of action and to a reproductive system (which we see existing in plants without apparent consciousness)—why may not there arise some new phase of mind which shall be as different from all present known phases, as the mind of animals is from that of vegetables?

"It would be absurd to attempt to define such a mental state (or whatever it may be called), inasmuch as it must be something so foreign to man that his experience can give him no help towards conceiving its nature; but surely when we reflect upon the manifold phases of life and consciousness which have been evolved already, it would be rash to say that no others can be developed, and that animal life is the end of all things. There was a time when fire was the end of all things: another when rocks and water were so."

The writer, after enlarging on the above for several pages, proceeded to inquire whether traces of the approach of such a new phase of life could be perceived at present; whether we could see any tenements preparing which might in a remote futurity be adapted for it; whether, in fact, the primordial cell of such a kind of life could be now detected upon earth. In the course of his work he answered this question in the affirmative and pointed to the higher machines.

"There is no security"—to quote his own words—"against the ultimate development of mechanical consciousness, in the fact of machines possessing little consciousness now. A mollusc has not much consciousness. Reflect upon the extraordinary advance which machines have made during the last few hundred years, and note how slowly the animal and vegetable kingdoms are advancing. The more highly organized machines are creatures not so much of yesterday, as of the last five minutes, so to speak, in comparison with past time. Assume for the sake of argument that conscious beings have existed for some twenty million years: see what strides machines have made in the last thousand! May not the world last twenty million years longer? If so, what will they not in the end become? Is it not safer to nip the mischief in the bud and to forbid them further progress?

"But who can say that the vapor-engine has not a kind of consciousness? Where does consciousness begin, and where end? Who can draw the line? Who can draw any line? Is not everything interwoven with everything? Is not machinery linked with animal life in an infinite variety of ways? The shell of a hen's egg is made of a delicate white ware and is a machine as much as an egg-cup is: the shell is a device for holding the egg, as much as the egg-cup for holding the shell: both are phases of the same function; the hen makes the shell in her inside, but it is pure pottery. She makes her nest outside of herself for convenience' sake, but the nest is not more of a machine than the egg-shell it. A 'machine' is only a 'device.' . . .

"Do not let me be misunderstood as living in fear of any actually existing machine; there is probably no known machine which is more than a prototype of future mechanical life. The present machines are to the future as the early Saurians to man. The largest of them will probably greatly diminish in size. Some of the lowest vertebrate attained a much greater bulk than has descended to their more highly organized living representatives, and in like manner a diminution in the size of machines has often attended their development and progress.

"Take the watch, for example; examine its beautiful structure; observe the intelligent play of the minute members which compose it: yet this little creature is but a development of the cumbrous clocks that preceded it; it is no deterioration from them. A day may come when clocks, which certainly at the present time are not diminishing in bulk, will be superseded owing to the universal use of watches, in which case they will become as extinct as ichthyosauri, while the watch, whose tendency has for some years been to decrease in size rather than the contrary, will remain the only existing type of an extinct race.

"But returning to the argument, I would repeat that I fear none of the existing machines; what I fear is the extraordinary rapidity with which they are becoming something very different to what they are at present. No class of beings have in any time past made so rapid a movement forward. Should not that movement be jealously watched, and checked while we can still check it? And is it not necessary for this end to destroy the more advanced of the machines which are in use at present, though it is admitted that they are in themselves harmless?

"As yet the machines receive their impressions through the agency of man's senses: one traveling machine calls to another in a shrill accent of alarm and the other instantly retires; but it is through the ears of the driver that the voice of the one has acted upon the other. Had there been no driver, the callee would have been deaf to the caller. There was a time when it must have seemed highly improbable that machines should learn to make their wants known by sound, even through the ears of man; may we not conceive, then, that a day will come when those ears will be no longer needed, and the hearing will be done by the delicacy of the machine's own construction?—when its language shall have been developed from the cry of animals to a speech as intricate as our own?

"It is possible that by that time children will learn the differential calculus—as they learn now to speak—from their mothers and nurses, or that they may talk in the hypothetical language, and work rule of three sums, as soon as they are born; but this is not probable; we cannot calculate on any corresponding advance in man's intellectual or physical powers which shall be a set-off against the far greater development which seems in store for the machines. Some people may say that man's moral influence will suffice to rule them; but I cannot think it will ever be safe to repose much trust in the moral sense of any machine.

"Again, might not the glory of the machines consist in their being without this same boasted gift of language? 'Silence,' it has been said by one writer, 'is a virtue which renders us agreeable to our fellow-creatures.'"

Chapter XXIV. The Book of the Machines—continued

"BUT other questions come upon us. What is a man's eye but a machine for the little creature that sits behind in his brain to look through? A dead eye is nearly as good as a living one for some time after the man is dead. It is not the eye that cannot see, but the restless one that cannot see through it. Is it man's eyes, or is it the big seeing-engine which has revealed to us the existence of worlds beyond worlds into infinity? What has made man familiar with the scenery of the moon, the spots on the sun, or the geography of the planets? He is at the mercy of the seeing-engine for these things, and is powerless unless he tack it on to his own identity, and make it part and parcel of himself. Or, again, is it the eye, or the little see-engine, which has shown us the existence of infinitely minute organisms which swarm unsuspected around us? . . .

"It can be answered that even though machines should hear never so well and speak never so wisely, they will still always do the one or the other for our advantage, not their own; that man will be the ruling spirit and the machine the servant; that as soon as a machine fails to discharge the service which man expects from it, it is doomed to extinction; that the machines stand to man simply in the relation of lower animals, the vapor-engine itself being only a more economical kind of horse; so that instead of being likely to be developed into a higher kind of life than man's, they owe their very existence and progress to their power of ministering to human wants, and must therefore both now and ever be man's inferiors.

"This is all very well. But the servant glides by imperceptible approaches into the master; and we have come to such a pass that, even now, man must suffer terribly on ceasing to benefit the machines. If all machines were to be annihilated at one moment, so that not a knife nor lever nor rag of clothing nor anything whatsoever were left to man but his bare body alone that he was born with, and if all knowledge of mechanical laws were taken from him so that he could make no more machines, and all machine-made food destroyed so that the race of man should be left as it were naked upon a desert island, we should become extinct in six weeks. A few miserable individuals might linger, but even these in a year or two would become worse than monkeys. Man's very soul is due to the machines; it is a machine-made thing: he thinks as he thinks, and feels as he feels, through the work that machines have wrought upon him, and their existence is quite as much a *sine quâ non* for his, as for theirs. This fact precludes us from proposing the complete annihilation of machinery, but surely it indicates that we should destroy as many of them as we can possibly dispense with, lest they should tyrannize over us even more completely.

"True, from a low materialistic point of view, it would seem that those thrive best who use machinery wherever its use is possible with profit; but this is the art of the machines—they serve that they may rule. They bear no malice towards man for destroying a whole race of them provided he creates a better instead; on the contrary, they reward him liberally for having hastened their development. It is for neglecting them that he incurs their wrath, or for using inferior machines, or for not making sufficient exertions to invent new ones, or for destroying them without replacing them; yet these are the very things we ought to do, and do quickly; for though our rebellion against their infant power will cause infinite suffering, what will not things come to, if that rebellion is delayed?

"They have preyed upon man's groveling preference for his material over his spiritual interests; and have betrayed him into supplying that element of struggle and warfare without which no race can advance. The lower animals progress because they struggle with one another; the weaker die, the stronger breed and transmit their strength. The machines being of themselves unable to struggle, have got man to do their struggling for them: as long as he fulfills this function duly, all goes well with him—at least he thinks so; but the moment he fails to do his best for the advancement of machinery by encouraging the good and destroying the bad, he is left behind in the race of competition; and this means that he will be made uncomfortable in a variety of ways, and perhaps die.

"So that even now the machines will only serve on condition of being served, and that too upon their own terms; the moment their terms are not complied with, they jib, and either smash both themselves and all whom they can reach, or turn churlish and refuse to work at all. How many men at this hour are living in a state of bondage to the machines? How many spend their whole lives, from the cradle to the grave, in tending them by night and day? Is it not plain that the machines are gaining ground upon us, when we reflect on the increasing number of those who are bound down to them as slaves, and of those who devote their whole souls to the advancement of the mechanical kingdom? . . .

"The main point, however, to be observed as affording cause for alarm is, that whereas animals were formerly the only stomachs of the machines, there are now many which have stomachs of their own, and consume their food themselves. This is a great step towards their becoming, if not animate, yet something so near akin to it, as not to differ more widely from our own life than animals do from vegetables. And though man should remain, in some respects, the higher creature, is not this in accordance with the practice of nature, which allows superiority in some things to animals which have, on the whole, been long surpassed? Has she not allowed the ant and the bee to retain superiority over man in the organization of their communities and social arrangements, the bird in traversing the air, the fish in swimming, the horse in strength and fleetness, and the dog in self-sacrifice?

"It is said by some with whom I have conversed upon this subject, that the machines can never be developed into animate or *quasi*-animate existences, inasmuch as they have no reproductive system, nor seem ever likely to possess one. If this be taken to mean that they cannot marry, and that we are never likely to see a fertile union between two vapor-engines with the young ones playing about the door of the shed, however greatly we might desire to do so, I will readily grant it. But the objection is not a very profound one. No one expects that all the features of the now existing organizations will be absolutely repeated in an entirely new class of life. The reproductive system of animals differs widely from that of plants, but both are reproductive systems. Has nature exhausted her phases of this power?

"Surely if a machine is able to reproduce another machine systematically, we may say that it has a reproductive system. What is a reproductive system, if it be not a system for reproduction? And how few of the machines are there which have not been produced systematically by other machines? But it is man that makes them do so. Yes; but is it not insects that make many of the plants reproductive, and would not whole families of plants die out if their fertilization was not effected by a class of agents utterly foreign to themselves? Does any one say that the red clover has no reproductive system because the humble bee (and the humble bee only) must aid and abet it before it can reproduce? No one. The humble bee is a part of the reproductive system of the clover. Each one of ourselves has sprung from minute animalcules whose entity was entirely distinct from our own, and which acted after their kind with no thought or heed of what we might think about it. These little creatures are part of our own reproductive system; then why not we part of that of the machines?

"But the machines which reproduce machinery do not reproduce machines after their own kind. A thimble may be made by machinery, but it was not made by, neither will it ever make, a thimble. Here, again, if we turn to nature we shall find abundance of analogies which will teach us that a reproductive system may be in full force without the thing produced being of the same kind as that which produced it. Very few creatures reproduce after their own kind; they reproduce something which has the potentiality of becoming that which their parents were. Thus the butterfly lays an egg, which egg can become a caterpillar, which caterpillar can become a chrysalis, which chrysalis can become a butterfly; and though I freely grant that the machines cannot be said to have more than the germ of a true reproductive system at present, have we not just seen that they have only recently obtained the germs of a mouth and stomach? And may not some stride be made in the direction of true reproduction which shall be as great as that which has been recently taken in the direction of true feeding?

"It is possible that the system when developed may be in many cases a vicarious thing. Certain classes of machines may be alone fertile, while the rest discharge other functions in the mechanical system, just as the great majority of ants and bees have nothing to do with the continuation of their species, but get food and store it, without thought of breeding. One cannot expect the parallel to be complete or nearly so; certainly not now, and probably never; but is there not enough analogy existing at the present moment, to make us feel seriously uneasy about the future, and to render it our duty to check the evil while we can still do so? Machines can within certain limits beget machines of any class, no matter how different to themselves, Every class of machines will probably have its special mechanical breeders, and all the higher ones will owe their existence to a large number of parents and not to two only.

Samuel Butler (1835–1902) was an English novelist.

Source: [Samuel Butler], Erewhon; or, Over the Range (London: Trübner, 1872), 206–19, 222–24, 228–31, 233–35, 238–41.

Edward Bellamy
Looking Backward: 2000–1887

One of the most influential events in the history of utopian literature was the publication of Edward Bellamy's novel *Looking Backward: 2000–1887*. This novel sold more copies than any other book (except religious books such as the Bible and the Koran) and inspired hundreds of imitators, commentators, and critics to write utopian novels in all Western languages. In addition, movements started in many countries to attempt to put Bellamy's ideas into practice. Bellamy, who had been a rather shy journalist and novelist, found himself leading one such movement.

Julian West, the hero of the novel, falls asleep in 1887 and wakes up in 2000, where he is shown around by members of the Leete family. This method of conveying someone to the future, while not original with Bellamy, becomes common in utopian literature after him.

Chapter 5

"THE movement toward the conduct of business by larger and larger aggregations of capital, the tendency toward monopolies, which had been so desperately and vainly resisted, was recognized at last, in its true significance, as a process which only needed to complete its logical evolution to open a golden future to humanity.

"Early in the last century the evolution was completed by the final consolidation of the entire capital of the nation. The industry and commerce of the country, ceasing to be conducted by a set of irresponsible corporations and syndicates of private persons at their caprice and for their profit, were intrusted to a single syndicate representing the people, to be conducted in the common interest for the common profit. The nation, that is to say, organized as the one great business corporation in which all other corporations were absorbed; it became the one capitalist in the place of all other capitalists, the sole employer, the final monopoly in which all previous and lesser monopolies were swallowed up, a monopoly in the profits and economies of which all citizens shared. The epoch of trusts had ended in The Great Trust. In a word, the people of the United States concluded to assume the conduct of their own business, just as one hundred odd years before they had assumed the conduct of their own government, organizing now for industrial purposes on precisely the same grounds that they had then organized for political purposes. At last, strangely late in the world's history, the obvious fact was perceived that no business is so essentially the public business as the industry and commerce on which the people's livelihood depends, and that to entrust it to private persons to be managed for private profit is a folly similar in kind, though vastly greater in magnitude, to that of surrendering the functions of political government to kings and nobles to be conducted for their personal glorification."

"Such a stupendous change as you describe," said I, "did not, of course, take place without great bloodshed and terrible convulsions."

"On the contrary," replied Dr. Leete, "there was absolutely no violence. The change had been long foreseen. Public opinion had become fully ripe for it, and the whole mass of the people was behind it. There was no more possibility of opposing it by force than by argument. On the other hand the popular sentiment toward the great corporations and those identified with them had ceased to be one of bitterness, as they came to realize their necessity as a link, a transition phase, in the evolution of the true industrial system. The most violent foes of the great private monopolies were now forced to recognize how invaluable and indispenable had been their office in educating the people up to the point of assuming control of their own business. Fifty years before, the consolidation of the industries of the country under national control would have seemed a very daring experiment to the most sanguine. But by a series of object lessons, seen and studied by all men, the great corporations had taught the people an entirely new set of ideas on this subject. They had seen for many years syndicates handling revenues greater than those of states, and directing the labors of hundreds of thousands of men with an efficiency and economy unattainable in smaller operations. It had come to be recognized as an axiom that the larger the business the simpler the principles that can be applied to it; that, as the machine is truer than the hand, so the system, which in a great concern does the work of the master's eye in a small business, turns out more accurate results. Thus it came about that, thanks to the corporations themselves, when it was proposed that the nation should assume their functions, the suggestion implied nothing which seemed impracticable even to the timid. To be sure it was a step beyond any yet taken, a broader generalization, but the very fact that the nation would be the sole corporation in the field would, it was seen, relieve the undertaking of many difficulties with which the partial monopolies had contended."

Chapter 6

DR. LEETE ceased speaking, and I remained silent, endeavoring to form some general conception of the changes in the arrangements of society implied in the tremendous revolution which he had described.

Finally I said, "The idea of such an extension of the functions of government is, to say the least, rather overwhelming."

"Extension!" he repeated, "where is the extension?"

"In my day," I replied, "it was considered that the proper functions of government, strictly speaking, were limited to keeping the peace and defending the people against the public enemy, that is, to the military and police powers."

"And, in heaven's name, who are the public enemies?" exclaimed Dr. Leete. "Are they France, England, Germany, or hunger, cold, and nakedness? In your day governments were accustomed, on the slightest international misunderstanding, to seize upon the bodies of citizens and deliver them over by hundreds of thousands to death and mutilation, wasting their treasures the while like water; and all this oftenest for no imaginable profit to the victims. We have no wars now, and our governments no war powers, but in order to protect every citizen against hunger, cold, and nakedness, and provide for all his physical and mental needs, the function is assumed of directing his industry for a term of years. No, Mr. West, I am sure on reflection you will perceive that it was in your age, not in ours, that the extension of the functions of governments was extraordinary. Not even for the best ends would men now allow their governments such powers as were then used for the most maleficent."

"Leaving comparisons aside," I said, "the demagoguery and corruption of our public men would have been considered, in my day, insuperable objections to any assumption by government, of the charge of the national industries. We should have thought that no arrangement could be worse than to entrust the politicians with control of the wealth-producing machinery of the country. Its material interests were quite too much the football of parties as it was."

"No doubt you were right," rejoined Dr. Leete, "but all that is changed now. We have no parties or politicians, and as for demagoguery and corruption, they are words having only an historical significance."

"Human nature itself must have changed very much," I said.

"Not at all," was Dr. Leete's reply, "but the conditions of human life have changed, and with them the motives of human action. The organization of society with you was such that officials were under a constant temptation to misuse their power for the private profit of themselves or others. Under such circumstances it seems almost strange that you dared entrust them with any of your affairs. Nowadays, on the contrary, society is so constituted that there is absolutely no way in which an official, however ill-disposed, could possibly make any profit for himself or any one else by a misuse of his power. Let him be as bad an official as you please, he cannot be a corrupt one. There is no motive to be. The social system no longer offers a premium on dishonesty. But these are matters which you can only understand as you come, with time, to know us better."

"But you have not yet told me how you have settled the labor problem. It is the problem of capital which we have been discussing," I said. "After the nation had assumed conduct of the mills, machinery, railroads, farms, mines, and capital in general of the country, the labor question still remained. In assuming the responsibilities of capital the nation had assumed the difficulties of the capitalist's position."

"The moment the nation assumed the responsibilities of capital those difficulties vanished," replied Dr. Leete. "The national organization of labor under one direction was the complete solution of what was, in your day and under your system, justly regarded as the insoluble labor problem. When the nation became the sole employer, all the citizens, by virtue of their citizenship, became employees, to be distributed according to the needs of industry."

"That is," I suggested, "you have simply applied the principle of universal military service, as it was understood in our day, to the labor question."

"Yes," said Dr. Leete, "that was something which followed as a matter of course as soon as the nation had become the sole capitalist. The people were already accustomed to the idea that the obligation of every citizen, not physically disabled, to contribute his military services to the defense of the nation was equal and absolute. That it was equally the duty of every citizen to contribute his quota of industrial or intellectual services to the maintenance of the nation was equally evident, though it was not until the nation became the employer of labor that citizens were able to render this sort of service with any pretence either of universality or equity. No organization of labor was possible when the employing power was divided among hundreds or thousands of individuals and corporations, between which concert of any kind was neither desired, nor indeed feasible. It constantly happened then that vast numbers who desired to labor could find no opportunity, and on the other hand, those who desired to evade a part or all of their debt could easily do so.

"Service, now, I suppose, is compulsory upon all," I suggested.

"It is rather a matter of course than of compulsion," replied Dr. Leete. "It is regarded as so absolutely natural and reasonable that the idea of its being compulsory has ceased to be thought of. He would be thought to be an incredibly contemptible person who should need compulsion in such a case. Nevertheless, to speak of service being compulsory would be a weak way to state its absolute inevitableness. Our entire social order is so wholly based upon and deduced from it that if it were conceivable that a man could escape it, he would be left with no possible way to provide for his existence. He would have excluded himself from the world, cut himself off from his kind, in a word, committed suicide."

"Is the term of service in this industrial army for life?"

"Oh, no; it both begins later and ends earlier than the average working period in your day. Your workshops were filled with children and old men, but we hold the period of youth sacred to education, and the period of maturity, when the physical forces begin to flag, equally sacred to ease and agreeable relaxation. The period of industrial service is twenty-four years, beginning at the close of the course of education at twenty-one and terminating at forty-five. After forty-five, while discharged from labor, the citizen still remains liable to special calls, in case of emergencies causing a sudden great increase in the demand for labor, till he reaches the age of fifty-five, but such calls are rarely, in fact almost never, made. The fifteenth day of October of every year is what we call Muster Day, because those who have reached the age of twenty-one are then mustered into the industrial service, and at the same time those who, after twenty-four years' service, have reached the age of forty-five, are honorably mustered out. It is the great day of the year with us, whence we reckon all other events, our Olympiad, save that it is annual."

Chapter 7

"It is after you have mustered your industrial army into service," I said, "that I should expect the chief difficulty to arise, for there its analogy with a military army must cease. Soldiers have all the same thing, and a very simple thing, to do, namely, to practice the manual of arms, to march and stand guard. But the industrial army must learn and follow two or three hundred diverse trades and avocations. What administrative talent can be equal to determining wisely what trade or business every individual in a great nation shall pursue?"

"The administration has nothing to do with determining that point."

"Who does determine it, then?" I asked.

"Every man for himself in accordance with his natural aptitude, the utmost pains being taken to enable him to find out what his natural aptitude really is. The principle on which our industrial army is organized is that a man's natural endowments, mental and physical, determine what he can work at most profitably to the nation and most satisfactorily to himself. While the obligation of service in some form is not to be evaded, voluntary election, subject only to necessary regulation, is depended on to determine the particular sort of service every man is to render. As an individual's satisfaction during his term of service depends on his having an occupation to his taste, parents and teachers watch from early years for indications of special aptitudes in children. A thorough study of the National industrial system, with the history and rudiments of all the great trades, is an essential part of our educational system. While manual training is not allowed to encroach on the general intellectual culture to which our schools are devoted, it is carried far enough to give our youth, in addition to their theoretical knowledge of the national industries, mechanical and agricultural, a certain familiarity with their tools and methods. Our schools are constantly visiting our workshops, and often are taken on long excursions to inspect particular industrial enterprises. In your day a man was not ashamed to be grossly ignorant of all trades except his own, but such ignorance would not be consistent with our idea of placing every one in a position to select intelligently the occupation for which he has most taste. Usually long before he is mustered into service a young man has found out the pursuit he wants to follow, has acquired a great deal of knowledge about it, and is waiting impatiently the time when he can enlist in its ranks."

"Surely," I said, "it can hardly be that the number of volunteers for any trade is exactly the number needed in that trade. It must be generally either under or over the demand."

"The supply of volunteers is always expected to fully equal the demand," replied Dr. Leete. "It is the business of the administration to see that this is the case. The rate of volunteering for each trade is closely watched. If there be a noticeably greater excess of volunteers over men needed in any trade, it is inferred that the trade offers greater attractions than others. On the other hand, if the number of volunteers for a trade tends to drop below the demand, it is inferred that it is thought more arduous. It is the business of the administration to seek constantly to equalize the attractions of the trades, so far as the conditions of labor in them are concerned, so that all trades shall be equally attractive to persons having natural tastes for them. This is done by making the hours of labor in different trades to differ according to their arduousness. The lighter trades, prosecuted under the most agreeable circumstances, have in this way the longest hours, while an arduous place, such as mining, has very short hours. There is no theory, no *a priori* rule, by which the respective attractiveness of industries is determined. The administration, in taking burdens off one class of workers and adding them to other classes, simply follows the fluctuations of opinion among the workers themselves as indicated by the rate of volunteering. The principle is that no man's work ought to be, on the whole, harder for him than any other man's for him, the workers themselves to be the judges. There are no limits to the application of this rule. If any particular occupation is in itself so arduous or so oppressive that, in order to induce volunteers, the day's work in it had to be reduced to ten minutes, it would be done. If, even then, no man was willing to do it, it would remain undone. But of course, in point of fact, a moderate reduction in the hours of labor, or addition of other privileges, suffices to secure all needed volunteers for any occupation necessary to men. If, indeed, the unavoidable difficulties and dangers of such a necessary pursuit were so great that no inducement of compensating advantages would overcome men's repugnance to it, the administration would only need to take it out of the common order of occupations by declaring it 'extra hazardous,' and those who pursued it especially worthy of the national gratitude, to be overrun with volunteers. Our young men are very greedy of honor, and do not let slip such opportunities. Of course you will see that dependence on the purely voluntary choice of avocations involves the abolition in all of anything like unhygienic conditions or special peril to life and limb. Health and safety are conditions common to all industries. The nation does not maim and slaughter its workmen by thousands, as did the private capitalists and corporations of your day."

"When there are more who want to enter a particular trade than there is room for, how do you decide between the applicants?" I inquired.

"Preference is given to those who have acquired the most knowledge of the trade they wish to follow. No man, however, who through successive years remains persistent in his desire to show what he can do at any particular trade, is in the end denied an opportunity. Meanwhile, if a man cannot at first win entrance into the business he prefers he has usually one or more alternative preferences, pursuits for which he has some degree of aptitude, although not the highest. Every one, indeed, is expected to study his aptitudes so as to have not only a first choice as to occupation, but a second or third, so that if, either at the outset of his career or subsequently, owing to the progress of invention or changes in demand, he is unable to follow his first vocation, he can still find reasonably congenial employment. This principle of secondary choices as to occupation is quite important in our system I should add, in reference to the counter-possibility of some sudden failure of volunteers in a particular trade, or some sudden necessity of an increased force, that the administration, while depending on the voluntary system for filling up the trades as a rule, holds always in reserve the power to call for special volunteers, or draft any force needed from any quarter. Generally, however, all needs of this sort can be met by details from the class of unskilled or common laborers."

"How is this class of common laborers recruited?" I asked? "Surely nobody voluntarily enters that."

"It is the grade to which all new recruits belong for the first three years of their service. It is not till after this period, during which he is assignable to any work at the discretion of his superiors, that the young man is allowed to elect a special avocation. These three years of stringent discipline none are exempt from, and very glad our young men are to pass from this severe school into the comparative liberty of the trades. If a man were so stupid as to have no choice as to occupation, he would simply remain a common laborer; but such cases, as you may suppose, are not common."

"Having once elected and entered on a trade or occupation," I remarked, "I suppose he has to stick to it the rest of his life."

"Not necessarily," replied Dr. Leete, "while frequent and merely capricious changes of occupation are not encouraged or even permitted, every worker is allowed, of course, under certain regulations and in accordance with the exigencies of the service, to volunteer for another industry which he thinks would suit him better than his first choice. In this case his application is received just as if he were volunteering for the first time, and on the same terms. Not only this, but a worker may likewise, under suitable regulations and not too frequently, obtain a transfer to an establishment of the same industry in another part of the country which for any reason he may prefer. Under your system a discontented man could indeed leave his work at will, but he left his means of support at the same time, and took his chances as to future livelihood. We find that the number of men who wish to abandon an accustomed occupation for a new one, and old friends and associations for strange ones, is small. It is only the poorer sort of workmen who desire to change even as frequently as our regulations permit. Of course transfers or discharges, when health demands them, are always given."

"As an industrial system, I should think this might be extremely efficient," I said, "but I don't see that it makes any provision for the professional classes, the men who serve the nation with brains instead of hands. Of course you can't get along without the brain-workers. How, then, are they selected from those who are to serve as farmers and mechanics? That must require a very delicate sort of sifting process, I should say."

"So it does," replied Dr. Leete, "the most delicate possible test is needed here, and so we leave the question whether a man shall be a brain or hand worker entirely to him to settle. At the end of the term of three years as a common laborer, which every man must serve, it is for him to choose, in accordance to his natural tastes, whether he will fit himself for an art or profession, or be a farmer or mechanic. If he feels that he can do better work with his brains than his muscles, he finds every facility provided for testing the reality of his supposed bent, of cultivating it, and if fit, of pursuing it as his avocation. The schools of technology, of medicine, of art, of music, of histrionics, and of higher liberal learning are always open to aspirants without condition."

"Are not the schools flooded with young men whose only motive is to avoid work?"

Dr. Leete smiled a little grimly.

"No one is at all likely to enter the professional schools for the purpose of avoiding work, I assure you," he said, "They are intended for those with special aptitude for the branches they teach, and any one without it would find it easier to do double hours at his trade than try to keep up with the classes. Of course many honestly mistake their vocation, and, finding themselves unequal to the requirements of the schools, drop out and return to the industrial service; no discredit attaches to such persons, for the public policy is to encourage all to develop suspected talents which only actual tests can prove the reality of. The professional and scientific schools of your day depended on the patronage of their pupils for support, and the practice appears to have been common of giving diplomas to unfit persons, who afterwards found their way into the professions. Our schools are national institutions, and to have passed their tests by a proof of special abilities not to be questioned.

"This opportunity for a professional training," the doctor continued, "remains open to every man till the age of thirty is reached, after which students are not received, as there would remain too brief a period before the age of discharge in which to serve the nation in their professions. In your day young men had to choose their professions very young, and therefore, in a large proportion of instances, wholly mistook their vocations. It is recognized nowadays that the natural aptitudes of some are later than those of others in developing, and therefore, while the choice of profession may be made as early as twenty-four, it remains open for six years longer."

A question which had a dozen times before been on my lips now found utterance, a question which touched upon what, in my time, had been regarded the most vital difficulty in the way of any final settlement of the industrial problem. "It is an extraordinary thing," I said, "that you should not yet have said a word about the method of adjusting wages. Since the nation is the sole employer, the government must fix the rate of wages and determine just how much everybody shall earn, from the doctors to the diggers. All I can say is, that this plan would never have worked with us, and I don't see how it can now unless human nature has changed. In my day, nobody was satisfied with his wages or salary. Even if he felt he received enough, he was sure his neighbor had too much, which was as bad. If the universal discontent on this subject, instead of being dissipated in curses and strikes directed against innumerable employers, could have been concentrated upon one, and that the government, the strongest ever devised would not have seen two pay days."

Dr. Leete laughed heartily.

"Very true, very true," he said, "a general strike would most probably have followed the first pay day, and a strike directed against a government is a revolution."

"How, then, do you avoid a revolution every pay day?" I demanded? "Has some prodigious philosopher devised a new system of calculus satisfactory to all for determining the exact and comparative value of all sorts of service, whether by brawn or brain, by hand or voice, by ear or eye? Or has human nature itself changed, so that no man looks upon his own things but 'every man on the things of his neighbor?' One or the other of these events must be the explanation."

"Neither one nor the other, however, is," was my host's laughing response. "And now, Mr. West," he continued, "you must remember that you are my patient as well as my guest, and permit me to prescribe sleep for you before we have any more conversation. It is after three o'clock."

"The prescription is, no doubt, a wise one," I said, "I only hope it can be filled."

"I will see to that," the doctor replied, and he did, for he gave me a wineglass of something or other which sent me to sleep as soon as my head touched the pillow. . . .

Chapter 9

Dr. and Mrs. Leete were evidently not a little startled to learn, when they presently appeared, that I had been all over the city alone that morning, and it was apparent that they were agreeably surprised to see that I seemed so little agitated after the experience.

"Your stroll could scarcely have failed to be a very interesting one," said Mrs. Leete, as we sat down to table soon after. "You must have seen a good many new things."

"I saw very little that was not new," I replied. "But I think what surprised me as much as anything was not to find any stores on Washington Street, or any banks on State. What have you done with the merchants and bankers? Hung them all, perhaps, as the anarchists wanted to do in my day?"

"Not so bad as that," replied Dr. Leete. "We have simply dispensed with them. Their functions are obsolete in the modern world."

"Who sells you things when you want to buy them?" I inquired.

"There is neither selling nor buying nowadays; the distribution of goods is effected in another way. As to the bankers, having no money we have no use for those gentry."

"Miss Leete," said I, turning to Edith, "I am afraid that your father is making sport of me. I don't blame him, for the temptation my innocence offers must be extraordinary. But, really, there are limits to my credulity as to possible alterations in the social system."

"Father has no idea of jesting, I am sure," she replied, with a reassuring smile.

The conversation took another turn then, the point of ladies' fashions in the nineteenth century being raised, if I remember rightly, by Mrs. Leete, and it was not till after breakfast, when the doctor had invited me up to the house-top, which appeared to be a favorite resort of his, that he recurred to the subject.

"You were surprised," he said, "at my saying that we got along without money or trade, but a moment's reflection will show that trade existed and money was needed in your day simply because the business of production was left in private hands, and that, consequently, they are superfluous now."

"I do not at once see how that follows," I replied.

"It is very simple," said Dr. Leete. "When innumerable different and independent persons produced the various things needful to life and comfort, endless exchanges between individuals were requisite in order that they might supply themselves with what they desired. These exchanges constituted trade, and money was essential as their medium. But as soon as the nation became the sole producer of all sorts of commodities, there was no need of exchanges between individuals that they might get what they required. Everything was procurable from one source, and nothing could be procured anywhere else. A system of direct distribution from the national storehouses took the place of trade, and for this money was unnecessary."

"How is this distribution managed?" I asked.

"On the simplest possible plan," replied Dr. Leete. "A credit corresponding to his share of the annual product of the nation is given to every citizen on the public books at the beginning of each year, and a credit card issued him with which he procures at the public storehouses, found in every community, whatever he desires whenever he desires it. This arrangement, you will see, totally obviates the necessity for business transactions of any sort between individuals and consumers. Perhaps you would like to see what our credit-cards are like.

"You observe," he pursued as I was curiously examining the piece of pasteboard he gave me, "that this card is issued for a certain number of dollars. We have kept the old word, but not the substance. The term, as we use it, answers to no real thing, but merely serves as an algebraical symbol for comparing the values of products with one another. For this purpose they are all priced in dollars and cents, just as in your day. The value of what I procure on this card is checked off by the clerk, who pricks out of these tiers of squares the price of what I order."

"If you wanted to buy something of your neighbor, could you transfer part of your credit to him as consideration?" I inquired.

"In the first place," replied Dr. Leete, "our neighbors have nothing to sell us, but in any event our credit would not be transferable, being strictly personal. Before the nation could even think of honoring any such transfer as you speak of, it would be bound to inquire into all the circumstances of the transaction, so as to be able to guarantee its absolute equity. It would have been reason enough, had there been no other, for abolishing money, that its possession was no indication of rightful title to it. In the hands of the man who had stolen it or murdered for it, it was as good as in those which had earned it by industry. People nowadays interchange gifts and favors out of friendship, but buying and selling is considered absolutely inconsistent with the mutual benevolence and disinterestedness which should prevail between citizens and the sense of community of interest which supports our social system. According to our ideas, buying and selling is essentially antisocial in all its tendencies. It is an education in self-seeking at the expense of others, and no society whose citizens are trained in such a school can possibly rise above a very low grade of civilization."

"What if you have to spend more than your card in any one year?" I asked.

"The provision is so ample that we are more likely not to spend it all," replied Dr. Leete. "But if extraordinary expenses should exhaust it, we can obtain a limited advance on the next year's credit, though this practice is not encouraged, and a heavy discount is charged to check it. Of course if a man showed himself a reckless spendthrift he would receive his allowance monthly or weekly instead of yearly, or if necessary not be permitted to handle it all."

"If you don't spend your allowance, I suppose it accumulates?"

"That is also permitted to a certain extent when a special outlay is anticipated. But unless notice to the contrary is given, it is presumed that the citizen who does not fully expend his credit did not have occasion to do so, and the balance is turned into the general surplus."

"Such a system does not encourage saving habits on the part of citizens," I said.

"It is not intended to," was the reply. "The nation is rich, and does not wish the people to deprive themselves of any good thing. In your day, men were bound to lay up goods and money against coming failure of the means of support and for their children. This necessity made parsimony a virtue. But now it would have no such laudable object, and, having lost its utility, it has ceased to be regarded as a virtue. No man any more has any care for the morrow, either for himself or his children, for the nation guarantees the nurture, education, and comfortable maintenance of every citizen from the cradle to the grave."

"That is a sweeping guarantee!" I said. "What certainty can there be that the value of a man's labor will recompense the nation for its outlay on him? On the whole, society may be able to support all its members, but some must earn less than enough for their support, and others more; and that brings us back once more to the wages question, on which you have hitherto said nothing. It was at just this point, if you remember, that our talk ended last evening; and I say again, as I did then, that here I should suppose a national industrial system like yours would find its main difficulty. How, I ask once more, can you adjust satisfactorily the comparative wages or remuneration of the multitude of avocations, so unlike and so incommensurable, which are necessary for the service of society? In our day the market rate determined the price of labor of all sorts, as well as of goods. The employer paid as little as he could, and the worker got as much. It was not a pretty system ethically, I admit; but it did, at least, furnish us a rough and ready formula for settling a question which must be settled ten thousand times a day if the world was ever going to get forward. There seemed to us no other practicable way of doing it."

"Yes," replied Dr. Leete, "it was the only practicable way under a system which made the interests of every individual antagonistic to those of every other; but it would have been a pity if humanity could never have devised a better plan, for yours was simply the application to the mutual relations of men of the devil's maxim, 'Your necessity is my opportunity.' The reward of any service depended not upon its difficulty, danger, or hardship, for throughout the world it seems that the most perilous, severe, and repulsive labor was done by the worst paid classes; but solely upon the strait of those who needed the service."

"All that is conceded," I said. "But, with all its defects, the plan of settling prices by the market rate was a practical plan; and I cannot conceive what satisfactory substitute you can have devised for it. The government being the only possible employer, there is of course no labor market or market rate. Wages of all sorts must be arbitrarily fixed by the government. I cannot imagine a more complex and delicate function than that must be, or one, however performed, more certain to breed universal dissatisfaction."

"I beg your pardon," replied Dr. Leete, "but I think you exaggerate the difficulty. Suppose a board of fairly sensible men were charged with settling the wages for all sorts of trades under a system which, like ours, guaranteed employment to all, while permitting the choice of avocations. Don't you see that, however unsatisfactory the first adjustment might be, the mistakes would soon correct themselves? The favored trades would have too many volunteers, and those discriminated against would lack them till the errors were set right. But this is aside from the purpose, for, though this plan would, I fancy, be practicable enough, it is no part of our system."

"How, then, do you regulate wages?" I once more asked.

Dr. Leete did not reply till after several moments of meditative silence. "I know, of course," he finally said, "enough of the old order of things to understand just what you mean by that question; and yet the present order is so utterly different at this point that I am a little at loss how to answer you best. You ask me how we regulate wages; I can only reply that there is no idea in the modern social economy which at all corresponds with what was meant by wages in your day."

"I suppose you mean that you have no money to pay wages in," said I. "But the credit given the worker at the government storehouse answers to his wages with us. How is the amount of the credit given respectively to the workers in different lines determined? By what title does the individual claim his particular share? What is the basis of allotment?"

"His title," replied Dr. Leete, "is his humanity. The basis of his claim is the fact that he is a man."

"The fact that he is a man!" I repeated, incredulously. "Do you possibly mean that all have the same share?" . . .

"We leave no possible ground for any complaint of injustice," replied Dr. Leete, "by requiring precisely the same measure of service from all."

"How can you do that, I should like to know, when no two men's powers are the same?"

"Nothing could be simpler," was Dr. Leete's reply. "We require of each that he shall make the same effort; that is, we demand of him the best service it is in his power to give."

"And supposing all do the best they can," I answered, "the amount of the product resulting is twice greater from one man than from another."

"Very true," replied Dr. Leete, "but the amount of the resulting product has nothing whatever to do with the question, which is one of desert. Desert is a moral question, and the amount of the product a material quantity. It would be an extraordinary sort of logic which should try to determine a moral question by a material standard. The amount of the effort alone is pertinent to the question of desert. All men who do their best, do the same. A man's endowments, however godlike, merely fix the measure of his duty. The man of great endowments who does not do all he might, though he may do more than a man of small endowments who does his best, is deemed a less deserving worker than the latter, and dies a debtor to his fellows. The Creator sets men's tasks for them by the faculties he gives them, we simply exact their fulfillment."

"No doubt that is very fine philosophy," I said; "nevertheless it seems hard that the man who produces twice as much as another, even if both do their best, should have only the same share."

"Does it, indeed, seem so to you?" responded Dr. Leete. "Now, do you know, that seems very curious to me? The way it strikes people nowadays is, that a man who can produce twice as much as another with the same effort, instead of being rewarded for doing so, ought to be punished if he does not do so. In the nineteenth century, when a horse pulled a heavier load than a goat, I suppose you rewarded him. Now, we should have whipped him soundly if he had not, on the ground that, being much stronger, he ought to. It is singular how ethical standards change." The doctor said this with such a twinkle in his eye that I was obliged to laugh.

"I suppose," I said, "that the real reason that we rewarded men for their endowments, while we considered those of horses and goats merely asking the service to be severally required of them, was that the animals, not being reasoning beings, naturally did the best they could, whereas men could only be induced to do so by rewarding them according to the amount of their product. That brings me to ask why, unless human nature has mightily changed in a hundred years, you are not under the same necessity."

"We are," replied Dr. Leete. "I don't think there has been any change in human nature in that respect since your day. It is still so constituted that special incentives in the form of prizes, and advantages to be gained, are requisite to call out the best endeavors of the average man in any direction."

"But what inducement," I asked, "can a man have to put forth his best endeavors when, however much or little he accomplishes, his income remains the same? High characters may be moved by devotion to the common welfare under such a system, but does not the average man tend to rest back on his oar, reasoning that it is of no use to make a special effort, since the effort will not increase his income, nor its withholding diminish it?"

"Does it then really seem to you," answered my companion, "that human nature is insensible to any motives save fear of want and love of luxury, that you should expect security and equality of livelihood to leave them without possible incentives to effort? Your contemporaries did not really think so, though they might fancy they did. When it was a question of the grandest class of efforts, the most absolute self-devotion, they depended on quite other incentives. Not higher wages, but honor and the hope of men's gratitude, patriotism and the inspiration of duty, were the motives which they set before their soldiers when it was a question of dying for the nation, and never was there an age of the world when those motives did not call out what is best and noblest in men. And not only this, but when you come to analyze the love of money which was the general impulse to effort in your day, you find that the dread of want and desire of luxury was but one of several motives which the pursuit of money, represented; the others, and with many the more influential, being desire of power, of social position and reputation for ability and success. So you see that though we have abolished poverty and the fear of it, and inordinate luxury with the hope of it, we have not touched the greater part of the motives which underlay the love of money in former times, or any of those which prompted the supremer sorts of effort. The coarser motives, which no longer move us, have been replaced by higher motives wholly unknown to the mere wage earners of your age. Now that industry of whatever sort is no longer self-service, but service of the nation, patriotism, passion for humanity, impel the worker as in your day they did the soldier. The army of industry is an army, not alone by virtue of its perfect organization, but by reason also of the ardor of self-devotion which animates its members.

"But as you used to supplement the motives of patriotism with the love of glory, in order to stimulate the valor of your soldiers, so do we. Based as our industrial system is on the principle of requiring the same unit of effort from every man, that is, the best he can do, you will see that the means by which we spur the workers to do their best must be a very essential part of our scheme. With us, diligence in the national service is the sole and certain way to public repute, social distinction, and official power. The value of a man's services to society fixes his rank in it. Compared with the effect of our social arrangements in impelling men to be zealous in business, we deem the object-lessons of biting poverty and wanton luxury on which you depended a device as weak and uncertain as it was barbaric. The lust of honor even in your sordid day notoriously impelled men to more desperate effort than the love of money could." . . .

Chapter 17

I FOUND the processes at the warehouse quite as interesting as Edith had described them, and became even enthusiastic over the truly remarkable illustration which is seen there of the prodigiously multiplied efficiency which perfect organization can give to labor. It is like a gigantic mill, into the hopper of which goods are being constantly poured by the train-load and ship-load, to issue at the other end in packages of pounds and ounces, yards and inches, pints and gallons, corresponding to the infinitely complex personal needs of half a million people. Dr. Leete, with the assistance of data furnished by me as to the way goods were sold in my day, figured out some astounding results in the way of the economies effected by the modern system.

As we set out homeward, I said, "After what I have seen to-day, together with what you have told me, and what I learned under Miss Leete's tutelage at the sample store, I have a tolerably clear idea of your system of distribution, and how it enables you to dispense with a circulating medium. But I should like very much to know something more about your system of production. You have told me in general how your industrial army is levied and organized, but who directs its efforts? What supreme authority determines what shall be done in every department, so that enough of everything is produced and yet no labor wasted? It seems to me that this must be a wonderfully complex and difficult function, requiring very unusual endowments."

"Does it indeed seem so to you?" responded Dr. Leete. "I assure you that it is nothing of the kind, but on the other hand so simple, and depending on principles so obvious and easily applied, that the functionaries at Washington to whom it is trusted require to be nothing more than men of fair abilities to discharge it to the entire satisfaction of the nation. The machine which they direct is indeed a vast one, but so logical in its principles and direct and simple in its workings, that it all but runs itself; and nobody but a fool could derange it, as I think you will agree after a few words of explanation. Since you already have a pretty good idea of the working of the distributive system, let us begin at that end. Even in your day statisticians were able to tell you the number of yards of cotton, velvet, woolen, the number of barrels of flour, potatoes, butter, number of pairs of shoes, hats, and umbrellas annually consumed by the nation. Owing to the fact that production was in private hands, and that there was no way of getting statistics of actual distribution, these figures were not exact, but they were nearly so. Now that every pin which is given out from a national warehouse is recorded, of course the figures of consumption for any week, month, or year, in the possession of the department of distribution at the end of that period, are precise. On these figures, allowing for tendencies to increase or decrease and for any special causes likely to affect demand, the estimates, say for a year ahead, are based. These estimates, with a proper margin for security, having been accepted by the general administration, the responsibility of the distributive department ceases until the goods are delivered to it. I speak of the estimates being furnished for an entire year ahead, but in reality they cover that much time only in case of the great staples for which the demand can be calculated on as steady. In the great majority of smaller industries for the product of which popular taste fluctuates, and novelty is frequently required, production is kept barely ahead of consumption, the distributive department furnishing frequent estimates based on the weekly state of demand.

"Now the entire field of productive and constructive industry is divided into ten great departments, each representing a group of allied industries, each particular industry being in turn represented by a subordinate bureau, which has a complete record of the plant and force under its control, of the present product, and means of increasing it. The estimates of the distributive department after adoption by the administration, are sent as mandates to the ten great departments, which allot them to the subordinate bureaus representing the particular industries, and these set the men at work. Each bureau is responsible for the task given it, and this responsibility is enforced by departmental oversight and that of the administration; nor does the distributive department accept the product without its own inspection; while even if in the hands of the consumer an article turns out unfit, the system enables the fault to be traced back to the original workman. The production of the commodities for actual public consumption does not, of course, require by any means all the national force of workers. After the necessary contingents have been detailed for the various industries, the amount of labor left for other employment is expended in creating fixed capital, such as buildings, machinery, engineering works, and so forth."

"One point occurs to me," I said, "on which I should think there might be dissatisfaction. Where there is no opportunity for private enterprise, how is there any assurance that the claims of small minorities of the people to have articles produced, for which there is no wide demand, will be respected? An official decree at any moment may deprive them of the means of gratifying some special taste, merely because the majority does not share it."

"That would be tyranny indeed," replied Dr. Leete, "and you may be very sure that it does not happen with us, to whom liberty is as dear as equality or fraternity. As you come to know our system better, you will see that our officials are in fact, and not merely in name, the agents and servants of the people. The administration has no power to stop the production of any commodity for which there continues to be a demand. Suppose the demand for any article declines to such a point that its production becomes very costly. The price has to be raised in proportion, of course, but as long as the consumer cares to pay it, the production goes on. Again, suppose an article not before produced is demanded. If the administration doubts the reality of the demand, a popular petition guaranteeing a certain basis of consumption compels it to produce the desired article. A government, or a majority, which should undertake to tell the people, or a minority, what they were to eat, drink, or wear, as I believe governments in America did in your day, would be regarded as a curious anachronism indeed. Possibly you had reasons for tolerating these infringements of personal independence, but we should not think them endurable. I am glad you raised this point, for it has given me a chance to show you how much more direct and efficient is the control over production exercised by the individual citizen now than it was in your day, when what you called private initiative prevailed, though it should have been called capitalist initiative, for the average private citizen had little enough share in it."

"You speak of raising the price of costly articles," I said. "How can prices be regulated in a country where there is no competition between buyers or sellers?"

"Just as they were with you," replied Dr. Leete. "You think that needs explaining," he added, as I looked incredulous, "but the explanation need not be long; the cost of the labor which produced it was recognized as the legitimate basis of the price of an article in your day, and so it is in ours. In your day, it was the difference in wages that made the difference in the cost of labor; now it is the relative number of hours constituting a day's work in different trades, the maintenance of the worker being equal in all cases. The cost of a man's work in a trade so difficult that in order to attract volunteers the hours have to be fixed at four a day is twice as great as that in a trade where the men work eight hours. The result as to the cost of labor, you see, is just the same as if the man working four hours were paid, under your system, twice the wages the other gets. This calculation applied to the labor employed in the various processes of a manufactured article gives its price relatively to other articles. Besides the cost of production and transportation, the factor of scarcity affects the prices of some commodities. As regards the great staples of life, of which an abundance can always be secured, scarcity is eliminated as a factor. There is always a large surplus kept on hand from which any fluctuations of demand or supply can be corrected, even in most cases of bad crops. The prices of the staples grow less year by year, but rarely, if ever, rise. There are, however, certain classes of articles permanently, and others temporarily, unequal to the demand, as, for example, fresh fish or dairy products in the latter category, and the products of high skill and rare materials in the other. All that can be done here is to equalize the inconvenience of the scarcity. This is done by temporarily raising the price if the scarcity be temporary, or fixing it high if it be permanent. High prices in your day meant restriction of the articles affected to the rich, but nowadays, when the means of all are the same, the effect is only that those to whom the articles seem most desirable are the ones who purchase them. Of course the nation, as any other caterer for the public needs must be, is frequently left with small lots of goods on its hands by changes in taste, unseasonable weather, and various other causes. These it has to dispose of at a sacrifice just as merchants often did in your day, charging up the loss to the expenses of the business. Owing, however, to the vast body of consumers to which such lots can be simultaneously offered, there is rarely any difficulty in getting rid of them at trifling loss. I have given you now some general notion of our system of production, as well as distribution. Do you find it as complex as you expected?"

I admitted that nothing could be much simpler.

"I am sure," said Dr. Leete, "that it is within the truth to say that the head of one of the myriad private businesses of your day, who had to maintain sleepless vigilance against the fluctuations of the market, the machinations of his rivals, and the failure of his debtors, had a far more trying task than the group of men at Washington who nowadays direct the industries of the entire nation. All this merely shows, my dear fellow, how much easier it is to do things the right way than the wrong. It is easier for a general up in a balloon, with perfect survey of the field, to manoeuvre a million men to victory than for a sergeant to manage a platoon in a thicket."

"The general of this army, including the flower of the manhood of the nation, must be the foremost man in the country, really greater even than the President of the United States," I said.

"He is the President of the United States," replied Dr. Leete, "or rather the most important function of the presidency is the headship of the industrial army."

"How is he chosen?" I asked.

"I explained to you before," replied Dr. Leete, "when I was describing the force of the motive of emulation among all grades of the industrial army, that the line of promotion for the meritorious lies through three grades to the officer's grade, and thence up through the lieutenancies to the captaincy or foremanship, and superintendency or colonel's rank. Next, with an intervening grade in some of the larger trades, come the general of the guild, under whose immediate control all the operations of the trade are conducted. This officer is at the head of the national bureau representing his trade, and is responsible for its work to the administration. The general of his guild holds a splendid position, and one which amply satisfies the ambition of most men, but above his rank, which may be compared—to follow the military analogies familiar to you—to that of a general of division or major-general, is that of the chiefs of the ten great departments, or groups of allied trades. The chiefs of these ten grand divisions of the industrial army may be compared to your commanders of army corps, or lieutenant-generals, each having from a dozen to a score of generals of separate guilds reporting to him. Above these ten great officers, who form his council, is the general-in-chief, who is the President of the United States.

"The general-in-chief of the industrial army must have passed through all the grades below him, from the common laborers up. Let us see how he rises.

As I have told you, it is simply by the excellence of his record as a worker that one rises through the grades of the privates and becomes a candidate for a lieutenancy. Through the lieutenancies he rises to the colonelcy, or superintendent's position, by appointment from above, strictly limited to the candidates of the best records. The general of the guild appoints to the ranks under him, but he himself is not appointed, but chosen by suffrage."

"By suffrage?" I exclaimed. "Is not that ruinous to the discipline of the guild, by tempting the candidates to intrigue for the support of the workers under them?"

"So it would be, no doubt," replied Dr. Leete, "if the workers had any suffrage to exercise, or anything to say about the choice. But they have nothing. Just here comes in a peculiarity of our system. The general of the guild is chosen from among the superintendents by vote of the honorary members of the guild, that is, of those who have served their time in the guild and received their discharge. As you know, at the age of forty-five we are mustered out of the army of industry, and have the residue of life for the pursuit of our own improvement or recreation. Of course, however, the associations of our active lifetime retain a powerful hold on us. The companionships we formed then remain our companionships till the end of life. We always continue honorary members of our former guilds, and retain the keenest and most jealous interest in their welfare and repute in the hands of the following generation. In the clubs maintained by the honorary members of the several guilds, in which we meet socially, there are no topics of conversation so common as those which relate to these matters, and the young aspirants for guild leadership who can pass the criticism of us old fellows are likely to be pretty well equipped. Recognizing this fact, the nation entrusts to the honorary members of each guild the election of its general, and I venture to claim that no previous form of society could have developed a body of electors so ideally adapted to their office, as regards absolute impartiality, knowledge of the special qualifications and record of candidates, solicitude for the best result, and complete absence of self-interest.

"Each of the ten lieutenant-generals or heads of departments is himself elected from among the generals of the guilds grouped as a department, by vote of the honorary members of the guilds thus grouped. Of course there is a tendency on the part of each guild to vote for its own general, but no guild of any group has nearly enough votes to elect a man not supported by most of the others. I assure you that these elections are exceedingly lively."

"The President, I suppose, is selected from among the ten heads of the great departments," I suggested.

"Precisely, but the heads of departments are not eligible to the presidency till they have been a certain number of years out of office. It is rarely that a man passes through all the grades to the headship of a department much before he is forty, and at the end of a five years' term he is usually forty-five. If more, he still serves through his term, and if less, he is nevertheless discharged from the industrial army at its termination. It would not do for him to return to the ranks. The interval before he is a candidate for the presidency is intended to give time for him to recognize fully that he has returned into the general mass of the nation, and is identified with it rather than with the industrial army. Moreover, it is expected that he will employ this period in studying the general condition of the army, instead of that of the special group of guilds of which he was the head. From among the former heads of departments who may be eligible at the time, the President is elected by vote of all the men of the nation who are not connected with the industrial army."

"The army is not allowed to vote for President?"

"Certainly not. That would be perilous to its discipline, which it is the business of the President to maintain as the representative of the nation at large. His right hand for this purpose is the inspectorate, a highly important department of our system; to the inspectorate come all complaints or information as to defects in goods, insolence or inefficiency of officials, or dereliction of any sort in the public service. The inspectorate, however, does not wait for complaints. Not only is it on the alert to catch and sift every rumor of a fault in the service, but it is its business, by systematic and constant oversight and inspection of every branch of the army, to find out what is going wrong before anybody else does. The President is usually not far from fifty when elected, and serves five years, forming an honorable exception to the rule of retirement at forty-five. At the end of his term of office, a national Congress is called to receive his report and approve or condemn it. If it is approved, Congress usually elects him to represent the nation for five years more in the international council. Congress, I should also say, passes on the reports of the outgoing heads of departments, and a disapproval renders any one of them ineligible for President. But it is rare, indeed, that the nation has occasion for other sentiments than those of gratitude toward its high officers. As to their ability, to have risen from the ranks, by tests so various and severe, to their positions, is proof in itself of extraordinary qualities, while as to faithfulness, our social system leaves them absolutely without any other motive than that of winning the esteem of their fellow citizens. Corruption is impossible in a society where there is neither poverty to be bribed nor wealth to bribe, while as to demagoguery or intrigue for office, the conditions of promotion render them out of the question." . . .

Chapter 19

IN the course of an early morning constitutional I visited Charlestown. Among the changes, too numerous to attempt to indicate, which mark the lapse of a century in that quarter, I particularly noted the total disappearance of the old state prison.

"That went before my day, but I remember hearing about it," said Dr. Leete, when I alluded to the fact at the breakfast table. "We have no jails nowadays. All cases of atavism are treated in the hospitals."

"Of atavism?" I exclaimed, staring.

"Why, yes," replied Dr. Leete. "The idea of dealing punitively with those unfortunates was given up at least fifty years ago, and I think more."

"I don't quite understand you," I said. "Atavism in my day was a word applied to the cases of persons in whom some trait of a remote ancestor recurred in a noticeable manner. Am I to understand that crime is nowadays looked upon the recurrence of an ancestral trait?"

"I beg your pardon," said Dr. Leete with a smile half humorous, half deprecating, "but since you have so explicitly asked the question, I am forced to say that the fact is precisely that."

After what I had already learned of the moral contrasts between the nineteenth and the twentieth centuries, it was doubtless absurd in me to begin to develop sensitiveness on the subject, and probably if Dr. Leete had not spoken with that apologetic air and Mrs. Leete and Edith shown a corresponding embarrassment, I should not have flushed, as I was conscious I did.

"I was not in much danger of being vain of my generation before," I said? "but, really————"

"This is your generation, Mr. West," interposed Edith. "It is the one in which you are living, you know, and it is only because we are alive now that we call it ours."

"Thank you. I will try to think of it so," I said, and as my eyes met hers their expression quite cured my senseless sensitiveness. "After all," I said, with a laugh, "I was brought up a Calvinist, and ought not to be startled to hear crime spoken of as an ancestral trait."

"In point of fact," said Dr. Leete, "our use of the word is no reflection at all on your generation, if, begging Edith's pardon, we may call it yours, so far as seeming to imply that we think ourselves, apart from our circumstances, better than you were. In your day fully nineteen twentieths of the crime, using the word broadly to include all sorts of misdemeanors, resulted from the inequality in the possessions of individuals; want tempted the poor, lust of greater gains, or the desire to preserve former gains, tempted the well-to-do. Directly or indirectly, the desire for money, which then meant every good thing, was the motive of all this crime, the taproot of a vast poison growth, which the machinery of law, courts, and police could barely prevent from choking your civilization outright. When we made the nation the sole trustee of the wealth of the people, and guaranteed to all abundant maintenance, on the one hand abolishing want, and on the other checking the accumulation of riches, we cut this root, and the poison tree that overshadowed your society withered, like Jonah's gourd, in a day. As for the comparatively small class of violent crimes against persons, unconnected with any idea of gain, they were almost wholly confined, even in your day, to the ignorant and bestial; and in these days, when education and good manners are not the monopoly of a few, but universal, such atrocities are scarcely ever heard of. You now see why the word "atavism" is used for crime. It is because nearly all forms of crime known to you are motiveless now, and when they appear can only be explained as the outcropping of ancestral traits. You used to call persons who stole, evidently without any rational motive, kleptomaniacs, and when the case was clear deemed it absurd to punish them as thieves. Your attitude toward the genuine kleptomaniac is precisely ours toward the victim of atavism, an attitude of compassion and firm but gentle restraint."

"Your courts must have an easy time of it," I observed. "With no private property to speak of, no disputes between citizens over business relations, no real estate to divide or debts to collect, there must be absolutely no civil business at all for them; and with no offenses against property, and mighty few of any sort to provide criminal cases, I should think you might almost do without judges and lawyers altogether."

"We do without the lawyers, certainly," was Dr. Leete's reply. "It would not seem reasonable to us, in a case where the only interest of the nation is to find out the truth, that persons should take part in the proceedings who had an acknowledged motive to color it."

"But who defends the accused?"

"If he is a criminal he needs no defence, for he pleads guilty in most instances," replied Dr. Leete. "The plea of the accused is not a mere formality with us, as with you. It is usually the end of the case."

"You don't mean that the man who pleads not guilty is thereupon discharged?"

"No, I do not mean that. He is not accused on light grounds, and if he denies his guilt, must still be tried. But trials are few, for in most cases the guilty man pleads guilty. When he makes a false plea and is clearly proved guilty, his penalty is doubled. Falsehood is, however, so despised among us that few offenders would lie to save themselves."

"That is the most astounding thing you have yet told me," I exclaimed. "If lying has gone out of fashion, this is indeed the 'new heavens and the new earth wherein dwelleth righteousness,' which the prophet foretold."

"Such is, in fact, the belief of some persons nowadays," was the doctor's answer. "They hold that we have entered upon the millennium, and the theory from their point of view does not lack plausibility. But as to your astonishment at finding that the world has outgrown lying, there is really no ground for it. Falsehood, even in your day, was not common between gentlemen and ladies, social equals. The lie of fear was the refuge of cowardice, and the lie of fraud the device of the cheat. The inequalities of men and the lust of acquisition offered a constant premium on lying at that time. Yet even then, the man who neither feared another nor desired to defraud him scorned falsehood. Because we are now all social equals, and no man either has anything to fear from another or can gain anything by deceiving him, the contempt of falsehood is so universal that it is rarely, as I told you, that even a criminal in other respects will be found willing to lie. When, however, a plea of not guilty is returned, the judge appoints two colleagues to state the opposite sides of the case. How far these men are from being like your hired advocates and prosecutors, determined to acquit or convict, may appear from the fact that unless both agree that the verdict found is just, the case is tried over, while anything like bias in the tone of either of the judges stating the ease would be a shocking scandal."

"Do I understand," I said, "that it is a judge who states each side of the case as well as a judge who hears it?"

"Certainly. The judges take turns in serving on the bench and at the bar, and are expected to maintain the judicial temper equally whether in stating or deciding a case. The system is indeed in effect that of trial by three judges occupying different points of view as to the case. When they agree upon a verdict, we believe it to be as near to absolute truth as men well can come."

"You have given up the jury system, then?"

"It was well enough as a corrective in the days of hired advocates, and a bench sometimes venal, and often with a tenure that made it dependent, but is needless now. No conceivable motive but justice could actuate our judges."

"How are these magistrates selected?"

"They are an honorable exception to the rule which discharges all men from service at the age of forty-five. The President of the nation appoints the necessary judges year by year from the class reaching that age. The number appointed is, of course, exceedingly few, and the honor so high that it is held an offset to the additional term of service which follows, and though a judge's appointment may be declined, it rarely is. The term is five years, without eligibility to reappointment. The members of the Supreme Court, which is the guardian of the constitution, are selected from among the lower judges. When a vacancy in that court occurs, those of the lower judges, whose terms expire that year, select, as their last official act, the one of their colleagues left on the bench whom they deem fittest to fill it."

"There being no legal profession to serve as a school for judges," I said, "they must, of course, come directly from the law school to the bench."

"We have no such things as law schools," replied the doctor, smiling. "The law as a special science is obsolete. It was a system of casuistry which the elaborate artificiality of the old order of society absolutely required to interpret it, but only a few of the plainest and simplest legal maxims have any application to the existing state of the world. Everything touching the relations of men to one another is now simpler, beyond any comparison, than in your day. We should have no sort of use for the hair-splitting experts who presided and argued in your courts. You must not imagine, however, that we have any disrespect for those ancient worthies because we have no use for them. On the contrary, we entertain an unfeigned respect, amounting almost to awe, for the men who alone understood and were able to expound the interminable complexity of the rights of property, and the relations of commercial and personal dependence involved in your system. What, indeed, could possibly give a more powerful impression of the intricacy and artificiality of that system than the fact that it was necessary to set apart from other pursuits the cream of the intellect of every generation, in order to provide a body of pundits able to make it even vaguely intelligible to those whose fates it determined. The treatises of your great lawyers, the works of Blackstone and Chitty, of Story and Parsons, stand in our museums, side by side with the tomes of Duns Scotus and his fellow scholastics, as curious monuments of intellectual subtlety devoted to subjects equally remote from the interests of modern men. Our judges are simply widely informed, judicious, and discreet men of ripe years. . . .

It occurred to me, as Dr. Leete was speaking, that in all his talk I had heard much of the nation and nothing of the state governments. Had the organization of the nation as an industrial unit done away with the states? I asked.

"Necessarily," he replied. "The state governments would have interfered with the control and discipline of the industrial army, which, of course, required to be central and uniform. Even if the state governments had not become inconvenient for other reasons, they were rendered superfluous by the prodigious simplification in the task of government since your day. Almost the sole function of the administration now is that of directing the industries of the country. Most of the purposes for which governments formerly existed no longer remain to be subserved. We have no army or navy, and no military organization. We have no departments of state or treasury, no excise or revenue services, no taxes or tax collectors. The only function proper of government, as known to you, which still remains, is the judiciary and police system. I have already explained to you how simple is our judicial system as compared with your huge and complex machine. Of course the same absence of crime and temptation to it, which make the duties of judges so light, reduces the number and duties of the police to a minimum."

"But with no state legislatures, and Congress meeting only once in five years, how do you get your legislation done?"

"We have no legislation," replied Dr. Leete, "that is, next to none. It is rarely that Congress, even when it meets, considers any new laws of consequence, and then it only has power to commend them to the following Congress, lest anything be done hastily. If you will consider a moment, Mr. West, you will see that we have nothing to make laws about. The fundamental principles on which our society is founded settle for all time the strifes and misunderstandings which in your day called for legislation.

"Fully ninety-nine hundredths of the laws of that time concerned the definition and protection of private property and the relations of buyers and sellers. There is neither private property, beyond personal belongings, now, nor buying and selling, and therefore the occasion of nearly all the legislation formerly necessary has passed away. Formerly, society was a pyramid poised on its apex. All the gravitations of human nature were constantly tending to topple it over, and it could be maintained upright, or rather upwrong (if you will pardon the feeble witticism), by an elaborate system of constantly renewed props and buttresses and guy-ropes in the form of laws. A central Congress and forty state legislatures, turning out some twenty thousand laws a year, could not make new props fast enough to take the place of those which were constantly breaking down or becoming ineffectual through some shifting of the strain. Now society rests on its base, and is in as little need of artificial supports as the everlasting hills."

"But you have at least municipal governments besides the one central authority?"

"Certainly, and they have important and extensive functions in looking out for the public comfort and recreation, and the improvement and embellishment of the villages and cities."

"But having no control over the labor of their people, or means of hiring it, how can they do anything?"

"Every town or city is conceded the right to retain, for its own public works, a certain proportion of the quota of labor its citizens contribute to the nation. This proportion, being assigned it as so much credit, can be applied in any way desired." . . .

Chapter 25

"I SUPPOSE," I said, "that women nowadays, having been relieved of the burden of housework, have no employment but the cultivation of their charms and graces."

"So far as we men are concerned," replied Dr. Leete, "we should consider that they amply paid their way, to use one of your forms of expression, if they confined themselves to that occupation, but you may be very sure that they have quite too much spirit to consent to be mere beneficiaries of society, even as a return for ornamenting it. They did, indeed, welcome their riddance from housework, because that was not only exceptionally wearing in itself, but also wasteful, in the extreme, of energy, as compared with the coöperative plan; but they accepted relief from that sort of work only that they might contribute in other and more effectual, as well as more agreeable, ways to the common weal. Our women, as well as our men, are members of the industrial army, and leave it only when maternal duties claim them. The result is that most women, at one time or another of their lives, serve industrially some five or ten or fifteen years, while those who have no children fill out the full term."

"A woman does not, then, necessarily leave the industrial service on marriage?" I queried.

"No more than a man," replied the doctor. "Why on earth should she? Married women have no housekeeping responsibilities now, you know, and a husband is not a baby that he should be cared for."

"It was thought one of the most grievous features of our civilization that we required so much toil from women," I said, "but it seems to me you get more out of them than we did."

Dr. Leete laughed. "Indeed we do, just as we do out of our men. Yet the women of this age are very happy, and those of the nineteenth century, unless contemporary references greatly mislead us, were very miserable. The reason that women nowadays are so much more efficient co-laborers with the men, and at the same time are so happy, is that, in regard to their work as well as men's, we follow the principle of providing every one the kind of occupation he or she is best adapted to. Women being inferior in strength to men, and further disqualified industrially in special ways, the kinds of occupation reserved for them, and the conditions under which they pursue them, have reference to these facts. The heavier sorts of work are everywhere reserved for men, the lighter occupations for women. Under no circumstances is a woman permitted to follow any employment not perfectly adapted, both as to kind and degree of labor, to her sex. Moreover, the hours of women's work are considerably shorter than those of men's, more frequent vacations are granted, and the most careful provision is made for rest when needed. The men of this day so well appreciate that they owe to the beauty and grace of women the chief zest of their lives and their main incentive to effort, that they permit them to work at all only because it is fully understood that a certain regular requirement of labor, of a sort adapted to their powers, is well for body and mind, during the period of maximum physical vigor. We believe that the magnificent health which distinguishes our women from those of your day, who seem to have been so generally sickly, is owing largely to the fact that all alike are furnished with healthful and inspiriting occupation."

"I understood you," I said, "that the women-workers belong to the army of industry, but how can they be under the same system of ranking and discipline with the men, when the conditions of their labor are so different."

"They are under an entirely different discipline," replied Dr. Leete, "and constitute rather an allied force than an integral part of the army of the men. They have a woman general-in-chief and are under exclusively feminine régime. This general, as also the higher officers, is chosen by the body of women who have passed the time of service, in correspondence with the manner in which the chiefs of the masculine army and the President of the nation are elected. The general of the women's army sits in the cabinet of the President and has a veto on measures respecting women's work, pending appeals to Congress. I should have said, in speaking of the judiciary, that we have women on the bench, appointed by the general of the women, as well as men. Causes in which both parties are women are determined by women judges, and where a man and a woman are parties to a case, a judge of either sex must consent to the verdict."

"Womanhood seems to be organized as a sort of *imperium in imperio* in your system," I said.

"To some extent," Dr. Leete replied, "but the inner *imperium* is one from which you will admit there is not likely to be much danger to the nation. The lack of some such recognition of the distinct individuality of the sexes was one of the innumerable defects of your society. The passional attraction between men and women has too often prevented a perception of the profound differences which make the members of each sex in many things strange to the other, and capable of sympathy only with their own. It is in giving full play to the differences of sex rather than in seeking to obliterate them, as was apparently the effort of some reformers in your day, that the enjoyment of each by itself and the piquancy which each has for the other, are alike enhanced. In your day there was no career for women except in an unnatural rivalry with men. We have given them a world of their own, with its emulations, ambitions, and careers, and I assure you they are very happy in it. It seems to us that women were more than any other class the victims of your civilization. There is something which, even at this distance of time, penetrates one with pathos in the spectacle of their ennuied, undeveloped lives, stunted at marriage, their narrow horizon, bounded so often, physically, by the four walls of home, and morally by a petty circle of personal interests. I speak now, not of the poorer classes, who were generally worked to death, but also of the well-to-do and rich. From the great sorrows, as well as the petty frets of life, they had no refuge in the breezy outdoor world of human affairs, nor any interests save those of the family. Such an existence would have softened men's brains or driven them mad. All that is changed to-day. No woman is heard nowadays wishing she were a man, nor parents desiring boy rather than girl children. Our girls are as full of ambition for their careers as our boys. Marriage, when it comes, does not mean incarceration for them, nor does it separate them in any way from the larger interests of society, the bustling life of the world. Only when maternity fills a woman's mind with new interests does she withdraw from the world for a time. Afterwards, and at any time, she may return to her place among her comrades, nor need she ever lose touch with them. Women are a very happy race nowadays, as compared with what they ever were before in the world's history, and their power of giving happiness to men has been of course increased in proportion."

"I should imagine it possible," I said, "that the interest which girls take in their careers as members of the industrial army and candidates for its distinctions might have an effect to deter them from marriage."

Dr. Leete smiled. "Have no anxiety on that score, Mr. West," he replied. "The Creator took very good care that whatever other modifications the dispositions of men and women might with time take on, their attraction for each other should remain constant. The mere fact that in an age like yours, when the struggle for existence must have left people little time for other thoughts, and the future was so uncertain that to assume parental responsibilities must have often seemed like a criminal risk, there was even then marrying and giving in marriage, should be conclusive on this point. As for love nowadays, one of our authors says that the vacuum left in the minds of men and women by the absence of care for one's livelihood has been entirely taken up by the tender passion. That, however, I beg you to believe, is something of an exaggeration. For the rest, so far is marriage from being an interference with a woman's career, that the higher positions in the feminine army of industry are intrusted only to women who have been both wives and mothers, as they alone fully represent their sex."

"Are credit cards issued to the women just as to the men?"

"Certainly."

"The credits of the women, I suppose, are for smaller sums, owing to the frequent suspension of their labor on account of family responsibilities."

"Smaller?" exclaimed Dr. Leete, "oh, no! The maintenance of all our people is the same. There are no exceptions to that rule, but if any difference were made on account of the interruptions you speak of, it would be by making the woman's credit larger, not smaller. Can you think of any service constituting a stronger claim on the nation's gratitude than bearing and nursing the nation's children? According to our view, none deserve so well of the world as good parents. There is no task so unselfish, so necessarily without return, though the heart is well rewarded, as the nurture of the children who are to make the world for one another when we are gone."

"It would seem to follow, from what you have said, that wives are in no way dependent on their husbands for maintenance."

"Of course they are not," replied Dr. Leete, "nor children on their parents either, that is, for means of support, though of course they are for the offices of affection. The child's labor, when he grows up, will go to increase the common stock, not his parents', who will be dead, and therefore he is properly nurtured out of the common stock. The account of every person, man, woman, and child, you must understand, is always with the nation directly, and never through any intermediary, except, of course, that parents, to a certain extent, act for children as their guardians. You see that it is by virtue of the relation of individuals to the nation, of their membership in it, that they are entitled to support; and this title is in no way connected with or affected by their relations to other individuals who are fellow members of the nation with them. That any person should be dependent for the means of support upon another would be shocking to the moral sense as well as indefensible on any rational social theory. What would become of personal liberty and dignity under such an arrangement? I am aware that you called yourselves free in the nineteenth century. The meaning of the word could not then, however, have been at all what it is at present, or you certainly would not have applied it to a society of which nearly every member was in a position of galling personal dependence upon others as to the very means of life, the poor upon the rich, or employed upon employer, women upon men, children upon parents. Instead of distributing the product of the nation directly to its members, which would seem the most natural and obvious method, it would actually appear that you had given your minds to devising a plan of hand to hand distribution, involving the maximum of personal humiliation to all classes of recipients.

"As regards the dependence of women upon men for support, which then was usual, of course natural attraction in case of marriages of love may often have made it endurable, though for spirited women I should fancy it must always have remained humiliating. What, then, must it have been in the innumerable cases where women, with or without the form of marriage, had to sell themselves to men to get their living? Even your contemporaries, callous as they were to most of the revolting aspects of their society, seem to have had an idea that this was not quite as it should be; but, it was still only for pity's sake that they deplored the lot of the women. It did not occur to them that it was robbery as well as cruelty when men seized for themselves the whole product of the world and left women to beg and wheedle for their share. Why—but bless me, Mr. West, I am really running on at a remarkable rate, just as if the robbery, the sorrow, and the shame which those poor women endured were not over a century since, or as if you were responsible for what you no doubt deplored as much as I do."

"I must bear my share of responsibility for the world as it then was," I replied. "All I can say in extenuation is that until the nation was ripe for the present system of organized production and distribution, no radical improvement in the position of woman was possible. The root of her disability, as you say, was her personal dependence upon man for her livelihood, and I can imagine no other mode of social organization than that you have adopted, which would have set woman free of man at the same time that it set men free of one another. I suppose, by the way, that so entire a change in the position of women cannot have taken place without affecting in marked ways the social relations of the sexes. That will be a very interesting study for me."

"The change you will observe," said Dr. Leete, "will chiefly be, I think, the entire frankness and unconstraint which now characterizes those relations, as compared with the artificiality which seems to have marked them in your time. The sexes now meet with the ease of perfect equals, suitors to each other for nothing but love. In your time the fact that women were dependent for support on men made the woman in reality the one chiefly benefited by marriage. This fact, so far as we can judge from contemporary records, appears to have been coarsely enough recognized among the lower classes, while among the more polished it was glossed over by a system of elaborate conventionalities which aimed to carry the precisely opposite meaning, namely, that the man was the party chiefly benefited. To keep up this convention it was essential that he should always seem the suitor. Nothing was therefore considered more shocking to the proprieties than that a woman should betray a fondness for a man before he had indicated a desire to marry her. Why, we actually have in our libraries books, by authors of your day, written for no other purpose than to discuss the question whether, under any conceivable circumstances, a woman might, without discredit to her sex, reveal an unsolicited love. All this seems exquisitely absurd to us, and yet we know that, given your circumstances, the problem might have a serious side. When for a woman to proffer her love to a man was in effect to invite him to assume the burden of her support, it is easy to see that pride and delicacy might well have checked the promptings of the heart. When you go out into our society, Mr. West, you must be prepared to be often cross-questioned on this point by our young people, who are naturally much interested in this aspect of old-fashioned manners."

"And so the girls of the twentieth century tell their love."

"If they choose," replied Dr. Leete. "There is no more pretence of a concealment of feeling on their part than on the part of their lovers. Coquetry would be as much despised in a girl as in a man. Affected coldness, which in your day rarely deceived a lover, would deceive him wholly now, for no one thinks of practicing it."

"One result which must follow from the independence of women I can see for myself," I said. "There can be no marriages now except those of inclination."

"That is a matter of course," replied Dr. Leete.

"Think of a world in which there are nothing but matches of pure love! Ah me, Dr. Leete, how far you are from being able to understand what an astonishing phenomenon such a world seems to a man of the nineteenth century!"

"I can, however, to some extent, imagine it," replied the doctor. "But the fact you celebrate, that there are nothing but love matches, means even more, perhaps, than you probably at first realize. It means that for the first time in human history the principle of sexual selection, with its tendency to preserve and transmit the better types of the race, and let the inferior types drop out, has unhindered operation. The necessities of poverty, the need of having a home, no longer tempt women to accept as the fathers of their children men whom they neither can love nor respect. Wealth and rank no longer divert attention from personal qualities. Gold no longer 'gilds the straitened forehead of the fool.' The gifts of person, mind, and disposition; beauty, wit, eloquence, kindness, generosity, geniality, courage, are sure of transmission to posterity. Every generation is sifted through a little finer mesh than the last. The attributes that human nature admires are preserved, those that repel it are left behind. There are, of course, a great many women who with love must mingle admiration, and seek to wed greatly, but these not the less obey the same law, for to wed greatly now is not to marry men of fortune or title, but those who have risen above their fellows by the solidity or brilliance of their services to humanity. These form nowadays the only aristocracy with which alliance is distinction.

"You were speaking, a day or two ago, of the physical superiority of our people to your contemporaries. Perhaps more important than any of the causes I mentioned then as tending to race purification has been the effect of untrammeled sexual selection upon the quality of two or three successive generations. I believe that when you have made a fuller study of our people you will find in them not only a physical, but a mental and moral improvement. It would be strange if it were not so, for not only is one of the great laws of nature now freely working out the salvation of the race, but a profound moral sentiment has come to its support. Individualism, which in your day was the animating idea of society, not only was fatal to any vital sentiment of brotherhood and common interest among living men, but equally to any realization of the responsibility of the living for the generation to follow. To-day this sense of responsibility, practically unrecognized in all previous ages, has become one of the great ethical ideas of the race, reinforcing, with an intense conviction of duty, the natural impulse to seek in marriage the best and noblest of the other sex. The result is, that not all the encouragements and incentives of every sort which we have provided to develop industry, talent, genius, excellence of whatever kind, are comparable in their effect on our young men with the fact that our women sit aloft as judges of the race and reserve themselves to reward the winners. Of all the whips, and spurs, and baits, and prizes, there is none like the thought of the radiant faces which the laggards will find averted.

"Celibates nowadays are almost invariably men who have failed to acquit themselves creditably in the work of life. The woman must be a courageous one, with a very evil sort of courage, too, whom pity for one of these unfortunates should lead to defy the opinion of her generation—for otherwise she is free—so far as to accept him for a husband. I should add that, more exacting and difficult to resist than any other element in that opinion, she would find the sentiment of her own sex. Our women have risen to the full height of their responsibility as the wardens of the world to come, to whose keeping the keys of the future are confided. Their feeling of duty in this respect amounts to a sense of religious consecration. It is a cult in which they educate their daughters from childhood."

After going to my room that night, I sat up late to read a romance of Berrian, handed me by Dr. Leete, the plot of which turned on a situation suggested by his last words, concerning the modern view of parental responsibility. A similar situation would almost certainly have been treated by a nineteenth century romancist so as to excite the morbid sympathy of the reader with the sentimental selfishness of the lovers, and his resentment toward the unwritten law which they outraged. I need not describe—for who has not read "Ruth Elton?"—how different is the course which Berrian takes, and with what tremendous effect he enforces the principle which he states: "Over the unborn our power is that of God, and our responsibility like His toward us. As we acquit ourselves toward them, so let Him deal with us."

Edward Bellamy (1850–1898) was a Springfield, Massachusetts, newspaperman and novelist who wrote the best-selling LOOKING BACKWARD: 2000–1887 and, as a result, became the leader of a worldwide reform movement.

Source: Edward Bellamy. LOOKING BACKWARD: 2000–1887, 2d ed. (Boston: Houghton Mifflin & Co., 1888), 126–39, 146–54, 210–19, 224–31, 262–71.

William Morris

News from Nowhere

William Morris wrote *News from Nowhere* (1890) as a direct response to Edward Bellamy's *Looking Backward* (1888), which he believed overemphasized work to the detriment of a more balanced life.

After a pause, I said: "Your big towns, now; how about them? London, which—which I have read about as the modern Babylon of civilisation, seems to have disappeared."

"Well, well," said old Hammond, "perhaps after all it is more like ancient Babylon now than the 'modern Babylon' of the nineteenth century was. But let that pass. After all, there is a good deal of population in places between here and Hammersmith; nor have you seen the most populous part of the town yet."

"Tell me, then," said I, "how is it towards the east?"

Said he: "Time was when if you mounted a good horse and rode straight away from my door here at a round trot for an hour and a half, you would still be in the thick of London, and the greater part of that would be 'slums', as they were called; that is to say, places of torture for innocent men and women; or worse, stews for rearing and breeding men and women in such degradation that that torture should seem to them mere ordinary and natural life."

"I know, I know," I said, rather impatiently, "That was what was; tell me something of what is. Is there any of that left?"

"Not an inch," said he; "but some memory of it abides with us, and I am glad of it. Once a year, on May-day, we hold a solemn feast in those easterly communes of London to commemorate The Clearing of Misery, as it is called. On that day we have music and dancing, and merry games and happy feasting on the site of some of the worst of the old slums, the traditional memory of which we have kept. On that occasion the custom is for the prettiest girls to sing some of the old revolutionary songs, and those which were the groans of the discontent, once so hopeless, on the very spots where those terrible crimes of class-murder were committed day by day for so many years. To a man like me, who has studied the past so diligently, it is a curious and touching sight to see some beautiful girl, daintily clad, and crowned with flowers from the neighbouring meadows standing amongst the happy people, on some mound where of old time stood the wretched apology for a house, a den in which men and women lived packed amongst the filth like pilchards in a cask; lived in such a way that they could only have endured it, as I said just now, by being degraded out of humanity—to hear the terrible words of threatening and lamentation coming from her sweet and beautiful lips, and she unconscious of their real meaning: to hear her, for instance, singing Hood's Song of the Shirt,[1] and to think that all the time she does not understand what it is all about—a tragedy grown in-

---

1. Thomas Hood's (1799–1845) "Song of the Shirt" was a popular song describing the poverty of a seamstress. For more information and a key stanza from the song, see William Morris, *News from Nowhere*, ed. James Redmond (London: Routledge, 1970), 189–90. *Ed.*

conceivable to her and her listeners. Think of that, if you can, and of how glorious life is grown!"

"Indeed," said I, "it is difficult for me to think of it."

And I sat watching how his eyes glittered, and how the fresh life seemed to glow in his face, and I wondered how at his age he should think of the happiness of the world, or indeed anything but his coming to dinner.

"Tell me in detail," said I, "what lies east of Bloomsbury now?"

Said he: "There are but few houses between this and the outer part of the old city; but in the city we have a thickly-dwelling population. Our forefathers, in the first clearing of the slums, were not in a hurry to pull down the houses in what was called at the end of the nineteenth century the business quarter of town, and what later got to be known as the Swindling Kens. You see, these houses, though they stood hideously thick on the ground, were roomy and fairly solid in building, and clean, because they were not used for living in, but as mere gambling booths; so the poor people from the cleared slums took them for lodgings and dwelt there, till the folk of those days had time to think of something better for them; so the buildings were pulled down so gradually that people got used to living thicker on the ground there than in most places; therefore it remains the most populous part of London, or perhaps of all these islands. But it is very pleasant there, partly because of the splendor of the architecture, which goes further than what you will see elsewhere. However, this crowding, if it may be called so, does not go further than a street called Aldgate, a name that perhaps you may have heard of. Beyond that the houses are scattered wide about the meadows there, which are very beautiful, especially when you get on to the lovely river Lea (where old Isaak Walton used to fish, you know) about the places called Stratford and Old Ford, names which of course you will not have heard of, though the Romans were busy there once upon a time."

Not heard of them! thought I to myself. How strange! that I who had seen the very last remnant of the pleasantness of the meadows by the Lea destroyed, should have heard them spoken of with pleasantness come back to them in full measure.

Hammond went on: "When you get down to the Thames side you come on the Docks, which are works of the nineteenth century, and are still in use, although not so thronged as they once were, since we discourage centralisation all we can, and we have long ago dropped the pretension to be the market of the world. About these Docks are a good few houses, which, however, are not inhabited by many people permanently; I mean, those who use them come and go a good deal, the place being too low and marshy for pleasant dwelling. Past the Docks eastward and landward it is all flat pasture, once marsh, except for a few gardens, and there are very few permanent dwellings there: scarcely anything but a few sheds, and cots for the men who come to look after the great herds of cattle pasturing there. But however, what with the beasts and the men, and the scattered red-tiled roofs and the big hayricks, it does not make a bad holiday to get a quiet pony and ride about there on a sunny afternoon of autumn, and look over the river and the craft passing up and down, and on to Shooters' Hill and the Kentish uplands, and then turn round to the wide green sea of the Essex marshland, with the great domed line of the sky, and the sun shining down in one flood of peaceful light over the long distance. There is a place called Canning's Town, and further out, Silvertown, where the pleasant meadows are at their pleasantest: doubtless they were once slums, and wretched enough."

The names grated on my ear, but I could not explain why to him. So I said: "And south of the river, what is it like?"

He said: "You would find it much the same as the land about Hammersmith. North, again, the land runs up high, and there is an agreeable and well-built town called Hampstead, which fitly ends London on that side. It looks down on the north-western end of the forest you passed through."

I smiled. "So much for what was once London," said I. "Now tell me about the other towns of the country."

He said: "As to the big murky places which were once, as we know, the centres of manufacture, they have, like the brick and mortar desert of London, disappeared; only, since they were the centres of nothing but 'manufacture', and served no purpose but that of the gambling market, they have left less signs of their existence than London. Of course, the great change in the use of mechanical force made this an easy matter, and some approach to their break-up as centres would probably have taken place, even if we had not changed our habits so much: but they being such as they were, no sacrifice would have seemed too great a price to pay for getting rid of the 'manufacturing districts', as they used to be called. For the rest, whatever coal or mineral we need is brought to grass and sent whither it is needed with as little as possible of dirt, confusion, and the distressing of quiet people's lives. One is tempted to believe from what one has read of the condition of those districts in the nineteenth century, that those who had them under their power worried, befouled, and degraded men out of malice prepense: but it was not so; like the miseducation of which we were talking just now, it came of their dreadful poverty. They were obliged to put up with everything, and even pretend that they liked it; whereas we can now deal with things reasonable, and refuse to be saddled with what we do not want."

I confess I was not sorry to cut short with a question his glorifications of the age he lived in. Said I: "How about the smaller towns? I suppose you have swept those away entirely?"

"No, no," said he, "it hasn't gone that way. On the contrary, there has been but little clearance, though much rebuilding in the smaller towns. Their suburbs, indeed, when they had any, have melted away into the general country, and space and elbow-room has been got in their centres: but there are the towns still with their streets and squares the market-places; so that it is by means of these smaller towns that we of to-day can get some kind of idea of what the towns of the older world were like;—I mean to say at their best."

"Take Oxford, for instance," said I.

"Yes," said he, "I suppose Oxford was beautiful even in the nineteenth century. At present it has the great interest of still preserving a great mass of pre-commercial building, and is a very beautiful place, yet there are many towns which have become scarcely less beautiful."

Said I: "In passing, may I ask if it is still a place of learning?"

"Still?" said he, smiling. "Well, it has reverted to some of its best traditions; so you may imagine how far it is from its nineteenth-century position. It is real learning, knowledge cultivated for its own sake—the Art of Knowledge, in short—which is followed there, not the Commercial learning of the past. Though perhaps you do not know that in the nineteenth century Oxford and its less interesting sister Cambridge became definitely commercial. They (and especially Oxford) were the breeding places of a peculiar class of parasites, who called themselves cultivated people; they were indeed cynical enough, as the so-called educated classes of the day generally were; but they affected an exaggeration of cynicism in order that they might be thought knowing and worldly-wise. The rich middle classes (they had no relation with the working-classes) treated them with the kind of contemptuous toleration with which a mediaeval baron treated his jester; though it must be said that they were by no means so pleasant as the old jesters were, being, in fact, *the* bores of society. They were laughed at, despised—and paid. Which last was what they aimed at."

Dear me! thought I, how apt history is to reverse contemporary judgements. Surely only the worst of them were as bad as that. But I must admit that they were mostly prigs, and they were *commercial.* I said aloud, though more to myself than to Hammond, "Well, how could they be better than the age that made them?"

"True," he said, "but their pretensions were higher."

"Were they?" said I, smiling.

"You drive me from corner to corner," said he, smiling in turn. "Let me say at least that they were a poor sequence to the aspirations of Oxford of 'the barbarous Middle Ages'."

"Yes, that will do," said I.

"Also," said Hammond, "what I have been saying of them is true in the main. But ask on!"

I said: "We have heard about London and the manufacturing districts and the ordinary towns: how about the villages?"

Said Hammond: "You must know that toward the end of the nineteenth century the villages were almost destroyed, unless where they became mere adjuncts to the manufacturing district themselves. Houses were allowed to fall into decay and actual ruin; trees were cut down for the sake of the few shillings which the poor sticks would fetch; the building became inexpressibly mean and hideous. Labour was scarce; but wages fell nevertheless. All the small country arts of life which once added to the little pleasures of country people were lost. The country produce which passed through the hands of the husbandmen never got so far as their mouths. Incredible shabbiness and niggardly pinching reigned over the fields and acres which, in spite of the rude and careless husbandry of the times, were so kind and bountiful. Had you any inkling of all this?"

"I have heard that it was so," said I; "but what followed?"

"The change," said Hammond, "which in these matters took place very early in our epoch, was most strangely rapid. People flocked into the country villages, and, so to say, flung themselves upon the freed land like a wild beast upon his prey; and in a very little time the villages of England were more populous than they had been since the fourteenth century, and were still growing fast. Of course, this invasion of the country was awkward to deal with, and would have created much misery, if the folk had still been under the bondage of class monopoly. But as it was, things soon righted themselves. People found out what they were fit for, and gave up attempting to push themselves into occupations in which they must needs fail. The town invaded the country; but the invaders, like the warlike invaders of early days, yielded to the influence of their surroundings, and became country people; and in their turn, as they became more numerous than the townsmen, influenced them also; so that the difference between town and country grew less and less; and it was indeed this world of town-bred folk which has produced that happy and leisurely but eager life of which you have had a first taste. Again I say, many blunders were made, but we have had time to set them right. Much was left for the men of my earlier life to deal with. The crude ideas of the first half of the twentieth century, when men were still oppressed by the fear of poverty, and did not look enough to the present pleasure of ordinary life, spoilt a great deal of what the commercial age had left us of external beauty: and I admit that it was but slowly that men recovered from the injuries they had inflicted on themselves even after they became free. But slowly as the recovery came, it did come; and the more you see of us, the clearer it will be to you that we are happy. That we live amidst beauty without any fear of becoming effeminate; that we have plenty to do, and on the whole enjoy doing it. What more can we ask of life?"

He paused, as if he were seeking for words with which to express his thought. Then he said:

"This is how we stand. England was once a country of clearings amongst the woods and wastes, with a few towns interspersed, which were fortresses for the feudal army, markets for the folk, gathering places for craftsmen. It then became a country of huge and foul workshops and fouler gambling-dens, surrounded by an ill-kept, poverty-stricken farm, pillaged by the masters of the workshops. It is now a garden, where nothing is wasted and nothing is spoilt, with the necessary dwellings, sheds, and workshops scattered up and down the country, all trim and neat and pretty. For, indeed, we should be too much ashamed of ourselves if we allowed the making of goods, even on a large scale, to carry with it the appearance, even, of desolation and misery. Why my friend, those housewives we were talking of just now would teach us better than that."

Said I: "This side of your change is certainly for the better. But though I shall soon see some of these villages, tell me in a word or two what they are like, just to prepare me."

"Perhaps," said he, "you have seen a tolerable picture of these villages as they were before the end of the nineteenth century. Such things exist."

"I have seen several of such pictures," said I.

"Well," said Hammond, "our villages are something like the best of such places, with the church or mote-house of the neighbours for their chief building. Only note that there are no tokens of poverty about them: no tumbledown picturesque; which, to tell you the truth, the artist usually availed himself of to veil his incapacity for drawing architecture. Such things do not please us, even when they indicate no misery. Like the mediaevals, we like everything trim and clean, and orderly and bright; as people always do when they have any sense of architectural power; because then they know that they can have what they want, and they won't stand any nonsense from Nature in their dealings with her."

"Besides the villages, are there any scattered country houses?" said I.

"Yes, plenty," said Hammond; "in fact, except in the wastes and forests and amongst the sand-hills (like Hindhead in Surrey), it is not easy to be out of sight of a house; and where the houses are thinly scattered they run large, and are more like the old colleges than ordinary houses as they used to be. That is done for the sake of society, for a good many people can dwell in such houses, as the country dwellers are not necessarily husbandmen; though they almost all help in such work at times. The life that goes on in these big dwellings in the country is very pleasant, especially as some of the most studious men of our time live in them, and altogether there is a great variety of mind and mood to be found in them which brightens and quickens the society there."

"I am rather surprised," said I, "by all this, for it seems to me that after all the country must be tolerably populous."

"Certainly," said he; "the population is pretty much the same as it was at the end of the nineteenth century; we have spread it, that is all. Of course, also, we have helped to populate other countries—where we were wanted and were called for."

Said I: "One thing, it seems to me, does not go with your word of 'garden' for the country. You have spoken of wastes and forests, and I myself have seen the beginning of your Middlesex and Essex forest. Why do you keep such things in a garden? and isn't it very wasteful to do so?"

"My friend," he said, "we like these pieces of wild nature, and can afford them, so we have them; let alone that as to forests, we need a great deal of timber, and suppose that our sons and our sons' sons will do the like. As to the land being a garden, I have heard that they used to have shrubberies and rockeries in gardens once; and though I might not like the artificial ones, I assure you that some of the natural rockeries of our garden are worth seeing. Go north this summer and look at the Cumberland and Westmoreland ones,—where, by the way, you will see some sheep feeding, so that they are not so wasteful as you think; not so wasteful as forcing-grounds for fruit out of season, *I* think. Go and have a look at the sheep-walks high up in the slopes between Ingleborough and Pen-y-gwent, and tell me if you think we *waste* the land there by not covering it with factories for making things that nobody wants, which was the chief business of the nineteenth century."

"I will try to go there," said I. "It won't take much trying," said he.

Chapter II. Concerning Government

"Now," said I, "I have come to the point of asking questions which I suppose will be dry for you to answer and difficult for you to explain; but I have foreseen for some time past that I must ask them, will I nill I. What kind of a government have you? Has republicanism finally triumphed? or have you come to a mere dictatorship, which some persons in the nineteenth century used to prophesy as the ultimate outcome of democracy? Indeed, this last question does not seem so very unreasonable, since you have turned your Parliament House into a dung-market. Or where do you house your present Parliament?"

The old man answered my smile with a hearty laugh, and said: "Well, well, dung is not the worst kind of corruption; fertility may come of that, whereas mere dearth came from the other kind, of which those walls once held the great supporters. Now, dear guest, let me tell you that our present parliament would be hard to house in one place, because the whole people is our parliament."

"I don't understand," said I.

"No, I suppose not," said he. "I must now shock you by telling you that we have no longer anything which you, a native of another planet, would call a government."

"I am not so much shocked as you might think," said I, "as I know something about governments. But tell me, how do you manage, and how have you come to this state of things?"

Said he: "It is true that we have to make some arrangements about our affairs, concerning which you can ask presently; and it is also true that everybody does not always agree with the details of these arrangements; but, further, it is true that a man no more needs an elaborate system of government, with its army, navy, and police, to force him to give way to the will of the majority of his *equals*, than he wants a similar machinery to make him understand that his head and a stone wall cannot occupy the same space at the same moment. Do you want further explanation?"

"Well, yes, I do," quoth I. Old Hammond settled himself in his chair with a look of enjoyment which rather alarmed me, and made me dread a scientific diquisition: so I sighed and abided. He said:

"I suppose you know pretty well what the process of government was in the bad old times?"

"I am supposed to know," said I.

Hammond. What was the government of those days? Was it really the Parliament or any part of it?

I. No.

H. Was not the Parliament on the one side a kind of watch-committee sitting to see that the interests of the Upper Classes took no hurt; and on the other side a sort of blind to delude the people into supposing that they had some share in the management of their own affairs?

I. History seems to show us this.

H. To what extent did the people manage their own affairs?

I. I judge from what I have heard that sometimes they forced the Parliament to make a law to legalize some alteration which had already taken place.

H. Anything else?

I. I think not. As I am informed, if the people made any attempt to deal with the cause of their grievances, the law stepped in and said, this is sedition, revolt, or what not, and slew or tortured the ringleaders of such attempts.

H. If Parliament was not the government then, nor the people either, what was the government?

I. Can you tell me?

H. I think we shall not be far wrong if we say that government was the Law-Courts, backed up by the executive, which handled the brute force that deluded people allowed them to use for their own purposes; I mean the army, navy, and police.

I. Reasonable men must needs think you are right.

H. Now as to those Law-Courts. Were they places of fair dealing according to the idea of the day? Had a poor man a good chance of defending his property and person in them?

I. It is a commonplace that even rich men looked upon a law suit as a dire misfortune even if they gained the case; and as for a poor one—why, it was considered a miracle of justice and beneficence if a poor man who had once got into the clutches of the law escaped prison or utter ruin.

H. It seems, then, my son, that the government by law-courts and police, which was the real government of the nineteenth century, was not a great success even to the people of that day, living under a class system which proclaimed inequality and poverty as the law of God and the bond which held the world together.

I. So it seems, indeed.

H. And now that all this is changed, and the "rights of property," which mean the clenching the fist on a piece of goods and crying out to the neighbours, You shan't have this!—now that all this has disappeared so utterly that it is no longer possible even to jest upon its absurdity, is such a Government possible?

I. It is impossible.

H. Yes, happily. But for what other purpose than the protection of the rich from the poor, the strong from the weak, did this Government exist?

I. I have heard that it was said that their office was to defend their own citizens against attack from other countries.

H. It was said; but was any one expected to believe this? For instance, did the English Government defend the English citizen against the French?

I. So it was said.

H. Then if the French had invaded England and conquered it, they would not have allowed the English workmen to live well?

I. (laughing) As far as I can make out, the English masters of the English workmen saw to that: they took from their workmen as much of their livelihood as they dared, because they wanted it for themselves.

H. But if the French had conquered, would they not have taken more still from the English workmen?

I. I do not think so; for in that case the English workmen would have died of starvation; and then the French conquest would have ruined the French, just as if the English horses and cattle had died of under-feeding. So that after all, the English *workmen* would have been no worse off for the conquest: their

French masters could have got no more from them than their English masters did.

H. This is true; and we may admit that the pretensions of the government to defend the poor (i.e. the useful) people against other countries come to nothing. But that is but natural; for we have seen already that it was the function of the government to protect the rich against the poor. But did not the government defend its rich men against other nations?

I. I do not remember to have heard that the rich needed defence; because it is said that even when two nations were at war, the rich men of each nation gambled with each other pretty much as usual, and even sold each other weapons wherewith to kill their own countrymen.

H. In short, it comes to this, that whereas the so-called government of protection of property by means of the law-courts meant destruction of wealth, this defence of the citizens of one country against those of another country by means of war or the threat of war meant pretty much the same thing.

I. I cannot deny it.

H. Therefore the government really existed for the destruction of wealth?

I. So it seems. And yet—

H. Yet what?

I. There were many rich people in those times.

H. You see the consequences of that fact?

I. I think I do. But tell me what they were.

H. If the government habitually destroyed wealth, the country must have been poor?

I. Yes, certainly.

H. Yet amidst this poverty the persons for the sake of whom the government existed insisted on being rich whatever might happen?

I. So it was.

H. What must happen if in a poor country some people insist on being rich at the expense of others?

I. Unutterable poverty for the others. All this misery, then, was caused by the destructive government of which we have been speaking?

H. Nay, it would be incorrect to say so. The government itself was but the necessary result of the careless, aimless tyranny of the times; it was but the machinery of tyranny. Now tyranny has come to an end, and we no longer need such machinery; we could not possibly use it since we are free. Therefore in your sense of the word we have no government. Do you understand this now?

I. Yes, I do. But I will ask you some more questions as to how you as free men manage your affairs.

H. With all my heart. Ask away.

"Well," I said, "about those 'arrangements' which you spoke of as taking the place of government, could you give me any account of them?"

"Neighbour," he said, "although we have simplified our lives a great deal from what they were, and have got rid of many conventionalities and many sham wants, which used to give our forefathers much trouble, yet our life is too complex for me to tell you in detail by means of words how it is arranged; you must find that out by living amongst us. It is true that I can better tell you what we don't do than what we do do.

"Well?" said I.

"This is the way to put it," said he: "We have been living for a hundred and fifty years, at least, more or less in our present manner, and a tradition or habit of life has been growing on us; and that habit has become a habit of acting on the whole for the best. It is easy for us to live without robbing each other. It would be possible for us to contend with and rob each other, but it would be harder for us than refraining from strife and robbery. That is in short the foundation of our life and our happiness."

"Whereas in the old days," said I, "it was very hard to live without strife and robbery. That's what you mean, isn't it, by giving me the negative side of your good conditions?"

"Yes," he said, "it was so hard, that those who habitually acted fairly to their neighbours were celebrated as saints and heroes, and were looked up to with the greatest reverence."

"While they were alive?" said I.

"No," said he, "after they were dead."

"But as to these days," I said; "you don't mean to tell me that no one ever transgresses this habit of good fellowship?"

"Certainly not," said Hammond, "but when the transgressions occur, everybody, transgressors and all, know them for what they are; the errors of friends, not the habitual actions of persons driven into enmity against society."

"I see," said I; "you mean that you have no 'criminal' classes."

"How could we have them," said he, "since there is no rich class to breed enemies against the state by means of the injustice of the state?"

Said I: "I thought that I understood from something that fell from you a little while ago that you had abolished civil law. Is that so, literally?"

"It abolished itself, my friend," said he. "As I said before, the civil law-courts were upheld for the defence of private property; for nobody ever pretended that it was possible to make people act fairly to each other by means of brute force. Well, private property being abolished, all the laws and all the legal 'crimes' which it had manufactured of course came to an end. Thou shalt not steal, had to be translated into, Thou shalt work in order to live happily. Is there any need to enforce that commandment by violence?"

"Well," said I, "that is understood, and I agree with it; but how about the crimes of violence? would not their occurrence (and you admit that they occur) make criminal law necessary?"

Said he: "In your sense of the word, we have no criminal law either. Let us look at the matter closer, and see whence crimes of violence spring. By far the greater part of these in past days were the result of the laws of private property, which forbade the satisfaction of their natural desires to all but a privileged few, and of the general visible coercion which came of those laws. All *that* cause of violent crime is gone. Again, many violent acts came from the artificial perversion of the sexual passions, which caused over-weening jealousy and the like miseries. Now, when you look carefully into these, you will find that what lay at the bottom of them was mostly the idea (a law-made idea) of the woman being the property of the man, whether he were husband, father, brother, or what not. That idea has of course vanished with private property, as well as certain follies about the 'ruin' of women for following their natural desires in an illegal way, which of course was a convention caused by the laws of private property."

"Another cognate cause of crimes of violence was the family tyranny, which was the subject of so many novels and stories of the past and which once more was the result of private property. Of course that is all ended, since families are held together by no bond of coercion, legal or social, but by mutual liking and affection, and everybody is free to come or go as he or she pleases. Furthermore, our standards of honour and public estimation are very different from the old ones; success in beating our neighbours is a road to renown now closed, let us hope for ever. Each man is free to exercise his special faculty to the utmost and every one encourages him in so doing. So that we have got rid of the scowling envy, coupled by the poets with hatred, and surely with good reason; heaps of unhappiness and ill-blood were caused by it, which with irritable and passionate men—i.e., energetic and active men—often led to violence."

I laughed, and said: "So that you now withdraw your admission, and say that there is no violence amongst you?"

"No," said he, "I withdraw nothing; as I told you, such things will happen. Hot blood will err sometimes. A man may strike another, and the stricken strike back again, and the result be a homicide, to put it at the worst. But what then? Shall the neighbours make it worse still? Shall we think so poorly of each other as to suppose that the slain man calls on us to revenge him, when we *know* that if he had been maimed, he would, when in cold blood and able to weigh all the circumstances, have forgiven his maimer? Or will the death of the slayer bring the slain man to life again and cure the unhappiness his death has caused?"

"Yes," I said, "but consider, must not the safety of society be safeguarded by some punishment?"

"There, neighbour!" said the old man, with some exultation. "You have hit the mark. That *punishment* of which men used to talk so wisely and act so foolishly, what was it but the expression of their fear? And they had no need to fear, since they—i.e., the rulers of society—were dwelling like an armed band in a hostile country. But we who live amongst our friends need neither fear nor punish. Surely if we, in dread of an occasional rare homicide, an occasional rough blow, were solemnly and legally to commit homicide and violence, we could only be a society of ferocious cowards. Don't you think so neighbour?"

"Yes, I do, when I come to think of it from that side," said I.

"Yet you must understand," said the old man, "that when any violence is committed, we expect the transgressor to make any atonement possible to him, and he himself expects it. But again, think if the destruction or serious injury of a man momentarily overcome by wrath or folly can be any atonement to the commonwealth? Surely it can only be an additional injury to it."

Said I: "But suppose the man has a habit of violence—kills a man a year, for instance?"

"Such a thing is unknown," said he. "In a society where there is no punishment to evade, no law to triumph over, remorse will certainly follow transgression."

"And lesser outbreaks of violence," said I "how do you deal with them? for hitherto we have been talking of great tragedies, I suppose?"

Said Hammond: "If the ill-doer is not sick or mad (in which case he must be restrained until his sickness or madness is cured) it is clear that grief and humiliation must follow the ill-deed; and society in general will make that pretty clear to the ill-done if he should chance to be dull to it; and again, some kind of atonement will follow,—at the least, an open acknowledgement of the grief and humiliation. Is it so hard to say, I ask your pardon, neighbour?—well, sometimes it is hard—and let it be.

"You think that enough?" said I.

"Yes," said he, "and moreover it is all that we *can* do. If in addition we torture the man, we turn his grief into anger, and the humiliation he would otherwise feel for *his* wrong-doing is swallowed up by a hope of revenge for *our* wrong-doing to him. He has paid the legal penalty, and can 'go and sin again' with comfort. Shall we commit such a folly, then? Remember Jesus had got the legal penalty remitted before he said 'Go and sin no more.' Let alone that in a society of equals you will not find any one to play the part of torturer or jailer, though many to act as nurse or doctor.

"So," said I, "you consider crime a mere spasmodic disease, which requires no body of criminal law to deal with it?"

"Pretty much so," said he; "and since, as I have told you we are a healthy people generally, so we are not likely to be much troubled with *this* disease."

"Well, you have no civil law, and no criminal law. But have you no laws of the market, so to say—no regulation for the exchange of wares? for you must exchange, even if you have no property."

Said he: "We have no obvious individual exchange, as you saw this morning when you went a-shopping; but of course there are regulations of the markets varying according to the circumstances and guided by general custom. But as these are matters of general assent which nobody dreams of objecting to, so also we have made no provision for enforcing them: therefore I don't call them laws. In law, whether it be criminal or civil, execution always follows judgment, and some one must suffer. When you see the judge on his bench, you see through him, as clearly as if he were made of glass, the policeman to emprison and the soldier to slay some actual living person. Such follies would make an agreeable market, wouldn't they?"

"Certainly," said I, "that means turning the market into a mere battlefield, in which many people must suffer as much as in the battlefield of bullet and bayonet. And from what I have seen, I should suppose that your marketing, great and little, is carried on in a way that makes it a pleasant occupation."

"You are right, neighbour," said he. "Although there are so many, indeed by far the greater number amongst us, who would be unhappy if they were not engaged in actually making things, and things which turn out beautiful under their hands,—there are many, like the housekeepers I was speaking of, whose delight is in administration and organization to use long-tailed words; I mean people who like keeping things together, avoiding waste, seeing that nothing sticks fast uselessly. Such people are thoroughly happy in their business, all the more as they are dealing with actual facts, and not merely passing counters round to see what share they shall have in the privileged taxation of useful people which was the business of the commercial folk in past days. Well, what are you going to ask me next?"

Chapter 13. Concerning Politics

Said I: "How do you manage with politics?"

Said Hammond, smiling: "I am glad that it is of me that you ask that question; I do believe that anybody else would make you explain yourself, or try to do so, till you were sick of asking questions. Indeed, I believe I am the only man in England who would know what you mean; and since I know, I will answer your question briefly by saying that we are very well off as to politics,—because we have none. If ever you make a book out of this conversation, put this in a chapter by itself, after the model of old Horrebow's Snakes in Iceland."

"I will," said I.

Chapter 14. How Matters Are Arranged

Said I: "How about your relations with foreign nations?"

"I will not affect not to know what you mean," said he, "but I will tell you at once that the whole system of rival and contending nations which played so great a part in the 'government' of the world of civilisation has disappeared along with the inequality betwixt man and man in society."

"Does not that make the world duller?" said I.

"Why?" said the old man.

"The obliteration of national variety," said I.

"Nonsense," he said, somewhat snappishly. "Cross the water and see. You will find plenty of variety: the landscape, the building, the diet, the amusements, all various. The men and women varying in looks as well as in habits of thought; the costume more various than in the commercial period. How should it add to the variety or dispel the dulness, to coerce certain families or tribes, often heterogeneous and jarring with one another into certain artificial and mechanical groups and call them nations, and stimulate their patriotism— i.e., their foolish and envious prejudices?"

"Well—I don't know how," said I.

"That's right," said Hammond cheerily; "you can easily understand that now we are freed from this folly it is obvious to us that by means of this very diversity the different strains of blood in the world can be serviceable and pleasant to each other, without in the least wanting to rob each other: we are all bent on the same enterprise, making the most of our lives. And I must tell you whatever quarrels or misunderstandings arise, they very seldom take place between people of different race; and consequently since there is less unreason in them, they are the more readily appeased."

"Good," said I, "but as to those matters of politics; as to general differences of opinion in one and the same community. Do you assert that there are none?"

"No, not at all," said he, somewhat snappishly; "but I do say that differences of opinion about real solid things need not, and with us do not, crystallise people into parties permanently hostile to one another, with different theories as to the build of the universe and the progress of time. Isn't that what politics used to mean?"

"H'm, well," said I, "I am not so sure of that."

Said he: "I take you, neighbour; they only *pretended* to this serious difference of opinion; for if it had existed they could not have dealt together in the ordinary business of life; couldn't have eaten together, bought and sold together, gambled together, cheated other people together, but must have fought whenever they met: which would not have suited them at all. The game of the masters of politics was to cajole or force the public to pay the expense of a luxurious life and exciting amusement for a few cliques of ambitious persons: and the *pretence* of serious difference of opinion belied by every action of their lives, was quite good enough for that. What has all that got to do with us?"

Said I: "Why nothing, I should hope. But I fear—In short, I have been told that political strife was a necessary result of human nature."

"Human nature!" cried the old boy, impetuously; "What human nature? The human nature of paupers, of slaves, of slave-holders, or the human nature of wealthy freemen? Which? Come tell me that!"

"Well." said I, "I suppose there would be a difference according to circumstances in people's action about these matters."

"I should think so, indeed," said he. "At all events, experience shows that it is so. Amongst us, our differences concern matters of business, and passing events as to them, and could not divide men permanently. As a rule, the immediate outcome shows which opinion on a given subject is the right one; it is a matter of fact, not of speculation. For instance, it is clearly not easy to knock up a political party on the question as to whether haymaking in such and such a countryside shall begin this week or next, when all men agree that it must at latest begin the week after next, and when any man can go down into the fields himself and see whether the seeds are ripe enough for the cutting."

Said I: "And you settle these differences, great and small, by the will of the majority, I suppose?"

"Certainly," said he; "how else could we settle them? You see in matters which are merely personal which do not affect the welfare of the community— how a man shall dress, what he shall eat and drink, what he shall write and read, and so forth—there can be no difference of opinion, and everybody does as he pleases. But when the matter is of common interest to the whole community, and the doing or not doing something affects everybody, the majority must have their way; unless the minority were to take up arms and show by force that they were the effective or real majority; which, however, in a society of men who are free and equal is little likely to happen; because in such a community the apparent majority *is* the real majority, and the others, as I have hinted before, know that too well to obstruct from mere pigheadedness; especially as they have had plenty of opportunity of putting forward their side of the question."

"How is that managed?" said I.

"Well," said he, "let us take one of our units of management, a commune, or a ward, or a parish (for we have all three names, indicating little real distinction between them now, though time was there was a good deal). In such a district, as you would call it, some neighbours think that something ought to be done or undone: a new town-hall built; a clearance of inconvenient houses; or say a stone bridge substituted for some ugly old iron one,—there you have undoing and doing in one. Well, at the next ordinary meeting of the neighbours, or Mote, as we call it, according to the ancient tongue of the times before bureaucracy, a neighbour proposes the change and of course, if everybody agrees, there is an end of discussion except about details. Equally, if no one backs the proposer—'seconds him,' it used to be called—the matter drops for the time being; a thing not likely to happen amongst reasonable men however, as the proposer is sure to have talked it over with others before the Mote. But supposing the affair proposed and seconded, if a few of the neighbours disagree to it, if they think that the beastly iron bridge will serve a little longer and they don't want to be bothered with building a new one just then, they don't count heads that time, but put off the formal discussion to the next Mote; and meantime arguments pro and con are flying about, and some get printed, so that everybody knows what is going on; and when the Mote comes together again there is a regular discussion and at last a vote by show of hands. If the division is a close one, the question is again put off for further discussion; if the division is a wide one, the minority are asked if they will yield to the more general opinion, which they often, nay, most commonly do. If they refuse, the question is debated a third time, when, if the minority has not perceptibly grown, they always give way; though I believe there is some half-forgotten rule by which they might still carry it on further; but I say, what always happens is that they are convinced not perhaps that their view is the wrong one, but they cannot persuade or force the community to adopt it."

"Very good," said I; "but what happens if the divisions are still narrow?"

Said he: "As a matter of principle and according to the rule of such cases, the question must then lapse, and the majority, if so narrow, has to submit to sitting down under the *status quo*. But I must tell you that in point of fact the minority very seldom enforces this rule, but generally yields in a friendly manner."

"But do you know," said I, "that there is something in all this very like democracy; and I thought that democracy was considered to be in a moribund condition many, many years ago."

The old boy's eyes twinkled. "I grant you that our methods have that drawback. But what is to be done? We can't get any one amongst us to complain of his not always having his own way in the teeth of the community, when it is clear that everybody cannot have that indulgence. What is to be done?"

"Well," said I, "I don't know."

Said he: "The only alternatives to our method that I can conceive of are these. First, that we should choose out, or breed, a class of superior persons capable of judging on all matters without consulting the neighbours; that, in short, we should get for ourselves what used to be called an aristocracy of intellect; or, secondly, that for the purpose of safe-guarding the freedom of the individual will, we should revert to a system of private property again, and have slaves and slave-holders once more. What do you think of those two expedients?"

"Well," said I, "there is a third possibility—to wit, that every man should be quite independent of every other and that thus the tyranny of society should be abolished."

He looked hard at me for a second or two, and then burst out laughing very heartily; and I confess that I joined him. When he recovered himself he nodded at me, and said: "Yes, yes, I quite agree with you—and so we all do."

"Yes," I said, "and besides, it does not press hardly on the minority: for, take this matter of the bridge, no man is obliged to work on it if he doesn't agree to its building. At least I suppose not."

He smiled, and said: "Shrewdly put; and yet from the point of view of another planet. If the man of the minority does find his feelings hurt, doubtless he may relieve them by refusing to help in building the bridge. But, dear neighbour, that is not a very effective salve for the wound caused by the 'tyranny of a majority' in our society; because all work that is done is either beneficial or hurtful to every member of the society. The man is benefited by the bridge-building if it turns out a good thing, and hurt by it if it turns out a bad one, whether he puts a hand to it or not; and meanwhile he is benefiting the bridge-builders by his work, whatever that may be. In fact, I see no help for him except the pleasure of saying 'I told you so' if the bridge-building turns out to be a mistake and hurts him; if it benefits him he must suffer in silence. A terrible tyranny our Communism, is it not? Folk used often to be warned against this very unhappiness in times past, when for every well-fed, contented person you saw a thousand miserable starvelings. Whereas for us, we grow fat and well-liking on the tyranny; a tyranny, to say the truth, not to be made visible by any to seek for troubles by calling our peace and plenty and happiness by ill names whose very meaning we have forgotten!" He sat musing for a little, and then started and said: "Are there any more questions, dear guest? The morning is waning fast amidst my garrulity."

William Morris (1834–1896) was the leader of the British arts and crafts movement. Though some label him as an anarchist theorist, he considered himself more indebted to Marx.

Source: William Morris, NEWS FROM NOWHERE (London: Reeves & Turner, 1891), 72–100.

Ignatius Donnelly
Caesar's Column

Caesar's Column (1892) by Ignatius Donnelly was both a warning of industrial turmoil if reform was not forthcoming in the United States and a suggestion of the direction that reform should take. Donnelly, a Minnesota politician, was instrumental in founding the People's Party, a populist political party that appealed to farmers and workers. Donnelly also wrote a second utopia, *The Golden Bottle* (1892), that directly addressed elements of the platform of the People's Party.

Chapter XII. Gabriel's Utopia

"But what would you do, my good Gabriel," said Maximilian, smiling, "if the reformation of the world were placed in your hands? Every man has an Utopia in his head. Give me some idea of yours."

"First," I said, "I should do away with all interest on money. Interest on money is the root and ground of the world's troubles. It puts one man in a position of safety, while another is in a condition of insecurity, and thereby it at once creates a radical distinction in human society."

"How do you make that out?" he asked.

"The lender takes a mortgage on the borrower's land or house, or goods, for, we will say, one-half or one-third their value; the borrower then assumes all the chances of life in his efforts to repay the loan. If he is a farmer, he has to run the risk of the fickle elements. Rains may drown, droughts may burn up his crops. If a merchant, he encounters all the hazards of trade; the bankruptcy of other tradesmen; the hostility of the elements sweeping away agriculture, and so affecting commerce; the tempests that smite his ships, etc. If a mechanic, he is still more dependent upon the success of all above him, and the mutations of commercial prosperity. He may lose employment; he may sicken; he may die. But behind all these risks stands the money-lender, in perfect security. The failure of his customer only enriches him; for he takes for his loan property worth twice or thrice the sum he has advanced upon it. Given a million of men and a hundred years of time, and the slightest advantage possessed by any one class among the million must result, in the long run, in the most startling discrepancies of condition. A little evil grows like a ferment—it never ceases to operate; it is always at work. Suppose I bring before you a handsome, rosy-cheeked young man, full of life and hope and health. I touch his lip with a single *bacillus* of *phthisis pulmonalis*—consumption. It is invisible to the eye; it is too small to be weighed. Judged by all the tests of the senses, it is too insignificant to be thought of; but it has the capacity to multiply itself indefinitely. The youth goes off singing. Months, perhaps years, pass before the deadly disorder begins to manifest itself; but in time the step loses its elasticity; the eyes become dull; the roses fade from the cheeks; the strength departs, and eventually the joyous youth is but a shell—a cadaverous, shrunken form, inclosing a shocking mass of putridity; and death ends the dreadful scene. Give one set of men in a community a financial advantage over the rest, however slight—it may be almost invisible—and at the end of centuries that class so favored will own everything and wreck the country. A penny, they say, put out at interest the day Columbus sailed from Spain, and compounded ever since, would amount now to more than all the assessed value of all the property, real, personal and mixed, on the two continents of North and South America."

"But," said Maximilian, "how would the men get along who wanted to borrow?"

"The necessity to borrow is one of the results of borrowing. The disease produces the symptoms. The men who are enriched by borrowing are infinitely less in number than those who are ruined by it; and every disaster to the middle class swells the number and decreases the opportunities of the helplessly poor. Money in itself is valueless. It becomes valuable only by use—by exchange for things needful for life or comfort. If money could not be loaned, it would have to be put out by the owner of it in business enterprises, which would employ labor; and as the enterprise would not then have to support a double burden— to wit, the man engaged in it and the usurer who sits securely upon his back— but would have to maintain only the former usurer-that is, the present employer—its success would be more certain; the general prosperity of the community would be increased thereby, and there would be therefore more enterprises, more demand for labor, and consequently higher wages. Usury kills off the enterprising members of a community by bankrupting them, and leaves only the very rich and the very poor; for every dollar the employers of labor pay to the lenders of money has to come eventually out of the pockets of the laborers. Usury is therefore the cause of the first aristocracy, and out of this grow all the other aristocracies. Inquire where the money came from that now oppresses mankind, in the shape of great corporations, combinations, etc., and in nine cases out of ten you will trace it back to the fountain of interest on money loaned. The coral island is built out of the bodies of dead coral insects; large fortunes are usually the accumulations of wreckage, and every dollar represents disaster."

"Well," said Maximilian, "having abolished usury, in your Utopia, what would you do next?"

"I would set to work to make a list of all the laws, or parts of laws, or customs, or conditions which, either by commission or omission, gave any man an advantage over any other man; or which tended to concentrate the wealth of the community in the hands of a few. And having found out just what these wrongs or advantages were, I would abolish them *instanter.*"

"Well, let us suppose," said Maximilian, "that you were not immediately murdered by the men whose privileges you had destroyed—even as the Gracchi were of old—what would you do next? Men differ in every detail. Some have more industry, or more strength, or more cunning, or more foresight, or more acquisitiveness than others. How are you to prevent these men from becoming richer than the rest?"

"I should not try to," I said. "These differences in men are fundamental, and not to be abolished by legislation; neither are the instincts you speak of in themselves injurious. Civilization, in fact, rests upon them. It is only in their excess that they become destructive. It is right and wise and proper for men to accumulate sufficient wealth to maintain their age in peace, dignity and plenty, and to be able to start their children into the arena of life sufficiently equipped. A thousand men in a community worth $10,000 or $50,000, or even $100,000 each, may be a benefit, perhaps a blessing; but one man worth fifty or one hundred millions, or, as we have them now-a-days, one thousand millions, is a threat against the safety and happiness of every man in the world. I should establish a maximum beyond which no man could own property. I should not stop his accumulations when he had reached that point, for with many men accumulation is an instinct; but I should require him to invest the surplus, under the direction of a governmental board of management, in great works for the benefit of the laboring classes. He should establish schools, colleges, orphan asylums, hospitals, model residences, gardens, parks, libraries, baths, places of amusement, music-halls, sea-side excursions in hot weather, fuel societies in cold weather, etc., etc. I should permit him to secure immortality by affixing his name to his benevolent works; and I should honor him still further by placing his statue in a great national gallery set apart to perpetuate forever the memory of the benefactors of the race."

"But," said Maximilian, with a smile, "it would not take long for your rich men, with their surplus wealth, to establish all those works you speak of. What would you do with the accumulations of the rest?"

"Well," said I, "we should find plenty to do. We would put their money, for instance, into a great fund and build national railroads, that would bring the productions of the farmers to the workmen, and those of the workmen to the farmers, at the least cost of transportation, and free from the exactions of speculators and middlemen. Thus both farmers and workmen would live better, at less expense and with less toil."

"All very pretty," said he; "but your middlemen would starve."

"Not at all," I replied; "the cunning never starve. There would be such a splendid era of universal prosperity that they would simply turn their skill and shrewdness into some new channels, in which, however, they would have to give something of benefit, as an equivalent for the benefits they received. Now they take the cream, and butter, and beef, while some one else has to raise, feed and milk the cow."

"But," said he, "all this would not help our farmers in their present condition—they are blotted off the land."

"True," I replied; "but just as I limited a man's possible wealth, so should I limit the amount of land he could own. I would fix a maximum of, say, 100 or 500 acres, or whatever amount might be deemed just and reasonable. I should abolish all corporations, or turn them back into individual partnerships. . . .

"Then," I replied, "I should invoke the power of the nation, as was done in that great civil war of 1861, and issue paper money, receivable for all taxes, and secured by the guarantee of the faith and power of five hundred million people; and make advances to carry these ruined peasants beyond the first years of distress—that money to be a loan to them, without interest, and to be repaid as a tax on their land. Government is only a machine to insure justice and help the people, and we have not yet developed half its powers. And we are under no more necessity to limit ourselves to the governmental precedents of our ancestors than we are to confine ourselves to the narrow boundaries of their knowledge, or their inventive skill, or their theological beliefs. The trouble is that so many seem to regard government as a divine something which has fallen down upon us out of heaven, and therefore not to be improved upon or even criticised; while the truth is, it is simply a human device to secure human happiness, and in itself has no more sacredness than a wheelbarrow or a cooking-pot. The end of everything earthly is the good of man; and there is nothing sacred on earth but man, because he alone shares the Divine conscience."

"But," said he, "would not your paper money have to be redeemed in gold or silver?"

"Not necessarily," I replied. "The adoration of gold and silver is a superstition of which the bankers are the high priests and mankind the victims. Those metals are of themselves of little value. What should make them so?" . . .

I sat down, and, after some thought, wrote, on the back of the wrapping-paper, these words:

THIS GREAT MONUMENT

IS

ERECTED BY

CÆSAR LOMELLINI,

It is composed of the bodies of a quarter of a million of human beings, who were once the rulers, or the instruments of the rulers, of this mighty, but, alas! this ruined city.

They were dominated by leaders who were altogether evil.

They corrupted the courts, the juries, the newspapers, the legislatures, the congresses, the ballot-boxes and the hearts and souls of the people.

They formed gigantic combinations to plunder the poor; to make the miserable more miserable: to take from those who had least and to give it to those who had most.

They used the machinery of free government to effect oppression; they made liberty a mockery, and its traditions a jest; they drove justice from the land and installed cruelty, ignorance, despair and vice in its place.

Their hearts were harder than the nether mill-stone; they degraded humanity and outraged God.

At length indignation stirred in the vasty courts of heaven; and overburdened human nature rose in universal revolt on earth.

By the very instruments which their own wickedness had created they perished; and here they lie, sepulchred in stone, and heaped around explosives as destructive as their own lives. We execrate their vices, while we weep for their misfortunes. They were the culmination of centuries of misgovernment; and they paid an awful penalty for the sins of generations of short-sighted and selfish ancestors, as well as for their own cruelty and wickedness.

Let this monument, O man! stand forever.

Should civilization ever revive on earth, let the human race come hither and look upon this towering shaft, and learn to restrain selfishness and live righteously. From this ghastly pile let it derive the great lesson, that no earthly government can endure which is not built on mercy, justice, truth and love. . . .

When we had formulated our scheme of government we called the people together again; and after several days of debate it was substantially agreed upon.

In our constitution, we first of all acknowledged our dependence on Almighty God; believing that all good impulses on earth spring from his heart, and that no government can prosper which does not possess his blessing.

We decreed, secondly, a republican form of government. Every adult man and woman of sound mind is permitted to vote. We adopted a system of voting that we believed would insure perfect secrecy and prevent bribery—something like that which had already been in vogue, in some countries, before the revolution of the Proletariat.

The highest offense known to our laws is treason against the state, and this consists not only in levying war against the government, but in corrupting the voter or the office-holder; or in the voter or office-holder selling his vote or his services. For these crimes the penalty is death. But, as they are in their very nature secret offenses, we provide, in these cases only, for three forms of verdict: "*guilty*," "*not guilty*" and "*suspected.*" This latter verdict applies to cases where the jury are morally satisfied, from the surrounding circumstances, that the man is guilty, although there is not enough direct and positive testimony to convict him. The jury then have the power—not as a punishment to the man, but for the safety of the community—to declare him incapable of voting or holding office for a period of not less than one nor more than five years. We rank bribery and corruption as high treason; because experience has demonstrated that they are more deadly in their consequences to a people than open war against the government, and many times more so than murder.

We decreed, next, universal and compulsory education. No one can vote who cannot read and write. We believe that one man's ignorance should not countervail the just influence of another man's intelligence. Ignorance is not only ruinous to the individual, but destructive to society. It is an epidemic which scatters death everywhere.

We abolish all private schools, except the higher institutions and colleges. We believe it to be essential to the peace and safety of the commonwealth that the children of all the people, rich and poor, should, during the period of growth, associate together. In this way, race, sectarian and caste prejudices are obliterated, and the whole community grow up together as brethren. Otherwise, in a generation or two, we shall have the people split up into hostile factions, fenced in by doctrinal bigotries, suspicious of one another, and antagonizing one another in politics, business and everything else.

But, as we believe that it is not right to cultivate the heads of the young to the exclusion of their hearts, we mingle with abstract knowledge a cult of morality and religion, to be agreed upon by the different churches; for there are a hundred points wherein they agree to one wherein they differ. And, as to the points peculiar to each creed, we require the children to attend school but five days in the week, thus leaving one day for the parents or pastors to take charge of their religious training in addition to the care given them on Sundays.

We abolish all interest on money, and punish with imprisonment the man who receives it.

The state owns all roads, streets, telegraph or telephone lines, railroads and mines, and takes exclusive control of the mails and express matter.

As these departments will in time furnish employment for a great many officials, who might be massed together by the party in power, and wielded for political purposes, we decree that any man who accepts office relinquishes, for the time being, his right of suffrage. The servants of the people have no right to help rule them; and he who thinks more of his right to vote than of an office is at liberty to refuse an appointment.

As we have not an hereditary nobility, as in England, or great geographical subdivisions, as in America, we are constrained, in forming our Congress or Parliament, to fall back upon a new device.

Our governing body, called *The People*, is divided into three branches. The first is elected exclusively by the producers, to wit: the workmen in the towns and the farmers and mechanics in the country; and those they elect must belong to their own class. As these constitute the great bulk of the people, the body that represents them stands for the House of Commons in England, or the House of Representatives in America. The second branch is elected exclusively by and from the merchants and manufacturers, and all who are engaged in trade, or as employers of labor. The third branch, which is the smallest of the three, is selected by the authors, newspaper writers, artists, scientists, philosophers and literary people generally. This branch is expected to hold the balance of power, where the other two bodies cannot agree. It may be expected that they will be distinguished by broad and philanthropic views and new and generous conceptions. Where a question arises as to which of these three groups or subdivisions a voter belongs to, the matter is to be decided by the president of the Republic.

No law can be passed, in the first instance, unless it receives a majority vote in each of the three branches, or a two-thirds vote in two of them. Where a difference of opinion arises upon any point of legislation, the three branches are to assemble together and discuss the matter at issue, and try to reach an agreement. As, however, the experience of the world has shown that there is more danger of the upper classes combining to oppress the producers than there is of the producers conspiring to govern them,—except in the last desperate extremity, as shown recently,—it is therefore decreed that if the Commons, by a three-fourths vote, pass any measure, it becomes a law, notwithstanding the veto of the other two branches.

The executive is elected by the Congress for a period of four years, and is not eligible for re-election. He has no veto and no control of any patronage. In the election of president a two-thirds vote of each branch is necessary.

Whenever it can be shown, in the future, that in any foreign country the wages of labor and the prosperity of the people are as high as in our own, then free trade with that people is decreed. But whenever the people of another country are in greater poverty, or working at a lower rate of wages than our own, then all commercial intercourse with them shall be totally interdicted. For impoverished labor on one side of a line, unless walled out, must inevitably drag down labor on the other side of the line to a like condition. Neither is the device of a tariff sufficient; for, although it is better than free trade, yet, while it tends to keep up the price of goods, it lets in the products of foreign labor; this diminishes the wages of our own laborers by decreasing the demand for their productions to the extent of the goods imported; and thus, while the price of commodities is held up for the benefit of the manufacturers, the price of labor falls. There can be no equitable commerce between two peoples representing two different stages of civilization, and both engaged in producing the same commodities. Thus the freest nations are constantly pulled down to ruin by the most oppressed. What would happen to heaven if you took down the fence between it and hell? We are resolved that our republic shall be of itself, by itself— "in a great pool, a swan's nest."

As a corollary to these propositions, we decree that our Congress shall have the right to fix the rate of compensation for all forms of labor, so that wages shall never fall below a rate that will afford the laborer a comfortable living, with a margin that will enable him to provide for his old age. It is simply a question of the adjustment of values. This experiment has been tried before by different countries, but it was always tried in the interest of the employers; the laborers had no voice in the matter; and it was the interest of the upper class to cheapen labor; and hence *Muscle* became a drug and *Cunning* invaluable and masterful; and the process was continued indefinitely until the catastrophe came. Now labor has its own branch of our Congress, and can defend its rights and explain its necessities.

In the comparison of views between the three classes some reasonable ground of compromise will generally be found; and if error is committed we prefer that it should enure to the benefit of the many, instead of, as heretofore, to the benefit of the few.

We declare in the preamble to our constitution that "this government is intended to be merely a plain and simple instrument, to insure to every industrious citizen not only liberty, but an educated mind, a comfortable home, an abundant supply of food and clothing, and a pleasant, happy life."

Are not these the highest objects for which governments can exist? And if government, on the old lines, did not yield these results, should it not have been so reformed as to do so?

We shall not seek to produce uniformity of recompense for all kinds of work; for we know that skilled labor is intrinsically worth more than unskilled; and there are some forms of intellectual toil that are more valuable to the world than any muscular exertion. The object will be not to drag down, but to lift up; and, above all, to prevent the masses from falling into that awful slough of wretchedness which has just culminated in world-wide disaster.

The government will also regulate the number of apprentices who shall enter any given trade or pursuit. For instance, there may be too many shoemakers and not enough farmers; if, now, more shoemakers crowd into that trade, they will simply help starve those already there; but if they are distributed to farming, and other employments, where there is a lack, then there is more work for the shoemakers, and in time a necessity for more shoemakers.

There is no reason why the ingenuity of man should not be applied to these great questions. It has conquered the forces of steam and electricity, but it has neglected the great adjustments of society, on which the happiness of millions depends. If the same intelligence which has been bestowed on perfecting the steam-engine had been directed to a consideration of the correlations of man to man, and pursuit to pursuit, supply and demand would have precisely matched each other, and there need have been no pauperism in the world—save that of the sick and imbecile. And the very mendicants would begin to rise when the superincumbent pressure of those who live on the edge of pauperism had been withdrawn.

We deny gold and silver any function as money except for small amounts—such as five dollars or less. We know of no supplies of those metals in our mountains, and if we tied our prosperity to their chariot, the little, comparatively, there is among us, would gradually gravitate into a few hands, and these men would become the masters of the country. We issue, therefore, a legal-tender paper money, receivable for all indebtedness, public and private, and not to be increased beyond a certain *per capita* of population.

We decree a limitation upon the amount of land or money any one man can possess. All above that must be used, either by the owner or the government, in works of public usefulness.

There is but one town in our colony—it is indeed not much more than a village—called Stanley. The republic has taken possession of all the land in and contiguous to it, not already built on—paying the owners the present price of the same; and hereafter no lots will be sold except to persons who buy to build homes for themselves; and these lots will be sold at the original cost price. Thus the opportunity for the poor to secure homes will never be diminished.

We further decree that when hereafter any towns or cities or villages are to be established, it shall only be by the nation itself. Whenever one hundred persons or more petition the government, expressing their desire to build a town, the government shall then take possession of a sufficient tract of land, paying the intrinsic, not the artificial, price therefor. It shall then lay the land out in lots, and shall give the petitioners and others the right to take the lots at the original cost price, provided they make their homes upon them. We shut out all speculators.

No towns started in any other way shall have railroad or mail facilities.

When once a municipality is created in the way I have described, it shall provide, in the plat of the town, parks for recreation; no lot shall contain less than half an acre; the streets shall be very wide and planted with fruit trees in double and treble rows. In the center of the town shall be erected a town hall, with an assembly chamber, arranged like a theater, and large enough to seat all the inhabitants. The building shall also contain free public baths, a library, a reading-room, public offices, etc. The municipality shall divide the people into groups of five hundred families each, and for each group they shall furnish a physician, to be paid for out of the general taxes. They shall also provide in the same way concerts and dramatic representations and lectures, free of charge. The hours of labor are limited to eight each day; and there are to be two holidays in the week, Wednesday and Sundays. Just as the state is able to carry the mails for less than each man could carry them for himself, so the cost of physicians and entertainments procured by the municipality will be much less than under the old system.

We do not give any encouragement to labor-saving inventions although we do not discard them. We think the end of government should be—not cheap goods or cheap men, but happy families. If any man makes a serviceable invention the state purchases it at a reasonable price for the benefit of the people.

Men are elected to whom all disputes are referred; each of the contestants selects a man, and the three act together as arbitrators. Where a jury is demanded the defeated party pays all the expenses. We hold that it is not right that all the peaceable citizens should be taxed to enable two litigious fellows to quarrel. Where a man is convicted of crime he is compelled to work out all the cost of his trial and conviction, and the cost of his support as a prisoner, before he can be discharged. If vice will exist, it must be made self-supporting.

Ignatius Donnelly (1831–1901) was a Minnesota politician and author.

Source: [Ignatius Donnelly], Caesar's Column: A Story of the Twentieth Century, by Edmund Boisgilbert, M.D. (pseud.) (Chicago: F. J. Schulte, 1890, reprint, London: Sampson, Low, Marston and Co., 1892), 116–22, 329–30, 353–62.

William Dean Howells
A Traveler from Altruria

A Traveler from Altruria **is a response to Edward Bellamy's** *Looking Back-*
ward **that projects a suburban, even a rural, utopia in contrast to Bellamy's**

essentially urban one. The key to this utopia is altruism—everyone in the society cares for everyone else. Much of this novel and its sequel, *Through the Eye of the Needle* (1907), describe the ways contemporary Americans failed to live up to this standard.

Chapter Twelve

"And so," the Altrurian continued, "when the labor of the community was emancipated from the bondage of the false to the free service of the true, it was also, by an inevitable implication, dedicated to beauty and rescued from the old slavery to the ugly, the stupid and the trivial. The thing that was honest and useful became, by the operation of a natural law, a beautiful thing. Once we had not time enough to make things beautiful, we were so overworked in making false and hideous things to sell; but now we had all the time there was, and a glad emulation arose among the trades and occupations to the end that everything done should be done finely as well as done honestly. The artist, the man of genius, who worked from the love of his work became the normal man, and in the measure of his ability and of his calling each wrought in the spirit of the artist. We got back the pleasure of doing a thing beautifully, which was God's primal blessing upon all his working children, but which we had lost in the horrible days of our need and greed. There is not a working man within the sound of my voice, but has known this divine delight, and would gladly know it always if he only had the time. Well, now we had the time, the Evolution had given us the time, and in all Altruria there was not a furrow driven or a swath mown, not a hammer struck on house or on ship, not a stitch sewn or a stone laid, not a line written or a sheet printed, not a temple raised or an engine built, but it was done with an eye to beauty as well as to use.

"As soon as we were freed from the necessity of preying upon one another, we found that *there was no hurry*. The good work would wait to be well done; and one of the earliest effects of the Evolution was the disuse of the swift trains which had traversed the continent, night and day, that one man might overreach another, or make haste to undersell his rival, or seize some advantage of him, or plot some profit to his loss. Nine-tenths of the railroads, which in the old times had ruinously competed, and then in the hands of the Accumulation had been united to impoverish and oppress the people, fell into disuse. The commonwealth operated the few lines that were necessary for the collection of materials and the distribution of manufactures, and for pleasure travel and the affairs of state: but the roads that had been built to invest capital, or parallel other roads, or 'make work,' as it was called, or to develop resources, or boom localities, were suffered to fall into ruin; the rails were stripped from the landscape, which they had bound as with shackles, and the road-beds became highways for the use of kindly neighborhoods, or nature recovered them wholly and hid the memory of their former abuse in grass and flowers and wild vines. The ugly towns that they had forced into being, as Frankenstein was fashioned, from the materials of the charnel, and that had no life in or from the good of the community, soon tumbled into decay. The administration used parts of them in the construction of the villages in which the Altrurians now mostly live; but generally these towns were built of materials so fraudulent, in form so vile, that it was judged best to burn them. In this way their sites were at once purified and obliterated.

"We had, of course, a great many large cities under the old egoistic conditions, which increased and fattened upon the country, and fed their cancerous life with fresh infusions of its blood. We had several cities of half a million, and one of more than a million; we had a score of them with a population of a hundred thousand or more. We were very proud of them, and vaunted them as a proof of our unparalleled prosperity, though really they never were anything but congeries of millionaires and the wretched creatures who served them and supplied them. Of course, there was everywhere the appearance of enterprise and activity, but it meant final loss for the great mass of the businessmen, large and small, and final gain for the millionaires. These, and their parasites dwelt together, the rich starving the poor and the poor plundering and mis-governing the rich; and it was the intolerable suffering in the cities that chiefly hastened the fall of the old Accumulation, and the rise of the Commonwealth.

"Almost from the moment of the Evolution the competitive and monopolistic centers of population began to decline. In the clear light of the new order it was seen that they were not fit dwelling-places for men, either in the complicated and luxurious palaces where the rich fenced themselves from their kind, or in the vast tenements, towering height upon height, ten and twelve stories up, where the swarming poor festered in vice and sickness and famine. If I were to tell you of the fashion of those cities of our egoistic epoch, how the construction was one error from the first, and every correction of an error bred a new defect, I should make you laugh, I should make you weep. We let them fall to ruin as quickly as they would, and their sites are still so pestilential, after the lapse of centuries, that travelers are publicly guarded against them. Ravening beasts and poisonous reptiles lurk in those abodes of the riches and the poverty that are no longer known to our life. A part of one of the less malarial of the old cities, however, is maintained by the commonwealth in the form of its prosperity, and is studied by antiquarians for the instruction, and by moralists for the admonition it affords. A section of a street is exposed, and you see the foundations of the houses; you see the filthy drains that belched into the common sewers, trapped and retrapped to keep the poison gases down; you see the sewers that rolled their loathsome tides under the streets, amidst a tangle of gas pipes, steam pipes, water pipes, telegraph wires, electric lighting wires, electric motor wires and grip-cables; all without a plan, but make-shifts, expedients, devices, to repair and evade the fundamental mistake of having any such cities at all.

"There are now no cities in Altruria, in your meaning, but there are capitals, one for each of the Regions of our country, and one for the whole commonwealth. These capitals are for the transaction of public affairs, in which every citizen of Altruria is schooled, and they are the residences of the administrative officials, who are alternated every year, from the highest to the lowest. A public employment with us is of no greater honor or profit than any other, for with our absolute economic equality, there can be no ambition, and there is no opportunity for one citizen to outshine another. But as the capitals are the centers of all the arts, which we consider the chief of our public affairs, they are oftenest frequented by poets, actors, painters, sculptors, musicians and architects. We regard all artists, who are in a sort creators, as the human type which is likest the divine, and we try to conform our whole industrial life to the artistic temperament. Even in the labors of the field and shop, which are obligatory upon all, we study the inspirations of this temperament, and in the voluntary pursuits we allow it full control. Each, in these, follows his fancy as to what he shall do, and when he shall do it, or whether he shall do anything at all. In the capitals are the universities, theaters, galleries, museums, cathedrals, laboratories and conservatories, and the appliances of every art and science, as well as the administration buildings; and beauty as well as use is studied in every edifice. Our capitals are as clean and quiet and healthful as the country, and these advantages are secured simply by the elimination of the horse, an animal which we should be as much surprised to find in the streets of a town as the plesiosaurus or the pterodactyl. All transportation in the capitals, whether for pleasure or business, is by electricity, and swift electrical expresses connect the capital of each region with the villages which radiate from it to the cardinal points. These expresses run at the rate of a hundred and fifty miles an hour, and they enable the artist, the scientist, the literary man, of the remotest hamlet, to visit the capital (when he is not actually resident there in some public use) every day, after the hours of the obligatory industries; or if he likes, he may remain there a whole week or fortnight, giving six hours a day instead of three to the obligatories, until the time is made up. In case of very evident merit, or for the purpose of allowing him to complete some work requiring continuous application, a vote of the local agents may release him from the obligatories indefinitely. Generally, however, our artists prefer not to ask this, but avail themselves of the stated means we have of allowing them to work at the obligatories, and get the needed exercise and variety of occupation, in the immediate vicinity of the capital.

"We do not think it well to connect the hamlets on the different lines of radiation from the capital, except by the good country roads which traverse each region in every direction. The villages are mainly inhabited by those who prefer a rural life; they are farming villages; but in Altruria it can hardly be said that one man is more a farmer than another. We do not like to distinguish men by their callings; we do not speak of the poet This or the shoemaker That, for the poet may very likely be a shoemaker in the obligatories, and the shoemaker a poet in the voluntaries. If it can be said that one occupation is honored above another with us, it is that which we all share, and that is the cultivation of the earth. We believe that this, when not followed slavishly, or for gain, brings man into the closest relations to the deity, through a grateful sense of the divine bounty, and that it not only awakens a natural piety in him, but that it endears to the worker that piece of soil which he tills, and so strengthens his love of home. The home is the very heart of the Altrurian system, and we do not think it well that people should be away from their homes very long or very often. In the competitive and monopolistic times men spent half their days in racing back and forth across our continent; families were scattered by the chase for fortune, and there was a perpetual paying and repaying of visits. One-half the income of those railroads which we let fall into disuse came from the ceaseless unrest. Now a man is born and lives and dies among his own kindred, and the sweet sense of neighborhood, of brotherhood, which blessed the golden age of the first Christian republic is ours again. Every year the people of each Region meet one another on Evolution day, in the Regionic capital; once in four years they all visit the national capital. There is no danger of the decay of patriotism among us; our country is our mother, and we love her as it is impossible to love the stepmother that a competitive or monopolistic nation must be to its citizens.

"I can only touch upon this feature and that of our system, as I chance to think of it. If any of you are curious about others, I shall be glad to answer questions as well as I can. We have, of course," the Altrurian proceeded, after a little indefinite pause, to let any speak who liked, "no money in your sense. As the whole people control affairs, no man works for another, and no man pays another. Every one does his share of labor, and receives his share of food, clothing and shelter, which is neither more nor less than another's. If you can imagine the justice and impartiality of a well-ordered family, you can conceive of the social and economic life of Altruria. We are, properly speaking, a family rather than a nation like yours.

"Of course, we are somewhat favored by our insular, or continental position; but I do not know that we are more so than you are. Certainly, however, we are self-sufficing in a degree unknown to most European countries; and we have within our borders the materials of every comfort and the resources of every need. We have no commerce with the egoistic world, as we call that outside, and I believe that I am the first Altrurian to visit foreign countries avowedly in my national character, though we have always had emissaries living abroad incognito. I hope that I may say without offense that they find it a sorrowful exile, and that the reports of the egoistic world, with its wars, its bankruptcies, its civic commotions and its social unhappiness, do not make us discontented with our own condition. Before the Evolution we had completed the round of your inventions and discoveries, impelled by the force that drives you on; and we have since disused most of them as idle and unfit. But we profit, now and then, by the advances you make in science, for we are passionately devoted to the study of the natural laws, open or occult, under which all men have their being. Occasionally an emissary returns with a sum of money, and explains to the students of the national university the processes by which it is lost and won; and at a certain time there was a movement for its introduction among us, not for its use as you know it, but for a species of counters in games of chance. It was considered, however, to contain an element of danger, and the scheme was discouraged. . . .

"But we do not regret the experience of competition and monopoly. They taught us some things in the operation of the industries. The labor-saving inventions which the Accumulation perverted to money-making, we have restored to the use intended by their inventors and the Creator of their inventors. After serving the advantage of socializing the industries which the Accumulation effected for its own purposes, we continued the work in large mills and shops, in the interest of the workers, whom we wished to guard against the evil effects of solitude. But our mills and shops are beautiful as well as useful. They look like temples, and they are temples, dedicated to that sympathy between the divine and human which expresses itself in honest and exquisite workmanship. They rise amid leafy boscages beside the streams, which form their only power: for we have disused steam altogether, with all the offenses to the eye and ear which its use brought into the world. Our life is so simple and our needs are so few that the handwork of the primitive toilers could easily supply our wants; but machinery works so much more thoroughly and beautifully, that we have in great measure retained it. Only, the machines that were once the workman's enemies and masters are now their friends and servants; and if any man chooses to work alone with his own hands, the state will buy what he makes at the same price that it sells the wares made collectively. This secures every right of individuality.

"The farm work, as well as the mill work and the shop work, is done by companies of workers; and there is nothing of that loneliness in our woods and fields which, I understand, is the cause of so much insanity among you. It is not good for man to be alone, was the first thought of his Creator when he considered him, and we act upon this truth in everything. The privacy of the family is sacredly guarded in essentials, but the social instinct is so highly developed with us that we like to eat together in large refectories, and we meet constantly to argue and dispute on questions of aesthetics and metaphysics. We do not, perhaps, read so many books as you do, for most of our reading, when not for special research, but for culture and entertainment, is done by public readers, to large groups of listeners. We have no social meetings which are not free to all; and we encourage joking and the friendly give and take of witty encounters." . . .

The Altrurian had paused to drink a glass of water, and now he went on. "But we try, in everything that does not inconvenience or injure others, to let everyone live the life he likes best. If a man prefers to dwell apart and have his meals in private for himself alone, or for his family, it is freely permitted; only, he must not expect to be served as in public, where service is one of the voluntaries; private service is not permitted; those wishing to live alone must wait upon themselves, cook their own food and care for their own tables. Very few, however, wish to withdraw from the public life, for most of the discussions and debates take place at our midday meal, which falls at the end of the obligatory labors, and is prolonged indefinitely, or as long as people like to chat and joke, or listen to the reading of some pleasant book.

"In Altruria *there is no hurry*, for no one wishes to out-strip another, or in any wise surpass him. We are all assured of enough, and are forbidden any and every sort of superfluity. If anyone, after the obligatories, wishes to be entirely idle, he may be so, but I cannot now think of a single person without some voluntary occupation; doubtless there are such persons, but I do not know them: It used to be said, in the old times, that 'it was human nature' to shirk, and malinger and loaf, but we have found that it is no such thing. We have found that it is human nature to work cheerfully, willingly, eagerly, at the tasks which all share for the supply of the common necessities. In like manner we have found out that it is not human nature to hoard and grudge, but that when the fear, and even the imagination, of want is taken away, it is human nature to give and to help generously. We used to say, 'A man will lie, or a man will cheat in his own interest; that is human nature,' but that is no longer human nature with us, perhaps because no man has any interest to serve; he has only the interests of others to serve, while others serve his. It is in nowise possible for the individual to separate his good from the common good; he is prosperous and happy only as all the rest are so; and therefore it is not human nature with us for anyone to lie in wait to betray another or seize an advantage. That would be ungentlemanly, and in Altruria every man is a gentleman, and every woman a lady." . . .

It is impossible to follow closely the course of the Altrurian's account of his country, which grew more and more incredible as he went on, and implied every insulting criticism of ours. Some one asked him about war in Altruria, and he said, "The very name of our country implies the absence of war. At the time of the Evolution our country bore to the rest of our continent the same relative proportion that your country bears to your continent. The egoistic nations to the north and the south of us entered into an offensive and defensive alliance to put down the new altruistic commonwealth, and declared war against us. Their forces were met at the frontier by our entire population in arms, and full of the martial spirit bred of the constant hostilities of the competitive and monopolistic epoch just ended. Negotiations began in the face of the imposing demonstration we made, and we were never afterward molested by our neighbors, who finally yielded to the spectacle of our civilization and united their political and social fate with ours. At present, our whole continent is Altrurian. For a long time we kept up a system of coast defences, but it is also a long time since we abandoned these; for it is a maxim with us that where every citizen's life is a pledge of the public safety, that country can never be in danger of foreign enemies.

"In this, as in all other things, we believe ourselves the true followers of Christ, whose doctrine we seek to make our life, as He made it His. We have several forms of ritual, but no form of creed, and our religious differences may be said to be æsthetic and temperamental rather than theological and essential. We have no denominations, for we fear in this as in other matters to give names to things lest we should cling to the names instead of the things. We love the realities, and for this reason we look at the life of a man rather than his profession for proof that he is a religious man.

"I have been several times asked, during my sojourn among you, what are the sources of compassion, of sympathy, of humanity, of charity with us, if we have not only no want, or fear of want, but not even any economic inequality. I suppose this is because you are so constantly struck by the misery arising from economic inequality, and want, or the fear of want, among yourselves, that you instinctively look in that direction. But have you ever seen sweeter compassion, tenderer sympathy, warmer humanity, heavenlier charity, than that shown in the family, where all are economically equal, and no one can want while any other has to give? Altruria, I say again, is a family, and as we are mortal, we are still subject to those nobler sorrows which God has appointed to men, and which are so different from the squalid accidents that they have made for themselves. Sickness and death call out the most angelic ministries of love; and those who wish to give themselves to others may do so without hindrance from those cares, and even those duties, resting upon men where each must look out first for himself and for his own. Oh, believe me, believe me, you can know nothing of the divine rapture of self-sacrifice while you must dread the sacrifice of another in it! You are not *free*, as we are, to do everything for others, for it is your *duty* to do rather for those of your own household! . . .

"But now everything is changed, and the change has taken place chiefly from one cause, namely, the disuse of money. At first, it was thought that some sort of circulating medium must be used, that life could not be transacted without it. But life began to go on perfectly well, when each dwelt in the place assigned him, which was no better and no worse than any other; and when, after he had given his three hours a day to the obligatory labors, he had a right to his share of food, light, heat, and raiment; the voluntary labors, to which he gave much time or little, brought him no increase of those necessaries, but only credit and affection. We had always heard it said that the love of money was the root of all evil, but we had taken this for a saying, merely; now we realized it as an active, vital truth. As soon as money was abolished, the power to purchase was gone, and even if there had been any means of buying beyond the daily needs, with overwork, the community had no power to sell to the individual. No man owned anything, but every man had the right to anything that he could use; when he could not use it, his right lapsed.

"With the expropriation of the individual, the whole vast catalogue of crimes against property shrank to nothing. The thief could only steal from the community; but if he stole, what was he to do with his booty? It was still possible for a depredator to destroy, but few men's hate is so comprehensive as to include all other men, and when the individual could no longer hurt some other individual in his property, destruction ceased.

"All the many murders done from love of money, or of what money could buy, were at an end. Where there was no want, men no longer bartered their souls, or women their bodies, for the means to keep themselves alive. The vices vanished with the crimes, and the diseases almost as largely disappeared. People were no longer sickened by sloth and surfeit, or deformed and depleted by overwork and famine. They were wholesomely housed in healthful places, and they were clad fitly for their labor and fitly for their leisure; the caprices of vanity were not suffered to attaint the beauty of the national dress.

"With the stress of superfluous social and business duties, and the perpetual fear of want which all classes felt, more or less; with the tumult of the cities and the solitude of the country, insanity had increased among us till the whole land was dotted with asylums, and the mad were numbered by hundreds of thousands. In every region they were an army, an awful army of anguish and despair. Now they have decreased to a number so small, and are of a type so mild, that we can hardly count insanity among our causes of unhappiness.

"We have totally eliminated chance from our economic life. There is still a chance that a man will be tall or short, in Altruria, that he will be strong or weak, well or ill, gay or grave, happy or unhappy in love, but none that he will be rich or poor, busy or idle, live splendidly or meanly. These stupid and vulgar accidents of human contrivance cannot befall us; but I shall not be able to tell you just how or why, or to detail the process of eliminating chance. I may say, however, that it began with the nationalization of telegraphs, expresses, railroads, mines and all large industries operated by stock companies. This at once struck a fatal blow at the speculation in values, real and unreal, and at the stock exchange, or bourse; we had our own name for that gambler's paradise, or gambler's hell, whose baleful influence penetrated every branch of business.

"There were still business fluctuations, as long as we had business, but they were on a smaller and smaller scale, and with the final lapse of business they necessarily vanished; all economic chance vanished. The founders of the commonwealth understood perfectly that business was the sterile activity of the function interposed between the demand and the supply; that it was nothing structural; and they intended its extinction, and expected it from the moment that money was abolished."

"This is all pretty tiresome," said the professor, to our immediate party. "I don't see why we oblige ourselves to listen to that fellow's stuff. As if a civilized state could exist for a day without money or business."

He went on to give his opinion of the Altrurian's pretended description, in a tone so audible that it attracted the notice of the nearest group of railroad hands, who were listening closely to Homos, and one of them sang out to the professor: "Can't you wait and let the first man finish?" and another yelled: "Put him out!" and then they all laughed with a humorous perception of the impossibility of literally executing the suggestion.

By the time all was quiet again I heard the Altrurian saying: "As to our social life, I cannot describe it in detail, but I can give you some notion of its spirit. We make our pleasures civic and public as far as possible, and the ideal is inclusive, and not exclusive. There are, of course, festivities which all cannot share, but our distribution into small communities favors the possibility of all doing so. Our daily life, however, is so largely social that we seldom meet by special invitation or engagement. When we do, it is with the perfect understanding that the assemblage confers no social distinction, but is for a momentary convenience. In fact, these occasions are rather avoided, recalling as they do the vapid and tedious entertainments of the competitive epoch, the receptions and balls and dinners of a semi-barbaric people striving for social prominence by shutting a certain number in and a certain number out, and overdressing, overfeeding and overdrinking. Anything premeditated in the way of a pleasure we think stupid and mistaken; we like to meet suddenly, or on the spur of the moment, out of doors, if possible, and arrange a picnic, or a dance, or a play; and let people come and go without ceremony. No one is more host than guest; all are hosts and guests. People consort much according to their tastes—literary, musical, artistic, scientific, or mechanical—but these tastes are made approaches, not barriers; and we find out that we have many more tastes in common than was formerly supposed.

"But, after all, our life is serious, and no one among us is quite happy, in the general esteem, unless he has dedicated himself, in some special way, to the general good. Our ideal is not rights, but duties."

"Mazzini!" whispered the professor.

"The greatest distinction which anyone can enjoy with us is to have found out some new and signal way of serving the community; and then it is not good form for him to seek recognition. The doing any fine thing is the purest pleasure it can give; applause flatters, but it hurts, too, and our benefactors, as we call them, have learned to shun it.

"We are still far from thinking our civilization perfect; but we are sure that our civic ideals are perfect. What we have already accomplished is to have given a whole continent perpetual peace; to have founded an economy in which there is no possibility of want; to have killed out political and social ambition; to have disused money and eliminated chance; to have realized the brotherhood of the race, and to have outlived the fear of death."

William Dean Howells (1837–1920) was an American author and editor.

Source: William Dean Howells, A Traveler from Altruria (New York: Harper and Bros., 1894; reprint, Edinburgh: David Douglas, 1894), 214–23, 225–29, 230–32, 235–39.

SEVEN

The Twentieth Century

Because of the central role played by texts such as Yevgeny Zamiatin's *We* (1924), Aldous Huxley's *Brave New World* (1932), and George Orwell's *Nineteen Eighty-Four* (1949), the twentieth century is generally known as the dystopian century. While the dystopia certainly played a central role in twentieth-century utopianism, the century began with positive works by H. G. Wells and has, since the mid-1960s, seen the publication of many positive utopias.

H. G. Wells
A Modern Utopia

H. G. Wells was the most prominent and prolific utopian author of the early twentieth century and was one of the founders of modern science fiction. A number of his novels—including *The Time Machine* (1895), *The Island of Doctor Moreau* (1896), *The Invisible Man* (1897), *War of The Worlds* (1898), and *The First Men in the Moon* (1901)—have been made into films. The novel excerpted here, *A Modern Utopia* (1905), reflects a time when Wells thought a better society could be created by human beings much like those we all know; no radical improvement in "human nature" would be necessary. A later utopia, *Men Like Gods* (1923), reflects a stage where he thought that a better society could be created only by the very best of the human community working together.

The World State in this ideal presents itself as the sole landowner of the earth, with the great local governments I have adumbrated, the local municipalities, holding, as it were, feudally under it as landlords. The State or these subordinates holds all the sources of energy, and either directly or through its tenants, farmers and agents, develops these sources, and renders the energy available for the work of life. It or its tenants will produce food, and so human energy, and the exploitation of coal and electric power, and the powers of wind and wave and water will be within its right. It will pour out this energy by assignment and lease and acquiescence and what not upon its individual citizens. It will maintain order, maintain roads, maintain a cheap and efficient administration of justice, maintain cheap and rapid locomotion and be the common carrier of the planet, convey and distribute labour, control, let, or administer all natural productions, pay for and secure healthy births and a healthy and vigorous new generation, maintain the public health, coin money and sustain standards of measurement, subsidise research, and reward such commercially unprofitable undertakings as benefit the community as a whole; subsidise when needful chairs of criticism and authors and publications, and collect and distribute information. The energy developed and the employment afforded by the State will descend like water that the sun has sucked out of the sea to fall upon a mountain range, and back to the sea again it will come at last, debouching in ground rent and royalty and license fees, in the fees of travellers and profits upon carrying and coinage and the like, in death duty, transfer tax, legacy and forfeiture, returning to the sea. Between the clouds and the sea it will run, as a river system runs, down through a great region of individual enterprise and interplay, whose freedom it will sustain. In that intermediate region between the kindred heights and deeps those beginnings and promises will arise that are the essential significance, the essential substance, of life. From our human point of view the mountains and sea are for the habitable lands that lie between. So likewise the State is for Individualities. The State is for Individuals, the law is for freedoms, the world is for experiment, experience, and change: these are the fundamental beliefs upon which a modern Utopia must go.

Within this scheme, which makes the State the source of all energy, and the final legatee, what will be the nature of the property a man may own? Under modern conditions—indeed, under any conditions—a man without some negotiable property is a man without freedom, and the extent of his property is very largely the measure of his freedom. Without any property, without even shelter or food, a man has no choice but to set about getting these things; he is in servitude to his needs until he has secured property to satisfy them. But with a certain small property a man is free to do many things, to take a fortnight's holiday when he chooses, for example, and to try this new departure from his work or that; with so much more, he may take a year of freedom and go to the ends of the earth; with so much more, he may obtain elaborate apparatus and try curious novelties, build himself houses and make gardens, establish businesses and make experiments at large. Very speedily, under terrestrial conditions, the property of a man may reach such proportions that his freedom oppresses the freedom of others. Here, again, is a quantitative question, an adjustment of conflicting freedoms, a quantitative question that too many people insist on making a qualitative one.

The object sought in the code of property laws that one would find in operation in Utopia would be the same object that pervades the whole Utopian organisation, namely, a universal maximum of individual freedom. Whatever far-reaching movements the State or great rich men or private corporations may make, the starvation by any complication of employment, the unwilling deportation, the destruction of alternatives to servile submissions, must not ensue. Beyond such qualifications, the object of Modern Utopian statesmanship will be to secure to a man the freedom given by all his legitimate property, that is to say, by all the values his toil or skill or foresight and courage have brought into being. Whatever he has justly made he has a right to keep, that is obvious enough; but he will also have a right to sell and exchange, and so this question of what may be property takes really the form of what may a man buy in Utopia?

A modern Utopian most assuredly must have a practically unqualified property in all those things that become, as it were, by possession, extensions and expressions of his personality; his clothing, his jewels, the tools of his employment, his books, the objects of art he may have bought or made, his personal weapons (if Utopia have need of such things), insignia, and so forth. All such things that he has bought with his money or acquired—provided he is not a professional or habitual dealer in such property—will be inalienably his, his to give or lend or keep, free even from taxation. So intimate is this sort of property that I have no doubt Utopia will give a man posthumous rights over it—will permit him to assign it to a successor with at the utmost the payment of a small redemption. A horse, perhaps, in certain districts, or a bicycle, or any such mechanical conveyance personally used, the Utopians might find it well to rank with these possessions. No doubt, too, a house and privacy owned and occupied by a man, and even a man's own household furniture, might be held to stand as high or almost as high in the property scale, might be taxed as lightly and transferred under only a slightly heavier redemption, provided he had not let these things on hire, or otherwise alienated them from his intimate self. A thorough-going, Democratic Socialist will no doubt be inclined at first to object that if the Utopians make these things a specially free sort of property in this way, men would spend much more upon them than they would otherwise do, but indeed that will be an excellent thing. We are too much affected by the needy atmosphere of our own mismanaged world. In Utopia no one will have to hunger because some love to make and have made and own and cherish beautiful things. To give this much of property to individuals will tend to make clothing, ornamentation, implements, books, and all the arts finer and more beautiful, because by buying such things a man will secure something inalienable—save in the case of bankruptcy—for himself and for those who belong to him. Moreover, a man may in his lifetime set aside sums to ensure special advantages of education and care for the immature children of himself and others, and in this manner also exercise a posthumous right. . . .[1]

It was several hundred years ago that the great organisation of the *samurai* came into its present form. And it was this organisation's widely sustained activities that had shaped and established the World State in Utopia.

This organisation of the *samurai* was a quite deliberate invention. It arose in the course of social and political troubles and complications, analogous to those of our own time on earth, and was, indeed, the last of a number of political and religious experiments dating back to the first dawn of philosophical state-craft in Greece. . . .

"Tell me about these *samurai*, who remind me of Plato's guardians, who look like Knights Templars, who bear a name that recalls the swordsmen of Japan . . . and whose uniform you yourself are wearing. What are they? Are they an hereditary caste, a specially educated order, an elected class? For, certainly, this world turns upon them as a door upon its hinges."

"I follow the Common Rule, as many men do," said my double, answering my allusion to his uniform almost apologetically. "But my own work is, in its nature, poietic; there is much dissatisfaction with our isolation of criminals upon islands, and I am analysing the psychology of prison officials and criminals in general with a view to some better scheme. I am supposed to be ingenious with expedients in this direction. Typically, the *samurai* are engaged in administrative work. Practically the whole of the responsible rule of the world is in their hands; all our head teachers and disciplinary heads of colleges, our judges, barristers, employers of labour beyond a certain limit, practising medical men, legislators, must be *samurai*, and all the executive committees, and so forth, that play so large a part in our affairs are drawn by lot exclusively from them. The order is not hereditary—we know just enough of biology and the uncertainties of inheritance to know how silly that would be—and it does not require an early consecration or novitiate or ceremonies and initiations of that sort. The *samurai* are, in fact, volunteers. Any intelligent adult in a reasonably healthy

---

1. But a Statute of Mortmain will set a distinct time limit to the continuance of such benefactions. A periodic revision of endowments is a necessary feature in any modern Utopia.

and efficient state may, at any age after five-and-twenty, become one of the *samurai*, and take a hand in the universal control."

"Provided he follows the Rule."

"Precisely—provided he follows the Rule."

"I have heard the phrase, 'voluntary nobility.'"

"That was the idea of our Founders. They made a noble and privileged order—open to the whole world. No one could complain of an unjust exclusion, for the only thing that could exclude from the order was unwillingness or inability to follow the Rule."

"But the Rule might easily have been made exclusive of special lineages and races."

"That wasn't their intention. The Rule was planned to exclude the dull, to be unattractive to the base, and to direct and co-ordinate all sound citizens of good intent."

"And it has succeeded? "

"As well as anything finite can. Life is still imperfect, still a thick felt of dis-satisfactions and perplexing problems, but most certainly the quality of all its problems has been raised, and there has been no war, no grinding poverty, not half the disease, and an enormous increase of the order, beauty, and resources of life since the *samurai*, who began as a private aggressive cult, won their way to the rule of the world."

"I would like to have that history," I said. "I expect there was fighting?" He nodded. " But first—tell me about the Rule."

"The Rule aims to exclude the dull and base altogether, to discipline the impulses and emotions, to develop a moral habit and sustain a man in periods of stress, fatigue, and temptation, to produce the maximum co-operation of all men of good intent, and, in fact, to keep all the *samurai* in a state of moral and bodily health and efficiency. It does as much of this as well as it can, but, of course, like all general propositions, it does not do it in any case with absolute precision. On the whole, it is so good that most men who, like myself, are doing poietic work, and who would be just as well off without obedience, find a satisfaction in adhesion. At first, in the militant days, it was a trifle hard and uncompromising; it had rather too strong an appeal to the moral prig and harshly righteous man, but it has undergone, and still undergoes, revision and expansion, and every year it becomes a little better adapted to the need of a general rule of life that all men may try to follow. We have now a whole literature, with many very fine things in it, written about the Rule."

He glanced at a little book on his desk, took it up as if to show it me, then put it down again.

"The Rule consists of three parts; there is the list of things that qualify, the list of things that must not be done, and the list of things that must be done.

Qualification exacts a little exertion, as evidence of good faith, and it is designed to weed out the duller dull and many of the base. Our schooling period ends now about fourteen, and a small number of boys and girls—about three per cent.—are set aside then as unteachable, as, in fact, nearly idiotic; the rest go on to a college or upper school."

"All your population?"

"With that exception."

"Free?"

"Of course. And they pass out of college at eighteen. There are several different college courses, but one or other must be followed and a satisfactory examination passed at the end—perhaps ten per cent. fail—and the Rule requires that the candidate for the *samurai* must have passed." . . .

"There is a Rule of Chastity here—but not of Celibacy. We know quite clearly that civilisation is an artificial arrangement, and that all the physical and emotional instincts of man are too strong, and his natural instinct of restraint too weak, for him to live easily in the civilised State. Civilisation has developed far more rapidly than man has modified. Under the unnatural perfection of security, liberty and abundance our civilisation has attained, the normal untrained human being is disposed to excess in almost every direction; he tends to eat too much and too elaborately, to drink too much, to become lazy faster than his work can be reduced, to waste his interest upon displays, and to make love too much and too elaborately. He gets out of training, and concentrates upon egoistic or erotic broodings. The past history of our race is very largely a history of social collapses due to demoralisation by indulgences following security and abundance. In the time of our Founders the signs of a world-wide epoch of prosperity and relaxation were plentiful. Both sexes drifted towards sexual excesses, the men towards sentimental extravagances, imbecile devotions, and the complication and refinement of physical indulgences; the women towards those expansions and differentiations of feeling that find expression in music and costly and distinguished dress. Both sexes became unstable and promiscuous. The whole world seemed disposed to do exactly the same thing with its sexual interest as it had done with its appetite for food and drink—make the most of it."

He paused.

"Satiety came to help you," I said.

"Destruction may come before satiety. Our Founders organised motives from all sorts of sources, but I think the chief force to give men self-control is Pride. Pride may not be the noblest thing in the soul, but it is the best King there, for all that. They looked to it to keep a man clean and sound and sane. In this matter, as in all matters of natural desire, they held no appetite must he glutted, no appetite must have artificial whets, and also and equally that no appetite should be starved. A man must come from the table satisfied, but not replete. And, in the matter of love, a straight and clean desire for a clean and straight fellow-creature was our Founders' ideal. They enjoined marriage between equals as the *samurai's* duty to the race, and they framed directions of the precisest sort to prevent that uxorious inseparableness, that connubiality which will reduce a couple of people to something jointly less than either. That Canon is too long to tell you now. A man under the Rule who loves a woman who does not follow it, must either leave the *samurai* to marry her, or induce her to accept what is called the Woman's Rule, which, while it excepts her from the severer qualifications and disciplines, brings her regimen of life into a working harmony with his."

"Suppose she breaks the Rule afterwards?"

"He must leave either her or the order."

"There is matter for a novel or so in that."

"There has been matter for hundreds."

"Is the Woman's Rule a sumptuary law as well as a regimen? I mean—may she dress as she pleases?"

"Not a bit of it," said my double. "Every woman who could command money used it, we found, to make underbred aggressions on other women. As men emerged to civilisation, women seemed going back to savagery—to paint and feathers. But the *samurai*, both men and women, and the women under the Lesser Rule also, all have a particular dress. No difference is made between women under either the Great or the Lesser Rule. You have seen the men's dress—always like this I wear. The women may wear the same, either with the hair cut short or plaited behind them, or they may have a high-waisted dress of very fine, soft woollen material, with their hair coiled up behind."

"I have seen it," I said. Indeed, nearly all the women had seemed to be wearing variants of that simple formula. "It seems to me a very beautiful dress. The other—I'm not used to. But I like it on girls and slender women."

I had a thought, and added, "Don't they sometimes, well—take a good deal of care, dressing their hair?"

My double laughed in my eyes. "They do," he said.

"And the Rule?"

"The Rule is never fussy," said my double, still smiling.

"We don't want women to cease to be beautiful, and consciously beautiful, if you like," he added. "The more real beauty of form and face we have, the finer our world. But costly sexualised trappings————"

"I should have thought," I said, "a class of women who traded on their sex would have arisen, women, I mean, who found an interest and an advantage in emphasising their individual womanly beauty. There is no law to prevent it. Surely they would tend to counteract the severity of costume the Rule dictates."

"There are such women. But for all that the Rule sets the key of everyday dress. If a woman is possessed by the passion for gorgeous raiment she usually satisfies it in her own private circle, or with rare occasional onslaughts upon the public eye. Her everyday mood and the disposition of most people is against being conspicuous abroad. And I should say there are little liberties under the Lesser Rule; a discreet use of fine needlework and embroidery, a wider choice of materials."

"You have no changing fashions?"

"None. For all that, are not our dresses as beautiful as yours? "

"Our women's dresses are not beautiful at all," I said, forced for a time towards the mysterious philosophy of dress. "Beauty? That isn't their concern."

"Then what are they after?"

"My dear man! What is all my world after?"

Herbert George Wells (1866–1946) was one of the best known English authors of the late nineteenth and early twentieth centuries.

Source: H[erbert] G[eorge] Wells, A Modern Utopia (London: Chapman & Hall, 1905), 89–94, 261, 277–81, 292–96. Reprint, Lincoln: University of Nebraska Press, 1967.

Charlotte Perkins Gilman
Herland

Charlotte Perkins Gilman is currently thought to have been the most important American author of the early twentieth-century women's movement. She edited a newspaper, *The Forerunner* (1909–1916), and wrote one of the first studies of women's role in the economic system, *Women and Economics* (1898). She also wrote a number of utopias, including her best-known utopia, *Herland* (1915, excerpted here), *Moving the Mountain* (1911), *With Her in Ourland* (1916), and a number of utopian short stories.

IT IS NO USE for me to try to piece out this account with adventures. If the people who read it are not interested in these amazing women and their history, they will not be interested at all.

As for us—three young men to a whole landful of women—what could we do? We did get away, as described, and were peacefully brought back again without, as Terry complained, even the satisfaction of hitting anybody.

There were no adventures because there was nothing to fight. There were no wild beasts in the country and very few tame ones. Of these I might as well stop to describe the one common pet of the country. Cats, of course. But such cats!

What do you suppose these lady Burbanks had done with their cats? By the most prolonged and careful selection and exclusion they had developed a race of cats that did not sing! That's a fact.

The most those poor dumb brutes could do was to make a kind of squeak when they were hungry or wanted the door open; and, of course, to purr, and make the various mother-noises to their kittens.

Moreover they had ceased to kill birds. They were rigorously bred to destroy mice and moles and all such enemies of the food supply; but the birds were numerous and safe.

While we were discussing birds, Terry asked them if they used feathers for their hats, and they seemed amused at the idea. He made a few sketches of our women's hats, with plumes and quills and those various tickling things that stick out so far; and they were eagerly interested, as at everything about our women.

As for them, they said they only wore hats for shade when working in the sun; and those were big light straw hats, something like those used in China and Japan. In cold weather they wore caps or hoods.

"But for decorative purposes—don't you think they would be becoming?" pursued Terry, making a picture as [best] he could of a lady with a plumed straw hat.

They by no means agreed to that, asking quite simply if the men wore the same kind. We hastened to assure her that they did not—and drew for them our kind of headgear.

"And do no men wear feathers in their hats?"

"Only Indians," Jeff explained, "savages, you know." And he sketched a war-bonnet to show them.

"And soldiers," I added, drawing a military hat with plumes.

They never expressed horror or disapproval, nor indeed much surprise—just a keen interest. And the notes they made!—miles of them!

But to return to our pussy-cats. We were a good deal impressed by this achievement in breeding, and when they questioned us—I can tell you we were well pumped for information—we told of what had been done for dogs and horses and cattle, but that there was no effort applied to cats, except for show purposes.

I wish I could represent the kind, quiet, steady, ingenious way they questioned us. It was not just curiosity—they weren't a bit more curious about us than we were about them, if as much. But they were bent on understanding our kind of civilization and their lines of interrogation would gradually surround us and drive us in till we found ourselves up against some admissions we did not want to make.

"Are all these breeds of dogs you have made useful?" they asked.

"Oh—useful! Why, the hunting dogs and watch-dogs and sheep-dogs are useful—and sled-dogs of course!—and ratters, I suppose, but we don't keep dogs for their *usefulness*. The dog is 'the friend of men,' we say—we love them."

That they understood. "We love our cats that way. They surely are our friends, and helpers too. You can see how intelligent and affectionate they are."

It was a fact. I'd never seen such cats, except in a few rare instances. Big, handsome silky things, friendly with everyone and devotedly attached to their special owners.

"You must have a heartbreaking time drowning kittens," we suggested.

But they said: "Oh, no! You see we care for them as you do for your valuable cattle. The fathers are few compared to the mothers, just a few very fine ones in each town; they live quite happily in walled gardens and the houses of their friends. But they only have a mating season once a year."

"Rather hard on Thomas, isn't it?" suggested Terry.

"Oh, no—truly! You see it is many centuries that we have been breeding the kind of cats we wanted. They are healthy and happy and friendly, as you see. How do you manage with your dogs? Do you keep them in pairs, or segregate the fathers, or what?"

Then we explained that—well, that it wasn't a question of fathers exactly; that nobody wanted a—a mother dog; that, well, that practically all our dogs were males—there was only a very small percentage of females allowed to live.

Then Zava, observing Terry with her grave sweet smile, quoted back at him: "Rather hard on Thomas, isn't it? Do they enjoy it—living without mates? Are your dogs as uniformly healthy and sweet-tempered as our cats?"

Jeff laughed, eyeing Terry mischievously. As a matter of fact we began to feel Jeff something of a traitor—he so often flopped over and took their side of things; also his medical knowledge gave him a different point of view somehow.

"I'm sorry to admit," he told them, "that the dog, with us, is the most diseased of any animal—next to man. And as to temper—there are always some dogs who bite people[,] especially children."

That was pure malice. You see children were the—the *raison d'être* in this country. All our interlocutors sat up straight at once. They were still gentle, still restrained, but there was a note of deep amazement in their voices.

"Do we understand that you keep an animal—an unmated male animal—that bites children? About how many are there of them, please?"

"Thousands—in a large city," said Jeff, "and nearly every family has one in the country."

Terry broke in at this. "You must not imagine they are all dangerous—it's not one in a hundred that ever bites anybody. Why, they are the best friends of the children—a boy doesn't have half a chance that hasn't a dog to play with!"

"And the girls?" asked Somel.

"Oh—girls—why they like them too," he said, but his voice flattened a little. They always noticed little things like that, we found later.

Little by little they wrung from us the fact that the friend of man, in the city, was a prisoner; was taken out for his meager exercise on a leash; was liable not only to many diseases, but to the one destroying horror of rabies, and, in many cases, for the safety of the citizens, he had to go muzzled. Jeff maliciously added vivid instances he had known or read of injury and death from mad dogs.

They did not scold or fuss about it. Calm as judges, those women were. But they made notes; Moadine read them to us.

"Please tell me if I have the facts correct," she said. "In your country—and in others too?"

"Yes," we admitted, "in most civilized countries."

"In most civilized countries a kind of animal is kept which is no longer useful—"

"They are a protection," Terry insisted. "They bark if burglars try to get in."

Then she made notes of "burglars" and went on: "because of the love which people bear to this animal."

Zava interrupted here. "Is it the men or the women who love this animal so much?"

"Both!" insisted Terry.

"Equally?" she inquired.

And Jeff said: "Nonsense, Terry—you know men like dogs better than women do—as a whole."

"Because they love it so much—especially men. This animal is kept shut up, or chained."

"Why?" suddenly asked Somel. "We keep our father cats shut up because we do not want too much fathering; but they are not chained—they have large grounds to run in."

"A valuable dog would be stolen if he was let loose," I said. "We put collars on them, with the owner's name, in case they do stray. Besides, they get into fights—a valuable dog might easily be killed by a bigger one."

"I see," she said. "They fight when they meet—is that common?" We admitted that it was.

"They are kept shut up, or chained." She paused again, and asked, "Is not a dog fond of running? Are they not built for speed?" That we admitted too, and Jeff, still malicious, enlightened them farther.

"I've always thought it was a pathetic sight, both ways—to see a man or a woman taking a dog to walk—at the end of a string."

"Have you bred them to be as neat in their habits as cats are?" was the next question. And when Jeff told them of the effect of dogs on sidewalk merchandise and the streets generally, they found it hard to believe.

You see their country was as neat as a Dutch kitchen, and as to sanitation—but I might as well start in now with as much as I can remember of the history of this amazing country before further description.

And I'll summarize here a bit as to our opportunities for learning it. I will not try to repeat the careful, detailed account I lost; I'll just say that we were kept in that fortress a good six months all told; and after that, three in a pleasant enough city where—to Terry's infinite disgust—there were only "Colonels" and little children—no young women whatever. Then we were under surveillance for three more—always with a tutor or a guard or both. But those months were pleasant because we were really getting acquainted with the girls. That was a chapter!—or will be—I will try to do justice to it.

We learned their language pretty thoroughly—had to; and they learned ours much more quickly and used it to hasten our own studies.

Jeff, who was never without reading matter of some sort, had two little books with him, a novel, and a little anthology of verse; and I had one of those pocket encyclopedias—a fat little thing, bursting with facts. These were used in our education—and theirs. Then as soon as we were up to it, they furnished us with plenty of their own books, and I went in for the history part—I wanted to understand the genesis of this miracle of theirs.

And this is what happened, according to their records:

As to geography—at about the time of the Christian era this land had a free passage to the sea. I'm not saying where, for good reasons. But there was a fairly easy pass through that wall of mountains behind us, and there is no doubt in my mind that these people were of Aryan stock, and were once in contact with the best civilization of the old world. They were "white," but somewhat darker than our northern races because of their constant exposure to sun and air.

The country was far larger then, including much land beyond the pass, and a strip of coast. They had ships, commerce, an army, a king—for at that time they were what they so calmly called us—a bi-sexual race.

What happened to them first was merely a succession of historic misfortunes such as have befallen other nations often enough. They were decimated by war, driven up from their coast line till finally the reduced population with many of the men killed in battle, occupied this hinterland, and defended it for years, in the mountain passes. Where it was open to any possible attack from below they strengthened the natural defences so that it became unscalably secure, as we found it.

They were a polygamous people, and a slave-holding people, like all of their time; and during the generation or two of this struggle to defend their mountain home they built the fortresses, such as the one we were held in, and other of their oldest buildings, some still in use. Nothing but earthquakes could destroy such architecture—huge solid blocks, holding by their own weight. They must have had efficient workmen and enough of them in those days.

They made a brave fight for their existence, but no nation can stand up against what the steamship companies call "an act of God." While the whole fighting force was doing its best to defend their mountain pathway, there occurred a volcanic outburst, with some local tremors, and the result was the complete filling up of the pass—their only outlet. Instead of a passage, a new ridge, sheer and high, stood between them and the sea; they were walled in, and beneath that wall lay their whole little army. Very few men were left alive, save the slaves; and these now seized their opportunity, rose in revolt, killed their remaining masters even to the youngest boy, killed the old women too, and the mothers, intending to take possession of the country with the remaining young women and girls.

But this succession of misfortunes was too much for those infuriated virgins. There were many of them, and but few of these would be masters, so the young women, instead of submitting, rose in sheer desperation, and slew their brutal conquerors.

This sounds like Titus Andronicus, I know, but that is their account. I suppose they were about crazy—can you blame them?

There was literally no one left on this beautiful high garden land but a bunch of hysterical girls and some older slave women.

That was about two thousand years ago.

At first there was a period of sheer despair. The mountains towered between them and their old enemies, but also between them and escape. There was no way up or down or out—they simply had to stay there. Some were for suicide, but not the majority. They must have been a plucky lot, as a whole, and they decided to live—as long as they did live. Of course they had hope, as youth must, that something would happen to change their fate.

So they set to work, to bury the dead, to plow and sow, to care for one another.

Speaking of burying the dead, I will set down while I think of it, that they had adopted cremation about the thirteenth century, for the same reason that they had left off raising cattle—they could not spare the room. They were much surprised to learn that we were still burying—asked our reasons for it, and were much dissatisfied with what we gave. We told them of the belief in the resurrection of the body, and they asked if our God was not as well able to resurrect from ashes as from long corruption. We told them of how people thought it repugnant to have their loved ones burn, and they asked if it was less repugnant to have them decay. They were inconveniently reasonable, those women.

Well—that original bunch of girls set to work to clean up the place and make their livings as best they could. Some of the remaining slave women rendered invaluable service, teaching such trades as they knew. They had such records as were then kept, all the tools and implements of the time, and a most fertile land to work in.

There were a handful of the younger matrons who had escaped slaughter, and a few babies were born after the cataclysm—but only two boys and they both died.

For five or ten years they worked together, growing stronger and wiser and more and more mutually attached, and then the miracle happened—one of these young women bore a child. Of course they all thought there must be a man somewhere, but none was found. Then they decided it must be a direct gift from the gods, and placed the proud mother in the Temple of Maaia—their Goddess of Motherhood—under strict watch. And there, as years passed, this wonder-woman bore child after child, five of them—all girls.

I did my best, keenly interested as I have always been in sociology and social psychology, to reconstruct in my mind the real position of these ancient women. There were some five or six hundred of them, and they were harem-bred; yet for the few preceding generations they had been reared in the atmosphere of such heroic struggle that the stock must have been toughened somewhat. Left alone in that terrific orphanhood, they had clung together, supporting one another and their little sisters, and developing unknown powers in the stress of new necessity. To this pain-hardened and work-strengthened group, who had lost not only the love and care of parents, but the hope of ever having children of their own, there now dawned the new hope.

Here at last was Motherhood, and though it was not for all of them personally, it might—if the Power was inherited—found here a new race.

It may be imagined how those five Daughters of Maaia, Children of the Temple, Mothers of the Future—they had all the titles that love and hope and reverence could give—were reared. The whole little nation of women surrounded them with loving service, and waited, between a boundless hope and an as boundless despair, to see if they too would be Mothers.

And they were! As fast as they reached the age of twenty-five they began bearing. Each of them, like her mother, bore five daughters. Presently there were twenty-five New Women, Mothers in their own right, and the whole spirit of the country changed from mourning and mere courageous resignation, to proud joy. The older women, those who remembered men, died off; the youngest of all the first lot of course died too, after a while, and by that time there were left one hundred and fifty-five parthenogenetic women, founding a new race.

They inherited all that the devoted care of that declining band of original ones could leave them. Their little country was quite safe. Their farms and gardens were all in full production. Such industries as they had were in careful order. The records of their past were all preserved, and for years the older women had spent their time in the best teaching they were capable of, that they might leave to the little group of sisters and mothers all they possessed of skill and knowledge.

There you have the start of Herland! One family, all descended from one mother! She lived to be a hundred years old; lived to see her hundred and twenty-five great-granddaughters born; lived as Queen-Priestess-Mother of them all; and died with a nobler pride and a fuller joy than perhaps any human soul has ever known—she alone had founded a new race!

The first five daughters had grown up in an atmosphere of holy calm, of awed watchful waiting, of breathless prayer. To them the longed-for Motherhood was not only a personal joy, but a nation's hope. Their twenty-five daughters in turn, with a stronger hope, a richer, wider outlook, with the devoted love and care of all the surviving population, grew up as a holy sisterhood, their whole ardent youth looking forward to their great office. And at last they were left alone; the white-haired First Mother was gone, and this one family, five sisters, twenty-five first cousins, and a hundred and twenty-five second cousins, began a new race.

Here you have human beings, unquestionably, but what we were slow in understanding was how these ultra-women, inheriting only from women, had eliminated not only certain masculine characteristics, which of course we did not look for; but so much of what we had always thought essentially feminine.

The tradition of men as guardians and protectors had quite died out. These stalwart virgins had no men to fear and therefore no need of protection. As to wild beasts—there were none in their sheltered land.

The power of mother-love, that maternal instinct we so highly laud, was theirs of course, raised to its highest power; and a sister-love which, even while recognizing the actual relationship, we found it hard to credit.

Terry, incredulous, even contemptuous, when we were alone, refused to believe the story. "A lot of traditions as old as Herodotus—and about as trustworthy!" he said. "It's likely women—just a pack of women—would have hung together like that! We all know women can't organize—that they scrap like anything—are frightfully jealous."

"But these New Ladies didn't have anyone to be jealous of, remember," drawled Jeff.

"That's a likely story," Terry sneered.

"Why don't you invent a likelier one?" I asked him. "Here *are* the women—nothing but women, and you admit yourself there's no trace of a man in the country." This was after we had been about a good deal.

"I'll admit that," he growled. "And it's a big miss, too. There's not only no fun without 'em—no real sport—no competition: but these women aren't *womanly*. You know they aren't."

That kind of talk always set Jeff going; and I gradually grew to side with him. "Then you don't call a breed of women whose one concern is Motherhood—womanly?" he asked.

"Indeed I don't," snapped Terry. "What does a man care for motherhood—when he hasn't a ghost of a chance at fatherhood? And besides—what's the good of talking sentiment when we are just men together? What a man wants of women is a good deal more than this 'motherhood'!"

We were as patient as possible with Terry. He had lived about nine months among the Colonels when he made that outburst; and with no chance at any more strenuous excitement than our gymnastics gave us—save for our escape fiasco. I don't suppose Terry had ever lived so long with neither Love, Combat, nor Danger to employ his superabundant energies, and he was irritable. Neither Jeff nor I found it so wearing. I was so much interested intellectually that our confinement did not wear on me; and as for Jeff, bless his heart!—he enjoyed the society of that tutor of his almost as much as if she had been a girl—I don't know but more.

As to Terry's criticism, it was true. These women, whose essential distinction of Motherhood was the dominant note of their whole culture, were strikingly deficient in what we call "femininity." This led me very promptly to the conviction that these "feminine charms" we are so fond of are not feminine at all, but mere reflected masculinity—developed to please us because they had to please us—and in no way essential to the real fulfillment of their great process. But Terry came to no such conclusion.

"Just you wait till I get out!" he muttered.

Then we both cautioned him. "Look here, Terry, my boy! You be careful! They've been mighty good to us—but do you remember the anaesthesia? If you do any mischief in this virgin land, beware of the vengeance of the Maiden Aunts! Come, be a man! It won't be forever."

To return to the history:

They began at once to plan and build for their children, all the Strength and intelligence of the whole of them devoted to that one thing. Each girl, of course, was reared in full knowledge of her Crowning Office, and they had, even then, very high ideas of the moulding powers of the mother as well as those of education.

Such high ideals as they had! Beauty, Health, Strength, Intellect, Goodness—for these they prayed and worked.

They had no enemies; they themselves were all sisters and friends; the land was fair before them, and a great Future began to form itself in their minds.

The religion they had to begin with was much like that of old Greece—a number of gods and goddesses; but they lost all interest in deities of war and plunder, and gradually centered on their Mother Goddess altogether. Then, as they grew more intelligent, this had turned into a sort of Maternal Pantheism.

Here was Mother Earth, bearing fruit. All that they ate was fruit of motherhood, from seed or egg or their product. By motherhood they were born and by motherhood they lived—life was, to them, just the long cycle of motherhood.

But very early they recognized the need of improvement as well as of mere repetition, and devoted their combined intelligence to that problem—how to make the best kind of people. First this was merely the hope of bearing better ones, and then they recognized that however the children differed at birth, the real growth lay later—through education.

Then things began to hum.

As I learned more and more to appreciate what these women had accomplished, the less proud I was of what we, with all our manhood, had done.

You see, they had had no wars. They had had no kings, and no priests, and no aristocracies. They were sisters, and as they grew, they grew together; not by competition, but by united action.

We tried to put in a good word for competition, and they were keenly interested. Indeed we soon found, from their earnest questions of us, that they were prepared to believe our world must be better than theirs. They were not sure; they wanted to know; but there was no such arrogance about them as might have been expected.

We rather spread ourselves, telling of the advantages of competition; how it developed fine qualities; that without it there would be "no stimulus to industry." Terry was very strong on that point.

"No stimulus to industry," they repeated, with that puzzled look we had learned to know so well. "*Stimulus? To Industry?* But don't you *like* to work?"

"No man would work unless he had to," Terry declared.

"Oh, no *man*! You mean that is one of your sex distinctions?"

"No, indeed!" he said hastily. "No one, I mean, man or woman, would work without incentive. Competition is the—the motor power, you see."

"It is not with us," they explained gently, "so it is hard for us to understand. Do you mean, for instance, that with you no mother would work for her children without the stimulus of competition?"

No, he admitted that he did not mean that. Mothers, he supposed, would of course work for their children in the home; but the world's work was different—that had to be done by men, and required the competitive element.

All our teachers were eagerly interested.

"We want so much to know—you have the whole world to tell us of, and we have only our little land! And there are two of you—the two sexes—to love and help one another. It must be a rich and wonderful world. Tell us—what is the work of the world,—that men do—which we have not here?"

"Oh, everything," Terry said, grandly. "The men do everything, with us." He squared his broad shoulders and lifted his chest. "We do not allow our women to work. Women are loved—idolized—honored—kept in the home to care for the children."

"What is 'the home'?" asked Somel a little wistfully.

But Zava begged: "Tell me first, do no women work, really?"

"Why, yes," Terry admitted. "Some have to, of the poorer sort."

"About how many—in your country?"

"About seven or eight million," said Jeff, as mischievous as ever.

Charlotte Perkins Gilman (1860–1935) was a leading American feminist writer.

Source: Charlotte Perkins Gilman, "A Unique History: From Herland," THE FORERUNNER 6, no. 5 (May 1915): 123–29.

Yevgeny Zamiatin
We

Yevgeny Zamiatin's *We* was the first of the major dystopias of the twentieth century, followed by Aldous Huxley's *Brave New World* (1932) and George Orwell's *Nineteen Eighty-four* (1949).

I looked over all that I wrote down yesterday and I find that my descriptions are not sufficiently clear. That is, everything would undoubtedly be clear to one of us, but who knows to whom my *Integral* will someday bring these records? Perhaps you, like our ancestors, have read the great book of civilization only up to the page of nine hundred years ago. Perhaps you don't know even such elementary things as the Hour Tables, Personal Hours, Maternal Norm, Green Wall, Well-Doer. It seems droll to me, and at the same time it is very difficult to explain these things. It is as though, let us say, a writer of the twentieth century should start to explain in his novel such words as coat, apartment, wife. Yet if his novel had been translated for primitive races, how could he have avoided explaining what a coat meant? I am sure that the primitive man would look at a coat and think, "What is this for? It is only a burden, an unnecessary burden." I am sure that you will feel the same, if I tell you that not one of us has ever stepped beyond the Green Wall since the Two-Hundred Years' War.

But, dear readers, you must think, at least a little. It helps.

It is clear that the history of mankind, as far as our knowledge goes, is a history of the transition from nomadic forms to more sedentary ones. Does it not follow that the most sedentary form of life (ours) is at the same time the most perfect one? There was a time when people rushed from one end of the earth to another, but this was the prehistoric time when such things as nations, wars, commerce, different discoveries of different Americas still existed. Who has need of these things now?

I admit that humanity acquired this habit of a sedentary form of life not without difficulty and not all at once. When the Two Hundred Years' War had destroyed all the roads, which later were overgrown with grass, it was probably very difficult at first. It must have seemed uncomfortable to live in cities which were cut off from each other by green debris. But what of it? Man soon after he lost his tail probably did not learn at once how to chase away flies without its help. I am almost sure that at first he was even lonesome without his tail; but now, can you imagine yourself with a tail? Or can you imagine yourself walking in the street naked, without clothes? (It is possible you go without clothes still.) Here we have the same case. I cannot imagine a city which is not surrounded by a Green Wall; I cannot imagine a life which is not surrounded by the figures of our Tables.

Tables. . . . Now even, purple figures look at me austerely yet kindly from the golden background of the wall. Involuntarily I am reminded of the thing which was called by the ancients "Sainted Image," and I feel a desire to compose verses, or prayers, which are the same. Oh, why am I not a poet, so as to be able to glorify the Tables properly, the heart and pulse of the United State!

All of us and perhaps all of you read in childhood, while in school, that greatest of all monuments of ancient literature, the Official Railroad Guide. But if you compare this with the Tables, you will see side by side graphite and diamonds. Both are the same, carbon. But how eternal, transparent, how shining the diamond! Who does not lose his breath when he runs through the pages of the Guide? The Tables transformed each one of us, actually, into a six-wheeled steel hero of a great poem. Every morning, with six-wheeled precision, at the same hour, at the same minute, we wake up, millions of us at once. At the very-same hour, millions like one, we begin our work, and millions like one we finish it. United into a single body with a million hands, at the very same second, designated by the Tables, we carry the spoons to our mouths; at the same second we all go to the auditorium, to the halls for the Taylor[1] exercises, and then to bed.

I shall be quite frank: even we have not attained the absolute, exact solution of the problem of happiness. Twice a day, from sixteen to seventeen o'clock and from twenty-one to twenty-two, our powerful united organism dissolves into separate cells; these are the personal hours designated by the Tables. During these hours you would see the curtains discreetly drawn in the rooms of some; others march slowly over the pavement of the main avenue or sit at their desks as I sit now. But I firmly believe, let them call me an idealist and a dreamer, I believe that sooner or later we shall somehow find a place in the general formula even for these hours. Somehow, all of the 86,400 seconds will be incorporated in the Tables of Hours.

I have had opportunity to read and hear many improbable things about those times when human beings still lived in the state of freedom, that is, in an unorganized primitive state. One thing has always seemed to me most improbable: how could a government, even a primitive government, permit people to live without anything like our Tables—without compulsory walks, without precise regulation of the time to eat, for instance? They would get up and go to bed whenever they liked. Some historians even say that in those days the streets were lighted all night, and all night people went about the streets.

That I cannot understand. True, their minds were rather limited in those days. Yet they should have understood, should they not, that such a life was actually wholesale murder, although slow murder, day after day? The State (humanitarianism) forbade in those days the murder of one person, but it did not forbid the killing of millions slowly and by inches. To kill one person, that is, to reduce the individual span of human life by fifty years, was considered criminal, but to reduce the general sum of human life by fifty million years was not considered criminal! Isn't it droll? Today this simple mathematical moral problem could easily be solved in half a minute's time by any ten-year-old Number, yet *they* couldn't do it! All their Immanuel Kants[2] together couldn't do it! It didn't enter the heads of all their Kants to build a system of scientific ethics, that is, ethics based on adding, subtracting, multiplying, and dividing.

Further, is it not absurd that their State (they called it State!) left sexual life absolutely without control? On the contrary, whenever and as much as they wanted . . . absolutely unscientific, like beasts! And like beasts they blindly gave birth to children! Is it not strange to understand gardening, chicken farming,

1. Frederick Wislow Taylor (1865–1915) was a U. S. engineer and efficiency expert. *Ed.*
2. Immanuel Kant (1724–1804) was a German philosopher. *Ed.*

fishery (we have definite knowledge that they were familiar with all these things)! and not to be able to reach the last step in this logical scale, namely, production of children—not to be able to discover such things as Maternal and Paternal Norms?

It is so droll, so improbable, that while I write this I am afraid lest you, my unknown future readers, should think I am merely a poor jester. I feel almost as if you may think I want simply to mock you and with a very serious face try to relate absolute nonsense to you. But first I am incapable of jesting, for in every joke a lie has its hidden function. And second, the science of the United State contends that the life of the ancients was exactly what I am describing, and the science of the United State does not make mistakes! Yet how could they have State logic, since they lived in a condition of freedom like beasts, like apes, like herds? What could one expect of them, since even in our day one hears from time to time, coming from the bottom, the primitive depths, the echo of the apes?

Fortunately it happens only from time to time, very seldom. Happily, it is only a case of small parts breaking; these may easily be repaired without stopping the eternal great march of the whole machine. And in order to eliminate a broken peg we have the skillful heavy hand of the Well-Doer, we have the experienced eyes of the Guardians.

By the way, I just thought of that Number whom I met yesterday, the double-curved one like the letter S; I think I have seen him several times coming out of the Bureau of Guardians. Now I understand why I felt such an instinctive respect for him and a kind of awkwardness when I saw that strange I-330 at his side. . . . I must confess that, that I . . . they ring the bell, time to sleep, it is twenty-two-thirty. Till tomorrow, then. . . .

Dear O- was to come in an hour. I felt agitated, agreeably and usefully. Home at last! I rushed to the house office, handed over to the controller on duty my pink ticket, and received a certificate permitting the use of the curtains. This right exists in our State only for the sexual days. Normally we live surrounded by transparent walls which seem to be knitted of sparkling air; we live beneath the eyes of everyone, always bathed in light. We have nothing to conceal from one another; besides, this mode of living makes the difficult and exalted task of the Guardians much easier. Without it many bad things might happen. It is possible that the strange opaque dwellings of the ancients were responsible for their pitiful cellish psychology. "My *(sic!)* home is my fortress!" How did they manage to think such things?

At twenty-two o'clock I lowered the curtain and at the same second o- came in smiling, slightly out of breath. She extended to me her rosy lips and her pink ticket. I tore off the stub but I could not tear myself away from the rosy lips up to the last moment, twenty-two-fifteen.

Then I showed her my diary and I talked; I think I talked very well on the beauty of a square, a cube, a straight line. At first she listened so charmingly, she was so rosy; then suddenly a tear appeared in her blue eyes, then another, and a third fell straight on the open page (page 7). The ink blurred; well, I shall have to copy it again. . . .

Again with you, my unknown reader; I talk to you as though you were, let us say, my old comrade, R-13, the poet with the lips of a Negro—well, everyone knows him. Yet you are somewhere on the moon, or on Venus, or on Mars. Who knows you? Where and who are you?

Imagine a square, a living, beautiful square. Imagine that this square is obliged to tell you about itself, about its life. You realize that this square would hardly think it necessary to mention the fact that all its four angles are equal. It knows this too well. This is such an ordinary, obvious thing. I am in exactly the same square position. Take the pink checks, for instance, and all that goes with them: for me they are as natural as the equality of the four angles of the square. But for you they are perhaps more mysterious and hard to understand than Newton's binomial theorem. Let me explain: an ancient sage once said a clever thing (accidentally, beyond doubt). He said, "Love and Hunger rule the World." Consequently, to dominate the world, man had to win a victory over hunger after paying a very high price. I refer to the great Two Hundred Years' War, the war between the city and the land. Probably on account of religious prejudices, the primitive peasants stubbornly held on to their "bread."[3]

In the thirty-fifth year before the foundation of the United State our contemporary petroleum food was invented. True, only about two tenths of the population of the globe did not die out. But how beautifully shining the face of the earth became when it was cleared of its impurities!

Accordingly the 0.2 which survived have enjoyed the greatest happiness in the bosom of the United State. But is it not clear that supreme bliss and envy are only the numerator and the denominator, respectively, of the same fraction, happiness? What sense would the innumerable sacrifices of the Two Hundred Years' War have for us if a reason were left in our life for jealousy? Yet such a reason persisted because there remained buttonlike noses and classical noses. . . . For there were some whose love was sought by everyone, and others whose love was sought by no one.

Naturally, having conquered hunger (that is, algebraically speaking, having achieved the total of bodily welfare), the United State directed its attack against the second ruler of the world, against love. At last this element also was

---

3. This word came down to us for use only as a poetic form, for the chemical constitution of this substance is unknown to us.

conquered, that is, organized and put into a mathematical formula. It is already three hundred years since our great historic *Lex Sexualis* was promulgated: "A Number may obtain a license to use any other Number as a sexual product."

The rest is only a matter of technique. You are carefully examined in the laboratory of the Sexual Department where they find the content of the sexual hormones in your blood, and they accordingly make out for you a Table of sexual days. Then you file an application to enjoy the services of Number so and so, or Numbers so and so. You get for that purpose a checkbook (pink). That is all.

It is clear that under such circumstances there is no reason for envy or jealousy. The denominator of the fraction of happiness is reduced to zero and the whole fraction is thus converted into a magnificent infiniteness. The thing which was for the ancients a source of innumerable stupid tragedies has been converted in our time into a harmonious, agreeable, and useful function of the organism, a function like sleep, physical labor, the taking of food, digestion, etc., etc. Hence you see how the great power of logic purifies everything it happens to touch. Oh, if only you unknown readers—can conceive this divine power! If you will only learn to follow it to the end!

It is very strange. While I was writing today of the loftiest summit of human history, all the while I breathed the purest mountain air of thought, but within me it was and remains cloudy, cobwebby, and there is a kind of cross-like, four-pawed X. Or perhaps it is my paws and I feel like that only because they are always before my eyes, my hairy paws. I don't like to talk about them. I dislike them. They are a trace of a primitive epoch. Is it possible that there is in me . . . ?

I wanted to strike out all this because it trespasses on the limits of my synopsis. But then I decided: no, I shall not! Let this diary give the curve of the most imperceptible vibrations of my brain, like a precise seismograph, for at times such vibrations serve as forewarnings . . . Certainly this is absurd! This certainly should be stricken out; we have conquered all the elements; catastrophes are not possible any more.

Now everything is clear to me. The peculiar feeling inside is a result of that very same square situation of which I spoke in the beginning. There is no X in me. There can be none. I am simply afraid lest some X will be left in you, my unknown readers. I believe you will understand that it is harder for me to write than it ever was for any author throughout human history. Some of them wrote for contemporaries, some for future generations, but none of them ever wrote for their ancestors, or for beings like their primitive, distant ancestors. . . .

I must repeat, I have made it my duty to write concealing nothing. Therefore I must point out now that, sad as it may be, the process of the hardening and crystallization of life has evidently not been completed even here in our

State. A few steps more and we will be within reach of our ideal. The ideal (it's clear) is to be found where nothing *happens*, but here. . . . I will give you an example: in the State paper I read that in two days the holiday of Justice will be celebrated on the Plaza of the Cube. This means that again some Number has impeded the smooth running of the great State machine. Again something that was not foreseen, or forecalculated, *happened*. . . .

It was long ago, during my school days, when I first encountered the square root of minus one. I remember it all very clearly: a bright globelike class hall, about a hundred round heads of children, and Plappa—our mathematician. We nicknamed him Plappa; it was a very much used-up mathematician, loosely screwed together; as the member of the class who was on duty that day would put the plug into the socket behind, we would hear at first from the loudspeaker, "Plap-plap-plap-plap-tshshsh. . . ." Only then the lesson would follow. One day Plappa told us about irrational numbers, and I remember I wept and banged the table with my fist and cried, "I do not want that square root of minus one; take that square root of minus one away!" This irrational root grew into me as something strange, foreign, terrible; it tortured me; it could not be thought out. It could not be defeated because it was beyond reason.

Now, that square root of minus one is here again. I read over what I have written and I see clearly that I was insincere with myself, that I lied to myself in order to avoid seeing that square root of minus one. My sickness is all nonsense! *I could go there.* I feel sure that if such a thing had happened a week ago I should have gone without hesitating. Why, then, am I unable to go now? . . .

Today, for instance, at exactly sixteen-ten I stood before the glittering Glass Wall. Above was the shining, golden, sun-like sign: "Bureau of Guardians." Inside, a long queue of bluish-grey unifs awaiting their turns, faces shining like the oil lamps in an ancient temple. They had come to accomplish a great thing: they had come to put on the altar of the United State their beloved ones, their friends, their own selves. My whole being craved to join them, yet . . . I could not; my feet were as though melted into the glass plates of the sidewalk. I simply stood there looking foolish.

"Hey, mathematician! Dreaming?"

I shivered. Black eyes varnished with laughter looked at me—thick Negro lips! It was my old friend the poet, R-13, and with him rosy O-. I fumed around angrily (I still believe that if they had not appeared I should have entered the Bureau and have torn the square root of minus one out of my flesh).

"Not dreaming at all. If you will, 'standing in adoration,'" I retorted quite brusquely.

"Oh, certainly, certainly! You, my friend, should never have become a mathematician; you should have become a poet, a great poet! Yes, come over to our trade, to the poets. Eh? If you will, I can arrange it in a jiffy. Eh?"

R-13 usually talks very fast. His words run in torrents, his thick lips sprinkle. Every "p" is a fountain, every "poets" a fountain.

"So far I have served knowledge, and I shall continue to serve knowledge."

I frowned. I do not like, I do not understand jokes, and R-13 has the bad habit of joking. . . .

It is pleasant to feel that somebody's penetrating eye is watching you from behind your shoulder, lovingly guarding you from making the most minute mistake, from the most minute incorrect step. It may seem to you too sentimental, but I do see in all this the materialization of the dream of the ancients about a Guardian Angel. How many things, of which the ancients had only dreams, are materialized in our life!

At the moment when I became aware of the presence of the Guardian Angel behind me, I was enjoying a poem entitled "Happiness." I think I am not mistaken when I say that it is a piece of rare beauty and depth of thought. These are the first four lines:

> Two times two—eternal lovers;
> Inseparable in passion four . . .
> Most flaming lovers in the world,
> Eternally welded, two times two.

And the rest is in the same vein: on the wisdom and the eternal happiness of the multiplication table. Every poet is inevitably a Columbus. America existed before Columbus for ages, but only Columbus found it. The multiplication table existed before R-13 for ages, but only R-13 could find in the virginal forest of figures a new Eldorado. Is it not true? Is there any happiness more wise and cloudless in this wonderful world? Steel may rust. The ancient god created ancient man i.e., the man capable of mistakes, *ergo*, the ancient god himself made a mistake. The multiplication table is more wise and more absolute than the ancient god, for the multiplication table never (do you understand—never) make mistakes! There are no more fortunate and happy people than those who live according to the correct, eternal laws of the multiplication table. No hesitation! No errors! There is but one truth, and there is but one path to it; and that truth is: four, and that path is: two times two. Would it not seem preposterous for these happily multiplied twos suddenly to begin thinking of some foolish kind of freedom?—i.e. (is it not clear?), of a mistake? It seems undeniable, axiomatic, that R-13 knows how to grasp the most fundamental, the most . . .

At that moment again I felt (first near the back of my head, then on my left ear) the warm, tender breath of the Guardian Angel. He apparently noticed that the book on my lap had long been closed and that my thoughts were somewhere very far. . . . Well, I am ready this minute to spread before him the pages of my brain. This gives one such a feeling of tranquillity and joy. I remember I even turned around and gazed long and questioningly into his eyes; but either he did not understand, or he did not want to understand me. He did not ask me anything. . . . The only thing left for me is to relate everything to you, my unknown readers. You are to me now as dear and as near and as far out of reach as he was at that moment.

This was my way of thinking: from the part to the whole—R-13 is the part, the whole is our Institution of State Poets and Authors. I thought: how was it that the ancients did not notice the utter absurdity of their prose and poetry? The gigantic, magnificent power of the artistic word was spent by them in vain. It is really funny; anybody wrote whatever happened to come into his head! It was as foolish as the fact that in the days of the ancients the ocean blindly splashed on the shore for twenty-four hours a day, without interruption or use. The millions of kilogram meters of energy which were hidden in the waves were used only for the stimulation of sweethearts! We obtained electricity from the amorous whisper of the waves! We made a domestic animal out of that sparkling, foaming, rabid one! And in the same manner, we domesticated and harnessed the wild element of poetry. Now poetry is no longer the unpardonable whistling of nightingales, but a State Service! Poetry is a commodity.

Our famous "Mathematical Norms"! Without them in our schools, how could we love so sincerely and dearly our four rules of arithmetic? And "Thorns"! This is a classical image: the Guardians are thorns about a rose, thorns that guard our tender State Flower from coarse hands. Whose heart could resist, could remain indifferent, when seeing and hearing the lips of our children recite like a prayer: "A bad boy caught the rose with his hand, but the thorn of steel pricked him like a needle; the bad boy cried and ran home," etc., etc. And the "Daily Odes to the Well-Doer!" Who, having read them, will not bow piously before the unselfish service of that Number of all Numbers? And the dreadful red "Flowers of Court Sentences!" And the immortal tragedy, "Those Who Come Late to Work!" And the popular book, *Stanzas on Sex Hygiene!*

Our whole life in all its complexity and beauty is thus stamped forever in the gold of words. Our poets do not soar any longer in the unknown; they have descended to earth and they march with us, keeping step to the accompaniment of our austere and mechanical March of the musical State Tower. Their lyre is the morning rubbing sound of the electric toothbrushes, and the threatening crack of the electric sparks coming from the Machine of the Well-Doer, and the magnificent echo of the Hymn of the United State, and the intimate ringing of the crystalline, shining washbasins, and the stimulating rustle of the falling curtains, and the joyous voices of the newest cookbooks, and the almost imperceptible whisper of the street membranes. . . .

Our gods are here, below. They are with us in the Bureau, in the kitchen, in the shops, in the rest rooms. The gods have become like us, ergo we have become like gods. And we shall come to you, my unknown readers on another planet, we shall come to you to make your life as godlike, as rational, and as correct as our own. . . .

Oh, how great and divinely limiting is the wisdom of walls and bars! This Green Wall is, I think, the greatest invention ever conceived. Man ceased to be a wild animal the day he built the first wall; man ceased to be a wild man only on the day when the Green Wall was completed, when by this wall we isolated our machine-like, perfect world from the irrational, ugly world of trees, birds, and beasts. . . .

The blunt snout of some unknown beast was to be seen dimly through the glass of the Wall; its yellow eyes kept repeating the same thought which remained incomprehensible to me. We looked into each other's eyes for a long while. Eyes are shafts which lead from the superficial world into a world which is beneath the surface. A thought awoke in me: "What if that yellow-eyed one, sitting there on that absurd dirty heap of leaves, is happier in his life which cannot be calculated in figures!" I waved my hand. The yellow eyes twinkled, moved back, and disappeared in the foliage. What a pitiful being! How absurd the idea that he might be happier! Happier than I he may be, but I am an exception, am I not? I am sick. . . .

Discharge is the best word for it. Now I see that it was actually like an electric discharge. The pulse of my last few days had been becoming dryer and dryer, more and more rapid, more intense. The opposite poles had been drawing nearer and nearer, and already I could hear the dry crackling; one millimeter more, and—an explosion! Then silence.

Within me there is quiet now, and emptiness like that of a house after everybody has left, when one lies ill, all alone, and hears so clearly the distinct, metallic tick-tock of thoughts.

Perhaps that "discharge" cured me at last of my torturing "soul." Again I am like all of us. At least at this moment as I write I can see, as it were, without any pain in my mental eye, how O-90 is brought to the steps of the Cube; or I see her in the Gas Bell. And if there in the Operation Department she should give my name, I do not care. Piously and gratefully I would kiss the punishing hand of the Well-Doer at the last moment. I have this right with regard to the United State: to receive my punishment. And I shall not give up this right. No Number ought, or dares, to refuse this one personal, and therefore most precious, privilege.

. . . Quietly, metallically, distinctly, do the thoughts rap in the head. An invisible aero carries me into the blue height of my beloved abstractions. And I see how there in the height, in the purest rarefied air, my judgment about the only "right" bursts with a crack, like a pneumatic tire. I see clearly that only an atavism, the absurd superstition of the ancients, gives me this idea of "right."

There are ideas of moulded clay and ideas moulded of gold, or of our precious glass. In order to know the material of which an idea is made, one needs only to let fall upon it a drop of strong acid. One of these acids was known to the ancients under the name of *reductio ad absurdum*. This was the name for it, I think. But they were afraid of this poison, they preferred to believe that they saw *heaven*, even though it was a toy made of clay, rather than confess to themselves that it was only a blue nothing. We, on the other hand (glory to the Well-Doer!), we are adults, and we have no need of toys. Now if we put a drop of acid on the idea of "right" . . . Even the ancients (the most mature of them) knew that the source of right was—might! Right is a function of might. Here we have our scale on the one side an ounce, on the other a ton. On one side "I," on the other "we," the United State. Is it not clear? To assume that I may have any "right" as far as the State is concerned is like assuming that an ounce may equilibrate a ton in a scale! Hence the natural distribution: tons—rights, grams—duties. And the natural road from nothingness to greatness is to forget that one is a gram and to feel that one is one millionth of a ton!

You ripe-bodied, bright Venerians; you sooty, blacksmith-like Uranians, I almost hear your protests in this silence. But only think, everything that is great is simple. Remember, Only the four rules of arithmetic are unshakable and eternal! And only that mortality will be unshakeable and eternal which is built upon those four rules. This is the superior wisdom, this is the summit of that pyramid around which people, red with sweat, fought and battled for centuries trying to crawl up!

Looking from this summit down to the bottom, where something is still left swarming like worms, from this summit all that is left over in us from the ancients seems alike. Alike are the unlawful coming motherhood of O-90, a murder, and the insanity of that Number who dared to throw verses into the face of the United State, and alike is the judgment for them—premature death. This is that divine justice of which those stone-housed ancients dreamed, lit by the naïve pink rays of the dawn of history. Their "God" punished sacrilege as a capital crime.

You Uranians, morose and as black as the ancient Spaniards, who were wise in knowing so well how to burn at the stake, you are silent; I think you agree with me. But I hear you, pink Venerians, saying something about "tortures, executions, return to barbarism." My dear Venerians, I pity you! You are incapable of philosophical mathematical thinking. Human history moves upward in circles, like an aero. The circles are at times golden, sometimes they are bloody, but all have 360 degrees. They go from 0° to 10°, 20°, 200°, 360°—and then again 0°. Yes, we have returned to zero. But for a mathematically working mind it is obvious that this zero is different: it is a perfectly new zero. We started from zero to the right and came to zero on the left. Hence instead of plus zero we are at minus zero. Do you understand?

This zero appears to me now as a silent, immense, narrow rock, sharp as a blade. In cruel darkness, holding our breath, we set sail from the black night side of the zero rock. For centuries we, Columbuses, floated and floated; we made the circuit of the whole world and at last! Hurrah! Salute! We climbed up the masts; before us now was a new side of the zero rock, hitherto unknown, bathed in the polar light of the United State—a blue mass covered with rainbow sparkles! Suns!—a hundred suns! A million rainbows! What does it matter if we are separated from the other black side of the zero rock only by the thickness of a blade? A knife is the most solid, the most immortal, the most inspired invention of man. The knife served on the guillotine. The knife is the universal tool for cutting knots. The way of paradoxes follows its sharp edge, the only way becoming to a fearless mind. . . .

I am like a motor set in motion at a speed of too many revolutions per second; the bearings have become too hot, and in one more minute the molten metal will begin to drip and everything will go to the devil. Cold water! Quick! Some logic! I pour on pailfuls of it, but my logic merely sizzles on the hot metal and disappears into the air in the form of vapor.

Of course it is clear that in order to establish the true meaning of a function one must establish its limit. It is also clear that yesterday's "dissolution in the universe" taken to its limit is death. For death is exactly the most complete dissolution of the self in the universe. Hence: L=f (D), love is the function of death.

Yes, exactly, exactly! That is why I am afraid of I-330; I struggle against her, I don't want . . . But why is it that within me "I don't want to" and "I want to" stand side by side? That is the chief horror of the matter; I continue to long for that happy death of yesterday. The horror of it is that even now, when I have integrated the logical function, when it becomes evident that that function contains death hidden within it, still I long for it with my lips, my arms, my heart, with every millimeter. . . .

Tomorrow is the Day of Unanimity. She will certainly be there and I shall see her, though from a distance. That distance will be painful to me, for I must be, I am inevitably drawn, close to her, so that her hands, her shoulder, her hair . . . I long for even that pain. . . . Let it come. . . . Great Well-Doer! How absurd to desire pain! Who is ignorant of the simple fact that pains are negative items that reduce that sum total we call happiness? Consequently . . . Well, no "consequently" . . . Emptiness. . . . Nakedness!

The Same Evening

Through the glass wall of the house I see a disquieting, windy, feverishly pink sunset. I move my armchair to avoid that pinkness and turn over these pages, and I find I am forgetting that I write this not for myself but for you unknown people whom I love and pity, for you who still lag centuries behind, below. Let me tell you about the Day of Unanimity, about that Great Day. I think it is for us what Easter was for the ancients. I remember I used to prepare an hour calendar on the eve of that day; solemnly I would cross out every time the figure of the hour elapsed: nearer by one hour! one hour less to wait! . . . If I were certain that nobody would discover it, I assure you I should now, too, make out such a calendar and carry it with me, and I should watch how many hours remain until tomorrow. . . . When I shall see, at least from a distance . . .

(I was interrupted. They brought me a new unif from the shop. As is customary, new unifs are given to us for tomorrow's celebration. Steps in the hall, exclamations of joy, noises.)

I shall continue; tomorrow I shall see the same spectacle which we see year after year, and which always awakes in us fresh emotions, as if we saw it for the first time: an impressive throng of piously lifted arms. Tomorrow is the day of the yearly election of the Well-Doer. Tomorrow we shall again hand over to our Well-Doer the keys to the impregnable fortress of our happiness. Certainly this in no way resembles the disorderly, unorganized election days of the ancients, on which (it seems so funny!) they did not even know in advance the result of the election. To build a state on some non-discountable contingencies, to build blindly—what could be more nonsensical? Yet centuries had to pass before this was understood!

Needless to say, in this respect as in all others we have no place for contingencies; nothing unexpected can happen. The elections themselves have rather a symbolic meaning. They remind us that we are a united, powerful organism of millions of cells, that—to use the language of the "gospel" of the ancients— we are a united church. The history of the United State knows not a single case in which upon this solemn day even a solitary voice has dared to violate the magnificent unison.

They say that the ancients used to conduct their elections secretly, stealthily like thieves. Some of our historians even assert that they would come to the electoral celebrations completely masked. Imagine the weird, fantastic spectacle! Night. A plaza. Along the walls the stealthily creeping figures covered with mantles. The red flame of torches dancing in the wind. . . . Why was such secrecy necessary? It has never been satisfactorily explained. Probably it resulted from the fact that elections were associated with some mystic and superstitious, perhaps even criminal, ceremonies. We have nothing to conceal or to be ashamed of; we celebrate our election openly, honestly, in daylight. I see them all vote for the Well-Doer, and everybody sees me vote for the Well-Doer. How could it be otherwise, since "all" and "I" are one "we"? How ennobling, sincere, lofty this is, compared with the cowardly, thievish "secrecy" of the ancients! . . . It is very strange that a kind of empty white page should be left in my hand. How I walked there, how I waited (I remember I had to wait), I know nothing about it; I remember not a sound, not a face, not a gesture, as if all communicating wires between me and the world were cut.

When I came to, I found myself standing before Him. I was afraid to raise my eyes; I saw only the enormous cast-iron hands upon His knees. Those hands weighed upon Him, bending His knees with their weight. He was slowly moving His fingers. His face was somewhere above, as if in fog. And, only because His voice came to my ears from such a height, it did not roar like thunder, it did not deafen me but appeared to be an ordinary, human voice.

"Then you, too, you, the Builder of the *Integral!* You, whose lot it was to become the greatest of all *conquistadores!* You, whose name was to have been at the head of a glorious new chapter in the history of the United State! You . . ."

Blood ran to my head, to my cheeks—and here again a white page; only the pulsation in my temples and the heavy voice from above; but I remember not a word. Only when He became silent, I came to and noticed how His hand moved heavily like a thousand pounds, and crawled slowly—His finger threatened me.

"Well? Why are you silent? Is it true, or not? Executioner? So!"

"So," I repeated submissively. And then I heard clearly every one of His words."

"Well, then? Do you think I am afraid of the Word? Did you ever try to take off its shell and look into its inner meaning? I shall tell you . . . Remember a blue hill, a crowd, a cross? Some up on the hill, sprinkled with blood, are busy nailing a body to the cross; others below, sprinkled with tears, are gazing upward. Does it not occur to you that the part which those above must play is the more difficult, the more important part? If it were not for them, how could that magnificent tragedy ever have been staged? True, they were hissed by the dark crowd, but for that the author of the tragedy, God, should have remunerated them the more liberally, should He not? And the most clement, Christian God himself, who burned all the infidels on a slow fire, is He not an executioner? Was the number of those burned by the Christians less than the number of burned Christians? Yet (you must understand this!), yet this God was for centuries glorified as the God of love! Absurd? Oh, no. Just the contrary. It is instead a testament to the imperishable wisdom of man, written in blood. Even at the time when he still was wild and hairy, man knew that real, algebraic love for humanity must inevitably be inhuman, and that the inevitable mark of truth is cruelty—just as the inevitable mark of fire is its property of causing the sensation of burning. Could you show me a fire that would not hurt? Well, now prove your point! Proceed! Argue!"

How could I argue? How could I argue when those thoughts were once mine, though I was never able to dress them in such a splendid, tempered armor? I remained silent.

"If your silence is intended to mean that you agree with me, then let us talk as adults do after the children have gone to bed; let us talk to the logical end. I ask: what was it that man from his diaper age dreamed of, tormented himself for, prayed for? He longed for that day when someone would tell him what happiness is, and then would chain him to it. What else are we doing now? The ancient dream about a paradise . . . Remember: there in paradise they know no desires any more, no pity, no love; there they are all—blessed. An operation has been performed upon their center of fancy; that is why they are blessed, angels, servants of God . . . And now, at the very moment when we have caught up with that dream, when we hold it like this" (He clenched his hand so hard, that if he had held a stone in it sap would have run out!) ". . . At the moment when all that was left for us was to adorn our prize and distribute it among all in equal pieces, at that very moment you you . . ."

The cast-iron roar was suddenly broken off. I was as red as a piece of iron on an anvil under the moulding sledge hammer. The hammer seemed to have stopped for a second, hanging in the air, and I waited, waited . . . until suddenly:

"How old are you?"

"Thirty-two."

"Just double the age, and as simple as at sixteen! Listen. Is it possible that it really never occurred to you that they (we do not yet know their names, but I am certain you will disclose them to us), that they were interested in you only as the Builder of the *Integral?* Only in order to be able, through the use of you—"

"Don't! Don't!" I cried. But it was like protecting yourself with your hands and crying to a bullet: you may still be hearing your own "don't," but meanwhile the bullet has burned you through, and writhing with pain you are prostrated on the ground.

Yes, yes: the Builder of the *Integral* . . . Yes, yes. . . . At once there came back to me the angry face of U- with twitching, brick-red gills, on that morning when both of them . . .

I remember now, clearly, how I raised my eyes and laughed. A Socrates-like, bald-headed man was sitting before me; and small drops of sweat dotted the bald surface of his head.

How simple, how magnificently trivial everything was! How simple . . . almost to the point of being ridiculous! Laughter was choking me and bursting forth in puffs; I covered my mouth with my hand and rushed wildly out. . . .

Steps. Wind. Damp, leaping fragments of lights and faces . . . And while running: "No! Only to see her! To see her once more!"

Here again an empty white page. All I remember is feet: not people, just feet, hundreds of feet, confusedly stamping feet, falling from somewhere in the pavement, a heavy rain of feet . . . And some cheerful, daring voice, and a shout that was probably for me: "Hey, hey! Come here! Come along with us!"

Afterward—a deserted square heavily overloaded with tense wind. In the middle of the square a dim, heavy, threatening mass—the Machine of the Well-Doer. And a seemingly unexpected image arose within me in response to the sight of the Machine: a snow-white pillow, and on the pillow a head thrown back, and half-closed eyes, and a sharp, sweet line of teeth. . . . All this seemed so absurdly, so terribly connected with the Machine. I know how this connection has come about, but I do not yet want to see it nor to say it aloud—I don't want to! I don't!

I closed my eyes and sat down on the steps which led upward to the Machine. I must have been running hard, for my face was wet. From somewhere far away cries were coming. But nobody heard them; nobody heard me crying: "Save me from it—save me!"

If only I had a mother as the ancients had—my mother, mine, for whom I should be not the Builder of the *Integral,* and not D-530, not a molecule of the United State but merely a living human piece, a piece of herself, a trampled, smothered, cast-off piece . . . And, though I were driving the nails into the cross, or being nailed to it (perhaps it is the same), she would hear what no one else could hear, her old, grown-together, wrinkled lips . . .

Yevgeny Zamiatin (1884–1937) was a Russian engineer and novelist.

Source: Yevgeny Zamiatin, WE, trans. Gregory Zilboorg (New York: E. P. Dutton, 1924), records 3, 4, 5–6, 8, 12, 17, 20, 24, 36.

Katherine Burdekin
Swastika Night

There were many anti-German or anti-Nazi dystopias written in the late 1930s. One of the most powerful condemnations of Hitler and his program is found

in *Swastika Night*. In Burdekin's novel, the Nazis have ruled most of the world for five hundred years. The following is from a religious service:

I believe . . .

In God the Thunderer, who made this physical earth on which men march in their mortal bodies and in His heaven where all the heroes are, and in His Son our Holy Adolf Hitler, the Only Man. Who was, not begotten, not born of a woman, but Exploded! . . .

From the Head of His Father, He the perfect the untainted Man-Child, whom we, mortals and defiled in our birth and in our conception, must ever worship and praise. Heil Hitler.

Who in our need, in Germany's need, in the World's need; for our sake, for Germany's sake, for the world's sake; came down from the Mountain, the holy Mountain, the German mountain, the nameless one, to march before us as Man who is God, to lead us, to deliver us, in darkness then in sin and chaos and impurity, ringed round by devils, by Lenin,[1] by Stalin,[2] by Roehm,[3] by Karl Barth,[4] the four archfiends, whose necks he set under His Holy Heel, grinding them into the dust. . . .

Who, when our Salvation was accomplished went into the Forest, the Holy Forest, the German Forest, the nameless one; and was there reunited to His Father, God the Thunderer, so that we men, the mortals, the defiled at birth, could see His Face no more. . . .

And I believe that when all things are accomplished and the last heathen man is enlisted in His Holy Army, that Adolf Hitler our God will come again in martial glory to the sound of guns and aeroplanes, to the sound of trumpets and drums.

And I believe in the Twin Arch-Heroes, Goering[5] and Goebbels,[6] who were found worthy even to be His Familiar Friends.

And I believe in courage in violence in brutality in bloodshed in ruthlessness and all other soldierly and heroic virtues. Heil Hitler.

---

1. Vladimir Ilich Lenin (b. Vladimir Ilich Ulyanov, 1870–1924) was the leader of the Russian Revolution of 1917 and ruled the Soviet Union after the revolution until his death. *Ed.*

2. Joseph Stalin (b. Iosif Vissarionovich Dzhugashvili, 1879–1953) was the leader of the Soviet Union after Lenin. *Ed.*

3. Ernst Roehm (1887–1934) was a Nazi leader assassinated by Hitler. *Ed.*

4. Karl Barth (1886–1968) was a Swiss theologian who refused to support Hitler. *Ed.*

5. Herman Goering (1893–1946) was the founder of the Gestapo and set up the concentration camps. *Ed.*

6. Joseph Goebbels (1897–1945) was Minister for Propaganda and National Enlightenment under Hitler. *Ed.*

The fundamental laws are then chanted:

> As a woman is above a worm,
> So is a man above a woman.
> As a woman is above a worm,
> So is a worm above a Christian.
>
> So, my comrades, the lowest thing,
> The meanest, filthiest thing
> That crawls on the face of the earth
> Is a Christian woman.
> To touch her is the uttermost defilement
> For a German man.
> To speak to her only is a shame.
> They are all outcast, the man, the woman, the child.
> My sons, forget it not!
> On pain of death or torture
> Or being cut off from the blood. Heil Hitler. . . .
>
> As a man is above a woman,
> So is a Nazi above any foreign Hitlerian.
> As a Nazi is above a foreign Hitlerian,
> So is a Knight above a Nazi.
> As a Knight is above a Nazi,
> So is Der Fuehrer (whom may Hitler bless)
> Above all Knights.
> Even above the Inner Ring of Ten.
> And as Der Fuehrer is above all Knights,
> So is God, our Lord Hitler, above Der Fuehrer.
>
> But of God the Thunderer and our Lord Hitler
> Neither is pre-eminent,
> Neither commands,
> Neither obeys.
> They are equal in this holy mystery.
> They are God.
> Heil Hitler.

Katherine Burdekin (1896–1963) was a British novelist and feminist.

Source: [Katherine Burdekin], Swastika Night, by Murray Constantine [pseud.] (London: Victor Gollancz, 1937, 6–9; reprint, under the author's real name, Old Westbury, N.Y.: Feminist Press, 1985.)

Aldous Huxley
Brave New World

Aldous Huxley's _Brave New World_ is the classic extrapolation dystopia, in which contemporary trends are projected into the future. In a foreword to the 1946 edition and in _Brave New World Revisited_ (1958), Huxley argued that the world he had projected was coming much faster than he expected. In the 1946 foreword, Huxley also criticized _Brave New World_ for the options it provided. In _Island_ (1962) he presents a utopia that is similar in many respects to the world found in _Brave New World_, but is transformed by, among other things, religion. It can be considered a working out of an option to _Brave New World_.

Chapter 1

A SQUAT grey building of only thirty-four stories. Over the main entrance the words, CENTRAL LONDON HATCHERY AND CONDITIONING CENTRE, and, in a shield, the World State's motto, COMMUNITY, IDENTITY, STABILITY.

The enormous room on the ground floor faced towards the north. Cold for all the summer beyond the panes, for all the tropical heat of the room itself, a harsh thin light glared through the windows, hungrily seeking some draped lay figure, some pallid shape of academic goose-flesh, but finding only the glass and nickel and bleakly shining porcelain of a laboratory. Wintriness responded to wintriness. The overalls of the workers were white, their hands gloved with a pale corpse-coloured rubber. The light was frozen, dead, a ghost. Only from the yellow barrels of the microscopes did it borrow a certain rich and living substance, lying along the polished tubes like butter, streak after luscious streak in long recession down the work tables.

"And this," said the Director opening the door, "is the Fertilizing Room."

Bent over their instruments, three hundred Fertilizers were plunged, as the Director of Hatcheries and Conditioning entered the room, in the scarcely breathing silence, the absent-minded, soliloquizing hum or whistle, of absorbed concentration. A troop of newly arrived students, very young, pink and callow, followed nervously, rather abjectly, at the Director's heels. Each of them carried a note-book, in which, whenever the great man spoke, he desperately scribbled. Straight from the horse's mouth. It was a rare privilege. The D. H. C. for Central London always made a point of personally conducting his new students round the various departments.

"Just to give you a general idea," he would explain to them. For of course some sort of general idea they must have, if they were to do their work intelligently—though as little of one, if they were to be good and happy members of society, as possible. For particulars, as every one knows, make for virtue and happiness; generalities are intellectually necessary evils. Not philosophers but fret-sawyers and stamp collectors compose the backbone of society.

"To-morrow," he would add, smiling at them with a slightly menacing geniality, "you'll be settling down to serious work. You won't have time for generalities. Meanwhile . . ."

Meanwhile, it was a privilege. Straight from the horse's mouth into the note-book. The boys scribbled like mad.

Tall and rather thin but upright, the Director advanced into the room. He had a long chin and big rather prominent teeth, just covered, when he was not talking, by his full, floridly curved lips. Old, young? Thirty? Fifty? Fifty-five? It was hard to say. And anyhow the question didn't arise; in this year of stability, A.F. 632, it didn't occur to you to ask it.

"I shall begin at the beginning," said the D.H.C. and the more zealous students recorded his intention in their note-books: *Begin at the beginning.* "These," he waved his hand, "are the incubators." And opening an insulated door he showed them racks upon racks of numbered test-tubes. "The week's supply of ova. Kept," he explained, "at blood heat; whereas the male gametes," and here he opened another door, "they have to be kept at thirty-five instead of thirty-seven. Full blood heat sterilizes." Rams wrapped in theremogene beget no lambs.

Still leaning against the incubators he gave them, while the pencils scurried illegibly across the pages, a brief description of the modern fertilizing process; spoke first, of course, of its surgical introduction—"the operation undergone voluntarily for the good of Society, not to mention the fact that it carries a bonus amounting to six months' salary"; continued with some account of the technique for preserving the excised ovary alive and actively developing; passed on to a consideration of optimum temperature, salinity, viscosity; referred to the liquor in which the detached and ripened eggs were kept; and, leading his charges to the work tables, actually showed them how this liquor was drawn off from the test-tubes; how it was let out drop by drop onto the specially warmed slides of the microscopes; how the eggs which it contained were inspected for abnormalities, counted and transferred to a porous receptacle; how (and he now took them to watch the operation) this receptacle was immersed in a warm bouillon containing free-swimming spermatozoa—at a minimum concentration of one hundred thousand per cubic centimetre, he insisted; and how, after ten minutes, the container was lifted out of the liquor and its contents re-examined; how, if any of the eggs remained unfertilized, it was again immersed, and, if necessary, yet again; how, the fertilized ova went back to the incubators; where the Alphas and Betas remained until definitely bottled; while the Gammas, Deltas and Epsilons were brought out again, after only thirty-six hours, to undergo Bokanovsky's Process.

"Bokanovsky's Process," repeated the Director, and the students underlined the words in their little note-books.

One egg, one embryo, one adult-normality. But a bokanovskified egg will bud, will proliferate, will divide. From eight to ninety-six buds, and every bud will grow into a perfectly formed embryo, and every embryo into a full-sized adult. Making ninety-six human beings grow where only one grew before. Progress.

"Essentially," the D.H.C. concluded, "bokanovskification consists of a series of arrests of development. We check the normal growth and, paradoxically enough, the egg responds by budding."

Responds by budding. The pencils were busy.

He pointed. On a very slowly moving band a rack-full of test-tubes was entering a large metal box, another, rack-full was emerging. Machinery faintly purred. It took eight minutes for the tubes to go through, he told them. Eight minutes of hard X-rays being about as much as an egg can stand. A few died; of the rest, the least susceptible divided into two; most put out four buds; some eight; all were returned to the incubators, where the buds began to develop; then, after two days, were suddenly chilled, chilled and checked. Two, four, eight, the buds in their turn budded; and having budded were dosed almost to death with alcohol; consequently burgeoned again and having budded—bud out of bud out of bud—were thereafter—further arrest being generally fatal—left to develop in peace. By which time the original egg was in a fair way to becoming anything from eight to ninety-six embryos—a prodigious improvement, you will agree, on nature. Identical twins—but not in piddling twos and threes as in the old viviparous days, when an egg would sometimes accidentally divide; actually by dozens, by scores at a time.

"Scores," the Director repeated and flung out his arms, as though he were distributing largesse. "Scores."

But one of the students was fool enough to ask where the advantage lay.

"My good boy!" The Director wheeled sharply round on him. "Can't you see? Can't you *see?*" He raised a hand; his expression was solemn. "Bokanovsky's Process is one of the major instruments of social stability!"

Major instruments of social stability.

Standard men and women; in uniform batches. The whole of a small factory staffed with the products of a single bokanovskified egg.

"Ninety-six identical twins working ninety-six identical machines!" The voice was almost tremulous with enthusiasm. "You really know where you are.

For the first time in history." He quoted the planetary motto. "Community, Identity, Stability." Grand words. "If we could bokanovskify indefinitely the whole problem would be solved."

Solved by standard Gammas, unvarying Deltas, uniform Epsilons. Millions of identical twins. The principle of mass production at last applied to biology.

"But, alas," the Director shook his head, "we can't bokanovskify indefinitely."

Ninety-six seemed to be the limit; seventy-two a good average. From the same ovary and with gametes of the same male to manufacture as many batches of identical twins as possible—that was the best (sadly a second best) that they could do. And even that was difficult.

"For in nature it takes thirty years for two hundred eggs to reach maturity. But our business is to stabilize the population at this moment, here and now. Dribbling out twins over a quarter of a century—what would be the use of that?"

Obviously, no use at all. But Podsnap's Technique had immensely accelerated the process of ripening. They could make sure of at least a hundred and fifty mature eggs within two years. Fertilize and bokanovskify—in other words, multiply by seventy-two—and you get an average of nearly eleven thousand brothers and sisters in a hundred and fifty batches of identical twins, all within two years of the same age.

"And in exceptional cases we can make one ovary yield us over fifteen thousand adult individuals."

Beckoning to a fair-haired, ruddy young man who happened to be passing at the moment. "Mr. Foster," he called. The ruddy young man approached. "Can you tell us the record for a single ovary, Mr. Foster?"

"Sixteen thousand and twelve in this Centre," Mr. Foster replied without hesitation. He spoke very quickly, had a vivacious blue eye, and took an evident pleasure in quoting figures. "Sixteen thousand and twelve; in one hundred and eighty-nine batches of identicals. But of course they've done much better," he rattled on, "in some of the tropical Centres. Singapore has often produced over sixteen thousand five hundred; and Mombasa has actually touched the seventeen thousand mark. But then they have unfair advantages. You should see the way a negro ovary responds to pituitary! It's quite astonishing, when you're used to working with European material. Still," he added, with a laugh (but the light of combat was in his eyes and the lift of his chin was challenging), "still, we mean to beat them if we can. I'm working on a wonderful Delta-Minus ovary at this moment. Only just eighteen months old. Over twelve thousand seven hundred children already, either decanted or in embryo. And still going strong. We'll beat them yet."

"That's the spirit I like!" cried the Director, and clapped Mr. Foster on the shoulder. "Come along with us, and give these boys the benefit of your expert knowledge."

Mr. Foster smiled modestly. "With pleasure." They went.

In the Bottling Room all was harmonious bustle and ordered activity. Flaps of fresh sow's peritoneum ready cut to the proper size came shooting up in little lifts from the Organ Store in the sub-basement. Whizz and then, click! the lift-hatches flew open; the bottle-liner had only to reach out a hand, take the flap, insert, smooth-down, and before the lined bottle had had time to travel out of reach along the endless band, whizz, click! another flap of peritoneum had shot up from the depths, ready to be slipped into yet another bottle, the next of that slow interminable procession on the band.

Next to the Liners stood the Matriculators. The procession advanced; one by one the eggs were transferred from their test-tubes to the larger containers; deftly the peritoneal lining was slit, the morula dropped into place, the saline solution poured in . . . and already the bottle had passed, and it was the turn of the labellers. Heredity, date of fertilization, membership of Bokanovsky Group—details were transferred from test-tube to bottle. No longer anonymous, but named, identified, the procession marched slowly on; on through an opening in the wall, slowly on into the Social Predestination Room.

"Eighty-eight cubic metres of card-index," said Mr. Foster with relish, as they entered.

"Containing *all* the relevant information," added the Director.

"Brought up to date every morning."

"And co-ordinated every afternoon."

"On the basis of which they make their calculations."

"So many individuals, of such and such quality," said Mr. Foster.

"Distributed in such and such quantities."

"The optimum Decanting Rate at any given moment."

"Unforeseen wastages promptly made good."

"Promptly," repeated Mr. Foster. "If you knew the amount of overtime I had to put in after the last Japanese earthquake!" He laughed good-humoredly and shook his head.

"The Predestinators send in their figures to the Fertilizers.

"Who give them the embryos they ask for."

"And the bottles come in here to be predestined in detail."

"After which they are sent down to the Embryo Store."

"Where we now proceed ourselves."

And opening a door Mr. Foster led the way down a staircase into the basement.

The temperature was still tropical. They descended into a thickening twilight. Two doors and a passage with a double turn ensured the cellar against any possible infiltration of the day.

"Embryos are like photograph film," said Mr. Foster waggishly, as he pushed open the second door. "They can only stand red light."

And in effect the sultry darkness into which the students now followed him was visible and crimson, like the darkness of closed eyes on a summer's afternoon. The bulging flanks of row on receding row and tier above tier of bottles glinted with innumerable rubies, and among the rubies moved the dim red spectres of men and women with purple eyes and the symptoms of lupus. The hum and rattle of machinery faintly stirred the air.

"Give them a few figures, Mr. Foster," said the Director, who was tired of talking.

Mr. Foster was only too happy to give them a few figures.

Two hundred and twenty metres long, two hundred wide, ten high. He pointed upwards. Like chickens drinking, the students lifted their eyes towards the distant ceiling.

Three tiers of racks: ground-floor level, first gallery, second gallery.

The spidery steelwork of gallery above gallery faded away in all directions into the dark. Near them three red ghosts were busily unloading demijohns from a moving staircase.

The escalator from the Social Predestination Room.

Each bottle could be placed on one of fifteen racks, each rack, though you couldn't see it, was a conveyor travelling at the rate of thirty-three and a third centimetres an hour. Two hundred and sixty-seven days at eight metres a day. Two thousand one hundred and thirty-six metres in all. One circuit of the cellar at ground level, one on the first gallery, half on the second, and on the two hundred and sixty-seventh morning, daylight in the Decanting Room. Independent existence—so called.

"But in the interval," Mr. Foster concluded, "we've managed to do a lot to them. Oh, a very great deal." His laugh was knowing and triumphant.

"That's the spirit I like," said the Director once more. "Let's walk round. You tell them everything, Mr. Foster."

Mr. Foster duly told them.

Told them of the growing embryo on its bed of peritoneum. Made them taste the rich blood-surrogate on which it fed. Explained why it had to be stimulated with placentin and thyroxin. Told them of the *corpus luteum* extract. Showed them the jets through which at every twelfth metre from zero to 2040 it was automatically injected. Spoke of those gradually increasing doses of pituitary administered during the final ninety-six metres of their course. Described the artificial maternal circulation installed on every bottle at Metre 112;

showed them the reservoir of blood-surrogate, the centrifugal pump that kept the liquid moving over the placenta and drove it through the synthetic lung and waste-product filter. Referred to the embryo's troublesome tendency to anaemia, to the massive doses of hog's stomach extract and foetal foal's liver with which, in consequence, it had to be supplied.

Showed them the simple mechanism by means of which, during the last two metres out of every eight, all the embryos were simultaneously shaken into familiarity with movement. Hinted at the gravity of the so-called "trauma of decanting," and enumerated the precautions taken to minimize, by a suitable training of the bottled embryo, that dangerous shock. Told them of the test for sex carried out in the neighborhood of Metre 200. Explained the system of labelling—a T for the males, a circle for the females and for those who were destined to become freemartins a question mark, black on a white ground.

"For of course," said Mr. Foster, "in the vast majority of cases, fertility is merely a nuisance. One fertile ovary in twelve hundred—that would really be quite sufficient for our purposes. But we want to have a good choice. And of course one must always have an enormous margin of safety. So we allow as many as thirty per cent of the female embryos to develop normally. The others get a dose of male sex-hormone every twenty-four metres for the rest of the course. Result: they're decanted as freemartins—structurally quite normal (except," he had to admit, "that they *do* have the slightest tendency to grow beards), but sterile. Guaranteed sterile. Which brings us at last," continued Mr. Foster, "out of the realm of mere slavish imitation of nature into the much more interesting world of human invention."

He rubbed his hands. For of course, they didn't content themselves with merely hatching out embryos: any cow could do that.

"We also predestine and condition. We decant our babies as socialized human beings, as Alphas or Epsilons, as future sewage workers or future . . ." He was going to say "future World controllers," but correcting himself, said "future Directors of Hatcheries," instead.

The D.H.C. acknowledged the compliment with a smile.

They were passing Metre 320 on Rack ll. A young Beta-Minus mechanic was busy with screw-driver and spanner on the blood-surrogate pump of a passing bottle. The hum of the electric motor deepened by fractions of a tone as he turned the nuts. Down, down . . . A final twist, a glance at the revolution counter, and he was done. He moved two paces down the line and began the same process on the next pump.

"Reducing the number of revolutions per minute," Mr. Foster explained. "The surrogate goes round slower; therefore passes through the lung at longer intervals; therefore gives the embryo less oxygen. Nothing like oxygen-shortage for keeping an embryo below par." Again he rubbed his hands.

"But why do you want to keep the embryo below par?" asked an ingenuous student.

"Ass!" said the Director, breaking a long silence. "Hasn't it occurred to you that an Epsilon embryo must have an Epsilon environment as well as an Epsilon heredity?"

It evidently hadn't occurred to him. He was covered with confusion.

"The lower the caste," said Mr. Foster, "the shorter the oxygen." The first organ affected was the brain. After that the skeleton. At seventy per cent of normal oxygen you got dwarfs. At less than seventy eyeless monsters.

"Who are no use at all," concluded Mr. Foster.

Whereas (his voice became confidential and eager), if they could discover a technique for shortening the period of maturation what a triumph, what a benefaction to Society!

"Consider the horse."

They considered it.

Mature at six; the elephant at ten. While at thirteen a man is not yet sexually mature; and is only full-grown at twenty. Hence, of course, that fruit of delayed development, the human intelligence.

"But in Epsilons," said Mr. Foster very justly, "we don't need human intelligence."

Didn't need and didn't get it. But though the Epsilon mind was mature at ten, the Epsilon body was not fit to work till eighteen. Long years of superfluous and wasted immaturity. If the physical development could be speeded up till it was as quick, say, as a cow's, what an enormous saving to the Community!

"Enormous!" murmured the students. Mr. Foster's enthusiasm was infectious.

He became rather technical; spoke of the abnormal endocrine co-ordination which made men grow so slowly; postulated a germinal mutation to account for it. Could the effects of this germinal mutation be undone? Could the individual Epsilon embryo be made a revert, by a suitable technique, to the normality of dogs and cows? That was the problem. And it was all but solved.

Pilkington, at Mombasa, had produced individuals who were sexually mature at four and full-grown at six and a half. A scientific triumph. But socially useless. Six-year-old men and women were too stupid to do even Epsilon work. And the process was an all-or-nothing one; either you failed to modify at all, or else you modified the whole way. They were still trying to find the ideal compromise between adults of twenty and adults of six. So far without success. Mr. Foster sighed and shook his head.

Their wanderings through the crimson twilight had brought them to the neighborhood of Metre 170 on Rack 9. From this point onwards Rack 9 was enclosed and the bottle performed the remainder of their journey in a kind of tunnel, interrupted here and there by openings two or three metres wide.

"Heat conditioning," said Mr. Foster.

Hot tunnels alternated with cool tunnels. Coolness was wedded to discomfort in the form of hard X-rays. By the time they were decanted the embryos had a horror of cold. They were predestined to emigrate to the tropics, to be miner and acetate silk spinners and steel workers. Later on their minds would be made to endorse the judgment of their bodies. "We condition them to thrive on heat," concluded Mr. Poster. "Our colleagues upstairs will teach them to love it."

"And that," put in the Director sententiously, "that is the secret of happiness and virtue—liking what you've got to do. All conditioning aims at that: making people like their unescapable social destiny."

In a gap between two tunnels, a nurse was delicately probing with a long fine syringe into the gelatinous contents of a passing bottle. The students and their guides stood watching her for a few moments in silence.

"Well, Lenina," said Mr. Foster, when at last she withdrew the syringe and straightened herself up.

The girl turned with a start. One could see that, for all the lupus and the purple eyes, she was uncommonly pretty.

Henry!" Her smile flashed redly at him—a row of coral teeth.

"Charming, charming," murmured the Director and, giving her two or three little pats, received in exchange a rather deferential smile for himself.

"What are you giving them?" asked Mr. Foster, making his tone very professional.

"Oh, the usual typhoid and sleeping sickness."

"Tropical workers start being inoculated at Metre 150, Mr. Foster explained to the students. "The embryos still have gills. We immunize the fish against the future man's diseases." Then, turning back to Lenina, "Ten to five on the roof this afternoon," he said, "as usual."

"Charming," said the Director once more, and, with a final pat, moved away after the others.

On Rack 10 rows of next generation's chemical workers were being trained in the toleration of lead, caustic soda, tar, chlorine. The first of a batch of two hundred and fifty embryonic rocket-plane engineers was just passing the eleven hundred metre mark on Rack 3. A special mechanism kept their containers in constant rotation. "To improve their sense of balance," Mr. Foster explained. "Doing repairs on the outside of a rocket in mid-air is a ticklish job. We slacken off the circulation when they're right way up, so that they're half starved, and double the flow of surrogate when they're upside down. They learn to associate topsy-turvydom with well-being; in fact, they're only truly happy when they're standing on their heads.

"And now," Mr. Foster went on, "I'd like to show you some very interesting conditioning for Alpha Plus Intellectuals. We have a big batch of them on Rack 5. First Gallery level," he called to two boys who had started to go down to the ground floor.

"They're round about Metre 900," he explained. "You can't really do any useful intellectual conditioning till the foetuses have lost their tails. Follow me."

But the Director had looked at his watch. "Ten to three," he said. "No time for the intellectual embryos, I'm afraid. We must go up to the Nurseries before the children have finished their afternoon sleep."

Mr. Foster was disappointed. "At least one glance at the Decanting Room," he pleaded.

"Very well then." The Director smiled indulgently. "Just one glance."

Chapter 2

MR. FOSTER was left in the Decanting Room. The D.H.C. and his students stepped into the nearest lift and were carried up to the fifth floor.

INFANT NURSERIES. NEO-PAVLOVIAN CONDITIONING ROOMS, announced the notice board.

The Director opened a door. They were in a large bare room, very bright and sunny; for the whole of the southern wall was a single window. Half a dozen nurses, trousered and jacketed in the regulation white viscose-linen uniform, their hair aseptically hidden under white caps, were engaged in setting out bowls of roses in a long row across the floor. Big bowls, packed tight with blossom. Thousands of petals, ripe-blown and silkily smooth, like the cheeks of innumerable little cherubs, but of cherubs, in that bright light, not exclusively pink and Aryan, but also luminously Chinese, also Mexican, also apoplectic with too much blowing of celestial trumpets, also pale as death, pale with the posthumous whiteness of marble.

The nurses stiffened to attention as the D.H.C. came in.

"Set out the books," he said curtly.

In silence the nurses obeyed his command. Between the rose bowls the books were duly set out—a row of nursery quartos opened invitingly each at some gaily coloured image of beast or fish or bird.

"Now bring in the children."

They hurried out of the room and returned in a minute or two, each pushing a kind of tall dumb-waiter laden, on all its four wire-netted shelves, with eight-month-old babies, all exactly alike (a Bokanovsky Group, it was evident) and all (since their caste was Delta) dressed in khaki.

"Put them down on the floor."

The infants were unloaded.

"Now turn them so that they can see the flowers and books."

Turned, the babies at once fell silent, then began to crawl towards those clusters of sleek colours, those shapes so gay and brilliant on the white pages. As they approached, the sun came out of a momentary eclipse behind a cloud. The roses flamed up as though with a sudden passion from within; a new and profound significance seemed to suffuse the shining pages of the books. From the ranks of the crawling babies came little squeals of excitement, gurgles and twitterings of pleasure.

The Director rubbed his hands. "Excellent!" he said. "It might almost have been done on purpose."

The swiftest crawlers were already at their goal. Small hands reached out uncertainly, touched, grasped, unpetaling the transfigured roses, crumpling the illuminated pages of the books. The Director waited until all were happily busy. Then, "Watch carefully," he said. And, lifting his hand, he gave the signal.

The Head Nurse, who was standing by a switchboard at the other end of the room, pressed down a little lever.

There was a violent explosion. Shriller and ever shriller, a siren shrieked. Alarm bells maddeningly sounded.

The children started, screamed; their faces were distorted with terror.

"And now," the Director shouted (for the noise was deafening), "now we proceed to rub in the lesson with a mild electric shock."

He waved his hand again, and the Head Nurse pressed a second lever. The screaming of the babies suddenly changed its tone. There was something desperate, almost insane, about the sharp spasmodic yelps to which they now gave utterance. Their little bodies twitched and stiffened; their limbs moved jerkily as if to the tug of unseen wires.

"We can electrify that whole strip of floor," bawled the Director in explanation. "But that's enough," he signalled to the nurse.

The explosions ceased, the bells stopped ringing, the shriek of the siren died down from tone to tone into silence. The stiffly twitching bodies relaxed, and what had become the sob and yelp of infant maniacs broadened out once more into a normal howl of ordinary terror.

"Offer them the flowers and the books again."

The nurses obeyed; but at the approach of the roses, at the mere sight of those gaily-coloured images of pussy and cock-a-doodle-doo and baa-baa black sheep, the infants shrank away in horror; the volume of their howling suddenly increased.

"Observe," said the Director triumphantly, "observe."

Books and loud noises, flowers and electric shocks—already in the infant mind these couples were compromisingly linked; and after two hundred repetitions of the same or a similar lesson would be wedded indissolubly. What man has joined, nature is powerless to put asunder.

"They'll grow up with what the psychologists used to call an 'instinctive' hatred of books and flowers. Reflexes unalterably conditioned. They'll be safe from books and botany all their lives." The Director turned to his nurses. "Take them away again."

Still yelling, the khaki babies were loaded on to their dumb-waiters and wheeled out, leaving behind them the smell of sour milk and a most welcome silence.

One of the students held up his hand; and though he could see quite well why you couldn't have lower-caste people wasting the Community's time over books, and that there was always the risk of their reading something which might undesirably decondition one of their reflexes, yet . . . well, he couldn't understand about the flowers. Why go to the trouble of making it psychologically impossible for Deltas to like flowers?

Patiently the D.H.C. explained. If the children were made to scream at the sight of a rose, that was on grounds of high economic policy. Not so very long ago (a century or thereabouts), Gammas, Deltas, even Epsilons, had been conditioned to like flowers—flowers in particular and wild nature in general. The idea was to make them want to be going out into the country at every available opportunity, and so compel them to consume transport.

"And didn't they consume transport?" asked the student.

"Quite a lot," the D.H.C. replied. "But nothing else."

Primroses and landscapes, he pointed out, have one grave defect: they are gratuitous. A love of nature keeps no factories busy. It was decided to abolish the love of nature, at any rate among the lower classes; to abolish the love of nature, but not the tendency to consume transport. For of course it was essential that they should keep on going to the country, even though they hated it. The problem was to find an economically sounder reason for consuming transport than a mere affection for primroses and landscapes. It was duly found.

"We condition the masses to hate the country," concluded the Director. "But simultaneously we condition them to love all country sports. At the same time, we see to it that all country sports shall entail the use of elaborate apparatus. So that they consume manufactured articles as well as transport. Hence those electric shocks."

"I see," said the student, and was silent, lost in admiration.

There was a silence; then, clearing his throat, "Once upon a time," the Director began, "while our Ford was still on earth, there was a little boy called

Reuben Rabinovitch. Reuben was the child of Polish-speaking parents." The Director interrupted himself. "You know what Polish is, I suppose?"

"A dead language."

"Like French and German," added another student, consciously showing off his learning.

"And 'parent'?" questioned the D.H.C.

There was an uneasy silence. Several of the boys blushed. They had not yet learned to draw the significant but often very fine distinction between smut and pure science. One, at last, had the courage to raise a hand.

"Human beings used to be . . ." he hesitated; the blood rushed to his cheeks. "Well, they used to be viviparous."

"Quite right." The Director nodded approvingly.

"And when the babies were decanted . . ."

"'Born,'" came the correction.

"Well, then they were the parents—I mean, not the babies, of course; the other ones." The poor boy was overwhelmed with confusion.

"In brief," the Director summed up, "the parents were the father and the mother." The smut that was really science fell with a crash into the boys' eye-avoiding silence. "Mother," he repeated loudly rubbing in the science; and, leaning back in his chair, "These," he said gravely, "are unpleasant facts; I know it. But then most historical facts are unpleasant."

He returned to Little Reuben—to Little Reuben, in whose room, one evening, by an oversight, his father and mother (crash, crash!) happened to leave the radio turned on.

("For you must remember that in those days of gross viviparous reproduction, children were always brought up by their parents and not in State Conditioning Centres.")

While the child was asleep, a broadcast programme from London suddenly started to come through; and the next morning, to the astonishment of his crash and crash (the more daring of the boys ventured to grin at one another), Little Reuben woke up repeating word for word a long lecture by that curious old writer ("one of the very few whose works have been permitted to come down to us"), George Bernard Shaw, who was speaking, according to a well-authenticated tradition, about his own genius. To Little Reuben's wink and snigger, this lecture was, of course perfectly incomprehensible and, imagining that their child had suddenly gone mad, they sent for a doctor. He, fortunately, understood English, recognized the discourse as that which Shaw had broadcasted the previous evening realized the significance of what had happened, and sent a letter to the medical press about it.

"The principle of sleep-teaching, or hypnopædia, had been discovered." The D.H.C. made an impressive pause.

The principle had been discovered; but many, many years were to elapse before that principle was usefully applied.

"The case of Little Reuben occurred only twenty-three years after Our Ford's first T-Model was put on the market. (Here the Director made a sign of the T on his stomach and all the students reverently followed suit.)

"And yet . . . !

Furiously the students scribbled, *"Hypnopædia, first used officially in* A.F. *214. Why not before? Two reasons. (a) . . ."*

"These early experimenters," the D.H.C. was saying, were on the wrong track. They thought that hypnopædia could be made an instrument of intellectual education . . ."

(A small boy asleep on his right side, the right arm stuck out, the right hand hanging limp over the edge of the bed. Through a round grating in the side of a box a voice speaks softly.

"The Nile is the longest river in Africa and the second in length of all the rivers of the globe. Though falling short of the length of the Mississippi-Missouri, the Nile is at the head of all rivers as regards the length of its basin, which extends through 35 degrees of latitude . . ."

At breakfast the next morning, "Tommy," some one says, "do you know which is the longest river in Africa?" A shaking of the head. "But don't you remember something that begins: The Nile is the . . ."

"The - Nile - is - the - longest - river - in - Africa - and - the - second - in - length - of - all - the - rivers - of - the - globe . . ." The words come rushing out. "Although - falling - short - of . . ."

"Well now, which is the longest river in Africa?"

The eyes are blank. "I don't know."

"But the Nile, Tommy."

"The - Nile - is - the - longest - river - in - Africa - and - second ..."

"Then which river is the longest, Tommy?"

Tommy burst into tears. "I don't know," he howls.)

That howl, the Director made it plain, discouraged the earliest investigators. The experiments were abandoned. No further attempt was made to teach children the length of the Nile in their sleep. Quite rightly. You can't learn a science unless you know what it's all about.

"Whereas, if they'd only started on *moral* education," said the Director, leading the way towards the door. The students followed him, desperately scribbling as they walked and all the way up in the lift. "Moral education, which ought never, in any circumstances, to be rational."

"Silence, silence," whispered a loud speaker as they stepped out at the fourteenth floor, and "Silence, silence," the trumpet mouths indefatigably repeated at intervals down every corridor. The students and even the Director himself rose automatically to the tips of their toes. They were Alphas, of course; but even Alphas have been well conditioned. "Silence, silence." All the air of the fourteenth floor was sibilant with the categorical imperative.

Fifty yards of tiptoeing brought them to a door which the Director cautiously opened. They stepped over the threshold into the twilight of a shuttered dormitory. Eighty cots stood in a row against the wall. There was a sound of light regular breathing and a continuous murmur, as of very faint voices remotely whispering.

A nurse rose as they entered and came to attention before the Director.

"What's the lesson this afternoon?" he asked.

"We had Elementary Sex for the first forty minutes," she answered. "But now it's switched over to Elementary Class Consciousness."

The Director walked slowly down the long line of cots. Rosy and relaxed with sleep, eighty little boys and girls lay softly breathing. There was a whisper under every pillow. The D.H.C. halted and, bending over one of the little beds, listened attentively.

"Elementary Class Consciousness, did you say? Let's have it repeated a little louder by the trumpet."

At the end of the room a loud speaker projected from the wall. The Director walked up to it and pressed a switch.

". . . all wear green," said a soft but very distinct voice, beginning in the middle of a sentence, "and Delta Children wear khaki. Oh no, I don't want to play with Delta children. And Epsilons are still worse. They're too stupid to be able to read or write. Besides they wear black, which is such a beastly colour. I'm *so* glad I'm a Beta."

There was a pause; then the voice began again.

"Alpha children wear grey. They work much harder than we do, because they're so frightfully clever. I'm really awfully glad I'm a Beta, because I don't work so hard. And then we are much better than the Gammas and Deltas. Gammas are stupid. They all wear green, and Delta children wear khaki. Oh no, I *don't* want to play with Delta children. And Epsilons are still worse. They're too stupid to be able . . ."

The Director pushed back the switch. The voice was silent. Only its thin ghost continued to mutter from beneath the eighty pillows.

"They'll have that repeated forty or fifty times more before they wake; then again on Thursday, and again on Saturday. A hundred and twenty times three times a week for thirty months. After which they go on to a more advanced lesson."

Roses and electric shocks, the khaki of Deltas and a whiff of asafoetida—wedded indissolubly before the child can speak. But wordless conditioning is crude and wholesale; cannot bring home the finer distinctions, cannot inculcate the more complex courses of behaviour. For that there must be words, but words without reason. In brief, hypnopædia.

"The greatest moralizing and socializing force of all time."

The students took it down in their little books. Straight from the horse's mouth.

Once more the Director touched the switch.

". . . so frightfully clever," the soft, insinuating, indefatigable voice was saying, "I'm really awfully glad I'm a Beta, because . . ."

Not so much like drops of water, though water, it is true, can wear holes in the hardest granite; rather, drops of liquid sealing-wax, drops that adhere, incrust, incorporate themselves with what they fall on, till finally the rock is all one scarlet blob.

"Till at last the child's mind *is* these suggestions, and the sum of the suggestions *is* the child's mind. And not the child's mind only. The adult's mind too—all his life long. The mind that judges and desires and decides—made up of these suggestions. But all these suggestions are *our* suggestions!" The Director almost shouted in his triumph. "Suggestions from the State." He banged the nearest table. "It therefore follows . . ."

A noise made him turn round.

"Oh, Ford!" he said in another tone, "I've gone and woken the children."

Brave New World Revisited

In 1931, when *Brave New World* was being written, I was convinced that there was still plenty of time. The completely organized society, the scientific caste system, the abolition of free will by methodical conditioning, the servitude made acceptable by regular doses of chemically induced happiness, the orthodoxies drummed in by nightly courses of sleep-teaching—these things were coming all right, but not in my time, not even in the time of my grandchildren. I forget the exact date of the events recorded in *Brave New World*; but it was somewhere in the sixth or seventh century A.F. (After Ford). We who were living in the second quarter of the twentieth century A.D. were the inhabitants, admittedly, of a gruesome kind of universe; but the nightmare of those depression years was radically different from the nightmare of the future, described in *Brave New World*. Ours was a nightmare of too little order; theirs, in the seventh century A.F., of too much. In the process of passing from one extreme to the other, there would be a long interval, so I imagined, during which the more fortunate third of the human race would make the best of both worlds—the disorderly world of liberalism and the much too orderly Brave New World where perfect efficiency left no room for freedom or personal initiative.

Twenty-seven years later, in this third quarter of the twentieth century A.D., and long before the end of the first century A.F., I feel a good deal less optimistic than I did when I was writing *Brave New World*. The prophecies made in 1931 are coming true much sooner than I thought they would. The blessed interval between too little order and the nightmare of too much has not begun and shows no sign of beginning. In the West, it is true, individual men and women still enjoy a large measure of freedom. But even in those countries that have a tradition of democratic government, this freedom and even the desire for this freedom seem to be on the wane. In the rest of the world freedom for individuals has already gone, or is manifestly about to go. The nightmare of total organization, which I had situated in the seventh century After Ford, has emerged from the safe, remote future and is now awaiting us, just around the next corner.

Aldous Huxley (1894–1963) was a British author who moved to the United States in 1937.

Source: Aldous Huxley, BRAVE NEW WORLD (Garden City, N.Y.: Doubleday, Doran, 1932) chaps. 1–2; Aldous Huxley, BRAVE NEW WORLD REVISITED (New York: Harper and Brothers, 1958), 3–4.

Olaf Stapledon
Darkness and the Light

Olaf Stapledon is remembered most for his far-ranging explorations of future human evolution. The chapter excerpted here is placed nearer in the future than many of his projections.

New World

1. A World of Villages

THE AGE that now dawned was one of almost explosive progress, explosive, yet controlled. Unlike the industrial revolution which is familiar to readers of this book, it was not dependent on licentious economic individualism. Its energy was derived, of course, very largely from the self-assertive itch of able individuals, but the means of satisfying this craving were now in the main centrally planned and socially useful. Superficially at least I was able to grasp the material achievement of the race in this period, but its cultural life henceforth increasingly escaped me, outranging my comprehension.

Nevertheless it seems worth while to describe the main features of the new order, not only because it was characteristic of the human race for a very long time but also because of its novelty and its significance for our own age. At the outset the innate calibre of the average human being was not appreciably higher than our own. Men were on the whole no more intelligent, and had no more capacity for generosity than we have; but, owing to the world-wide victory of the will for the light and the founding of a new tradition of moral integrity and a more wholesome economy, average individuals behaved far better. They lived normally far nearer the upper limit of their capacity. Instead of being constantly degraded by their environment, they were constantly braced and humanized. The rulers of the new world were not content with this. The whole social organization was dominated by the aim of continuously raising the average human capacity far beyond its present level.

The social order of the new world was very different from any earlier form. It might be described as at once 'super-modern' and yet in a way medieval. At bottom it depended on the special characters of the new source of mechanical power. Two contrary but harmonized tendencies were at work. On the one hand mechanization was being steadily pushed forward; on the other there was a surprising recovery of manual skill and versatility in the life of the ordinary human being. On the one hand came the fulfilment of social unity and harmony, on the other the development of the individual's self-sufficiency and all-roundness.

This balanced economy was greatly assisted by the fact that power came to be accessible almost anywhere and was derived from quite ordinary materials. In our own age, no doubt, such an order would be far more difficult to establish, since in our stage of industrial evolution, power and manufacture both demand far-reaching organization, and the reducing of individuals to specialized cogs in the great machine. But even we, had we clear sight and the will for change, could at least set our faces in this direction.

Though at first the generators had been exceedingly cumbersome and delicate, the method was later transformed by a series of brilliant inventions, resulting from world-wide co-operative research. The standard generator, which supported the new civilization as combustion engines of all sorts support our own, was a subtle little machine which could be housed in a small barn. All the skill of the most expert physicists was needed for the making of this instrument; but the finished article, if not fool-proof, was reliable, potent, and versatile. It could be used not only for the production of power but also for the transmutation of the elements, and the synthesizing of a vast range of materials for use. As a power-unit it demanded little more skill than we use in motoring; but as an instrument for the varied synthesizing of materials it could employ every range of ability. Some elements and compounds could be produced easily by any competent person, some demanded rather special aptitude and training, some could be attempted only by the most brilliant masters, and some had to be undertaken in the great electro-chemical factories.

Little by little every village came to have its own power plant. Even isolated houses generated their own power and could produce the simpler materials. In the main, however, the village was the unit of the new social system. Its strength was due to the scope and limitations of the standard generator, which employed directly and indirectly in village industry and agriculture between fifty and five hundred persons. The population of the average village consisted of the electro-magnetic engineers who saw to the generating of power, a number of craftsmen specialized in the production of the different kinds of material needed by the village, and another set of craftsmen who worked up the materials into articles of use. The former class of craftsmen, who were called 'atomic weavers', used as their raw material ingredients in the local earth. These they bombarded with sub-atomic particles, fired out by their mighty power plant, and thus they produced a great range of elements and compounds. The process demanded the same kind of skill as that of the old-time hand-spinners and weavers, the craftsmen vying with each other to produce the subtlest and most serviceable compounds and mixtures free from all impurities. These products were then worked up by craftsmen of the other class into crockery, furniture, cutting tools, building materials, clothing, and so on. The village textile workers clothed their fellow villagers in a great variety of simple but pleasing fabrics. Even isolated households, with their smaller plant, could provide themselves with many of the simpler materials. On the other hand some villages excelled so much in a particular line of craftsmanship that their products were in demand throughout the countryside. Only the most difficult materials and articles had to be brought to the village from the local factory, itself but a large and highly specialized village or cluster of villages around a great power house and synthesis station.

The food of the village was not produced by the synthesis of organic compounds under sub-atomic power. Agriculture was still practised. But the old kind of agriculture was rapidly giving way to direct photosynthesis of the essential food factors under sunlight. The village was surrounded by its private gardens and communal fields. The earth was impregnated with appropriate chemicals and sprinkled with the spore of an artificial 'organic molecule', which absorbed light and propagated itself till it covered the field with a green exfoliation. It was then gathered by a tractor armed with a sort of vacuum cleaner, washed, and worked up with other materials (similarly produced) into a great variety of foodstuffs. Throughout the summer the fields were harvested at intervals of about a week. The advantage of this system over the old-fashioned agriculture was that the land produced nearly ten times its former yield in food value.

Certain luxury foods, and every villager demanded his share of luxury, had to be procured from the local or national factory, and some specially choice articles from foreign lands. But any village with any pretension to taste and local pride could produce characteristic local variants of the essential synthetic 'meats', 'breads', 'cheeses', 'fruits', and drinks. Many an isolated homestead, if its food-making was managed with intelligence and artistry, could produce a simple but elegant meal to delight the most fastidious traveller.

Little by little the new processes transformed the whole economy of the world. A miniature aeroplane, driven by sub-atomic power derived from one of the rarer elements in the air, made it possible for every one to travel any-where at a speed which we should regard as more than adequate. For very long fast journeys people had to resort to air-liners and stratosphere-liners; but enterprising young men, and young women also, often went to the far-thest countries in their own miniature planes. These little vehicles, com-monly called 'flies', were rather smaller than our smallest gliders. The flyer lay full length on his stomach in the coffin-like fuselage, which was padded to form a sort of bed.

Towns such as we know were disappearing. It was no longer necessary for people to live in great warrens, and there was a general demand for spacious-ness. Owing to the invaluable fly, this was no longer incompatible with con-stant social intercourse. Many of the old towns were being demolished or thinned out so as to display to better advantage their few but valued archi-tectural treasures. Slums had long since been turned into parks or agricul-tural land, with here and there a village. Of the old towns, the great ports alone fulfilled their old function, but these too were transformed. Save where ground space was restricted, as in New York, the congested area gave place to a host of villages separated by parks, market gardens, orchards, and fields. The great increase of local self-sufficiency might have been expected to kill sea-borne trade, but though at first the ports declined, a new tendency soon appeared. Sub-atomic power had released so great a fund of human energy and skill that many of the peoples began to specialize once more, not indeed in the production of basic necessities, but in luxury foodstuffs, luxury hand-icrafts, superfine machines and tools. A new and fierce competition arose be-tween peoples that vied with each other to produce the very best articles of some particular type, such as optical instruments, textiles, furniture, and so on. This competition was not of the capitalist sort. Its motive was sheer pride of workmanship and enlightened patriotism. In consequence of all this new industrial specialization, sea-borne and air-borne trade, and the trans-port of goods along the great arterial roads of the continents, were still im-portant social services. Every village in this new and prosperous world de-manded that, in addition to its self-sufficiency in essentials and its pride in local craftsmanship, it should have a share in the choicest products of the ex-cess energy of all peoples.

The average individual in the new order, in whatever land he lived, was either a village craftsman in one of the specialized sub-atomic skills or a sort of glorified subsistence farmer. On his personal acre or in the communal village fields he produced enough food for his family or co-operated in the communal production of the village. Enough was left over for taxes, bartering, trade with foreign lands, and lavish hospitality. As he would not be fully occupied by the new agriculture, unless he specialized in some difficult luxury product, he might also be enough of a craftsman with the sub-atomic machinery to make many of his household goods. His wife, possibly aided by the daughters, would prepare the food and keep the house in order. With the new power and the new labour-saving devices this would occupy no more than a couple of hours a day. The women would therefore lend a hand on the farm and probably spend a good deal of time on the production of clothes for the household. The children also would help on the farm, chiefly for their education. They would learn crafts for future use. The difference between the village agriculturalists and the village craftsmen was only one of emphasis. Both classes practised both activities, but while the agriculturalists supplemented their main occupation with simple crafts, the craftsmen were tillers and gardeners in their spare time.

As in the period that we call the Middle Ages, the great majority of men were agriculturalists to some extent; though minorities specialized completely, working in the factories, laboratories, and so on. In some districts specialism was more common than elsewhere. The different countries retained much of their characteristic pattern of life, but native customs were transmuted to accord with the general pattern and spirit of the new world. In some lands the ordinary village included, along with the houses of the village craftsmen, those of the local agriculturalists, who went to the communal or private fields each day by fly. Elsewhere the villages were populated mainly by craftsmen. The agriculturalists lived in scattered farm-houses throughout the countryside. In some countries there were few specialists, in others many. In some, agriculture was mainly individualistic, though subject to strict control by the state or the village; in others it was carried on by communal village enterprise. In some, where population was sparse, the grown sons would set up new farms in the untamed land. In others, densely populated, the sons might either decide among themselves who was to take over the paternal farm, or all might stay on in the old home with their wives and families, supplementing its produce by trade in handicrafts. Sometimes the individual homestead expanded into a clan village. Sometimes a dwelling-house would be little more than a dormitory, all social activity being centred upon the village. Sometimes the villages themselves tended to be mentally dominated by some neighbouring town or metropolis. But even the greatest cities of the world were now organic clusters of villages, each making its own special contribution to the city's life.

2. Village Culture

One remarkable institution was almost universal, namely the village 'meeting', a gathering of all the villagers for the planning of their communal life. The 'meeting' took a great variety of forms in different lands; but nearly always it centred on a building which combined many of the characters of a village hall, a church, and a public-house. By some freak of the evolution of language it was known in all countries as the 'poob' [pub—the standard British term for a public house or tavern]. In it the village met every evening to yarn, play games, sing, drink their synthetic elixirs, smoke their synthetic tobaccos. It was also the communal eating-house where friends could meet over a meal, where many of the more sociable villagers fed every day, where the guests of the village were entertained, where village banquets were held. In it also the villagers met for concerts and lectures. In it at regular intervals they held their formal 'meetings' to discuss communal business and settle disputes. There they also held their sacred ceremonies, such as marriages, funerals, initiations into citizenship, commemorations of great events, local, national, or cosmopolitan.

The poob housed the village sports trophies, historical relics, and art treasures. It contained also, normally behind curtains, but displayed on great occasions, the village 'ark'. This was at once a safe where valuable documents were preserved, a mascot, a sacred symbol, and a shrine. The ark was a great carved chest, often surmounted by a symbolic statue or picture. Sometimes it was the work of local craftsmen, sometimes it was a much treasured import from the near-by city or some foreign land. These objects varied greatly in aesthetic value and in symbolic power. A few were visited by pilgrims from every part of the planet. Others, though dear and sacred to the hearts of their own villagers, drew no attention from elsewhere. These symbols sometimes represented in a stylized manner incidents of special significance in the life of the village or the nation or mankind. Sometimes they symbolized love or reason or family, or the unity of the human race, or man's relation to the cosmos. On any solemn occasion, such as a marriage or one of the regular 'days of contemplation', the ark would be unveiled, and the assembled villagers would sit in silence for a few minutes before it. Music would follow, choral or instrumental, and then the brief and simple ceremony would be performed by the village headman or some specially deputed villager or stranger, either with some well-established form of words or impromptu, or perhaps with silent gesture. When the ceremony was over the ark would be once more veiled, and the villagers would drink or feed together.

Often the poob was simply the ancient village church or temple. In cities it might be the cathedral or the city hall or some other historic building. Meetings of essentially the same type as the village meetings but more ritualistic, took place in all the cities and in each national metropolis. Specially important meetings occurred in the four great cultural world-centres, Peking, Benares, Moscow, and San Francisco. But most exalted of all were the annual commemorations in sacred Lhasa.

Now that the economic problem had been solved, public attention was more and more directed to the cultural life of the race. Education was no longer dominated by the need to equip the young for the individualistic economic 'battle of life', nor yet by the demand for efficient and docile robots. Vocational training was still an important element in education, but it no longer devoured the whole time and attention of the young people. All children were brought up mainly in their native village. There were no boarding schools, great swarms of young things living in monastic isolation from the life of the world. Normally every child lived at home, and grew up in the normal environment of farm life, acquiring the various skills which were demanded by the varied life of adults. The village schools, though some were severely criticized for inefficiency or laxity, were in the main inspired by the new tradition of the race. In every country the teachers were jealously selected, and carefully trained in the great residential universities. In some countries a group of a score or a hundred neighbouring villages might combine to set up a common school for the brighter children of the whole district. Elsewhere this principle was rejected as tending to create a class division between the bright and the dull. Instead, both types were kept in the village school, but those who showed superior capacity were allowed to absent themselves from classes so long as they kept pace with the class work. The time thus gained they spent on developing their special powers or interests. A searching system of vocational selection skimmed off from the village schools those children of leaving age who had superior aptitude for particular occupations, and those who, through high general intelligence were fitted to become teachers or research workers in some branch of science or in technical philosophy, and also those whose special talents for organizing and social intercourse were needed for industrial management, large-scale economic planning, and political leadership.

Potential artists were also selected. These might either go into residence at one of the great art schools or universities; or else, living on the maintenance grant, they could allow their genius to pursue its own course, eking out their meagre grant by selling their works. Of set purpose, and not through mere niggardliness, the state allowed the young man or woman who chose to avoid all state-organized professions only a bare minimum of help, whether his field of adventure was art or science or philosophy. Thus it was hoped to weed out those who had not actually 'got it in them' to produce creative work. On the other hand, no matter how preposterous or shocking to the public his products might be, the adventurer was at least assured of his minimum grant. And if it had any real merit (unperceived by the majority), and indeed often if it had no real merit at all, he might well succeed in selling. For, unless his work was both technically feeble and quite extravagantly idiosyncratic, it was very likely to find some sort of market in the new culturally conscious world. For in this new world-society pictures, statues, music, and writing were in demand, in some cases by the national, in others by the world-wide public, and in yet others by one or other of the special publics, each interested in some particular sphere or *genre* of art. It was not uncommon for a neglected young painter to leap from penury to affluence and fame on the sale of a single work. Many artists, however, had no such luck, and were forced to live on the maintenance grant alone throughout their lives. Some of these, ahead of their time, became world-famous after death, but the great majority were merely untalented enthusiasts. No one dreamed of grudging them their futile but harmless careers, since the community could well afford to maintain them. Indeed, since most farms kept open house for any stray travellers, and all villages provided meals and beds for a constant flow of visitors, these artistic failures could eat and sleep their way over the face of the earth and use their maintenance grant wholly for clothing and extra comforts.

3. The Forwards

One class of persons in the new world-order it is very difficult to describe. They cannot be fitted into any of our categories. Moreover their function gradually changed and increased in importance. In the earlier period of the continually developing world-Utopia they were merely tramps with a bent for self-observation, observation of their fellow men and speculation about the universe. Later, they became a recognized and increasingly respected profession. They were called by an Indian name which was translated into the English of that period as the 'forwards'. In some respects they were the equivalent of the ancient 'Servants of the Light' who had played so great a part in the overthrow of the Tyranny, but their function was not to overthrow a social order and found another. In some ways they were a religious body, but they had no common creed save their common loyalty to the spirit. Like the medieval friars they were under a vow of poverty. A forward's belongings were never to be more than such as could be carried easily in a moderate-sized rucksack. They spent much of their time wandering from village to village and from continent to continent, much also in retreat in the austere and beautiful hostels which they themselves had built with their own hands. There they occupied themselves with communal farming and craftsmanship, and also with meditation and discussion. They practised 'psychic exercise', a form of self-discipline leading to super-normal clarity and depth of experience and to profound personal integration. On their travels they often helped in harvesting or other emergency work, and they took part in the social and religious life of the villages where they stayed, absorbing the atmosphere of the local poob and in return giving whatever was communicable in their own life of contemplation and discipline. They were under no vow of chastity, but marriage and domesticity were rare among them. A few married couples lived in the hostels or wandered together, gipsy-like, with their children. The celibate sometimes permitted themselves sexual love, either with colleagues of the opposite sex or with persons outside the order. Women who bore children from these unions were not disgraced but honoured. The extra-marital sexual relationships of the forwards were mostly passionate and brief. Long before their fire was quenched the consecrated partner would hear the call to pass on. Then in grief but without rancour, and in thankfulness for the past, the lovers would part.

It was the aim of every member of the order to participate so far as possible in all the great emotional experiences of the awakened human life, while at the same time remaining in his innermost self detached from all save fundamental loyalty to the spirit. Thus sexual love, and even marriage and the responsibilities of parenthood, must be broken off at the first sign of enthralment, and on the other hand before the deep and pure current of emotion was contaminated by disillusionment. Every partner who entered into relation with one of the forwards knew well that this was the stern condition of the union. But the agony of these separations could be a fruitful agony for both members. It was the claim of many of the forwards themselves that in the desolate recovery from these partings they sometimes rose to their states of clearest vision. On the other hand those few who lived in permanent marriage were apt to pity rather than admire the majority, saying, 'Well, for each there is an appropriate way; but for us the undying, the life-giving union.'

In addition to the duty of detachment from ordinary human experiences, the forwards laid upon themselves a complementary obligation. They must in a manner preserve detachment even from their supreme consecrated task of spiritual adventure. This too, if it should become enthralling to the hungry individual spirit, or lead to any slightest withdrawal of active sympathy from the life of the world, or again if it should be poisoned by any faint breath of self-pride, must be at once abandoned. The penitent would then impose on himself some weeks or months or even years of mundane life, as a farm worker or craftsman, a factory-hand, organizer, or teacher.

The twofold aim of the forwards was to explore the highest capacities of the human spirit and to impart their findings to the world. They were very widely respected, but not universally. There were some intellectuals of sceptical temper and also some hard-headed men of affairs who regarded the whole enterprise of the forwards as futile. These critics pointed out that in the perfecting of society and the raising of average intelligence and the endless developing of intellectual culture the race would be able to occupy itself fully for centuries to come, and probably for ever. There was no need, they said, to peer into the black fog of mystery.

For hundreds, perhaps thousands, of years I seemed to watch the successful carrying out of this policy, the patient perfecting of the social organization, the amplification of human life, the slow but universal rise of intelligence, the proliferation of culture in a thousand novel directions. Throughout this long period the forwards played an unostentatious but valuable part. Their spiritual researches led to no striking discovery, but they formed mankind's permanent outposts towards the superhuman; and their influence in keeping the daily lives of ordinary men and women sweet, and in preventing the temper of the race from becoming merely mundane, was probably very great. Of course there were fluctuations in their integrity and in their usefulness, phases of corruption and regeneration, of stagnation and of significant change; periods too, when their presence was barely tolerated or even actively resented, and others when their influence was very great. But on the whole throughout this age their part was never central and dominant, as it was later to become.

[William] Olaf Stapledon (1886–1950) was a British philosopher and science fiction writer.

Source: [William] Olaf Stapledon, Darkness and the Light (London: Methuen, 1942), 143–46.

B. F. Skinner
Walden Two

B. F. Skinner was a Harvard University psychologist who pioneered behaviorism in psychology. Skinner hoped to discover determinants of behavior and believed that, once discovered, these could be used to improve society. His novel *Walden Two* was his attempt to represent a society governed by the principles of behaviorism. In the essay "Walden Two Revisted" (1976), he argued for the principles presented in the novel. *Walden Two* inspired a number of communal societies. The two best known, Twin Oaks in Virginia and East Wind in Missouri, have largely abandoned the details of this model. Los Horcones, a small community in Mexico, still uses Skinner's model.

Castle got his chance to take up "general issues" that afternoon. A walk to the summit of Stone Hill had been planned for a large party, which included Mr. and Mrs. Meyerson and three or four children. It seemed unlikely that any serious discussion would be possible. But a storm had been threatening all morning, and at lunch we heard it break. The afternoon was again open. I detected a certain activity in the dining room as plans were changed. As we were finishing dinner two young people approached our table and spoke to Rodge, Steve, and the girls.

"Do you play? Cornet, sax, trombone? We're getting up a concert. We even have a lonely tuba."

"You play, Steve," said Mary

"Steve was the best little old trombone in the Philippines," said Rodge.

"Good! Anybody else? It's strictly amateur."

It appeared that Barbara could play popular tunes on the piano, mostly by ear, and it was thought that something might be arranged. They departed for the theater to look over the common stock of instruments, and Frazier, Castle, and I were left alone.

Castle immediately began to warm up his motors. He picked up an empty cigarette package which Barbara had left on the table, tore it in two, placed the halves together, and tore them again. Various husky noises issued from his throat. It was obvious that something was about to happen, and Frazier and I waited in silence.

"Mr. Frazier," Castle said at last, in a sudden roar, "I accuse you of one of the most diabolical machinations in the history of mankind!" He looked as steadily as possible at Frazier, but he was trembling, and his eyes were popping.

"Shall we go to my room?" Frazier said quietly.

It was a trick of Frazier's to adopt a contrasting tone of voice, and in this instance it was devastating. Castle came down to earth with a humiliating bump. He had prepared himself for a verbal battle of heroic dimensions, but he found himself humbly carrying his tray to the service window and trailing Frazier along the Walk.

I was not sure of the line Castle was going to take. Apparently he had done some thinking since morning, probably during the service, but I could not guess the result. Frazier's manner was also puzzling. His suggestion that we go to his room had sounded a little as if he were inviting a truculent companion to "step outside and say that again!" He had apparently expected the attack from Castle and had prepared the defenses to his satisfaction.

When we had settled ourselves in Frazier's room, with Frazier full-length on the bed, over which he had hastily pulled a cover, Castle began again in an unsuccessful attempt to duplicate the surprise and force of his first assault.

"A modern, mechanized, managerial Machiavelli—that is my final estimate of you, Mr. Frazier," he said, with the same challenging stare.

"It must be gratifying to know that one has reached a 'final estimate,'" said Frazier.

"An artist in power," Castle continued, "whose greatest art is to conceal art. The silent despot."

"Since we are dealing in 'M's,' why not sum it all up and say 'Mephistophelian'?" said Frazier, curiously reviving my fears of the preceding afternoon.

"I'm willing to do that!" said Castle. "And unless God is very sure of himself, I suspect He's by no means easy about this latest turn in the war of the angels. So far as I can see, you've blocked every path through which man was to struggle upward toward salvation. Intelligence, initiative—you have filled their places with a sort of degraded instinct, engineered compulsion. Walden Two is a marvel of efficient coordination—as efficient as an anthill!"

"Replacing intelligence with instinct—" muttered Frazier. "I had never thought of that. It's an interesting possibility. How's it done?" It was a crude maneuver. The question was a digression, intended to spoil Castle's timing and to direct our attention to practical affairs in which Frazier was more at home.

"The behavior of your members is carefully shaped in advance by a Plan," said Castle, not to be taken in, "and it's shaped to perpetuate that Plan. Intellectually Walden Two is quite as incapable of a spontaneous change of course as the life within a beehive."

"I see what you mean," said Frazier distantly. But he returned to his strategy. "And have you discovered the machinery of my power?"

"I have, indeed. We were looking in the wrong place. There's no *current* contact between you and the members of Walden Two. You threw us off the track very skillfully on that point last night. But you were behaving as a despot when you first laid your plans—when you designed the social structure and drew up the contract between community and member, when you worked out your educational practices and your guarantees against despotism—What a joker! Don't tell me you weren't in control *then*! Burris saw the point. What about your career as organizer? *There* was leadership! And the most damnable leadership in history, because you were setting the stage for the withdrawal of yourself as a personal force, knowing full well that everything that happened would still be your doing. Hundreds—you predicted millions—of unsuspecting souls were to fall within the scope of your ambitious scheme."

Castle was driving his argument home with great excitement, but Frazier was lying in exaggerated relaxation, staring at the ceiling, his hands cupped behind his head.

"Very good, Mr. Castle," he said softly. "I gave you the clue, of course, when we parted last night."

"You did, indeed. And I've wondered why. Were you led into that fatal error by your conceit? Perhaps that's the ultimate answer to your form of despotism. No one could enjoy the power you have seized without wishing to display it from time to time."

"I've admitted neither power nor despotism. But you're quite right in saying that I've exerted an influence and in one sense will continue to exert it forever.

I believe you called me a *primum mobile*—not quite correctly, as I found upon looking the term up last night. But I did plan Walden Two—not as an architect plans a building, but as a scientist plans a long-term experiment, uncertain of the conditions he will meet but knowing how he will deal with them when they arise. In a sense, Walden Two is predetermined, but not as the behavior of a beehive is determined. Intelligence, no matter how much it may be shaped and extended by our educational system, will still function as intelligence. It will be used to puzzle out solutions to problems to which a beehive would quickly succumb. What the plan does is to keep intelligence on the right track, for the good of society rather than of the intelligent individual—or for the eventual rather than the immediate good of the individual. It does this by making sure that the individual will not forget his personal stake in the welfare of society."

"But you are forestalling many possibly useful acts of intelligence which aren't encompassed by your plan.

"You have ruled out points of view which may be more productive. You are implying that T. E. Frazier, looking at the world from the middle of the twentieth century, understands the best course for mankind forever."

"Yes, I suppose I do."

"But that's absurd!"

"Not at all. I don't say I foresee the course man will take a hundred years hence, let alone forever, but I know which he should take now."

"How can you be sure of it? It's certainly not a question you have answered experimentally."

"I think we're in the course of answering it," said Frazier. "But that's beside the point. There's no alternative. We must take that course."

"But that's fantastic. You who are taking it are in a small minority."

Frazier sat up.

"And the majority are in a big quandary," he said. "They're not on the road at all, or they're scrambling back toward their starting point, or sidling from one side of the road to the other like so many crabs. What do you think two world wars have been about? Something as simple as boundaries or trade? Nonsense. The world is trying to adjust to a new conception of man in relation to men."

"Perhaps it's merely trying to adjust to despots whose ideas are incompatible with the real nature of man."

"Mr. Castle," said Frazier very earnestly, "let me ask you a question. I warn you, it will be the most terrifying question of your life. *What would you do if you found yourself in possession of an effective science of behavior?* Suppose you suddenly found it possible to control the behavior of men as you wished. What would you do?"

"That's an assumption?"

"Take it as one if you like. *I* take it as a fact. And apparently you accept it as a fact too. I can hardly be as despotic as you claim unless I hold the key to an extensive practical control."

"What would I do?" said Castle thoughtfully. "I think *I* would dump your science of behavior in the ocean."

"And deny men all the help you could otherwise give them?"

"How could you give them freedom?"

"By refusing to control them!"

"But you would only be leaving the control in other hands."

"Whose?"

"The charlatan, the demagogue, the salesman, the ward heeler, the bully; the cheat, the educator, the priest—all who are now in possession of the techniques of behavioral engineering."

"A pretty good share of the control would remain in the hands of the individual himself."

"That's an assumption, too, and it's your only hope. It's your only possible chance to avoid the implications of a science of behavior. If man is free, then a technology of behavior is impossible. But I'm asking you to consider the other case."

"Then my answer is that your assumption is contrary to fact and any further consideration idle."

"And your accusations—?"

"—were in terms of intention, not of possible achievement."

Frazier sighed dramatically.

"It's a little late to be proving that a behavioral technology is well advanced. How can you deny it? Many of its methods and techniques are really as old as the hills. Look at their frightful misuse in the hands of the Nazis! And what about the techniques of the psychological clinic? What about education? Or religion? Or practical politics? Or advertising and salesmanship? Bring them all together and you have a sort of rule-of-thumb technology of vast power. No, Mr. Castle, the science is there for the asking. But its techniques and methods are in the wrong hands—they are used for personal aggrandizement in a competitive world or, in the case of the psychologist and educator, for futilely corrective purposes. My question is, have you the courage to take up and wield the science of behavior for the good of mankind? You answer that you would dump it in the ocean!"

"I'd want to take it out of the hands of the politicians and advertisers and salesmen, too."

"And the psychologists and educators? You see, Mr. Castle, you can't have that kind of cake. The fact is, we not only *can* control human behavior, we *must*. But who's to do it, and what's to be done?"

"So long as a trace of personal freedom survives, I'll stick to my position," said Castle, very much out of countenance.

"Isn't it time we talked about freedom?" I said. "We parted a day or so ago on an agreement to let the question of freedom ring. It's time to answer don't you think?"

"My answer is simple enough." said Frazier. "I deny that freedom exists at all. I must deny it—or my program would be absurd. You can't have a science about a subject matter which hops capriciously about. Perhaps we can never *prove* that man isn't free: it's an assumption. But the increasing success of a science of behavior makes it more and more plausible."

"On the contrary, a simple personal experience makes it untenable." said Castle. "The experience of freedom. I *know* that I'm free."

"It must be quite consoling," said Frazier.

"And what's more—you do, too," said Castle hotly. "When you deny your own freedom for the sake of playing with a science of behavior, you're acting in plain bad faith. That's the only way I can explain it." He tried to recover himself and shrugged his shoulders. "At least you'll grant that you *feel* free."

"The 'feeling of freedom' should deceive no one," said Frazier. "Give me a concrete case.

"Well, right now," Castle said. He picked up a book of matches. "I'm free to hold or drop these matches."

"You will, of course, do one or the other," said Frazier. "Linguistically or logically there seem to be two possibilities, but I submit that there's only one in fact. The determining forces may be subtle but they are inexorable. I suggest that as an orderly person you will probably hold—ah! you drop them! Well, you see, that's all part of your behavior with respect to me. You couldn't resist the temptation to prove me wrong. It was all lawful. You had no choice. The deciding factor entered rather late, and naturally you couldn't foresee the result when you first held them up. There was no strong likelihood that you would act in either direction, and so you said you were free."

"That's entirely too glib," said Castle. "It's easy to argue lawfulness after the fact. But let's see you predict what I will do in advance. Then I'll agree there's law."

"I didn't say that behavior is always predictable, any more than the weather is always predictable. There are often too many factors to be taken into account. We can't measure them all accurately, and we couldn't perform the mathematical operations needed to make a prediction if we had the measurements. The legality is usually an assumption—but none the less important in judging the issue at hand."

"Take a case where there's no choice, then," said Castle. "Certainly a man in jail isn't free in the sense in which I am free now."

"Good! That's an excellent start. Let us classify the kinds of determiners of human behavior. One class, as you suggest, is physical restraint—handcuffs, iron bars, forcible coercion. These are ways in which we shape human behavior according to our wishes. They're crude, and they sacrifice the affection of the controllee, but they often work. Now, what other ways are there of limiting freedom?"

Frazier had adopted a professorial tone and Castle refused to answer.

"The threat of force would be one," I said.

"Right. And here again we shan't encourage any loyalty on the part of the controllee. He has perhaps a shade more of the feeling of freedom, since he can always 'choose to act and accept the consequences,' but he doesn't feel exactly free. He knows his behavior is being coerced. Now what else?"

I had no answer.

"Force or the threat of force—I see no other possibility," said Castle after a moment.

"Precisely," said Frazier.

"But certainly a large part of my behavior has no connection with force at all. There's my freedom!" said Castle.

"I wasn't agreeing that there was no other possibility—merely that *you* could see no other. Not being a good behaviorist—or a good Christian, for that matter—you have no feeling for a tremendous power of a different sort."

"What's that?"

"I shall have to be technical," said Frazier. "But only for a moment. It's what the science of behavior calls 'reinforcement theory.' The things that can happen to us fall into three classes. To some things we are indifferent. Other things we like—we want them to happen, and we take steps to make them happen again. Still other things we don't like—we don't want them to happen and we take steps to get rid of them or keep them from happening again.

"*Now,*" Frazier continued earnestly, "if it's in our power to create any of the situations which a person likes or to remove any situation he doesn't like, we can control his behavior. When he behaves as we want him to behave, we simply create a situation he likes, or remove one he doesn't like. As a result, the probability that he will behave that way again goes up, which is what we want. Technically it's called 'positive reinforcement.'

"The old school made the amazing mistake of supposing that the reverse was true, that by removing a situation a person likes or setting up one he doesn't like—in other words by punishing him—it was possible to *reduce* the probability that he would behave in a given way again. That simply doesn't hold. It has been established beyond question. What is emerging at this critical stage in the evolution of society is a behavioral and cultural technology based on positive reinforcement alone. We are gradually discovering—at an untold cost in human suffering—that in the long run punishment doesn't reduce the probability that an act will occur. We have been so preoccupied with the contrary that we always take 'force' to mean punishment. We don't say we're using force when we send shiploads of food into a starving country, though we're displaying quite as much *power* as if we were sending troops and guns."

"I'm certainly not an advocate of force," said Castle "But I can't agree that it's not effective."

"It's *temporarily* effective, that's the worst of it. That explains several thousand years of bloodshed. Even nature has been fooled. We 'instinctively' punish a person who doesn't behave as we like—we spank him if he's a child or strike him if he's a man. A nice distinction! The immediate effect of the blow teaches us to strike again. Retribution and revenge are the most natural things on earth. But in the long run the man we strike is no less likely to repeat his act."

"But he won't repeat it if we hit him hard enough," said Castle.

"He'll still *tend* to repeat it. He'll want to repeat it. We haven't really altered his potential behavior at all. That's the pity of it. If he doesn't repeat it in our presence, he will in the presence of someone else. Or it will be repeated in the disguise of a neurotic symptom. If we hit hard enough, we clear a little place for ourselves in the wilderness of civilization, but we make the rest of the wilderness still more terrible.

"Now, early forms of government are naturally based on punishment. It's the obvious technique when the physically strong control the weak. But we're in the throes of a great change to positive reinforcement—from a competitive society in which one man's reward is another man's punishment, to a cooperative society in which no one gains at the expense of anyone else.

"The change is slow and painful because the immediate, temporary effect of punishment overshadows the eventual advantage of positive reinforcement. We've all seen countless instances of the temporary effect of force, but clear evidence of the effect of not using force is rare. That's why I insist that Jesus, who was apparently the first to discover the power of refusing to punish, must have hit upon the principle by accident. He certainly had none of the experimental evidence which is available to us today, and I can't conceive that it was possible, no matter what the man's genius, to have discovered the principle from casual observation."

"A touch of revelation, perhaps?" said Castle.

"No, accident. Jesus discovered one principle because it had immediate consequences, and he got another thrown in for good measure."

I began to see light.

"You mean the principle of 'love your enemies'?"

"Exactly! To 'do good to those who despitefully use you' has two unrelated consequences. You gain the peace of mind we talked about the other day. Let the stronger man push you around—at least you avoid the torture of your own rage. *That's* the immediate consequence. What an astonishing discovery it must have been to find that in the long run you could *control the stronger man* in the same way!"

"It's generous of you to give so much credit to your early colleague," said Castle, "but why are we still in the throes of so much misery? Twenty centuries should have been enough for one piece of behavioral engineering."

"The conditions which made the principle difficult to discover made it difficult to teach. The history of the Christian Church doesn't reveal many cases of doing good to one's enemies. To inoffensive heathens, perhaps, but not enemies. One must look outside the field of organized religion to find the principle in practice at all. Church governments are devotees of *power*, both temporal and bogus."

"But what has all this got to do with freedom?" I said hastily.

Frazier took time to reorganize his behavior. He looked steadily toward the window, against which the rain was beating heavily.

"Now that we *know* how positive reinforcement works and why negative doesn't," he said at last, "we can be more deliberate, and hence more successful, in our cultural design. We can achieve a sort of control under which the controlled, though they are following a code much more scrupulously than was ever the case under the old system, nevertheless *feel free*. They are doing what they want to do, not what they are forced to do. That's the source of the tremendous power of positive reinforcement—there's no restraint and no revolt. By a careful cultural design, we control not the final behavior, but the *inclination* to behave—the motives, the desires, the wishes.

"The curious thing is that in that case *the question of freedom never arises.* Mr. Castle was free to drop the matchbook in the sense that nothing was preventing him. If it had been securely bound to his hand he wouldn't have been free. Nor would he have been quite free if I'd covered him with a gun and threatened to shoot him if he let it fall. The question of freedom arises when there is restraint—either physical or psychological.

"But restraint is only one sort of control, and absence of restraint isn't freedom. It's not control that's lacking when one feels 'free,' but the objectionable control of force. Mr. Castle felt free to hold or drop the matches in the sense that he felt no restraint—no threat of punishment in taking either course of action. He neglected to examine his positive reasons for holding or letting go, in spite of the fact that these were more compelling in this instance than any threat of force.

"We have no vocabulary of freedom in dealing with what we want to do," Frazier went on. "The question never arises. When men strike for freedom, they strike against jails and the police, or the threat of them—against oppression. They never strike against forces which make them want to act the way they do. Yet, it seems to be understood that governments will operate only through force or the threat of force, and that all other principles of control will be left to education, religion, and commerce. If this continues to be the case, we may as well give up. A government can never create a free people with the techniques now allotted to it.

"The question is: Can men live in freedom and peace? And the answer is: Yes, if we can build a social structure which will satisfy the needs of everyone and in which everyone will want to observe the supporting code. But so far this has been achieved only in Walden Two. Your ruthless accusations to the contrary, Mr. Castle, this is the freest place on earth. And it is free precisely because we make no use of force or the threat of force. Every bit of our research, from the nursery through the psychological management of our adult membership, is directed toward that end—to exploit every alternative to forcible control. By skillful planning, by a wise choice of techniques we *increase* the feeling of freedom.

"It's not planning which infringes upon freedom, but planning which uses force. A sense of freedom was practically unknown in the planned society of Nazi Germany, because the planners made a fantastic use of force and the threat of force.

"No, Mr. Castle, when a science of behavior has once been achieved, there's no alternative to a planned society. We can't leave mankind to an accidental or biased control. But by using the principle of positive reinforcement—carefully avoiding force or the threat of force—we can preserve a personal sense of freedom."

Frazier threw himself back upon the bed and stared at the ceiling.

"But you haven't denied that you are in complete control," said Castle. "You are still the long-range dictator."

"As you will," said Frazier, waving his hands loosely in the air and then cupping them behind his head. "In fact, I'm inclined to agree. When you have once grasped the principle of positive reinforcement, you can enjoy a sense of unlimited power. It's enough to satisfy the thirstiest tyrant."

"There you are, then," said Castle. "That's my case."

"But it's a limited sort of despotism," Frazier went on. "And I don't think anyone should worry about it. The despot must wield his power for the good of others. If he takes any step which reduces the sum total of human happiness, his power is reduced by a like amount. What better check against a malevolent despotism could you ask for?"

"The check I ask for," said Castle, "is nothing less than democracy. Let the people rule and power will not be misused. I can't see that the nature of the power matters. As a matter of fact, couldn't this principle of 'positive reinforcement,' as you call it, be used by a democratic government just as well as by your dictatorship?"

"No principle is consistently used by a democratic government. What do you mean by democracy, anyway?"

"Government by the people or according to the will of the people, naturally," said Castle.

"As exemplified by current practices in the United States?"

"I suppose so. Yes, I'll take my stand on that. It's not a perfect democracy, but it's the best there is at the moment."

"Then I say that democracy is a pious fraud," said Frazier. "In what sense is it 'government by the people'?"

"In an obvious sense, I should say."

"It isn't obvious at all. How is the people's will ascertained? In an election. But what a travesty! In a small committee meeting, or even a town hall, I can see some point in voting, especially on a yes-or-no question. But fifty million voters choosing a president—that's quite another thing."

"I can't see that the number of voters changes the principle," said Castle.

"The chance that one man's vote will decide the issue in a national election," said Frazier, speaking very deliberately, "is less than the chance that he will be killed on his way to the polls. We pay no attention whatsoever to chances of that magnitude in our daily affairs. We should call a man a fool who bought a sweepstakes ticket with similar odds against him."

"It must mean something or people wouldn't vote," said Castle.

"How many of them would go on voting if they were free of a lot of extraneous pressures? Do you think a man goes to the polls because of any effect which casting a vote has ever had? By no means. He goes to avoid being talked about by his neighbors, or to 'knife' a candidate whom he dislikes, marking his X as he might defile a campaign poster—and with the same irrational spite. No, a man has no logical reason to vote whatsoever. The chances of affecting the issue are too small to alter his behavior, in any appreciable way."

"I believe the mathematicians have a name for that fallacy," said Castle. "It's true that your chances of deciding the issue get smaller as the number of voters increases, but the stakes get larger at the same rate."

"But do they? Is a national election really an important issue? Does it really matter very much who wins? The platforms of the two parties are carefully made as much alike as possible, and when the election is over we're all advised to accept the result like good sports. Only a few voters go on caring very much after a week or two. The rest know there's no real threat. Things will go on pretty much the same. Elections are sometimes turned by a few million voters who can't make up their minds until election day. It can't be much of an issue if that's the case."

"Even so, it's important that the people feel they've chosen the government they want," said Castle.

"On the contrary, that's the worst of it. Voting is a device for blaming conditions on the people. The people aren't rulers, they're scapegoats. And they file to the polls every so often to renew their right to the title."

"I daresay there are defects in the machinery of democracy," said Castle. "No one wholly approves of the average presidential campaign. The will of the people is likely to be unduly influenced, and perhaps incorrectly determined. But that's a matter of technique. I think we will eventually work out a better system for ascertaining what the people want done. Democracy isn't a method of polling opinion, it's the assignment of power to that opinion. Let's assume that the will of the people can be ascertained. What then?"

"I should ask you that. What then, indeed? Are the people skilled governors? No. And they become less and less skilled, relatively speaking, as the science of government advances. It's the same point I raised in our discussion of the group nursery: when we've once acquired a behavioral technology, we can't leave the control of behavior to the unskilled. Your answer is to deny that the technology exists—a very feeble answer, it seems to me.

"The one thing the people know," Frazier continued, "and the one thing about which they should be heard is how they like the existing state of affairs, and perhaps how they would like some other state of affairs. What they conspicuously don't know is how to get what they want. That's a matter for specialists."

"But the people have solved some pretty important problems," I said

"Have they, in fact? The actual practice in a democracy is to vote, not for a given state of affairs, but for a man who claims to be able to achieve that state. I'm not a historian"—Frazier laughed explosively—"quite the contrary—but I suspect that that's always what is meant by the rule of the people—rule by a man chosen by the people."

"Isn't that a possible way out, though?" said Castle. "Suppose we need experts. Why not elect them?"

"For a very simple reason. The people are in no position to evaluate experts. And elected experts are never able to act as they think best. They can't experiment. The amateur doesn't appreciate the need for experimentation. He wants his expert to know. And he's utterly incapable of sustaining the period of doubt during which an experiment works itself out. The experts must either disguise their experiments and pretend to know the outcome in advance or stop experimenting altogether and struggle to maintain the *status quo*."

"'With all her faults, I love her still,'" said Castle. "I'll take democracy. We may have to muddle through. We may seem laughable to your streamlined Planners. But we have one thing on our side—freedom."

"I thought we had settled that," said Frazier.

"We had. But apparently not as you thought," said Castle. "I don't like despotism."

Frazier got up and went to the window. The rain had stopped, and the distant hills beyond the river had become visible. He stood with his back to us for perhaps a minute, which seemed very long against the energetic tempo of our conversation. Finally he turned.

"Can't I make you understand?" he said, holding out his hands in a gesture of appeal. "*I don't like despotism either!* I don't like the despotism of ignorance I don't like the despotism of neglect, of irresponsibility, the despotism of accident, even. And I don't like the despotism of democracy!"

He turned back to the window.

"I don't think I follow you," said Castle, somewhat softened by Frazier's evident emotion.

"Democracy is the spawn of despotism," Frazier said, continuing to look out the window. "And like father, like son. Democracy is power and rule. It's not the will of the people, remember; it's the will of the majority." He turned and, in a husky voice which broke in flight like a tumbler pigeon on the word "out," he added, "My heart goes out to the everlasting minority." He seemed ready to cry, but I could not tell whether it was in sympathy for the oppressed or in rage at his failure to convince Castle.

"In a democracy," he went on, "there is *no* check against despotism, because the principle of democracy is supposed to be itself a check. But it guarantees only that the *majority* will not be despotically ruled."

"I don't agree that the minority has no say," said Castle. "But in any case it's better that at least half the people get what they want, instead of a small élite."

"There you are!" said Frazier, jumping up again just as he had started to sit down. "The majority are an élite. And they're despots. I want none of them! Let's have government for the benefit of all."

"But that isn't always possible," said Castle.

"It's possible much oftener than under a democracy. There are seldom any issues which have to be decided in an all-or-none fashion. A careful planner could work out a compromise which would be reasonably satisfying to everyone. But in a democracy, the majority solve the problem to their satisfaction, and the minority can be damned.

"The government of Walden Two," he continued, "has the virtues of democracy, but none of the defects. It's much closer to the theory or intent of democracy than the actual practice in America today. The will of the people is carefully ascertained. We have no election campaigns to falsify issues or obscure them with emotional appeals, but a careful study of the satisfaction of the membership is made. Every member has a direct channel through which he may protest to the Managers or even the Planners. And these protests are taken as seriously as the pilot of an airplane takes a sputtering engine. We don't need laws and a police force to compel a pilot to pay attention to a defective engine. Nor do we need laws to compel our Dairy Manager to pay attention to an epidemic among his cows. Similarly, our Behavioral and Cultural Managers need not be compelled to consider grievances. A grievance is a wheel to be oiled, or a broken pipe line to be repaired.

"Most of the people in Walden Two take no active part in running the government. And they don't want an active part. The urge to have a say in how the country should be run is a recent thing. It was not part of early democracy. The original victory over tyranny was a constitutional guarantee of personal rights, including the right to protest if conditions were not satisfactory. But the business of ruling was left to somebody else. Nowadays, everybody fancies himself an expert in government and wants to have a say. Let's hope it's a temporary cultural pattern. I can remember when everyone could talk about the mechanical principles according to which his automobile ran or failed to run. Everyone was an automotive specialist and knew how to file the points of a magneto and take the shimmy out of front wheels. To suggest that these matters might be left to experts would have been called Fascism, if the term had been invented. But today no one knows how his car operates and I can't see that he's any the less happy.

"In Walden Two no one worries about the government except the few to whom that worry has been assigned. To suggest that everyone should take an interest would seem as fantastic as to suggest that everyone should become familiar with our Diesel engines. Even the constitutional rights of the members are seldom thought about, I'm sure. The only thing that matters is one's day-to-day happiness and a secure future. Any infringement there would undoubtedly 'arouse the electorate.'"

"I assume that your constitution at least can't be changed without a vote of the members," I said.

"Wrong again. It can be changed by a unanimous vote of the Planners and a two-thirds vote of the Managers. You're still thinking about government by the people. Get that out of your head. The people are in no better position to change the constitution than to decide upon current practices."

"Then what's to prevent your Planners from becoming despots?" I said. "Wouldn't it really be possible?"

"How?" said Frazier.

"Oh, in many ways, I imagine."

"Such as?"

"Well, if I were a Planner with a yen for despotism I would begin by insinuating into the culture the notion that Planners were exceptional people. I would argue that they should be personally known to members, and should therefore wear an identifying badge or uniform. This could be done under the guise of facilitating service to the members, but eventually the Planners would be set off as a separate caste. Then they'd be relieved from menial work on the ground that they were too busy with the affairs of the community. Then special quarters, perhaps quite luxurious, would be built for them. I'd bring the Managers around to this change in the constitution by giving them better quarters also. It would all be carefully propagandized, of course. Eventually more and more of the wealth of the community would be diverted to this élite, and I would come out with a true despotism. Isn't that possible?"

"If you mean, 'Isn't despotism possible?' the answer is yes," said Frazier. "Cultures which work for the advantage of a few last a long time. Look at India, where the oppressed aren't even aware that they are sick and miserable. But are the people strong, productive, progressive? If not, then the culture will eventually be replaced by competing cultures which work more efficiently. Our Planners know this. They know that any usurpation of power would weaken the community as a whole and eventually destroy the whole venture."

"A group of despotic planners might be willing to sacrifice the community," I said. "They wouldn't necessarily suffer if it failed. They could simply abscond with the funds."

"That would be a catastrophe. Like an earthquake, or a new and frightful epidemic, or a raid from another world. All we can do is take reasonable precautions. Your hypothetical case strikes me as implausible, that's all I can say."

"But isn't that just the weakness of your antidemocratic attitude?" Castle said. "Haven't you lost your guarantee against the usurpation of power?"

"There's no power to usurp," said Frazier. "There's no police, no military, no guns or bombs—tear-gas or atomic—to give strength to the few. In point of physical force the members are always clearly in power. Revolt is not only easy, it's inevitable if real dissatisfaction arises.

"And there's little real wealth to tempt anyone. It isn't true that the Planners could abscond with the funds. Our wealth is our happiness. The physical plant of the community would be practically worthless without the members.

"And then remember that the Planners are part of a noncompetitive culture in which a thirst for power is a curiosity. They have no reason to usurp. Their tradition is against it. Any gesture of personal domination would stand out as conspicuously as the theft of the bulletin board."

"But it's human to dominate," said Castle, "in any culture."

"That's an experimental question, Mr. Castle. You can't answer it from your armchair. But let's see what a usurpation of power would amount to. Insofar as the Planners rule at all, they do so through positive reinforcement. They don't use or threaten to use force. They have no machinery for that. In order to extend their power they would have to provide more and more satisfying conditions. A curious sort of despotism, Mr. Castle."

"But they might change to a different sort of power."

"That would require a unanimous vote. But the Planners are eventually demoted to simple citizenship. Their terms of office are staggered, and some of them are always so close to retirement that they wouldn't share in the selfish consequences. Why should they vote for the change?

"Usurpation of power is a threat only in a competitive culture," Frazier continued. "In Walden Two power is either destroyed or so diffused that usurpation is practically impossible. Personal ambition isn't essential in a good governor. As governmental technology advances, less and less is left to the decisions of governors, anyway. Eventually we shall have no use for Planners at all. The Managers will suffice."

Frazier turned to me in an open gesture of appeasement.

"Democracy is not a guarantee against despotism, Burris. Its virtues are of another sort. It has proved itself clearly superior to the despotic rule of a small élite. We have seen it survive in conflict with the despotic pattern in World War II. The democratic peoples proved themselves superior just because of their democracy. They could enlist the support of other peoples, who had less to fear from them than from an aggressive élite. They could marshal greater manpower in the long run because everyone had a stake in victory and few were suffering from the strain of forcible coercion. The despots couldn't convert the people they conquered while pretending to be a superior race. Every principle which seemed to strengthen the governmental structure of Fascism when the war began proved to be an eventual weakness.

"But the triumph of democracy doesn't mean it's the best government. It was merely the better in a contest with a conspicuously bad one. Let's not stop with democracy. It isn't, and can't be, the best form of government, because it's based on a scientifically invalid conception of man. It fails to take account of the fact that in the long run *man is determined by the state*. A *laissez-faire* philosophy which trusts to the inherent goodness and wisdom of the common man is incompatible with the observed fact that men are made good or bad and wise or foolish by the environment in which they grow."

"But which comes first," I asked, "the hen or the egg? Men build society and society builds men. Where do we start?"

"It isn't a question of starting. The start has been made. It's a question of what's to be done from now on."

"Then it's to be revolution, is that it?" said Castle. "If democracy can't change itself into something better."

"Revolution? You're not a very rewarding pupil, Mr. Castle. The change won't come about through power politics at all. It will take place at another level altogether."

"What level?"

Frazier waved his hand toward the window, through which we could see the drenched landscape of Walden Two.

"Well," said Castle, "you'd better hurry up. It's not a job to be done on four hours a day."

"Four hours a day is exactly what it needs," said Frazier with a smile. He lay back upon the bed, looking rather tired.

"I can think of a conspicuous case in which the change you're advocating is coming about at the level of power politics," I said.

Frazier sat up quickly, with obvious effort. He looked at me suspiciously.

"Russia," I said.

"Ah, Russia," he said with relief. He showed no inclination to go on.

"What about Russia, though?"

"What about it, indeed?"

"Isn't there a considerable resemblance between a Russian communism and your own philosophy?"

"Russia, Russia," Frazier murmured evasively. "Our visitors always ask that. Russia is our rival. It's very flattering—if you consider the resources and the numbers of people involved."

"But you're dodging my question. Hasn't Russia done what you're trying to do, but at the level of power politics? I can imagine what a Communist would say of your program at Walden Two. Wouldn't he simply tell you to drop the experiment and go to work for the Party?"

"He would and he does."

"And what's your answer?"

"I can see only four things wrong with Russia," Frazier said, clearly enjoying the condescension. "As originally conceived, it was a good try. It sprang from humanitarian impulses which are a commonplace in Walden Two. But it quickly developed certain weaknesses. There are four of them, and they were inevitable. They were inevitable just because the attempt was made at the level of power politics." He waited for me to ask him what the weaknesses were.

"The first," he said, as soon as I had done so, "is a decline in the experimental spirit. Many promising experiments have simply been dropped. The group care of children, the altered structure of the family, the abandonment of religion, new kinds of personal incentives—all these problems were 'solved' by dropping back to practices which have prevailed in capitalistic societies for centuries. It was the old difficulty. A government in power can't experiment. It must know the answers or at least pretend to know them. Today the Russians contend that an optimal cultural pattern has been achieved, if not yet fully implemented. They dare not admit to any serious need for improvement. Revolutionary experimentation is dead.

"In the second place, Russia has overpropagandized both to its own people and to the outside world. Their propaganda is much more extensive than any which ever enslaved a working class. That's a serious defect, for it has made it impossible to evaluate their success. We don't know how much of the current vigor of Russian communism is due to a strong, satisfying way of life, and how much to indoctrination. You may call it a temporary expedient, to counteract the propaganda embedded in an older culture. But that need has long since passed, yet the propaganda continues. So long as it goes on, no valid data on the effectiveness of Russian communism can be obtained. For all we know, the whole culture would fall apart if the supporting attitudes were taken away. And what is worse, it's hard to see how they can ever be taken away. Propaganda makes it impossible to progress toward a form of society in which it is unnecessary.

"The third weakness of the Russian government is its use of heroes. The first function of the hero, in Russia as elsewhere, is to piece out a defective governmental structure. Important decisions aren't made by appeal to a set of principles; they are personal acts. The process of governing is an art, not a science, and the government is only as good or as long-lasting as the artist. As to the second function of the hero—how long would communism last if all the pictures of Lenin and Stalin were torn down? It's a question worth asking.

"But most important of all, the Russian experiment was based on power. You may argue that the seizure of power was also a temporary expedient, since the people who held it were intolerant and oppressive. But you can hardly defend the continued use of power in that way. The Russians are still a long way from a culture in which people behave as they *want* to behave, for their mutual good. In order to get its people to act as the communist pattern demands, the Russian government has had to use the techniques of capitalism. On the one hand it resorts to extravagant and uneven rewards. But an unequal distribution of wealth destroys more incentives than it creates. It obviously can't operate for the *common* good. On the other hand, the government also uses punishment or the threat of it. What kind of behavioral engineering do you call that?"

Frazier spat into the flowerpot in a gesture of disgust. Then he held out his hands with an exaggerated shrug and drew himself slowly to his feet. He had evidently had enough of Castle's "general issues."

"Walden Two Revisited"

THE EARLY summer of 1945 when I wrote *Walden Two* was not a bad time for Western Civilization. Hitler was dead, and one of the most barbaric regimes in history was coming to an end. The Depression of the thirties had been forgotten. Communism was no longer a threat, for Russia was a trusted ally. It would be another month or two before Hiroshima would be the testing ground for a horrible new weapon. A few cities had a touch of smog but no one worried about the environment as a whole. There were wartime shortages, but industry would soon turn again to devoting unlimited resources to the fulfillment of unlimited desires. The industrial revolution was said to have stilled the voice of Thomas Robert Malthus.[1]

The dissatisfactions which led me to write *Walden Two* were personal. I had seen my wife and her friends struggling to save themselves from domesticity, wincing as they printed "housewife" in those blanks asking for occupation. Our older daughter had just finished first grade, and there is nothing like a first child's first year in school to turn one's thoughts to education. We were soon to leave Minnesota and move to Indiana—and I had been in search of housing. I would be leaving a group of talented young string players who had put up with my inadequacies at the piano and I was not sure I could ever replace them. I had just finished a productive year on a Guggenheim Fellowship, but I had accepted the chairmanship of a department at Indiana and was not sure when I would again have time for science or scholarship. Was there not something to be done about problems of that sort? Was there not by any chance something a science of behavior could do?

It was probably a good thing that these were small provincial problems, because I might not have had the courage to tackle bigger ones. In *Behavior of Organisms*, published seven years earlier, I had refused to apply my results outside the laboratory. "Let him extrapolate who will," I had said. But, of course, I had speculated about the technology that a science of behavior implied and about the differences it could make. I had recently been taking the implications seriously because I had been meeting once a month with a group of philosophers and critics (among them Herbert Feigl, Alburey Castell, and Robert Penn Warren) where the control of human behavior had emerged as a central topic.

That all this should come together in a novel about a utopian community was probably due to the fact that a colleague, Alice F. Tyler, had sent me a copy of her new book, *Freedom's Ferment*, a study of perfectionist movements in

---

1. Thomas Robert Malthus (1766–1834) was an English economist and clergyman who wrote on the problems of population growth. *Ed.*

America in the nineteenth century.[2] With two months to spare before moving to Indiana, I decided to write an account of how I thought a group of, say, a thousand people might have solved the problems of their daily lives with the help of behavioral engineering.

Two publishers turned *Walden Two* down, and Macmillan published it only on condition that I write an introductory text for them. These editorial judgments were, at the time, quite correct. One or two distinguished critics took the book seriously, but the public left it alone for a dozen years. Then it began to sell, and the annual sales rose steadily on a compound interest curve.

There were, I think, two reasons for the awakened interest. The "behavioral engineering" I had so frequently mentioned in the book was, at the time, little more than science fiction. I had thought that an experimental analysis of behavior could be applied to practical problems, but I had not proved it. The 1950's, however, saw the beginnings of what the public has come to know as behavior modification. There were early experiments on psychotic and retarded persons, and then on teaching machines and programmed instruction, and some of the settings in which these experiments were conducted were in essence communities. And in the sixties applications to other fields, such as counseling and the design of incentive systems, came even close to what I had described in *Walden Two*. A technology of behavior was no longer a figment of the imagination. Indeed, to many people it was altogether too real.

But there was, I think, a better reason why more and more people began to read the book. The world was beginning to face problems of an entirely new order of magnitude—the exhaustion of resources, the pollution of the environment, overpopulation, and the possibility of a nuclear holocaust, to mention only four. Physical and biological technologies could, of course, help. We could find new sources of energy and make better use of those we had. The world could feed itself by growing more nutritious grains and eating grain rather than meat. More reliable methods of contraception could keep the population within bounds. Impregnable defences could make a nuclear war impossible. But that would happen only if human behavior changed, and how it could be changed was still an unanswered question. How were people to be induced to use new forms of energy, to eat grain rather than meat, and to limit the size of their families; and how were atomic stockpiles to be kept out of the hands of desperate leaders?

From time to time policy makers in high places have been urged to pay more attention to the behavioral sciences. The National Research Council, the operative arm of the National Academy of Sciences, made one such proposal a num-

---

2. Tyler, A. F. *Freedom's Ferment.* Minneapolis, Univ. of Minnesota Press. 1944.

ber of years ago, pointing out that useful "insights in policy formulation" had been developed. But it implied that the chief role of the behavioral sciences was to collect facts and insisted, possibly to re-assure policy makers who might be alarmed by the ambitions of scientists, that "knowledge is no substitute for wisdom or common sense in making decisions." Science would get the facts but Congress or the President would make the decisions—with wisdom and common sense.

It is true that when the behavioral sciences have gone beyond the collection of facts to recommend courses of action and have done so by predicting consequences, they have not been too helpful. Not all economists agree, for example, on how an increase or reduction in taxes or a change in interest rates will affect business, prices, or unemployment, and political scientists are no more likely to agree on the consequences of domestic or international policies. In anthropology, sociology, and psychology the preferred formulations are those that do not dictate action. A thoroughgoing developmentalism, for example, almost denies the possibility of effective action. Applied psychology is usually a mixture of science and common sense, and Freud regarded therapy as a minor contribution of psychoanalysis.

From the very beginning the application of an experimental analysis of behavior was different. It was doubly concerned with consequences. Behavior could be changed by changing its consequences—that was operant conditioning—but it could be changed because other kinds of consequences would then follow. Psychotic and retarded persons would lead better lives, time and energy of teachers and students would be saved, homes would be pleasanter social environments, people would work more effectively while enjoying what they were doing, and so on.

These are the kinds of achievements traditionally expected from wisdom and common sense, but Frazier, the protagonist of *Walden Two*, insists that they are within reach of a special behavioral science which can take the place of wisdom and common sense and with happier results. And what has happened in the past twenty-five years has increased the plausibility of his achievement—a community in which the most important problems of daily life, as well as certain aspects of economics and government, are solved.

Frazier's critics will protest. What can we conclude from a successful community of a thousand people? Try those principles on New York City, say, or on the State Department and see what happens. The world is a vast and complex space. What works for a small group will be far short of what is needed for a nation or the world as a whole.

Frazier might answer by calling Walden Two a pilot experiment. Industries do not invest in large plants until they have tried a new process on a smaller scale. If we want to find out how people can live together without quarreling, can produce the goods they need without working too hard, or can raise and educate their children more efficiently, let us start with units of manageable size before moving on to larger problems.

But a more cogent answer is this: what is so wonderful about being big? It is often said that the world is suffering from the ills of bigness, and we now have some clinical examples in our large cities. Many cities are probably past the point of good government because too many things are wrong. Should we not rather ask whether we need cities? With modern systems of communication and transportation, businesses do not need to be within walking or taxicab distances of each other, and how many people must one be near in order to live a happy life? People who flock to cities looking for jobs and more interesting lives will flock back again if jobs and more interesting lives are to be found where they came from. It has been suggested that, with modern systems of communication, the America of the future may be simply a network of small towns. But should we not say Walden Twos? A few skeletons of cities may survive, like the bones of dinosaurs in museums, as the remains of a passing phase in the evolution of a way of life.

The British economist E. F. Schumacher, in his remarkable book *Small Is Beautiful*,[3] has discussed the problems that come from bigness and—has outlined a technology appropriate to systems of intermediate size. Many current projects dealing with new sources of energy and new forms of agriculture seem ideally suited to development by small communities. A network of small towns or Walden Twos would have its own problems, but the astonishing fact is that it could much more easily solve many of the crucial problems facing the world today. Although a small community does not bring out "human nature in all its essential goodness" (small towns have never supported that romantic dream), it makes it possible to arrange more effective "contingencies of reinforcement" according to the principles of an applied behavior analysis. We need not look too closely at practices derived from such principles to survey some of those which could solve basic problems in a small community.

To induce people to adapt to new ways of living which are less consuming and hence less polluting, we do not need to speak of frugality or austerity as if we meant sacrifice. There are contingencies of reinforcement in which people continue to pursue (and even overtake) happiness while consuming far less than they now consume. The experimental analysis of behavior has clearly shown that it is not the quantity of goods that counts (as the law of supply and demand suggests) but the contingent relation between goods and behavior. That is why, to the amazement of the American tourist, there are people in the

---

3. Schumacher, E. F. *Small Is Beautiful.* New York, Harper Torchbooks, 1973.

world who are happier than we are, while possessing far less. Inflation is said to be the most serious problem in the world today. It has been defined, not ineptly, as spending more than one has. In an experimental community contingencies of reinforcement which encourage unnecessary spending can be corrected. As for pollution, small communities are optimal for recycling materials and avoiding wasteful methods of distribution.

The basic research has also shown how important it is for everyone, young and old, women and men, not only to receive goods but to engage in their production. That does not mean that we should all work like eager beavers according to the Protestant work-ethic. There are many ways of saving labor, but they should not, as Frazier points out, be used to save laborers and hence to increase unemployment. Simply by dividing the total amount of wages Americans receive each year by the number of people who want jobs, we arrive at a perfectly reasonable annual wage for everyone. But that means a reduction in the standard of living for many people, which, as things now stand, is probably impossible. In a series of small communities, however, everyone would have a job because work, as well as wages, could be divided among workers. And good incentive conditions—for example, those in which people make not money, but the things that money buys—do not require what we call hard work.

If the world is to save any part of its resources for the future, it must reduce not only consumption but the number of consumers. It should be easy to change the birth rate in an experimental community. Parents would not need children for economic security, the childless could spend as much time with children as they liked, and the community would function as a large and affectionate family in which everyone would play parental and filial roles. Blood ties would then be a minor issue.

People are more likely to treat each other with friendship and affection if they are not in competition for personal or professional status. But good personal relations also depend upon immediate signs of commendation or censure, supported perhaps by simple rules or codes. The bigness of a large city is troublesome precisely because we meet so many people whom we shall never see again and whose commendation or censure is therefore meaningless. The problem cannot really be solved by delegating censure to a police force and the law courts. Those who have used behavior modification in family counseling or in institutions know how to arrange the face-to-face conditions which promote interpersonal respect and love.

We could solve many of the problems of delinquency and crime if we could change the early environment of offenders. One need not be a bleeding heart to argue that many young people today have simply not been prepared by their homes or school to lead successful lives within the law or, if prepared, do not have the chance to do so by getting jobs. Offenders are seldom improved by being sent to prison, and judges therefore tend to reduce or suspend sentences, but crime, unpunished, then increases. We all know how early environments can be improved, and a much neglected experiment reported by Cohen and Filipczak[4] has demonstrated that occasional offenders can be rehabilitated.

Children are our most valuable resources and they are now shamefully wasted. Wonderful things can be done in the first years of life, but we leave them to people whose mistakes range all the way from child abuse to overprotection and the lavishing of affection on the wrong behavior. We give small children little chance to develop good relationships with their peers or with adults, especially in the single-parent home, which is on the increase. That is all changed when children are, from the very first, part of a larger community.

City schools show how much harm bigness can do to education, and education is important because it is concerned with the transmission and hence the survival of a culture. We know how to solve many educational problems with programmed instruction and good contingency management, saving resources and the time and effort of teachers and students. Small communities are ideal settings for new kinds of instruction, free from interference by administrators, politicians, and organizations of teachers.

In spite of our lip service to freedom, we do very little to further the development of the individual. How many Americans can say that they are doing the kinds of things they are best qualified to do and most enjoy doing? What opportunities have they had to choose fields related to their talents or to the interests and skills they acquired in early life? Women, only just beginning to be able to choose not to be housewives, can now discover how hard it is to choose the right profession when they are young or to change to a different one later on.

And once one is lucky enough to be doing what one likes, what are the chances of being successful? How easily can artists, composers, and writers bring their work to the attention of those who will enjoy it and whose reactions will shape behavior in creative ways? Those who know the importance of contingencies of reinforcement know how people can be led to discover the things they do best and the things from which they will get the greatest satisfaction.

Although sometimes questioned, the survival value of art, music, literature, games, and other activities not tied to the serious business of life is clear enough. A culture must positively reinforce the behavior of those who support it and must avoid creating negative reinforcers from which its members will escape through defection. A world which has been made beautiful and exciting

---

4. Cohen, H. L., and Filipczak, J. *A New Learning Environment.* San Francisco, Jossey-Bass, 1971.

by artists, composers, writers, and performers is as important for survival as one which satisfies biological needs.

The effective use of leisure is almost completely neglected in modern life. We boast of our short workday and week, but what we do with the free time we have to spend is nothing of which we can be very proud. The leisure classes have almost always turned to alcohol and other drugs, to gambling, and to watching other people lead exhausting or dangerous lives, and we are no exception. Thanks to television millions of Americans now lead the exciting and dangerous lives of other people. Many states are legalizing gambling and have set up lotteries of their own. Alcohol and drugs are consumed in ever-increasing quantities. One may spend one's life in these ways and be essentially unchanged at the end of it. These uses of leisure are due to some basic behavioral processes, but the same processes, in a different environment, lead people to develop their skills and capacities to the fullest possible extent.

Are we quite sure of all this? Perhaps not, but Walden Two can help us make sure. Even as part of a larger design, a community serves as a pilot experiment. The question is simply whether it works, and one way or the other, the answer is usually clear. When that is the case, we can increase our understanding of human behavior with the greatest possible speed. Here is possibly our best chance to answer the really important questions facing the world today—questions not about economics or government but about the daily lives of human beings.

Yes, but what about economics and government? Must we not answer those questions too? I am not sure we must. Consider the following economic propositions. The first is from Henry David Thoreau's *Walden*: by reducing the amount of goods we consume, we can reduce the amount of time we spend in unpleasant labor. The second appears to assert just the opposite: we must all consume as much as possible so that everyone can have a job. I submit that the first is more reasonable, even though the second is defended by many people today. Indeed, it might be argued that if America were to convert to a network of small communities, our economy would be wrecked. But something is wrong when it is the system that must be saved rather than the way of life that the system is supposed to serve.

But what about government? Surely I am not suggesting that we can get along without a federal government? But how much of it is needed? One great share of our national budget goes to the Department of Health, Education, and Welfare. Health? Education? Welfare? But an experimental community like Walden Two *is* health, education, and welfare! The only reason we have a vast federal department is that millions of people find themselves trapped in overgrown, unworkable living spaces.

Another large share of the budget goes to the Department of Defense. Am I suggesting that we can get along without that? How can we preserve the peace of the world if we do not possess the most powerful weapons, together with an industry that continues to develop even more powerful ones? But we have weapons only because other countries have them, and although we feel threatened by countries with comparable military power, particularly the Bomb, the real threat may be the countries that have next to nothing. A few highly industrialized nations cannot long continue to face the rest of the world while consuming and polluting the environment as they do. A way of life in which each person used only a fair share of the resources of the world and yet somehow enjoyed life would be a real step toward world peace. It is a pattern that could easily be copied, and I was heartened recently when someone from the State Department called to tell me that he thought America ought to stop trying to export the "American way of life" and export Walden Twos instead. A state defined by repressive, formal, legal, social controls based on physical force is not necessary in the development of civilization,[5] and although such a state has certainly figured in our own development, we may be ready to move on to another stage.

Suppose we do know what is needed for the good life; how are we to bring it about? In America we almost instinctively move to change things by political action: we pass laws, we vote for new leaders. But a good many people are beginning to wonder. They have lost faith in a democratic process in which the so-called will of the people is obviously controlled in undemocratic ways. And there is always the question whether a government based on punitive sanctions is inappropriate if we are to solve problems nonpunitively.

It has been argued that the solution might be socialism, but it has often been pointed out that socialism, like capitalism, is committed to growth, and hence to overconsumption and pollution. Certainly Russia after fifty years is not a model we wish to emulate. China may be closer to the solutions I have been talking about, but a Communist revolution in America is hard to imagine. It would be a bloody affair, and there is always Lenin's question to be answered: How much suffering can one impose upon those now living for the sake of those who will follow? And can we be sure that those who follow will be any better off?

Fortunately, there is another possibility. An important theme in *Walden Two* is that political action is to be avoided. Historians have stopped writing about wars and conquering heroes and empires, and what they have turned to instead, though far less dramatic, is far more important. The great cultural revolutions

---

5. See Service, Elman. *Origins of the State and Civilization.* New York, Norton, 1975.

have not started with politics. The great men who are said to have made a difference in human affairs—Confucius, Buddha, Jesus, the scholars and scientists of the Revival of Learning, the leaders of the Enlightenment, Marx—were not political leaders. They did not change history by running for office. We need not aspire to their eminence in order to profit from their example. What is needed is not a new political leader or a new kind of government but further knowledge about human behavior and new ways of applying that knowledge to the design of cultural practices.

It is now widely recognized that great changes must be made in the American way of life. Not only can we not face the rest of the world while consuming and polluting as we do, we cannot for long face ourselves while acknowledging the violence and chaos in which we live. The choice is clear: either we do nothing and allow a miserable and probably catastrophic future to overtake us, or we use our knowledge about human behavior to create a social environment in which we shall live productive and creative lives and do so without jeopardizing the chances that those who follow us will be able to do the same. Something like a Walden Two would not be a bad start.

B[urrhus] F[rederick] Skinner (1904–1990) was a professor of psychology at Harvard University whose behavioralism dominated psychology in the United States for many years.

Source: B[urrhus] F[rederick] Skinner, WALDEN TWO (New York: Macmillan, 1948), 251–76; B[urrhus] F[rederick] Skinner, "Walden Two Revisited," in WALDEN TWO (New York: Macmillan, 1976), vii–xvi.

George Orwell
Nineteen Eighty-Four

George Orwell's *Nineteen Eighty-Four* (Orwell insisted that the title be spelled out) is one of the best known dystopias ever written. A central aspect of this future world is the alteration of language in order to reshape thought.

Appendix: The Principles of Newspeak

Newspeak was the official language of Oceania and had been devised to meet the ideological needs of Ingsoc, or English Socialism. In the year 1984 there was not as yet anyone who used Newspeak as his sole means of communication, either in speech or writing. The leading articles in *The Times* were written in it, but this was a *tour de force* which could only be carried out by a specialist. It was expected that Newspeak would have finally superseded Oldspeak (or Standard English, as we should call it) by about the year 2050. Meanwhile it gained ground steadily, all Party members tending to use Newspeak words and grammatical constructions more and more in their everyday speech. The version in use in 1984, and embodied in the Ninth and Tenth Editions of the Newspeak Dictionary, was a provisional one, and contained many superfluous words and archaic formations which were due to be suppressed later. It is with the final, perfected version, as embodied in the Eleventh Edition of the Dictionary, that we are concerned here.

The purpose of Newspeak was not only to provide a medium of expression for the world-view and mental habits proper to the devotees of Ingsoc, but to make all other modes of thought impossible. It was intended that when Newspeak had been adopted once and for all and Oldspeak forgotten, a heretical thought—that is, a thought diverging from the principles of Ingsoc—should be literally unthinkable, at least so far as thought is dependent on words. Its vocabulary was so constructed as to give exact and often very subtle expression to every meaning that a Party member could properly wish to express, while excluding all other meanings and also the possibility of arriving at them by indirect methods. This was done partly by the invention of new words, but chiefly by eliminating undesirable words and by stripping such words as remained of unorthodox meanings, and so far as possible of all secondary meanings whatever. To give a single example. The word *free* still existed in Newspeak, but it could only be used in such statements as 'This dog is free from lice' or 'This field is free from weeds'. It could not be used in its old sense of 'politically free' or 'intellectually free', since political and intellectual freedom no longer existed even as concepts, and were therefore of necessity nameless. Quite apart from the suppression of definitely heretical words, reduction of vocabulary was regarded as an end in itself and no word that could be dispensed with was allowed to survive. Newspeak was designed not to extend but to *diminish* the range of thought, and this purpose was indirectly assisted by cutting the choice of words down to a minimum.

Newspeak was founded on the English language as we now know it, though many Newspeak sentences, even when not containing newly-created words, would be barely intelligible to an English-speaker of our own day. Newspeak words were divided into three distinct classes, known as the A vocabulary, the B vocabulary (also called compound words), and the C vocabulary. It will be simpler to discuss each class separately, but the grammatical peculiarities of the language can be dealt with in the section devoted to the A vocabulary, since the same rules held good for all three categories.

The A vocabulary. The A vocabulary consisted of the words needed for the business of everyday life—for such things as eating, drinking, working, putting on one's clothes, going up and down stairs, riding in vehicles, gardening, cooking, and the like. It was composed almost entirely of words that we already possess—words like *hit, run, dog, tree, sugar, house, field*—but in comparison with the present-day English vocabulary their number was extremely small, while their meanings were far more rigidly defined. All ambiguities and shades of meaning had been purged out of them. So far as it could be achieved, a Newspeak word of this class was simply a staccato sound expressing *one* clearly understood concept. It would have been quite impossible to use the A vocabulary for literary purposes or for political or philosophical discussion. It was intended only to express simple, purposive thoughts, usually involving concrete objects or physical actions.

The grammar of Newspeak had two outstanding peculiarities. The first of these was an almost complete interchangeability between different parts of speech. Any word in the language (in principle this applied even to very abstract words such as *if* or *when*) could be used either as verb, noun, adjective, or adverb. Between the verb and the noun form, when they were of the same root, there was never any variation, this rule of itself involving the destruction of many archaic forms. The word *thought*, for example, did not exist in Newspeak. Its place was taken by *think*, which did duty for both noun and verb. No etymological principle was followed here: in some cases it was the original noun that was chosen for retention, in other cases the verb. Even where a noun and verb of kindred meaning were not etymologically connected, one or other of them was frequently suppressed. There was, for example, no such word as *cut*, its meaning being sufficiently covered by the noun-verb *knife*. Adjectives were formed by adding the suffix *-ful* to the noun-verb, and adverbs by adding *-wise*. Thus for example, *speedful* meant 'rapid' and *speedwise* meant 'quickly'. Certain of our present-day adjectives, such as *good, strong, big, black, soft*, were retained, but their total number was very small. There was little need for them, since almost any adjectival meaning could be arrived at by adding *-ful* to a noun-verb. None of the now-existing adverbs was retained, except for a very few already ending in *-wise*: the -wise termination was invariable. The word well, for example, was replaced by *goodwise*.

In addition, any word—this again applied in principle to every word in the language—could be negatived by adding the affix *un-*, or could be strengthened by the affix *plus-*, or, for still greater emphasis, *doubleplus-*. Thus, for example, *uncold* meant 'warm', while *pluscold* and *doublepluscold* meant, respectively, 'very cold' and 'superlatively cold'. It was also possible, as in present-day English, to modify the meaning of almost any word by prepositional affixes such as *ante-, post-, up-, down-*, etc. By such methods it was found possible to bring about an enormous diminution of vocabulary. Given, for instance, the word *good*, there was no need for such a word as *bad*, since the required meaning was equally well—indeed, better—expressed by *ungood*. All that was necessary, in any case where two words formed a natural pair of opposites, was to decide which of them to suppress. *Dark,* for example, could be replaced by *unlight,* or *light* by *undark,* according to preference.

The second distinguishing mark of Newspeak grammar was its regularity. Subject to a few exceptions which are mentioned below all inflexions followed the same rules. Thus, in all verbs the preterite and the past participle were the same and ended in *-ed.* The preterite of *steal* was *stealed,* the preterite of *think* was *thinked,* and so on throughout the language, all such forms as *swam, gave, brought, spoke, taken,* etc., being abolished. All plurals were made by adding *-s* or *-es* as the case might be. The plurals of *man, ox, life,* were *mans, oxes, lifes.* Comparison of adjectives was invariably made by adding *-er, -est (good, gooder, goodest),* irregular forms and the *more, most* formation being suppressed.

The only classes of words that were still allowed to inflect irregularly were the pronouns, the relatives, the demonstrative adjectives, and the auxiliary verbs. All of these followed their ancient usage, except that *whom* had been scrapped as unnecessary, and the *shall, should* tenses had been dropped, all their uses being covered by *will* and *would.* There were also certain irregularities in word-formation arising out of the need for rapid and easy speech. A word which was difficult to utter, or was liable to be incorrectly heard, was held to be *ipso facto* a bad word: occasionally therefore, for the sake of euphony, extra letters were inserted into a word or an archaic formation was retained. But this need made itself felt chiefly in connexion with the B vocabulary. *Why* so great an importance was attached to ease of pronunciation will be made clear later in this essay.

The B vocabulary. The B vocabulary consisted of words which had been deliberately constructed for political purposes: words, that is to say, which not only had in every case a political implication, but were intended to impose a desirable mental attitude upon the person using them. Without a full understanding of the principles of Ingsoc it was difficult to use these words correctly. In some cases they could be translated into Oldspeak, or even into words taken from the A vocabulary, but this usually demanded a long paraphrase and always involved the loss of certain overtones. The B words were a sort of verbal shorthand, often packing whole ranges of ideas into a few syllables, and at the same time more accurate and forcible than ordinary language.

The B words were in all cases compound words.[1] They consisted of two or more words, or portions of words, welded together in an easily pronounceable

---

1. Compound words such as *speakwrite,* were of course to be found in the A vocabulary, but these were merely convenient abbreviations and had no special ideological colour.

form. The resulting amalgam was always a noun-verb, and inflected according to the ordinary rules. To take a single example: the word *goodthink*, meaning, very roughly, 'orthodoxy', or, if one chose to regard it as a verb, 'to think in an orthodox manner'. This inflected as follows: noun-verb, *goodthink*; past tense and past participle, *goodthinked*; present participle, *goodthinking*; adjective, *goodthinkful*; adverb, *goodthinkwise*; verbal noun, *goodthinker*.

The B words were not constructed on any etymological plan. The words of which they were made up could be any parts of speech, and could be placed in any order and mutilated in any way which made them easy to pronounce while indicating their derivation. In the word *crimethink* (thoughtcrime), for instance, the *think* came second, whereas in *thinkpol* (Thought Police) it came first, and in the latter word *police* had lost its second syllable. Because of the greater difficulty in securing euphony, irregular formations were commoner in the B vocabulary than in the A vocabulary. For example, the adjective forms of *Minitrue, Minipax,* and *Miniluv* were, respectively, *Minitruthful, Minipeaceful,* and *Minilovely,* simply because *-trueful, -paxful,* and *-loveful* were slightly awkward to pronounce. In principle, however, all B words could inflect, and all inflected in exactly the same way.

Some of the B words had highly subtilized meanings, barely intelligible to anyone who had not mastered the language as a whole. Consider, for example, such a typical sentence from a *Times* leading article as *Oldthinkers unbellyfeel Ingsoc.* The shortest rendering that one could make of this in Oldspeak would be: 'Those whose ideas were formed before the Revolution cannot have a full emotional understanding of the principles of English Socialism.' But this is not an adequate translation. To begin with, in order to grasp the full meaning of the Newspeak sentence quoted above, one would have to have a clear idea of what is meant by *Ingsoc.* And in addition, only a person thoroughly grounded in Ingsoc could appreciate the full force of the word *bellyfeel,* which implied a blind, enthusiastic acceptance difficult to imagine to-day; or of the word *oldthink,* which was inextricably mixed up with the idea of wickedness and decadence. But the special function of certain Newspeak words, of which *oldthink* was one, was not so much to express meanings as to destroy them. These words, necessarily few in number, had had their meanings extended until they contained within themselves whole batteries of words which, as they were sufficiently covered by a single comprehensive term, could now be scrapped and forgotten. The greatest difficulty facing the compilers of the Newspeak Dictionary was not to invent new words, but, having invented them, to make sure what they meant: to make sure, that is to say, what ranges of words they cancelled by their existence.

As we have already seen in the case of the word *free*, words which had once borne a heretical meaning were sometimes retained for the sake of convenience, but only with the undesirable meanings purged out of them. Countless other words such as *honour, justice, morality, internationalism, democracy, science*, and *religion* had simply ceased to exist. A few blanket words covered them, and, in covering them, abolished them. All words grouping themselves round the concepts of liberty and equality, for instance, were contained in the single word *crimethink*, while all words grouping themselves round the concepts of objectivity and rationalism were contained in the single word *oldthink*. Greater precision would have been dangerous. What was required in a Party member was an outlook similar to that of the ancient Hebrew who knew, without knowing much else, that all nations other than his own worshipped 'false gods'. He did not need to know that these gods were called Baal, Osiris, Moloch, Ashtaroth, and the like: probably the less he knew about them the better for his orthodoxy. He knew Jehovah and the commandments of Jehovah: he knew, therefore, that all gods with other names or other attributes were false gods. In somewhat the same way, the Party member knew what constituted right conduct, and in exceedingly vague, generalized terms he knew what kinds of departure from it were possible. His sexual life, for example, was entirely regulated by the two Newspeak words *sexcrime* (sexual immorality) and *goodsex* (chastity). *Sexcrime* covered all sexual misdeeds whatever. It covered fornication, adultery, homosexuality, and other perversions, and, in addition, normal intercourse practised for its own sake. There was no need to enumerate them separately, since they were all equally culpable, and, in principle, all punishable by death. In the C vocabulary, which consisted of scientific and technical words, it might be necessary to give specialized names to certain sexual aberrations, but the ordinary citizen had no need of them. He knew what was meant by *goodsex*—that is to say, normal intercourse between man and wife, for the sole purpose of begetting children, and without physical pleasure on the part of the woman: all else was *sexcrime*. In Newspeak it was seldom possible to follow a heretical thought further than the perception that it *was* heretical: beyond that point the necessary words were nonexistent.

No word in the B vocabulary was ideologically neutral. A great many were euphemisms. Such words, for instance, as *joycamp* (forced-labour camp) or *Minipax* (Ministry of Peace, i.e. Ministry of War) meant almost the exact opposite of what they appeared to mean. Some words, on the other hand, displayed a frank and contemptuous understanding of the real nature of Oceanic society. An example was *prolefeed*, meaning the rubbishy entertainment and spurious news which the Party handed out to the masses. Other words, again, were ambivalent, having the connotation 'good' when applied to the Party and 'bad' when applied to its enemies. But in addition there were great numbers of words which at first sight appeared to be mere abbreviations and which derived their ideological colour not from their meaning, but from their structure.

So far as it could be contrived, everything that had or might have political significance of any kind was fitted into the B vocabulary. The name of every organization, or body of people, or doctrine, or country, or institution, or public building, was invariably cut down into the familiar shape; that is, a single easily pronounced word with the smallest number of syllables that would preserve the original derivation. In the Ministry of Truth, for example, the Records Department, in which Winston Smith worked, was called *Recdep*, the Fiction Department was called *Ficdep*, the Tele-programmes Department was called *Teledep*, and so on. This was not done solely with the object of saving time. Even in the early decades of the twentieth century, telescoped words and phrases had been one of the characteristic features of political language; and it had been noticed that the tendency to use abbreviations of this kind was most marked in totalitarian countries and totalitarian organizations. Examples were such words as *Nazi, Gestapo, Comintern, Inprecorr, Agitprop*. In the beginning the practice had been adopted as it were instinctively, but in Newspeak it was used with a conscious purpose. It was perceived that in thus abbreviating a name one narrowed and subtly altered its meaning, by cutting out most of the associations that would otherwise cling to it. The words *Communist International*, for instance, call up a composite picture of universal human brotherhood, red flags, barricades, Karl Marx, and the Paris Commune. The word *Comintern*, on the other hand, suggests merely a tightly-knit organization and a well-defined body of doctrine. It refers to something almost as easily recognized, and as limited in purpose, as a chair or a table. *Comintern* is a word that can be uttered almost without taking thought, whereas *Communist International* is a phrase over which one is obliged to linger at least momentarily. In the same way, the associations called up by a word like *Minitrue* are fewer and more controllable than those called up by *Ministry of Truth*. This accounted not only for the habit of abbreviating whenever possible, but also for the almost exaggerated care that was taken to make every word easily pronounceable.

In Newspeak, euphony outweighed every consideration other than exactitude of meaning. Regularity of grammar was always sacrificed to it when it seemed necessary. And rightly so, since what was required, above all for political purposes, was short clipped words of unmistakable meaning which could be uttered rapidly and which roused the minimum of echoes in the speaker's mind. The words of the B vocabulary even gained in force from the fact that nearly all of them were very much alike. Almost invariably these words—*goodthink, Minipax, prolefeed, sexcrime joycamp, Ingsoc, bellyfeel, thinkpol*, and countless others—were words of two or three syllables, with the stress distributed equally between the first syllable and the last. The use of them encouraged a gabbling style of speech, at once staccato and monotonous. And this was exactly what was aimed at. The intention was to make speech, and especially speech on any subject not ideologically neutral, as nearly as possible independent of consciousness. For the purposes of everyday life it was no doubt necessary, or sometimes necessary, to reflect before speaking, but a Party member called upon to make a political or ethical judgement should be able to spray forth the correct opinions as automatically as a machine gun spraying forth bullets. His training fitted him to do this, the language gave him an almost foolproof instrument, and the texture of the words, with their harsh sound and a certain wilful ugliness which was in accord with the spirit of Ingsoc, assisted the process still further.

So did the fact of having very few words to choose from. Relative to our own, the Newspeak vocabulary was tiny, and new ways of reducing it were constantly being devised. Newspeak, indeed, differed from most all other languages in that its vocabulary grew smaller instead of larger every year. Each reduction was a gain, since the smaller the area of choice, the smaller the temptation to take thought. Ultimately it was hoped to make articulate speech issue from the larynx without involving the higher brain centres at all. This aim was frankly admitted in the Newspeak word *duckspeak*, meaning 'to quack like a duck'. Like various other words in the B vocabulary, *duckspeak* was ambivalent in meaning. Provided that the opinions which were quacked out were orthodox ones, it implied nothing but praise, and when *The Times* referred to one of the orators of the Party as a *doubleplusgood duckspeaker* it was paying a warm and valued compliment.

The C vocabulary. The C vocabulary was supplementary to the others and consisted entirely of scientific and technical terms. These resembled the scientific terms in use to-day, and were constructed from the same roots, but the usual care was taken to define them rigidly and strip them of undesirable meanings. They followed the same grammatical rules as the words in the other two vocabularies. Very few of the C words had any currency either in everyday speech or in political speech. Any scientific worker or technician could find all the words he needed in the list devoted to his own speciality, but he seldom had more than a smattering of the words occurring in the other lists. Only a very few words were common to all lists, and there was no vocabulary expressing the function of Science as a habit of mind, or a method of thought, irrespective of its particular branches. There was, indeed, no word for 'Science', any meaning that it could possibly bear being already sufficiently covered by the word *Ingsoc*.

From the foregoing account it will be seen that in Newspeak the expression of unorthodox opinions, above a very low level, was well-nigh impossible. It was of course possible to utter heresies of a very crude kind, a species of blasphemy. It would have been possible, for example, to say *Big Brother is ungood*.

But this statement, which to an orthodox ear merely conveyed a self-evident absurdity, could not have been sustained by reasoned argument, because the necessary words were not available. Ideas inimical to Ingsoc could only be entertained in a vague wordless form, and could only be named in very broad terms which lumped together and condemned whole groups of heresies without defining them in doing so. One could, in fact, only use Newspeak for unorthodox purposes by illegitimately translating some of the words back into Oldspeak. For example, *All mans are equal* was a possible Newspeak sentence, but only in the same sense in which *All men are redhaired* is a possible Oldspeak sentence. It did not contain a grammatical error, but it expressed a palpable untruth—i.e. that all men are of equal size, weight, or strength. The concept of political equality no longer existed, and this secondary meaning had accordingly been purged out of the word *equal*. In 1984, when Oldspeak was still the normal means of communication, the danger theoretically existed that in using Newspeak words one might remember their original meanings. In practice it was not difficult for any person well grounded in *doublethink* to avoid doing this, but within a couple of generations even the possibility of such a lapse would have vanished. A person growing up with Newspeak as his sole language would no more know that *equal* had once had the secondary meaning of 'politically equal', or that *free* had once meant 'intellectually free', than for instance, a person who had never heard of chess would be aware of the secondary meanings attaching to *queen* and *rook*. There would be many crimes and errors which it would be beyond his power to commit, simply because they were nameless and therefore unimaginable. And it was to be foreseen that with the passage of time the distinguishing characteristics of Newspeak would become more and more pronounced—its words growing fewer and fewer, their meanings more and more rigid, and the chance of putting them to improper uses always diminishing.

When Oldspeak had been once and for all superseded, the last link with the past would have been severed. History had already been rewritten, but fragments of the literature of the past survived here and there, imperfectly censored, and so long as one retained one's knowledge of Oldspeak it was possible to read them. In the future such fragments, even if they chanced to survive, would be unintelligible and untranslatable. It was impossible to translate any passage of Oldspeak into Newspeak unless it either referred to some technical process or some very simple everyday action, or was already orthodox (*goodthinkful* would be the Newspeak expression) in tendency. In practice this meant that no book written before approximately 1960 could be translated as a whole. Prerevolutionary literature could only be subjected to ideological translation—that is, alteration in sense as well as language. Take for example the well-known passage from the Declaration of Independence:

We hold these truths to be self-evident, that all men are created equal, that they are endowed by their creator with certain inalienable rights, that among these are life, liberty, and the pursuit of happiness. That to secure these rights, Governments are instituted among men, deriving their powers from the consent of the governed. That whenever any form of Government becomes destructive of those ends, it is the right of the People to alter or abolish it, and to institute new Government. . . .

It would have been quite impossible to render this into Newspeak while keeping to the sense of the original. The nearest one could come to doing so would be to swallow the whole passage up in the single word *crimethink*. A full translation could only be an ideological translation, whereby Jefferson's words would be changed into a panegyric on absolute government.

A good deal of the literature of the past was, indeed, already being transformed in this way. Considerations of prestige made it desirable to preserve the memory of certain historical figures, while at the same time bringing their achievements into line with the philosophy of Ingsoc. Various writers such as Shakespeare, Milton, Swift, Byron, Dickens, and some others were therefore in process of translation: when the task had been completed, their original writings, with all else that survived of the literature of the past, would be destroyed. These translations were a slow and difficult business, and it was not expected that they would be finished before the first or second decade of the twenty-first century. There were also large quantities of merely utilitarian literature—indispensable technical manuals, and the like—that had to be treated in the same way. It was chiefly in order to allow time for the preliminary work of translation that the final adoption of Newspeak had been fixed for so late a date as 2050.

George Orwell was the pseudonym of Eric Blair (1903–1950), an English journalist and author.

Source: George Orwell, Nineteen Eighty-Four (London: Secker and Warburg, 1948), 299–312.

Ursula K. Le Guin
"The Day before the Revolution"

Ursula K. Le Guin's many utopias are among the most important additions to the genre in the last half of the twentieth century. Her earliest, *The Left Hand of Darkness* (1969), is an exploration of gender relations in a society in which they are not stable. *The Dispossessed* (1974) and "The Day before the

Revolution" (1974), which serves as an introduction to *The Dispossessed*, illustrate the events leading to the creation of an anarchist utopia and the society created. Le Guin has called this society "an ambiguous utopia" to signal to the reader that the society still has problems with which it must deal. Her other major utopias include *Always Coming Home* (1985) and *Four Ways to Forgiveness* (1995).

In memoriam, Paul Goodman, 1911–1972

THE speaker's voice was as loud as empty beer-trucks in a stone street, and the people at the meeting were jammed up close, cobble-stones, that great voice booming over them. Taviri was somewhere on the other side of the hall. She had to get to him. She wormed and pushed her way among the dark-clothed, close-packed people. She did not hear the words, nor see the faces: only the booming, and the bodies pressed one behind the other. She could not see Taviri, she was too short. A broad black-vested belly and chest loomed up, blocking her way. She must get through to Taviri. Sweating, she jabbed fiercely with her fist. It was like hitting stone, he did not move at all, but the huge lungs let out right over her head a prodigious noise, a bellow. She cowered. Then she understood that the bellow had not been at her. Others were shouting. The speaker had said something, something fine about taxes or shadows. Thrilled, she joined the shouting—"Yes! Yes!"—and shoving on, came out easily into the open expanse of the Regimental Drill Field in Parheo. Overhead the evening sky lay deep and colorless, and all around her nodded the tall weeds with dry, white, close-floreted heads. She had never known what they were called. The flowers nodded above her head, swaying in the wind that always blew across the fields in the dusk. She ran among them, and they whipped lithe aside and stood up again swaying, silent. Taviri stood among the tall weeds in his good suit, the dark grey one that made him look like a professor or a play-actor, harshly elegant. He did not look happy, but he was laughing, and saying something to her. The sound of his voice made her cry, and she reached out to catch hold of his hand, but she did not stop, quite. She could not stop. "Oh, Taviri," she said, "it's just on there!" The queer sweet smell of the white weeds was heavy as she went on. There were thorns, tangles underfoot, there were slopes, pits. She feared to fall, she stopped.

∞

Sun, bright morning-glare, straight in the eyes, relentless. She had forgotten to pull the blind last night. She turned her back on the sun, but the right side wasn't comfortable. No use. Day. She sighed twice, sat up, got her legs over the edge of the bed, and sat hunched in her nightdress looking down at her feet.

The toes, compressed by a lifetime of cheap shoes, were almost square where they touched each other, and bulged out above in corns; the nails were discolored and shapeless. Between the knob-like ankle bones ran fine, dry wrinkles. The brief little plain at the base of the toes had kept its delicacy, but the skin was the color of mud, and knotted veins crossed the instep. Disgusting. Sad, depressing. Mean. Pitiful. She tried on all the words, and they all fit, like hideous little hats. Hideous: yes, that one too. To look at oneself and find it hideous, what a job! But then, when she hadn't been hideous, had she sat around and stared at herself like this? Not much! A proper body's not an object, not an implement, not a belonging to be admired, it's just you, yourself. Only when it's no longer you, but yours, a thing owned, do you worry about it—Is it in good shape? Will it do? Will it last?

"Who cares'?" said Laia fiercely, and stood up.

It made her giddy to stand up suddenly. She had to put out her hand to the bedtable, for she dreaded falling. At that she thought of reaching out to Taviri, in the dream.

What had he said? She could not remember. She was not sure if she had even touched his hand. She frowned, trying to force memory. It had been so long since she had dreamed about Taviri; and now not even to remember what he had said!

It was gone, it was gone. She stood there hunched in her nightdress, frowning, one hand on the bedtable. How long was it since she had thought of him—let alone dreamed of him—even thought of him, as "Taviri"? How long since she had said his name?

Asieo said. When Asieo and I were in prison in the North. Before I met Asieo; Asieo's theory of reciprocity. Oh yes, she talked about him, talked about him too much no doubt, maundered, dragged him in. But as "Asieo," the last name, the public man. The private man was gone, utterly gone. There were so few left who had even known him. They had all used to be in jail. One laughed about it in those days, all the friends in all the jails. But they weren't even there, these days. They were in the prison cemeteries. Or in the common graves.

"Oh, oh my dear," Laia said out loud, and she sank down onto the bed again because she could not stand up under the remembrance of those first weeks in the Fort, in the cell, those first weeks of the nine years in the Fort in Drio, in the cell, those first weeks after they told her that Asieo had been killed in the fighting in Capitol Square and had been buried with the Fourteen Hundred in the lime-ditches behind Oring Gate. In the cell. Her hands fell into the old position on her lap, the left clenched and locked inside the grip of the right, the right thumb working back and forth a little pressing and rubbing on the knuckle of the left first finger. Hours, days, nights. She had thought of them all, each one, each one of the Fourteen Hundred, how they lay, how the quick-lime worked on the flesh, how the bones touched in the burning dark. Who touched him? How did the slender bones of the hand lie now? Hours, years.

"Taviri, I have never forgotten you!" she whispered, and the stupidity of it brought her back to morning-light and the rumpled bed. Of course she hadn't forgotten him. These things go without saying between husband and wife. There were her ugly old feet flat on the floor again, just as before. She had got nowhere at all, she had gone in a circle. She stood up with a grunt of effort and disapproval, and went to the closet for her dressing gown.

The young people went about the halls of the House in becoming immod-esty, but she was too old for that. She didn't want to spoil some young man's breakfast with the sight of her. Besides, they had grown up in the principle of freedom of dress and sex and all the rest, and she hadn't. All she had done was invent it. It's not the same.

Like speaking of Asieo as "my husband." They winced. The word she should use as a good Odonian, of course, was "partner." But why the hell did she have to be a good Odonian?

She shuffled down the hall to the bathrooms. Mairo was there, washing her hair in a lavatory. Laia looked at the long, sleek, wet hank with admiration. She got out of the House so seldom now that she didn't know when she had last seen a respectably shaven scalp, but still the sight of a full head of hair gave her pleasure, vigorous pleasure. How many times had she been jeered at, *Longhair*, *Longhair*, had her hair pulled by policemen or young toughs, had her hair shaved off down to the scalp by a grinning soldier at each new prison? And then had grown it all over again, through the fuzz, to the frizz, to the curls, to the mane . . . In the old days. For God's love, couldn't she think of anything today but the old days?

Dressed, her bed made, she went down to commons. It was a good breakfast, but she had never got her appetite back since the damned stroke. She drank two cups of herb tea, but couldn't finish the piece of fruit she had taken. How she had craved fruit as a child, badly enough to steal it; and in the Fort—oh for God's love stop it! She smiled and replied to the greetings and friendly inquiries of the other breakfasters and big Aevi who was serving the counter this morn-ing. It was he who had tempted her with the peach. "Look at this, I've been sav-ing it for you," and how could she refuse? Anyway she had always loved fruit, and never got enough; once when she was six or seven she had stolen a piece on a vendor's cart in River Street. But it was hard to eat when everyone was talk-ing so excitedly. There was news from Thu, real news. She was inclined to dis-count it at first, being wary of enthusiasms, but after she had read the article in the paper, and read between the lines of it, she thought, with a strange kind of certainty, deep but cold, Why, this is it; it has come. And in Thu, not here. That will break before this country does; the Revolution will first prevail there. As if that mattered! There will be no more nations. And yet it did matter somehow, it made her a little cold and sad-envious, in fact. Of all the infinite stupidities. She did not join in the talk much, and soon got up to go back to her room, feeling sorry for herself. She could not share their excitement. She was out of it, really out of it. It's not easy, she said to herself in justification, laboriously climbing the stairs, to accept being out of it when you've been in it, in the center of it, for fifty years. Oh for God's love. Whining!

She got the stairs and the self-pity behind her, entering her room. It was a good room, and it was good to be by herself. It was a great relief. Even if it wasn't strictly fair. Some of the kids in the attics were living five to a room no bigger than this. There were always more people wanting to live in an Odonian House than could be properly accommodated. She had this big room all to herself only because she was an old woman who had had a stroke. And maybe because she was Odo. If she hadn't been Odo, but merely the old woman with a stroke, would she have had it? Very likely. After all, who the hell wanted to room with a drooling old woman? But it was hard to be sure. Favoritism, elitism, leader-worship, they crept back and cropped out everywhere. But she had never hoped to see them eradicated in her lifetime, in one generation; only Time works the great changes. Meanwhile this was a nice, large, sunny room, proper for a drooling, old woman who had started a world revolution.

Her secretary would be coming in an hour to help her despatch the day's work. She shuffled over to the desk, a beautiful, big piece, a present from the Noi Cabinetmakers' Syndicate because somebody had heard her remark once that the only piece of furniture she had ever really longed for was a desk with drawers and enough room on top . . . damn, the top was practically covered with papers with notes clipped to them, mostly in Noi's small clear handwriting: Urgent.—Northern Provinces.—Consult w/R.T.?

Her own handwriting had never been the same since Asieo's death. It was odd, when you thought about it. After all, within five years after his death she had written the whole *Analogy*. And there were those letters, which the tall guard with the watery grey eyes, what was his name, never mind, had smuggled out of the Fort for her for two years. *The Prison Letters* they called them now, there were a dozen different editions of them. All that stuff, the letters which people kept telling her were so full of "spiritual strength"—which probably meant she had been lying herself blue in the face when she wrote them, trying to keep her spirits up—and the *Analogy* which was certainly the solidest intellectual work she had ever done, all of that had been written in the Fort in Drio, in the cell, after Asieo's death. One had to do something, and in the Fort they let one have paper and pens . . . But it had all been written in the hasty, scribbling hand which she had never felt was hers, not her own like the round, black scrollings of the manuscript of *Society Without Government*, forty-five years old. Taviri had taken not only her body's and her heart's desire to the quicklime with him, but even her good clear handwriting.

∞

But he had left her the Revolution.

How brave of you to go on, to work, to write, in prison, after such a defeat for the Movement, after your partner's death, people had used to say. Damn fools. What else had there been to do? Bravery, courage—what was courage? She had never figured it out. Not fearing, some said. Fearing yet going on, others said. But what could one do but go on? Had one any real choice, ever?

To die was merely to go on in another direction.

If you wanted to come home you had to keep going on, that was what she meant when she wrote, "True journey is return," but it had never been more than an intuition, and she was farther than ever now from being able to rationalize it. She bent down, too suddenly, so that she grunted a little at the creak in her bones, and began to root in a bottom drawer of the desk. Her hand came to an age-softened folder and drew it out, recognizing it by touch before sight confirmed: the manuscript of *Syndical Organization in Revolutionary Transition*. He had printed the title on the folder and written his name under it, Taviri Odo Asieo, IX 741. There was an elegant handwriting, every letter well-formed, bold, and fluent. But he had preferred to use a voiceprinter. The manuscript was all in voiceprint, and high quality too, hesitancies adjusted and idiosyncrasies of speech normalized. You couldn't see there how he had said "o" deep in his throat as they did on the North Coast. There was nothing of him there but his mind. She had nothing of him at all except his name written on the folder. She hadn't kept his letters, it was sentimental to keep letters. Besides, she never kept anything. She couldn't think of anything that she had ever owned for more than a few years, except this ramshackle old body, of course, and she was stuck with that . . .

Dualizing again. "She" and "it." Age and illness made one dualist, made one escapist; the mind insisted, *It's not me, it's not me.* But it was. Maybe the mystics could detach mind from body, she had always rather wistfully envied them the chance, without hope of emulating them. Escape had never been her game. She had sought for freedom here, now, body and soul.

First self-pity, then self-praise, and here she still sat, for God's love, holding Asieo's name in her hand, why? Didn't she know his name without looking it up? What was wrong with her? She raised the folder to her lips and kissed the hand-written name firmly and squarely, replaced the folder in the back of the bottom drawer, shut the drawer, and straightened up in the chair. Her right hand tingled. She scratched it, and then shook it in the air, spitefully. It had never quite got over the stroke. Neither had her right leg, or right eye, or the right corner of her mouth. They were sluggish, inept, they tingled. They made her feel like a robot with a short circuit.

And time was getting on, Noi would be coming, what had she been doing ever since breakfast?

She got up so hastily that she lurched, and grabbed at the chairback to make sure she did not fall. She went down the hall to the bathroom and looked in the big mirror there. Her grey knot was loose and droopy, she hadn't done it up well before breakfast. She struggled with it a while. It was hard to keep her arms up in the air. Amai, running in to piss, stopped and said, "Let me do it!" and knotted it up tight and neat in no time, with her round, strong, pretty fingers, smiling and silent. Amai was twenty, less than a third of Laia's age. Her parents had both been members of the Movement, one killed in the insurrection of '60, the other still recruiting in the South Provinces. Amai had grown up in Odonian Houses, born to the Revolution, a true daughter of anarchy. And so quiet and free and beautiful a child, enough to make you cry when you thought: this is what we worked for, this is what we meant, this is it, here she is, alive, the kindly, lovely future.

Laia Asieo Odo's right eye wept several little tears, as she stood between the lavatories and the latrines having her hair done up by the daughter she had not borne; but her left eye, the strong one, did not weep, nor did it know what the right eye did.

She thanked Amai and hurried back to her room. She had noticed, in the mirror, a stain on her collar. Peach juice, probably. Damned old dribbler. She didn't want Noi to come in and find her with drool on her collar.

As the clean shirt went on over her head, she thought, What's so special about Noi?

She fastened the collar-frogs with her left hand, slowly.

Noi was thirty or so, a slight, muscular fellow with a soft voice and alert dark eyes. That's what was special about Noi. It was that simple. Good old sex. She had never been drawn to a fair man or a fat one, or the tall fellows with big biceps, never, not even when she was fourteen and fell in love with every passing fart. Dark, spare, and fiery, that was the recipe. Taviri, of course. This boy wasn't a patch on Taviri for brains, nor even for looks, but there it was: she didn't want him to see her with dribble on her collar and her hair coming undone.

Her thin, grey hair.

Noi came in, just pausing in the open doorway—my God, she hadn't even shut the door while changing her shirt!—She looked at him and saw herself. The old woman.

You could brush your hair and change your shirt, or you could wear last week's shirt and last night's braids, or you could put on cloth of gold and dust your shaven scalp with diamond powder. None of it would make the slightest difference. The old woman would look a little less, or a little more, grotesque.

One keeps oneself neat out of mere decency, mere sanity, awareness of other people.

And finally even that goes, and one dribbles unashamed.

"Good morning," the young man said in his gentle voice.

"Hello, Noi."

No, by God, it was *not* out of mere decency. Decency be damned. Because the man she had loved, and to whom her age would not have mattered—because he was dead, must she pretend she had no sex? Must she suppress the truth, like a damned puritan authoritarian? Even six months ago, before the stroke, she had made men look at her and like to look at her; and now, though she could give no pleasure, by God she could please herself.

When she was six years old, and Papa's friend Gadeo used to come by to talk politics with Papa after dinner, she would put on the gold-colored necklace that Mama had found on a trash-heap and brought home for her. It was so short that it always got hidden under her collar where nobody could see it. She liked it that way. She knew she had it on. She sat on the doorstep and listened to them talk, and knew that she looked nice for Gadeo. He was dark, with white teeth that flashed. Sometimes he called her "pretty Laia." "There's my pretty Laia!" Sixty-six years ago.

"What? My head's dull. I had a terrible night." It was true. She had slept even less than usual.

"I was asking if you'd seen the papers this morning."

She nodded.

"Pleased about Soinehe?"

Soinehe was the province in Thu which had declared its secession from the Thuvian State last night.

He was pleased about it. His white teeth flashed in his dark, alert face. Pretty Laia.

"Yes. And apprehensive."

"I know. But it's the real thing, this time. It's the beginning of the end of the Government in Thu. They haven't even tried to order troops into Soinehe, you know. It would merely provoke the soldiers into rebellion sooner, and they know it."

She agreed with him. She herself had felt that certainty. But she could not share his delight. After a lifetime of living on hope because there is nothing but hope, one loses the taste for victory. A real sense of triumph must be preceded by real despair. She had unlearned despair a long time ago. There were no more triumphs. One went on.

"Shall we do those letters today?"

"All right. Which letters?"

"To the people in the North," he said without impatience.

"In the North?"

"Parheo, Oaidun."

She had been born in Parheo, the dirty city on the dirty river. She had not come here to the capital till she was twenty-two and ready to bring the Revolution. Though in those days, before she and the others had thought it through, it had been a very green and puerile revolution. Strikes for better wages, representation for women. Votes and wages—Power and Money, for the love of God! Well, one does learn a little, after all, in fifty years.

But then one must forget it all.

"Start with Oaidun," she said, sitting down in the armchair. Noi was at the desk ready to work. He read out excerpts from the letters she was to answer. She tried to pay attention, and succeeded well enough that she dictated one whole letter and started on another. "Remember that at this stage your brotherhood is vulnerable to the threat of . . . no, to the danger . . . to . . ." She groped till Noi suggested, "The danger of leader-worship?"

"All right. And that nothing is so soon corrupted by power-seeking as altruism. No. And that nothing corrupts altruism—no. Oh for God's love you know what I'm trying to say, Noi, you write it. They know it too, it's just the same old stuff, why can't they read my books!"

"Touch," Noi said gently, smiling, citing one of the central Odonian themes.

"All right, but I'm tired of being touched. If you'll write the letter I'll sign it, but I can't be bothered with it this morning." He was looking at her with a little question or concern. She said, irritable, "There is something else I have to do!"

∞

When Noi had gone she sat down at the desk and moved the papers about, pretending to be doing something, because she had been startled, frightened, by the words she had said. She had nothing else to do. She never had had anything else to do. This was her work: her lifework. The speaking tours and the meetings and the streets were out of reach for her now, but she could still write, and that was her work. And anyhow if she had had anything else to do, Noi would have known it; he kept her schedule, and tactfully reminded her of things, like the visit from the foreign students this afternoon.

Oh, damn. She liked the young, and there was always something to learn from a foreigner, but she was tired of new faces, and tired of being on view. She learned from them, but they didn't learn from her; they had learnt all she had to teach long ago, from her books, from the Movement. They just came to look, as if she were the Great Tower in Rodarred, or the Canyon of the Tulaevea. A phenomenon, a monument. They were awed, adoring. She snarled at them: Think your own thoughts!—That's not anarchism, that's mere obscurantism.—You don't think liberty and discipline are incompatible, do you?—They accepted their tonguelashing meekly as children, gratefully, as if she were some kind of All-Mother, the idol of the Big Sheltering Womb. She! She who had mined the shipyards at Seissero, and had cursed Premier Inoilte to his face in front of a crowd of seven thousand, telling him he would have cut off his own balls and had them bronzed and sold as souvenirs, if he thought there was any profit in it—she who had screeched, and sworn, and kicked policemen, and spat at priests, and pissed in public on the big brass plaque in Capitol Square that said HERE WAS FOUNDED THE SOVEREIGN NATION STATE OF A-IO ETC, pssssssss to all that! And now she was everybody's grandmama, the dear old lady, the sweet old monument, come worship at the womb. The fire's out, boys, it's safe to come up close.

"No, I won't," Laia said out loud. "I will not." She was not self-conscious about talking to herself, because she always had talked to herself. "Laia's invisible audience," Taviri had used to say, as she went through the room muttering. "You needn't come, I won't be here," she told the invisible audience now. She had just decided what it was she had to do. She had to go out. To go into the streets.

It was inconsiderate to disappoint the foreign students. It was erratic, typically senile. It was un-Odonian. Pssssss to all that. What was the good working for freedom all your life and ending up without any freedom at all? She would go out for a walk.

"What is an anarchist? One who, choosing, accepts the responsibility of choice."

On the way downstairs she decided, scowling, to stay and see the foreign students. But then she would go out.

They were very young students, very earnest: doe-eyed, shaggy, charming creatures from the Western Hemisphere, Benbili and the Kingdom of Mand, the girls in white trousers, the boys in long kilts, warlike and archaic. They spoke of their hopes. "We in Mand are so very far from the Revolution that maybe we are near it," said one of the girls, wistful and smiling: "The Circle of Life!" and she showed the extremes meeting, in the circle of her slender, dark-skinned fingers. Amai and Aevi served them white wine and brown bread, the hospitality of the House. But the visitors, unpresumptuous, all rose to take their leave after barely half an hour. "No, no, no," Laia said, "stay here, talk with Aevi and Amai. It's just that I get stiff sitting down, you see. I have to change about. It has been so good to meet you, will you come back to see me, my little brothers and sisters, soon?" For her heart went out to them, and theirs to her, and she exchanged kisses all round, laughing, delighted by the dark young cheeks, the affectionate eyes, the scented hair, before she shuffled off. She was really a little tired, but to go up and take a nap would be a defeat. She had wanted to go out. She would go out. She had not been alone outdoors since—when? since winter! before the stroke. No wonder she was getting morbid. It had been a regular jail sentence. Outside, the streets, that's where she lived.

She went quietly out the side door of the House, past the vegetable patch, to the street. The narrow strip of sour city dirt had been beautifully gardened and was producing a fine crop of beans and ceëa, but Laia's eye for farming was unenlightened. Of course it had been clear that anarchist communities, even in the time of transition, must work towards optimal self-support, but how that was to be managed in the way of actual dirt and plants wasn't her business. There were farmers and agronomists for that. Her job was the streets, the noisy, stinking streets of stone, where she had grown up and lived all her life, except for the fifteen years in prison.

She looked up fondly at the façade of the House. That it had been built as a bank gave peculiar satisfaction to its present occupants. They kept their sacks of meal in the bombproof money-vault, and aged their cider in kegs in safe deposit boxes. Over the fussy columns that faced the street, carved letters still read, NATIONAL INVESTORS AND GRAIN FACTORS BANKING ASSOCIATION. The Movement was not strong on names. They had no flag. Slogans came and went as the need did. There was always the Circle of Life to scratch on walls and pavements where Authority would have to see it. But when it came to names they were indifferent, accepting and ignoring whatever they got called, afraid of being pinned down and penned in, unafraid of being absurd. So this best known and second oldest of all the cooperative Houses had no name except The Bank.

It faced on a wide and quiet sheet, but only a block away began the Temeba, an open market, once famous as a center for black market psychogenics and teratogenics, now reduced to vegetables, secondhand clothes, and miserable sideshows. Its crapulous vitality was gone, leaving only half-paralyzed alcoholics, addicts, cripples, hucksters, and fifth-rate whores, pawnshops, gambling dens, fortune-tellers, body-sculptors, and cheap hotels. Laia turned to the Temeba as water seeks its level.

She had never feared or despised the city. It was her country. There would not be slums like this, if the revolution prevailed. But there would be misery. There would always be misery, waste, cruelty. She had never pretended to be changing the human condition, to be Mama taking tragedy away from the children so they won't hurt themselves. Anything but. So long as people were free to choose, if they chose to drink flybane and live in sewers, it was their business. Just so long as it wasn't the business of Business, the source of profit and the means of power for other people. She had felt all that before she knew anything; before she wrote the first pamphlet, before she left Parheo, before she knew what "capital" meant, before she'd been farther than River Street where she played roll-taggie kneeling on scabby knees on the pavement with the other six-year-olds, she had known it: that she, and the other kids, and her parents, and their parents, and the drunks and whores and all of River Street, were at the bottom of something—were the foundation, the reality, the source.

But will you drag civilization down into the mud? cried the shocked decent people, later on, and she had tried for years to explain to them that if all you had was mud, then if you were God you made it into human beings, and if you were human you tried to make it into houses where human beings could live. But nobody who thought he was better than mud would understand. Now, water seeking its level, mud to mud, Laia shuffled through the foul, noisy street, and all the ugly weakness of her old age was at home. The sleepy whores, their lacquered hair-arrangements dilapidated and askew, the one-eyed woman wearily yelling her vegetables to sell, the halfwit beggar slapping flies, these were her countrywomen. They looked like her, they were all sad, disgusting, mean, pitiful, hideous. They were her sisters, her own people.

She did not feel very well. It had been a long time since she had walked so far, four or five blocks, by herself, in the noise and push and stinking summer heat of the streets. She had wanted to get to Koly Park, the triangle of scruffy grass at the end of the Temeba, and sit there for a while with the other old men and women who always sat there, to see what it was like to sit there and be old; but it was too far. If she didn't turn back now, she might get a dizzy spell, and she had a dread of falling down, falling down and having to lie there and look up at the people come to stare at the old woman in a fit. She turned and started home, frowning with effort and self-disgust. She could feel her face very red, and a swimming feeling came and went in her ears. It got a bit much. She was really afraid she might keel over. She saw a doorstep in the shade and made for it, let herself down cautiously, sat, sighed.

Nearby was a fruit-seller, sitting silent behind his dusty, withered stock. People went by. Nobody bought from him. Nobody looked at her. Odo, who was Odo? Famous revolutionary, author of *Community*, *The Analogy*, etc. etc. She, who was she?

An old woman with grey hair and a red face sitting on a dirty doorstep in a slum, muttering to herself.

True? Was that she? Certainly it was what anybody passing her saw. But was it she, herself, any more than the famous revolutionary, etc., was? No. It was not. But who was she, then?

The one who loved Taviri.

Yes. True enough. But not enough. That was gone; he had been dead so long.

"Who am I?" Laia muttered to her invisible audience, and they knew the answer and told it to her with one voice. She was the little girl with scabby knees, sitting on the doorstep staring down through the dirty golden haze of River Street in the heat of late summer, the six-year-old, the sixteen-year-old, the fierce, cross, dream-ridden girl, untouched, untouchable. She was herself. Indeed she had been the tireless worker and thinker, but a bloodclot in a vein had taken that woman away from her. Indeed she had been the lover, the swimmer in the midst of life, but Taviri, dying, had taken that woman away with him. There was nothing left, really, but the foundation. She had come home; she had never left home. "True voyage is return." Dust and mud and a doorstep in the slums. And beyond, at the far end of the street, the field full of tall dry weeds blowing in the wind as night came.

"Laia! What are you doing here? Are you all right?"

One of the people from the House, of course, a nice woman, a bit fanatical and always talking. Laia could not remember her name though she had known her for years. She let herself be taken home, the woman talking all the way. In the big cool common-room (once occupied by tellers counting money behind polished counters supervised by armed guards) Laia sat down in a chair. She was unable just as yet to face climbing the stairs, though she would have liked to be alone. The woman kept on talking, and other excited people came in. It appeared that a demonstration was being planned. Events in Thu were moving so fast that the mood here had caught fire, and something must be done. Day after tomorrow, no, tomorrow, there was to be a march, a big one, from Old Town to Capitol Square—the old route, "Another Ninth Month Uprising," said a young man, fiery and laughing, glancing at Laia. He had not even been born at the time of the Ninth Month Uprising, it was all history to him. Now he wanted to make some history of his own. The room had filled up. A general meeting would be held here, tomorrow, at eight in the morning. "You must talk, Laia."

"Tomorrow? Oh, I won't be here tomorrow," she said brusquely. Whoever had asked her smiled, another one laughed, though Amai glanced round at her with a puzzled look. They went on talking and shouting. The Revolution. What on earth had made her say that? What a thing to say on the eve of the Revolution, even if it was true.

She waited her time, managed to get up, for all her clumsiness, to slip away unnoticed among the people busy with their planning and excitement. She got to the hall, to the stairs, and began to climb them one by one. "The general strike," a voice, two voices, ten voices were saying in the room below, behind her. "The general strike," Laia muttered, resting for a moment on the landing.

Above, ahead, in her room, what awaited her? The private stroke. That was mildly funny. She started up the second flight of stairs, one by one, one leg at a time, like a small child. She was dizzy, but she was no longer afraid to fall. On ahead, on there, the dry white flowers nodded and whispered in the open fields of evening. Seventy-two years and she had never had time to learn what they were called.

Ursula K. Le Guin (1929–) is a major science fiction, fantasy, and children's author whose novel THE DISPOSSESSED (1974) is a contribution to anarchist theory.

Source: Ursula K. Le Guin, "The Day before the Revolution," GALAXY 35, no. 8 (August 1974): 17–30.

About the Editors

Gregory Claeys is Professor of the History of Political Thought at the University of London and author of several books. Lyman Tower Sargent, Professor of Political Science at the University of Missouri, St. Louis, is author and editor of numerous books including *Extremism in America* and *Political Thought in the United States* (also available from NYU Press).